Women of Bible Lands

A Pilgrimage to Compassion and Wisdom

Martha Ann Kirk, C.C.V.I.

Kim, woman of compassion and wisdom,

blessings,

Martha Ann Kirk

 *(MG logo)*

A Michael Glazier Book

LITURGICAL PRESS
Collegeville, Minnesota

www.litpress.org

A Michael Glazier Book published by the Liturgical Press

Cover design by David Manahan, O.S.B. Front cover: St. Barbara, St. Macrina, St. Thecla painted by Michel and Gabriel Morochan of Romania, 1975. The Greek Catholic Patriarchate, Jerusalem. Used through the kind permission of Patriarch Lutfi Laham. Photos by James Heinsch, O.F.M. Spine: Painting, "Friend," by Salwa Arnous of Jaffa, living in San Antonio, Texas.

Interior illustrations by Brother Steve Erspamer, S.M. Reprinted from *Clip Art Year A* © 1992, *Clip Art Year B* © 1993, and *Clip Art Year C* © 1994 Archdiocese of Chicago: Liturgy Training Publications, 1800 North Hermitage Avenue, Chicago, IL 60622-1101; 1-800-933-1800, fax 1-800-933-7094, email orders@ltp.org. All rights reserved.

1	2	3	4	5	6	7	8

Library of Congress Cataloging-in-Publication Data

Kirk, Martha Ann.
    Women of Bible lands : a pilgrimage to compassion and wisdom / Martha Ann Kirk.
        p. cm.
    "A Michael Glazier book."
    Includes bibliographical references and index.
    ISBN 0-8146-5156-9 (pbk. : alk. paper)
    1. Women in the Bible. 2. Women in Christianity. 3. Women in Judaism. 4. Women in Islam. 5. Bible—Feminist criticism. 6. Feminist theology. I. Title.

BS575.K575 2004
220.9'2'082—dc22   2003021132

To Meredith Ambers Kirk
and Morgen Ann Kirk,
who carry forward
the history of women
in whom God delights

CONTENTS

PART TWO
STORIES, SITES, AND MAPS

Old names of places are in regular type and modern names that are sub-
stantially different are in italics. Because different political periods are covered there is sometimes more than one ancient name and more than one
modern name from different cultural groups today. A helpful source for
understanding the geography is *The Collegeville Atlas of the Bible* (Collegeville: The Liturgical Press, 1998).

ACKNOWLEDGMENTS

I am grateful to the University of the Incarnate Word in San Antonio, Texas, where I am a professor, for supporting me for a sabbatical of research at Tantur Ecumenical Institute between Jerusalem and Bethlehem. Many persons there including Father Thomas Stransky and in other places of biblical lands helped me as I integrated ideas from my past research on women's stories with the insights from the land itself, the archaeological sites, the liturgical experiences, and the contemporary peoples. The methods and insights of Dr. Jim Flemming of the Biblical Resources Center in Jerusalem and the wisdom and contacts of Dr. Betty Jane Bailey, Dr. Martin Bailey, Vivi Senora, and Wisam T. Salsaa have helped me immensely. I wish to thank the librarians, the staffs, and other gracious hosts at Tantur, Bethlehem University, Hebrew University, Bir Zeit University of the Holy Land; of the Graduate Theological Union and the Franciscan School of Theology in Berkeley, California; and of the University of the Incarnate Word. The Melkite Sisters of Emmanuel Convent in Bethlehem, the Loretto Sisters Kathleen Tighe and Kay Lane, my congregation the Sisters of Charity of the Incarnate Word of San Antonio, Texas, and especially Sisters Maria Teresa Flores, Mary T. Phelan, and Cathy Vetter with whom I live at Annunciation Community all reveal to me aspects of the sisterly face of the divine and dimensions of the holiness of the ancient saints of whom I write. The artworks of Brother Steve Erspamer, S.M., and Salwa Arnous enrich this book. The friendships of these compassionate creators have enriched my life. I am grateful to the many who have assisted me in gathering material, typing, and editing, especially Bridget Korenek, Susan Brown, Penny Davis, Linda Etter, Adela Gott, Mary Lance, Troy Knickenbocker, John Carolla, Linda Maloney, and especially my mother Ada Sophie Koenig Kirk. She brought not only knowledge and skill as a teacher of literature and writing, but a face of Sophia—the wisdom, holiness, and deep love of an immanent God. My father, Bert Ambers Kirk, of Baptist background taught me to love the Bible, diverse peoples, and travel. Brother Rufino Zaragoza, O.F.M., and my brother Robert Kirk and his family, Cindy, Meredith, and Morgen encourage me in the journey of my life.

The author gratefully acknowledges copyright permission for the use of the following texts:

Ah Ahmadiyya Anjuman Ishaat Islam Lahore, Inc.

Holy Qur²an (The), (Columbus: Ahmadiyya Anjuman Ishaat Islam Lahore, Inc., 1991) 140–41.

Cambridge University Press

Smith, Margaret. *Rabi²a the Mystic and Her Fellow Saints in Islam* (Cambridge: Cambridge University Press, 1928). Reprinted with the permission of Cambridge University Press.

Cistercian Publications

"A Letter from Gregory, Bishop of Nyssa on the Life of Saint Macrina" as translated in Joan M. Petersen, *Handmaids of the Lord: Contemporary Descriptions of Feminine Asceticism in the First Six Centuries* (Kalamazoo: Cistercian Publications, Inc., 1996) 67–70.

Handmaids of the Lord, "Lusiac History of Palladius," as translated by Joan M. Petersen, 303–36.

Handmaids of the Lord, "Melanie the Younger" by Gerontius as translated by Joan M. Petersen, 327.

The Continuum International Publishing Group

"Life of Maria the Harlot" written by the Archdeacon Ephraim; translated into Latin by an anonymous translator, found in PL 73, col. 651–60. (BHL 12). English translation from Benedicta Ward, *Harlots of the Desert, A Study of Repentance in Early Monastic Sources* (London: Mowbray, 1987). Reprinted by permission of The Continuum International Publishing Group.

"Life of Saint Pelagia the Harlot" written by Deacon James and translated into Latin by Eustochius from *Vitas Sanctae Pelagiae, Meretricis* in PL 73, col. 663–72. English translation from Benedicta Ward. Reprinted by permission of The Continuum International Publishing Group.

"Life of St. Mary of Egypt" written by Sophronius, bishop of Jerusalem, translated into Latin by Paul, deacon of the holy church of Naples from PG 87 (3), col. 3693–3726. English translation by Benedicta Ward. Reprinted by permission of The Continuum International Publishing Group.

"Life of St. Thais the Harlot" from a Latin translation of a Greek text by an anonymous author from PL 73, cols. 661–62. English translation by Benedicta Ward. Reprinted by permission of The Continuum International Publishing Group.

José de Vinck

Raya, Most Rev. Joseph, and Baron José de Vinck. *Byzantine Daily Worship* (Allendale: Alleluia Press, 1969) 538–39, 658–59, 755–56, 971.

Dumbarton Oaks Research Library and Collection

"Life of St. Matrona of Perge," Talbot, Alice-Mary, ed., *Holy Women of Byzantium: Ten Saints' Lives in English Translation* (Washington, D.C.: Dumbarton Oaks, 1996) 34–38. Edition used for translation, *Acta Sanctorum Novembris,* 3 (Brussels: Societe des Bollandistes, 1910) 790–813.

Niketas the Most Glorious Magistros, *The Life of Our Blessed Mother Theoktiste of Lesbos Who Practiced Asceticiasm and Died on the Island Named Paros.* Trans., Angela C. Hero, as cited by Alice-Mary Talbot, ed. *Holy Women of Byzantium* (Washington, D.C.: Dumbarton Oaks, 1966) 224–33.

"The Life and Conduct of the Blessed Mary Who Changed Her Name to Marinos," *Holy Women of Byzantium,* Alice-Mary Talbot, ed. (Washington, D.C.: Dumbarton Oaks, 1966) 7–11 (131 lines). Edition used for translation: M. Richard, "La Vie Ancienne de Sainte Marie surnommee Marinos," on *Caorona Gratiarun, Miscellanae paatristica, historica et liturgica Eligio Dekkers* OSB *XII Lustra complenti oblata.* I (Brugge, 1975) 83–94; reprinted in M. Richard, *Opera minora,* III (Leuven, 1977) no. 67.

"St. Athanasia of Aegina" *Holy Women of Byzantium,* Mary-Alice Talbot (Washington, D.C.: Dumbarton Oaks, 1996) 142–46 of Edition used for translation, F. Halkin, "Vie de sainte Anthansie d'eegine" in *Six inedits d'hagiologie byzantie* [=SubsHag, 74] (Brussels, 1987) 179–95.

Edwin Mellen Press

Clark, Elizabeth A., *Jerome, Chrysostom, and Friends* (Lewiston, N.Y.: The Edwin Mellen Press, 1982, 1979) 130–33, 138–40.

Kluwer Academic Press, Kari E. Børresen, Kari Vogt

Børresen, Kari Elizabeth, "Ancient and Medieval Church Mothers" in Børresen, Kari Elizabeth, and Kari Vogt. *Women's Studies of the Christian and Islamic Traditions: Ancient, Medieval, and Renaissance Foremothers* (Boston: Kluwer Academic Press, 1993) 247. Reprinted with the kind permission of Kluwer Academic Publishers.

Socrates Scholasticus as cited in Kari Vogt, "The Hierophant of Philosophy" "Hypatia of Alexander" in Kari Elisabeth

Børrensen and Kari Vogt, *Women's Studies of the Christian and Islamic Traditions* (Boston: Kluwer Academic Press, 1993) 156–57, 165. Reprinted with the kind permission of Kluwer Academic Publishers and the authors.

Ross S. Kraemer for translations of

"Epitaph of the Deaconess Athanasia," 223. "Acts of Paul and Thecla," 285–88.

Kraemer, Ross S., *Maenads, Martyrs, Matrons, Monastics: A Sourcebook on Women's Religions in the Greco-Roman World* (Philadelphia: Fortress Press, 1988).

"Letter 108, Jerome to Eustochium," in Kraemer, 142–45, 147–50, 156–59, 164, 166.

Loeb Classical Library, Harvard University Press

Josephus, *Antiquitites of the Jews XX.* 53, 92–96. Reprinted with permission of the publishers and Trustees of the Loeb Classical Library from Josephus, *Antiquities of the Jews XX,* Loeb Classical Library Vol. 9, translated by Louis Feldman, Cambridge, Mass.: Harvard University Press, 1965. The Loeb Classical Library® is a registered trademark of the President and Fellows of Harvard College.

Philo, *On the Contemplative Life,* 32–33. Reprinted with permission of the publishers and Trustees of the Loeb Classical Library from Philo, Loeb Classical Library Vol. 9, translated by F. H. Colson, Cambridge, Mass.: Harvard University Press, 1941. The Loeb Classical Library® is a registered trademark of the President and Fellows of Harvard College.

Michael Glazier, Inc.

Didascalia et Constitutiones Apostolorum, ed. F. X. Funk (Paderborn, 1905) II, 26, 6, 105, as cited in Elizabeth Clark, *Women of the Early Church* (Wilmington: Michael Glazier, Inc., 1983) 177–78.

Proba, Faltonia Betitia. "A Cento" from Corpus Scriptorum Ecclisiasticorum Latinorum 16.576, as cited in *Women of the Early Church,* Elizabeth Clark (Wilmington: Michael Glazier, Inc., 1983) 167–68.

Socrates Scholasticus, Ecclesiastica Historia, ed. R. Hussey (Wilmington: Michael Glazier, Inc., 1983) 184–86.

New Directions Publishing Corporation

"Lament for a Brother" (excerpts) by Omar Pound, *Arabic and Persian Poems* (New Directions Publishing, 1970) © 1970 by

Omar Pound. Used by permission of New Directions Publishing Corporation.

New Revised Standard Version Bible

The Scripture quotations contained herein are from the New Revised Standard Version Bible, Catholic Anglicized Edition, © 1999, 1995, 1989, Division of Christian Education of the National Council of the Churches of Christ in the United States of America, and are used by permission. All rights reserved.

Oxford University Press

"Acts of Perpetua and Feliciatas," *The Acts of the Christian Martyrs.* Translation by Hubert Musurillo. (Oxford: The Clarendon Press, 1972) 107–8, 123, 133–35. Reprinted by permission of Oxford University Press.

"Acts of Sts. Agape, Chione, and Companions," *The Acts of the Christian Martyrs,* translation by Hubert Musurillo (Oxford: The Clarendon Press, 1972) 287–93. Reprinted by permission of Oxford University Press.

Corpus Scriptorum Ecclesiasticorum Latinorum (Vienna, 1866–) 108.23, 5–21 as quoted in Susanna Elm, *Virgins of God: The Making of Asceticism in Late Antiqua* (Oxford: The Clarendon Press, 1994) 5–21, 303, 290, 307. Reprinted by permission of Oxford University Press.

Paulist Press

Excerpts from *Augustine of Hippo: Selected Writings,* from The Classics of Western Spirituality, translated by Mary T. Clark, copyright © 1984 by Mary T.. Clark, Paulist Press, Inc., New York/Mahwah, N.J. Used with permission of Paulist Press. www.paulistpress.com

Excerpts from *Palladius: the Lausiac History* by Palladius, translated by Robert T. Meyer, © 1965 Newman Press. Paulist Press, Inc., New York/Mahwah, N.J. Used with permission of Paulist Press. www.paulistpress.com

John Chrysostom, *Homily on Romans 16:1–2, 6–7,* MPG *60.663–70,* translated by Carolyn Osiek in Barbara Bowe, Kathleen Hughes, Sharon Karam, and Carolyn Osiek, eds., *Silent Voices, Sacred Lives. Women's Readings for the Liturgical Year* (New York: Paulist, 1992) 216–17.

Didascalia Apostolorum 3.12.1–13.1, as cited in Barbara Bowe, et al., eds., *Silent Voices, Sacred Lives* (Mahwah, N.J.: Paulist) 156–57.

SPCK

Egeria, *Egeria's Travels.* Newly translated with supporting documents and notes by John Wilkinson. London: SPCK, 1971.

University of California Press

"Anastasia" in Peeters (ed.)., *Bibliotheca Hagiographica Orientalis* 242 (Bruxelles, 1910) translated from F. Nau's edition of the Syriac in *Revue de l'Orient Chretien* 5 (1900) 391–401 in *Holy Women of the Syrian Orient* introduced and translated by Sebasian P. Brock and Susan Ashbrook Harvey (Berkeley: University of California Press, 1987) 146–49.

Also in *Holy Women of the Syrian Orient*, "Martha" introduced and translated by Sebasian P. Brock and Susan Ashbrook Harvey, from P. Peeters, ed., *Bibliotheca Hagiographica Orentalis 698* (Bruxelles, 1910) translated from *Acta Sanctorum martyrum et Sanctorum* 2, 233–41.

University of Chicago

Nabia Abbott, *Aishah, the Beloved of Muhammad* (Chicago: University of Chicago Press, 1942) 46.

University of Texas Press

Elizabeth Warnock Fernea and Basima Qattan Bezergan, *Middle Eastern Muslim Women Speak* (Austin: University of Texas Press, 1977) 4.

Benedicta Ward

The Desert Christians: The Sayings of the Desert Fathers, trans. Benedicta Ward, S.L.G. (Kalamazoo: Cistercian Publications, revised ed., 1984, © Benedicta Ward, 1975) 82–84, 229–35.

Westminster John Knox Press, James Clarke & Co., and Mohr Siebeck Verlag

The Gospel of Bartholomew 2:1-14, trans. by Felix Scheidweiler and Wilhelm Schneemelcher. In Wilhelm Schneemelcher, ed., *New Testament Apocrypha* (English trans. edited by R. McL. Wilson; rev. ed. Louisville: Westminster, 1991) vol. 1: *Gospels and Related Writings* (Philadelphia: The Westminster Press, 1963) 537–53, at 543–44.

Westminster John Knox Press

I Esdras 4:13-32. From *Biblical Affirmations of Women* by Leonard Swidler. © 1979 The Westminster Press. Used by permission of John Knox Press.

LIST OF MAPS

Some maps include both ancient and modern names of places. Various cultural groups may have different names for the same place.

Maps 1–5 by Audrey Gould.
Maps 6–8 by Jennifer E. Sobin.

ABBREVIATIONS

ACW   Ancient Christian Writers

EGERIA   *Egeria's Travels*, Newly translated with supporting
           documents and notes by John Wilkinson. London:
           S.P.C.K., 1971.

PAULA   "Letter 108, Jerome to Eustochium" in Ross S.
           Kraemer, *Maenads, Martyrs, Matrons, Monastics*.
           Philadelphia: Fortress, 1988.

MPG   *Patrologia Graeca*, ed. J. P. Migne *et al.* Paris, 1857– .

MPL   *Patrologia Latina*, ed. J. P. Migne *et al.* Paris, 1844– .

INTRODUCTION

In the last decade I have been on many journeys in the Americas, Asia, Africa, and the Middle East. After one long, hot day my friend Trish and I sought a room in Jordan. We were brought into the home of a large Muslim family and put in the room of the aunt and uncle who were camping out with the sheep in this season of new lambs. The room filled with half a dozen interested little daughters, sons, and cousins. Smiles were our only common language. They sat on the carpet, for the room had no furniture except a storage chest and mats to roll out for sleeping. As the children kept refilling our teacups all evening, I began to understand the biblical virtue of hospitality with Sarah and Abraham welcoming and entertaining complete strangers. My weariness from the heat of the desert outside began to fade.

Another night I sat in the back seat of a car with an older woman, Esther, who at the end of the conference in Tel Aviv had asked for a ride back home to Jerusalem. As we drove up to Jerusalem she spoke of her happy youth in Poland, then the growing fear of the Nazis. When she was sixteen her parents had heard of a train that took children to England for safety. Though she knew no one on the train, her parents felt that it was better for her to go. Her mother corresponded with Esther for three years—until the mother was killed at Auschwitz. While many stories are written today about conflicts between mothers and daughters, Esther had just edited for publication her mother's letters, which reflected a deep, loving relationship that brought empowerment and freedom. I read my Bible before going to bed, but I had no need to that night, for I had received holy words, the kind of loving wisdom about survival shared by Ruth and Naomi.

The radio of the shared taxi was blaring loud pop music in Arabic. The car shocks and seats had worn out long ago and we would have bounced if we had not been so tightly crowded together in the back seat going from the Damascus Gate to Bethlehem. How uncomfortable it was to be surrounded by women in their white Muslim veils and long black embroidered Palestinian dresses with no way to communicate. Then one of them began to sort through bundles from the market. She pulled out the most succulent grapes and was a most gracious hostess as she offered them to me. The discomfort changed to communion. Sisterhood is so much stronger than barriers of culture and language.

The Orthodox Patriarch and his assistants were finishing the early morning liturgy in the Cave of the Nativity under the Church in Bethlehem. Of course I knew the reasons why I was not welcome for Communion. I am a teacher of the theologies of the Eucharist and the dates of the splits between Eastern and Western Christians. All that doesn't make it any easier to stand at the same table but not be a part of the banquet. As people began to leave, the Ethiopian nun who seemed to be so deep in prayer that she was totally unaware of the rest of us came toward me with a gracious smile, pressing half of her blessed bread in my hand. Did she feel the hunger in my heart? Through the ages hasn't it been the women who would watch and be sure that everyone was fed? No, we were not able to speak a word to each other, but her simple gesture seemed to embody all of the gospel stories of healing, reconciling, nurturing, transforming, transfiguring, dying, and rising.

All of my journeys have come to be pilgrimages, seeking and finding the divine, finding the divine in sisters as well as in brothers. One receives compassion. One learns compassion. One learns to see more and more. Peace is built as people travel across modern borders, as women talk to women of other cultures, as women remember ancient women. Peace is built as men and women learn to have historical perspectives. Uncovering and recovering women's stories can contribute to a more egalitarian, less domineering world. Stories of ancient women travelers give people today courage to travel. Women's history is as important for men as for women.

This book is like a handful of potsherds. I had to dig deeply for some of them, but others were on the surface unnoticed. The fragments were in Hebrew, Greek, Latin, Syriac, Coptic, and Arabic. The biblical texts have been available, but women's stories have not been emphasized. The ancient collections of the writings of the "Latin Fathers" and the "Greek Fathers," and the Latin "Acts of the Martyrs" containing some women have been accessible in scholarly collections in English in the twentieth century. The Syriac, Coptic, and Arabic stories of ancient women have rarely been available, and some have only been translated into English in the last two decades. Women's stories were not considered valuable and were not accessible for ordinary people, only for specialists.

This book emphasizes the Christian tradition but looks with respect to others. Besides the women of the Bible and Christian holy women, a few examples of Jewish and Muslim women have been included. The "peoples of the book," Jews, Christians, and Muslims, have a common heritage of a God of compassion that is more important than the differences that separate. What are the challenges modern women have in common with women through the ages? Economic inequality and violence continue. Whether we consider the story of Tamar raped by her stepbrother in the tenth century B.C.E. or the stories of Byzantine women saints abused by men in the ninth century C.E., we know that women have suffered. Few have questioned the suffering as the patriarchal narratives continue the stories of male heroes. Is this suffering what God wills? Or is God more like a sister who invites women to share stories, listens to them, weeps with them, and invites all peoples to turn their hearts of stone to hearts of flesh? In these stories women are the victims, the survivors, and the heroes.

Literary analysis of the hero's quest seems to apply predominantly to the male heroes. Feminist literary criticism is grappling with the little-explored world of female heroism. While men in their heroic stories go out and confront dragons, women's heroism seems to be in confronting the dragons of the limitations of their lives and abilities imposed by patriarchal culture. Sometimes this confrontation of dragons involves external challenge, but more often it involves facing dragons within, in confronting self-internalization of the limits. Women questioning oppression take the first step of the heroic journey. True heroism is not in situations of winners and losers, but in situations encouraging the well-being of all, especially the disadvantaged.

Women have, to a large extent, been invisible within history and literature as developed and preserved by patriarchal societies. But the issue is not just lack of visibility; it is also a lack of knowledge of female heroes. Heroines, that is, women who are supporting characters for male heroes, have been used extensively. Female heroes have rarely been developed or analyzed. Many studies of children's literature, of literary masterpieces, and of the Bible reveal that traditionally stories of powerful or independent females are rare and that powerful females are often shown as evil. Stories that get preserved and stories that reveal women as good are usually stories of women as mothers, wives, caretakers of men or children, or women waiting to be helped or rescued by men. The Roman Catholic Lectionary has patterns of selecting women's stories similar to patterns of selection in other literature. Orthodoxy and Catholicism are often lauded for having a female symbol in Mary. The symbol of Mary is better than no feminine symbol at all, yet she is usually extolled as a heroine, the supporting character for the male heroes imaged as Son, Father, and Spouse. It is crucial to have female symbols of wholeness, not just symbols of complementarity, supportiveness, or passivity. Biblical female images of God can be symbols of wholeness.

Only when prophets vehemently lament the old order is there a possibility for a new creation. Lament carries within itself the seed of hope. People who begin to be aware of evils begin to get in touch with anger and grief. People must not deny or suppress the tears of rage, but rather bring them before Jesus, who also wept. In the midst of tears and anger one has, like Martha, an opportunity to make a profession of faith, the profession that reveals apostolic primacy. Jesus gave new life to Lazarus, but he invited the community to go and unbind the one who had been dead. Communities today are being given the gift of mutual discipleship. The world has been called from the tomb of patriarchy. "Unbind him and let him go free."

This book is an invitation to the reader in her or his incarnational reality to listen deeply within and to begin to tell one's own story. How is God's grace working through one's own experiences and feelings about them on the journey of life? How would a woman tell her own story as a woman? How would she tell stories of other women? If over ninety-nine per cent of both biblical and ancient stories of women are actually men's stories of women rather than the women's own interpretations of experience, do contemporary women have the tools needed to recognize their own experiences? If women had written ninety-nine percent of history would struggles for political power and military victories be primary subjects, as they are now? Are these the big things that matter in God's eyes? Jesus said that what really matters is feeding the hungry, clothing the naked, sheltering the homeless, visiting the sick, and burying the dead. When asked by the disciples about who was the greatest in the reign of God, Jesus put a little child in their midst. Serving those in need, noticing, learning from, and caring for little ones—these are the central issues in history. Those who did these things should get the most attention so that they might be role models for the future.

Ancient church history often chronicles the councils that defined dogmas and the philosophical and theological debates associated with them. Heretics were condemned. People were defined as right or wrong, orthodox or heterodox, in terms of what they believed. How much difference did the dogma defined at a council make in the life of an ordinary Christian woman in antiquity? This does not deny that right actions are motivated by thought. However, in studying the gospel we see that Jesus repeatedly emphasizes orthopraxis, right action, while respecting orthodoxy, right belief. The men of church history spend much time and energy studying and debating orthodoxy. Having more history of women could give more examples of orthopraxis. While the Peoples of the Book, Jewish, Muslim, and Christian, do not agree on orthodoxy, focusing on and coming to agree on some aspects of orthopraxis is a reasonable goal. Agreeing that all children should live in safety with food, shelter, education, and health care and that the work of creating this reality is part of the divine plan is a reasonable goal. In the face of continuing violence and environmental degradation, orthopraxis seems to be a more urgent priority for religious groups than agreeing on orthodoxy.

PART ONE

**RECLAIMING WOMEN'S STORIES
AND WOMEN'S JOURNEYS**

CHAPTER 1

SHARDS AND STORIES

In archaeological sites in Israel, if pot shards are loose on the surface and not in enclosed areas it is permissible to pick them up. At Meggido I held in my hand a thick shard of the Canaanite period. What is known of the woman who used the pot from which this shard came? Was it full of olive oil? Like a later Good Samaritan, did she pour oil on the wounds of those scarred from the repeated battles that took place at this crossroads of the continents? Is the woman's name remembered? Is the healing she brought celebrated?

This fragment from Samaria may have been part of a pot to hold water. Was the water brought to wash a new baby, but alas, the child was stillborn? There is no reason to think that the prayers of this mother to Astarte for another child after painful and frustrating labor were any less devout or less sincere than those my friend prayed to Christ after her child was stillborn.

If I listen with my heart, each of the shards has a story. "We are earthen vessels, but we contain a treasure," Paul wrote. Women are sometimes compared to vessels. Women have open space, wombs within. They can carry a precious treasure of new life in their wombs. They carry a treasure of wisdom in their hearts. The pot shards connect me with my ancient sisters. They carry nourishment, medicine, and beauty. So few of the women's words remain, but each pot shard carries some of the mystery of their "ordinary lives." Pottery has been the traditional and amazingly effective method of dating cultures. The ordinary vessels of ordinary people have documented the human story as much as the ruins of temples of the gods, the monuments of monarchs, and the palaces of the patriarchs. The vessels were probably used more by women than by men.

At Arad I held a shard from a pot made a thousand years before Christ. Perhaps a woman made the pot to store the bitumen made there from chemicals of the Dead Sea. Her pots with their valuable cargo went to Egypt and all around the sea. Like God, described by Jeremiah as a potter, she shaped and re-shaped the pot, seeking not only function but also beauty.

In Jerusalem I picked up a shard. Perhaps it was from a lamp of the second century B.C.E. that a woman trimmed and brought to her husband, a priest, so that he could continue to read the Torah as the dusk fell. Her husband offered sacrifices to God. He spent long hours studying God's word. She was only a woman and could spend long hours preparing food. She could not offer sacrifice as he did. Did her life matter as much in the eyes of God?

In Caesarea Philippi I found a fine thin shard with painted decoration, perhaps from the cosmetic container of a wealthy woman. Had this woman come to believe that looking beautiful for men was the most important thing? Did she spend much of her time and energy trying to do that while slaves cared for her home and her children? Was she happy?

At Nimrud castle, where Muslims tried to defend the land where they had lived for nearly five hundred years, I found a green glazed shard of pottery. Did it come from a lovely plate that a wife set out with fruit, trying to please her husband who was greatly troubled as he made plans for the defense of his family?

More shards remain than whole pots or plates, just as more fragments than whole stories of women remain. This book gathers some fragments. They can be pieced together to reveal more of the whole, but even the most isolated or tiniest fragment is precious and can have its own beauty. Humankind is only beginning to claim women's history, but their stories could be even more important than pottery dating. Did the swords and spears in a museum save a culture or bring better life? Or did the bowls, plates, cups, and jars serve the human family best? All need to be considered and respected.

Women as Tellers and Writers of Their Own Stories

Were some parts of the Bible stories told by women? Were some parts written down by women editors? The first two chapters of Exodus and the book of Ruth (except the emphasis on male genealogy at the end) seem to have been stories that women told each other for encouragement. Some of the psalms, with lines such as "like a weaned child on its mother's lap," may have originally been poems or songs of women. Some scholars have suggested that Priscilla was the author of the letter to the Hebrews, but this is very hard to determine.

In Hebrew culture there was the role of "singing women" such as Miriam, Deborah, and the daughter of Jephthah, who shared the ballads and poetry and often the dance. Many references to women transmitting culture orally can be found (2

Sam 19:35-6; 2 Chr 35:25; Isa 23:16; Eccl 2:8; Zeph 3:14; Zech 2:10). Both ballads and religious songs were part of women's tradition. The Song of Songs seems to have come out of that tradition of women's poetry and song.

What parts of early Christian texts might have come from women's oral stories or writings? In the modern period distinctions have been made between "orthodox" and "heterodox" groups and texts, but it is more realistic to say that many people of faith touched by Christ gave voice to their experiences as best they could. The victors wrote the history books at later dates and labeled the "others" and attributed motives and qualities to them from the point of view of the victors' values and interests. Biblical scholar Stevan Davies has put forth a thesis proposing that several apocryphal New Testament Acts of the Apostles, such as the Acts of John, Peter, Paul, Andrew, Thomas, and of Xanthippe and Polyxeus, were authored by women and for women.[1] In *Chastity as Autonomy* Virginia Burrus makes a strong case that the Acts of Paul and Thecla originated with women's oral stories.[2] Many groups, now labeled as unorthodox or heretical, had some women leaders. Were those who labeled the groups "wrong" willing to enter into serious theological dialogues with women to see if common ground could be found? Were those who wrote the histories later too embedded in patriarchy to consider women seriously as a part of history?

Few writings by Christian women survive from antiquity, but about a hundred letters to women from John Chrysostom, Jerome, and Augustine have survived. Not a single letter of the women was preserved, though three letters in the collection of letters attributed to Jerome seem to be by women. While Jerome's letters often praise Paula the Elder (d. 404) who financially supported him, Palladius in his *Lausiac History* written in 419–20 gives a different picture of him. "A certain Jerome of Dalmatia stood in her way, for she was well able to surpass everyone else, being a genius of a woman. He thwarted her with his jealousy and prevailed upon her to work to his own end and purpose."[3]

Palladius also respected the scholarship of Melania the Elder, who died in 406. He wrote, "She was most erudite and fond of literature, and she turned night into day going through every writing of the ancient commentators—three million lines of Origen and two and a half million of Gregory, Stephen, Pierius, Basil, and other worthy men. And she did not read them once only and in an offhand way, but she worked on them, dredging through each work seven or eight times."[4]

New discoveries may be made, but near the beginning of the twenty-first century the only extant writings by Christian women of antiquity seem to be:

1. Vibia Perpetua's words from prison in Carthage (North Africa) before she was martyred in 203 C.E., which were put into the longer "Acts of Perpetua and Felicity."

2. Faltonia Betitia Proba's "Cento" from about 306 C.E., which speaks of God's action through history in poetic form.

3. Egeria's Diary of her pilgrimage in the 380's C.E. to the Middle East, with extensive descriptions of liturgy, monasticism, and places visited by pilgrims. This was only discovered in 1884 after being lost for centuries.

4. Melania the Elder's eleven letters to Evagrius Ponticus, translated from an Armenian version.

5. Among Jerome's letters is one that is actually from Paula and Eustochium to Marcella from about 392 C.E.

6. Among Jerome's letters are two that are actually by a Spanish woman ascetic, written to a woman friend around 400.

7. Sayings from the Desert Mothers Theodora, Sarah, Syncletica, and Eugenia are in the fifth-century collection *Sayings of the Desert Fathers*.

8. The "Martyrdom of Saint Cyprian" by the Empress Eudocia, who died in 460 has survived, but unfortunately not her other six works that are mentioned in other sources. Her biblical paraphrases, including a sequence on the Octateuch and hexameter versions of Daniel and Zechariah, have been praised by literary critics.[5]

In comparison to thousands and thousands of pages by the Church Fathers, this is a small collection. As archaeologists have picked up pieces of ancient pottery and tried not only to put together a pot but to give contexts to the sites, the cultures, the trade patterns, and the work methods, so this book claims some of the fragments of women's stories that do exist. Slowly a more complete understanding of the human story, not just the male story, may be grasped.

A question remains: Were women's stories accidentally lost or deliberately destroyed? Probably both. If they were destroyed, why? Were men jealous of women because women give birth and have intimate relationships with the new life through nurturing? Was this power of birthing so awesome, so mysterious and close to the divine, that males tried to denigrate and obscure it?

Within ancient Christian literature there are contradictions. Women are considered redeemed by Christ. Paul wrote in Gal 3:28 that there is no longer male and female, for all are one in Christ Jesus. Yet in contradiction to this, classical theological anthropology said that God created females subordinate to males; for women to be good they must be like males. This concept had significant influence on many of the types of women discussed in this book. The ideal was to be like men, so women chose ascetic defeminization, or they overcame their female inferiority by virginity or widowhood. Writings praised Perpetua, Thecla, Syncletica, Melania, and Olympias by saying that they were like men in some way. Palladius, in his *Lausiac History* 9.1, lauded an outstanding ascetic woman as a "female man of God."

In many ways the modern world has been trapped in values shaped by that anthropology. What is male is good. A modern concept is that women should have opportunities to be like men and to do what men do. A more sensible and balanced approach would say that men should have opportunities to be like women, to do things that women do. On modern journeys through life can men lead at some times and women at others? How do they support each other along the way, bearing each others' burdens?

Stories That Have Survived by and About Women

Within both Judaism and Christianity certain Bible texts have been held up by patriarchal interpreters to mean that women should not speak publicly and consequently should not have a voice in worship. Susan Grossman and Rivka Haut have looked extensively at the use of Psalm 45:14 and they note:

> "The king's daughter is all glorious within,
> Her clothing is of wrought gold."
>
> Psalm 45:14

> This verse has been cited as proof that, according to tradition, women have divinely ordained roles that preclude any public activity. Rabbis through the ages, including our own, have cited this beautiful image to justify excluding women from public life, restricting their dress, and stressing that women's sole legitimate sphere of activity is *within* the home. The use of this phrase has become so widespread that it surfaces in most discussions about broadening women's role in Jewish ritual and communal life. It is often cited by Orthodox, Conservative, and other scholars who seek to exclude women from elected office in Israel, from praying together in public places, and from the rabbinate. Psalm 45 is a

beautiful hymn written in praise of an earthly king. It describes the "king's daughters" of other nations who have come to wait upon the Israelite king (Psalm 45:10). They are advised to forget their own people and devote themselves to the king.[6]

Within Christianity 1 Cor 14:34 has been held up as a universal prohibition against women speaking rather than a comment within a particular context in which some women may have been thought disruptive. Despite these prohibitions women have spoken in Judaism and Christianity, and stories of women have survived. God's Wisdom has been poured out on women as well as men.

> In every generation she passes into holy souls
> and makes them friends of God, and prophets (Wis 7:27).

Generally women's stories have fallen into these categories in the early centuries of Christianity:

> 1st–2nd centuries: Evangelists, leaders of house churches, servers of the needy
> 2nd–3rd centuries: Martyrs
> 4th–7th centuries: Ascetics, spiritual directors, monastic organizers
> 4th century onward: Pilgrims, patrons
> 8th, 9th, and later centuries: Nuns, wives, mothers

In the first few hundred years the folk heroes came to be called saints. Locally the people would flock to the tomb of someone they remembered as holy. The day of the saint's death would be remembered and stories of the person's life would be told. Storytelling is an art, and facts were put to the service of the dramatic craft. The local church leaders might record the holy person's name with the designation of saint. Canonization, as official acknowledgment by the larger church, did not happen in the Western church until the tenth century and in the Eastern church until the thirteenth century. Elizabeth A. Johnson has noted the importance of women saints and of the communion of saints, which cuts across nations, classes, and centuries giving people a sense of meaning and of strength. Johnson writes of holy women: "Friends of God and prophets in their own right, they have known spiritual power coming to them from God out of the struggles of their own life. They have expressed this power in fights for self-worth, in wide and deep hospitality, in unremitting service with and to the poor, in struggles for justice, in tongues touched with fire that announce the Holy Spirit, in continuous assertive patterns of compassionate ministry."[7]

Women martyrs are frequently recalled in the listed saints of the second, third, and early fourth centuries. Many of the stories of the martyrs are written in a literary form that can be called an "epic passion." These describe gruesome suffering in great detail. Do the authors have some type of perverse delight in pain? Probably not, but they have a deep-seated sense that initiations are transitions that involve some type of suffering. Since the martyrs are being initiated into the greatest place, the presence of Christ, the sufferings of the initiation must be very great.

During late antiquity and the early medieval period the literary genre of hagiography developed. The form was influenced by the legends of the Christian martyrs and the genre of Greek philosophical biography. This form does not aim to be factual, but rather edifying. While the main aim is not historicity, hagiography can be valuable for understanding everyday life and the context of ordinary people. For instance, in Constantinople, the center of the Byzantine empire, histories primarily focused on important political and military events. Hagiography can give some understanding of rural areas and of people who are not members of the elite. Since women usually did not have major political or military positions they appear very little in the histories, but women do appear in some of the hagiographies.

After Christianity became legal and martyrdom was no longer considered the main way to heaven, some people chose asceticism. Much Christian literature was preserved and transmitted through monastic groups in the Middle East. Stories of women survive, but most of them are males' interpretations of women rather than women's interpretations of women. In the first six centuries of the Christian era stories of transvestite nuns and female ascetics were popular in monastic oral tradition and then in literature. In the eighth through tenth centuries stories of married women and cenobite nuns predominate. Some women, like Theodora of Thessalonica and Theodora of Arta, became nuns after being widowed. A number of women saints, including Matrona, Mary the Younger, and Thomais, all suffered abuse from their husbands, and even Monica, the mother of Augustine, was psychologically abused. Marriage was like martyrdom. This theological approach needs to be questioned. Are women meant to suffer from male violence and so win their sanctity? Is this a way for males to rationalize sinfulness, rather than the plan of God?

Mary as the Theotokos, the Mother of God, was always honored, especially from the sixth century on. In the Eastern church calendars biblical women are recalled as saints and have particular feast days and visual commemoration in the icons. Until recently there were few English translations of the lives of Byzantine women saints. Their stories, which reveal the general ambivalence about women, are beginning to be an interesting area of women's studies. Genesis said that both females and males are made in God's image, but patriarchal interpretation has focused on Eve as the source of evil in the world. In Galatians, Paul wrote that there is no longer male and female, but all are one in Christ Jesus. Yet patriarchal interpretation has chosen to focus on the statement that women should remain silent in church and cover their heads.

The *Synaxarion of Constantinople,* the tenth-century collection of saints arranged for the church year, has 55 individual women martyrs from the third and fourth centuries, 14 women of the fourth and fifth centuries, four women from the sixth century, then none from the seventh, and eight from the ninth and tenth centuries, while 64 male saints are mentioned from the eighth and ninth centuries. Within the contemporary Roman Catholic tradition dictionaries of saints list about 2700 men and 500 women. Are women less holy, or do these numbers just reveal the politics of churches?

Notes

[1] Stevan L. Davies, *The Revolt of the Widows: The Social World of the Apocryphal Acts* (Carbondale: Southern Illinois University Press, 1980).

[2] Virginia Burrus, *Chastity as Autonomy: Women in the Stories of the Apocryphal Acts* (Lewiston: Edwin Mellen, 1987).

[3] Palladius, *The Lausiac History,* trans. Robert T. Meyer, ACW 34 (Westminster, Md.: Newman Press, 1965) 118.

[4] Ibid., 136.

[5] Kari Elisabeth Børresen, "Ancient and Medieval Church Mothers," in Kari Elisabeth Børresen and Kari Vogt, *Women's Studies of the Christian and Islamic Traditions: Ancient, Medieval, and Renaissance Foremothers* (Boston: Kluwer Academic, 1993) 247.

[6] Susan Grossman and Rivka Haut, *Daughters of the King: Women and the Synagogue* (Philadelphia: Jewish Publication Society, 1992) xxii–xxiii.

[7] Elizabeth A. Johnson, *Friends of God and Prophets, A Feminist Theological Reading of the Communion of Saints* (New York: Continuum, 1999) 175.

CHAPTER TWO

"AS A HEN GATHERS HER BROOD UNDER HER WINGS . . ."

Jesus stood on the Mount of Olives and looked down on the city and said, "Jerusalem, Jerusalem, the city that kills the prophets and stones those who are sent to it! How often have I desired to gather your children together as a hen gathers her brood under her wings, and you were not willing!" (Luke 13:34). He was grieving that the people were not following a God of compassion. He wept. He used a female image to describe himself, and in doing so entered into the rich tradition of female divine images in the Hebrew Scriptures. Mother bird images can be found in Exod 19:4; Deut 32:11-13; Ruth 2:12; Pss 36:7-9; 61:4; 63:7. One has only to look at human relations around the globe today to see that the idols of phallus and spear predominate. Will the Peoples of the Book cling to the idols of masculinity or seek the true God beyond the images? A gift of the Peoples of the Book to the religious consciousness of humankind is the emphasis in Judaism, Christianity, and Islam on a transcendent God. Now is the time for these traditions to face honestly the idol of the warrior from outmoded tribal eras. In journeys to Bible lands one encounters huge pantheons of deities who are "dead," including Marduk, Tiamat, Innana, Horus, Isis, Osiris, Baal, Zeus, Diana, Bacchus, and Artemis. The test of the truth of the religions of the Peoples of the Book is whether their God lives. Living deities undergo metamorphosis relating to the human family in different forms and ways sympathetic to people's needs. The living God can cross international borders, cultures, and languages. The true living God is no more womb and breast than phallus and spear. While this book points out some images of womb and breast that might stand by those of phallus and spear, in the end all idols and images are inadequate. Are modern people courageous enough to go on the pilgrimages seeking the living God, the God who offers life and peace? The heavy idols of claims to dominance can keep them from traveling freely and joyfully and from meeting sisters and brothers all along the way.

The Bible begins by describing a dark, formless void, but then God's wind or spirit sweeps over the chaos, and from all that creation comes (Gen 1:2). The Hebrew word for wind, breath, or spirit, which develops into the concept of God's Holy Spirit, is *ruach,* a feminine word. The first biblical image of God is associated with the female, and the first chapter of Genesis continues with people who are created in God's own image "male and female," implying the equality of the sexes. The feminine *ruach* can be seen in Isa 11:1-2; 61:1-2; Ezek 36:24-27; 37:4-6, 10; Joel 2:28-29; Luke 4:18; John 3:5-8. The second account of creation in Genesis 2 describes God creating the person, *"ʾādām,"* originally neither male nor female. Then from "flesh of flesh" and "bone of bone," in other words of the same human substance, another person is made; then there is sexual differentiation. This text itself does not imply the inferiority of the female, though it has often been interpreted that way.

The Hebrew word for God's compassion, *rachămim,* is from the root word meaning womb. Arabic has a similar root word sounding like *"r-h-m."* Muslims meditate on the "Ninety-nine names of God"; one of the names, the attributes, is Merciful or Compassionate. A favored Arabic name for a son is Rahim, that is, benevolent or merciful. God's compassion for creatures is like the womb-love of a woman for her child. Phyllis Trible in *God and the Rhetoric of Sexuality* discusses the beauty of this imagery at some length.[1] The womb protects and nurtures, but then gives forth life. It does not permanently control, but selflessly gives. The root word for womb is a part of the word for merciful. In many different periods and types of biblical literature, God is described by the adjective *rahûm,* meaning "merciful." The two words "merciful" and "gracious" are used to describe God, but never creatures: "The LORD, the LORD, a God merciful and gracious, slow to anger, and abounding in steadfast love and faithfulness" (Exod 34:6); "Return to the LORD, your God, for he is gracious and merciful . . ." (Joel 2:13); "a gracious God and merciful, slow to anger, and abounding in steadfast love . . ." (Jonah 4:2b). This phrase has been used in different ways throughout the ages; in hymns (Pss 111:4; 112:4; 145:8), in a thanksgiving song (Ps 103:8), and in lament (Ps 86:5, 15). Ezra emphasizes the compassion of God who takes care of the wandering people even when they are evil, "But you are a God ready to forgive, gracious and merciful, slow to anger and abounding in steadfast love, and you did not forsake them" (Neh 9:17b). Further use can be seen in 2 Chr 30:9, Jonah 4:2, Ps 78:38, and Deut 4:31.

In the "Song of Moses," which calls God "a rock" to indicate stability and faithfulness in contrast to the people's unfaithfulness, there are masculine and feminine metaphors for God:

> Is not he your father, who created you,
> who made you and established you? (Deut 32:6)

Trible translates the other metaphor:

> The Rock who gave you birth you forgot,
> and you lost remembrance of the God
> who writhed in labor pains with you (v. 18).[2]

Another use of the image of birth is found in Isaiah 42. Destruction and confusion have prevailed, but now a new creation will be born:

> See, the former things have come to pass,
> and new things I now declare;
> before they spring forth,
> I tell you of them. (Isa 42:9)

God enters into labor pains that the new creation may emerge:

> For a long time I have held my peace,
> I have kept still and restrained myself;
> now I will cry out like a woman in labor,
> I will gasp and pant. (Isa 42:14)

Third, Isaiah uses the image of birthing to describe Zion as a nation bringing forth children (Isa 66:1-9). God also serves as a midwife who helps the mother and then puts the child at her breasts to nurse:

> Shall I open the womb and not deliver?
> says the LORD;
> shall I, the one who delivers, shut the womb?
> says your God.
> Rejoice with Jerusalem, and be glad for her,
> all you who love her;
> rejoice with her in joy,
> all you who mourn over her—
> that you may nurse and be satisfied
> from her consoling breast;
> that you may drink deeply with delight
> from her glorious bosom. (Isa 66:9-11)

Then there is a poem about the joy of Jerusalem:

> I will extend prosperity to her like a river,
> and the wealth of the nations like an overflowing stream;
> and you shall nurse and be carried on her arm,
> and dandled on her knees. (Isa 66:12)

As God has made Jerusalem a comforting mother, so God describes Herself:

> As a mother comforts her child,
> so I will comfort you;
> you shall be comforted in Jerusalem. (Isa 66:13)

God also is called to nurturing responsibility for the offspring. Moses is angry because the people in the wilderness of Sinai are like babies needing care, and he says it is God's obligation and not his to mother and nurse them:

> Did I conceive all this people? Did I give birth to them, that you should say to me, "Carry them in your bosom, as a nurse carries a sucking child," to the land that you promised on oath to their ancestors? (Num 11:12).

Forty-eight times in the Bible God is called El Shaddai. While this is often explained as "God of the high places" from the Akkadian word *shadu,* which means mountain, El Shaddai can also be explained as "God, the breasted one" from the Hebrew word *shad,* which means breasts, with the old Ugaritic feminine ending *-ai.* (Abraham's wife was called "Sarai.") El Shaddai promises many children (Gen 17:1-22). El Shaddai brings blessings of the covenant with intimacy and fertility (Gen 28:3; 35:11; 48:3; 49:25).

The psalm Jesus quoted from the cross is a plea from a person in great pain, asking God to help because God was the midwife who brought the person to birth.

> Yet it was you who took me from the womb;
> you kept me safe on my mother's breast.
> On you I was cast from my birth,
> and since my mother bore me you have been my God.
> (Ps 22:9-10)

Christ's "time had come" and as a "woman in labor suffers," he was in travail that a new creation might be born through his death (John 17:1; 16:21).

Women do most of the childcare in the world. God is imaged as one caring for an unruly child:

When Israel was a child, I loved him,
and out of Egypt I called my son.
The more I called them,
the more they went from me;
they kept sacrificing to the Baals,
and offering incense to idols.
Yet it was I who taught Ephraim to walk,
I took them up in my arms;
but they did not know that I healed them.
I led them with cords of human kindness,
with bands of love.
I was to them like those
who lift infants to their cheeks.
I bent down to them and fed them. (Hos 11:1-4)

God, who has cared for people in childhood, also does so in old age:

Listen to me, O house of Jacob,
all the remnant of the house of Israel,
who have been borne by me from your birth,
carried from the womb;
even to your old age I am he,
even when you turn gray I will carry you.
I have made, and I will bear;
I will carry and will save. (Isa 46:3-4)

Women do most of the cleaning of both people and things in the world. God is imaged as one who cleanses: "I will sprinkle clean water upon you, and you shall be clean from all your uncleanness, and from all your idols I will cleanse you" (Ezek 36:25). Women traditionally have been the ones who clothed their families. God is imaged as one who clothes: "And the LORD God made garments of skins for the man and for his wife, and clothed them" (Gen 3:21). Nehemiah images the Exodus God as one who does the woman's work of seeing that her family has food, water, and clothes (Neh 9:20-21). God brings comfort and wipes away tears.

On this mountain the LORD of hosts will make for all peoples
a feast of rich food, a feast of well-aged wines,
of rich food filled with marrow, of well-aged wines strained
    clear . . .
Then the Lord GOD will wipe away the tears from all faces,
and the disgrace of his people he will take away from all
    the earth,
for the LORD has spoken. (Isa 25:6, 8)

Revelation also uses this imagery. God "will wipe every tear from their eyes. Death will be no more; mourning and crying and pain will be no more, for the first things have passed away" (Rev 21:4; cf. Rev 7:17).

Metaphors of God who conceives, is pregnant, writhes in labor pains, brings forth a child, and nurses the child abound. God is further imaged doing work that certainly could be done by men, but in biblical times—and to a large extent today—is done predominantly by women; God washes, cares for children, clothes, and wipes away the tears of one who is weeping.

The poetry of Jer 31:15-22 elaborates on the womb metaphor. The poem begins with Rachel, a mother whose womb was blessed by God, weeping for her children:

> A voice is heard in Ramah,
> lamentation and bitter weeping.
> Rachel is weeping for her children;
> she refuses to be comforted for her children,
> because they are no more. (Jer: 31:15)

God sees the straying child, Ephraim. God, like the mother Rachel, laments. Phyllis Trible reflects on this passage: "As Rachel mourns the loss of the fruit of her womb, so Yahweh, from the divine womb, mourns the same child. Yet there is a difference. The human mother refuses consolation; the divine mother changes grief into grace. As a result, the power has moved from the desolate lamentation of Rachel to the redemptive compassion of God. Female imagery surrounds Ephraim; words of a mother embrace her son."[3]

In the last verse the imagery changes and the son Ephraim becomes the daughter Israel. The climax of the poem is, "For the LORD has created a new thing on the earth: a woman encompasses a man" (v. 22). This could have many meanings; Rachel embracing her son, God consoling Rachel. The whole shape of the poem is like an embracing womb. Women's wisdom and compassion are needed to enclose and protect our world. Women who have wombs know the bonds of relationships, and these bonds extend more and more to all the human family. Women's sense of relationship, bondedness, and interdependence needs to be explored.

The Wisdom literature, including the books of Job, Psalms, Proverbs, Ecclesiastes, Song of Songs, Wisdom, and Sirach in the Septuagint collection, reveals ancient people's desires to collect the understanding that comes from human experience as well as their reflections on the divine. While the historical books help people's understanding, the Wisdom books (excepting Psalms and the Song of Songs, which are poetry about God and celebrating love) were particularly developed to instruct people. Though biblical Wisdom literature has similarities to such literature in other ancient Middle Eastern cultures, the biblical tradition moves toward the concept of the greatest wisdom as a personification of the divine.

God in the manifestation of Wisdom is often personified as female. The Hebrew word *ḥokmah* and the Greek *sophia* are developed both in the Bible and in extrabiblical Jewish and later Christian writings. A significant personification of God's Wisdom as female is in Sirach (also called Ben Sira or Ecclesiasticus), which was written about 190 B.C.E. In Jewish writings *Ḥokmah* is often identified with the Torah; God's wisdom is God's word.[4]

> Wisdom praises herself,
>> and tells of her glory in the midst of her people.
> In the assembly of the Most High she opens her mouth,
>> and in the presence of his hosts she tells of her glory . . .
> "Come to me, you who desire me,
>> and eat your fill of my fruits.
> For the memory of me is sweeter than honey,
>> and the possession of me sweeter than the honeycomb."
>> (Sir 24:1-2, 19-20)

God's female personification or manifestation comes in many ways in Sacred Scripture, as Creator (Prov 8:27-31; Sir 1:14; 8:34; 24:3-5; Bar 3:29-32), as Wisdom (Prov 4:1-6; Wis 6:12), as Teacher (Prov 1:20-22; 8:1-11; Sir 1:17-20; Wis 8:3-5), as Lover (Sir 4:11-18; 6:26-28; Wis 8:2-3, 9, 16), as a fruitful, sheltering Tree (Sir 24:12-19; 14:20-27), and as the Designer of History (Wis 10:9-12). Is Sophia, Wisdom God? Yes and no, as God is beyond any name, image, or description. The divine in deference to human weakness and limited understanding gives sacred texts that help humans grasp something of the incomprehensible mystery. Yes, in this way Sophia is God. Texts of Job and of Wisdom grapple with this hard question.

> Where then does wisdom come from?
> And where is the place of understanding?
> It is hidden from the eyes of all living,
> and concealed from the birds of the air. (Job 28:20-24)

> Because of her pureness she pervades and penetrates all things.
> For she is a breath of the power of God,
> and a pure emanation of the glory of the Almighty;

therefore nothing defiled gains entrance into her.
For she is a reflection of eternal light,
a spotless mirror of the working of God,
and an image of his goodness. (Wis 7:25-26)

In Christian Scriptures Jesus Christ is Sophia according to Paul in 1 Corinthians 1 and 2:

> For Jews demand signs and Greeks desire wisdom, but we proclaim Christ crucified, a stumbling block to Jews and foolishness to Gentiles, but to those who are the called, both Jews and Greeks, Christ the power of God and the wisdom [sophia] of God. For God's foolishness is wiser than human wisdom, and God's weakness is stronger than human strength. . . . He is the source of your life in Christ Jesus, who became for us wisdom [sophia] from God, and righteousness and sanctification and redemption. (1 Cor 1:22-25, 30)

> Yet among the mature we do speak wisdom [sophia], though it is not a wisdom of this age or of the rulers of this age, who are doomed to perish. But we speak God's wisdom [sophia], secret and hidden, which God decreed before the ages for our glory. None of the rulers of this age understood this; for if they had, they would not have crucified the Lord of glory. But, as it is written,

> > "What no eye has seen, nor ear heard,
> > nor the human heart conceived,
> > what God has prepared for those who love him—"
> > (1 Cor 2:6-9)

The gospel writers, the early theologians like Paul, tried to describe the mystery of Christ beyond any descriptions used so far. They struggled with this Jewish Messiah and king who had "failed" to fulfill those functions and who seemed divine; wouldn't such an assertion contradict cherished monotheism? Jesus speaks like *Sophia:*

> "Come to me, all you that are weary and are carrying heavy burdens, and I will give you rest. Take my yoke upon you, and learn from me; for I am gentle and humble in heart, and you will find rest for your souls. For my yoke is easy, and my burden is light." (Matt 11:28-29)

That passage is reminiscent of Sir 51:26:

> Put your neck under her yoke,
> and let your souls receive instruction;
> it is to be found close by.

Sirach 6 also uses the imagery of the yoke:

> Search out and seek, and she will become known to you;
> and when you get hold of her, do not let her go.
> For at last you will find the rest she gives,
> and she will be changed into joy for you.
> Then her fetters will become for you a strong defense,
> and her collar a glorious robe.
> Her yoke is a golden ornament,
> and her bonds a purple cord. (Sir 6:27-30)

Jesus speaks of himself as the hidden *Sophia* of God:

> At that time Jesus said, "I thank you, Father, Lord of heaven
> and earth, because you have hidden these things from the
> wise and the intelligent and have revealed them to infants;
> yes, Father, for such was your gracious will. All things have
> been handed over to me by my Father; and no one knows
> the Son except the Father, and no one knows the Father ex-
> cept the Son and anyone to whom the Son chooses to reveal
> him. (Matt 11:25-27)

Jesus' words sound like Wis 9:17-18:

> Who has learned your counsel,
> unless you have given wisdom
> and sent your holy spirit from on high?
> And thus the paths of those on earth were set right,
> and people were taught what pleases you,
> and were saved by wisdom.

The Wisdom, the *Sophia* of God is further revealed in the synop-
tic gospels in the words of Jesus, such as Matt 11:16-19 (Luke
7:31-35), Luke 10:21-22, Matt 23:34-36 (Luke 11:49-51), Matt
23:37-39 (Luke 13:34). The writer of John's gospel often enters
into the poetic beauty and imagery of the Wisdom tradition as
in John 1:1-3; 3:31-33; 5:19-20; 7:28-29; 8:23-24; 10:37-38; 12:44-48.

Christ is described with Sophia imagery in an early church
hymn recorded in Colossians:

> He is the image of the invisible God, the firstborn of all crea-
> tion; for in him all things in heaven and on earth were cre-
> ated, things visible and invisible, whether thrones or
> dominions or rulers or powers—all things have been created
> through him and for him. He himself is before all things, and
> in him all things hold together. (Col 1:15-17)

The historical Jesus was male, but the Christ is the fullness of humanity and of divinity that encompasses all so-called female and

male images of wisdom and goodness. In Matt 11:15-19 Jesus invites people not to be blinded to how *Sophia* manifests the Christ:

> Let anyone with ears listen! But to what will I compare this generation? It is like children sitting in the marketplaces and calling to one another, "We played the flute for you, and you did not dance; we wailed, and you did not mourn." For John came neither eating nor drinking, and they say, "He has a demon"; the Son of Man came eating and drinking, and they say, "Look, a glutton and a drunkard, a friend of tax collectors and sinners!" Yet wisdom is vindicated by her deeds.

Jesus' deeds were nurturing, helping the poor and the needy, healing, giving life, calling for justice, and describing a God infinitely more tolerant and compassionate than people could ever imagine. *Sophia*'s delight was to play among the children and *Sophia* "played the flute" and invited the dance.[5] *Sophia* prepared a banquet and Christ continues to do so. These images contrast with those of the warrior. *Sophia* reveals a God who allures the human family with delights rather than threatening them with retribution. Elizabeth A. Johnson writes extensively about the *Sophia* and christology and notes:

> Christ crucified and risen, the Wisdom of God, manifests the truth that divine justice and renewing power leavens the world in a way different from the techniques of dominating violence. The victory of *shalom* is won not by the sword of the warrior god but by the awesome power of compassionate love, in and through solidarity with those who suffer. The unfathomable depths of evil and suffering are entered into in friendship with Sophia-God, in trust that this is the path to life.[6]

A religious tradition does not drop from heaven in one day, but is part of the evolving consciousness of humankind. Christian images of the divine are a part of that larger history of human development. The Ten Commandments forbid graven images of the divine. The sin, the evil or danger is to think that any image of the divine, whether graven, verbal, or theological, can grasp the reality. God is always more than human descriptions. The God of the past, present, and future beckons the human family to see more and more of the limitless love imaging the divine.

Raphael Patai writes in *The Hebrew Goddess* that, though monotheism emphasized the masculine, there was never a period in Hebrew history without some imaging of the divine as feminine among the people.[7] Often in religious traditions there is a relationship between the sexual imagery of the divine and the persons who lead religious rituals. Hebrew Scriptures negatively describe women who participate in syncretistic rites. Phyllis Bird has noted that the rites are connected with female deities or deities whose cults were predominantly female (Deut 23:18; Hos 4:14; Gen 38:21-22; 2 Kgs 23:7; Ezek 8:14; Jer 7:18 and 44:17-19).[8] Was it zeal for the one God or for male supremacy that prompted opposition to these women honoring and leading worship of the divine image as female?[9] A similar question could be asked of opposition to female leadership and female images today.

After the egalitarian Jesus movement including female as well as male disciples, early communities of followers of Christ had both female leadership in ministry and female imagery of the divine. While there was a plurality of theologies and ministries in early Christianity, the male, hierarchical, authorized patterns prevailed and much of the female leadership and imagery were suppressed. Many contemporary scholars are working on reconstructions of early Christian origins, including women's participation in ministry, which has usually been omitted. These roots can strengthen the tree of Christianity. Biblical female images of the divine are beautiful and have potential for spiritually healing and balancing the overemphasis on masculinity. Part Two of this book gives examples of female leadership and imagery.

Biblical development of a God of compassion and justice, interwoven with the Wisdom tradition, forms a basis for critiquing violence between and among the religions of the world today. Violence is never a solution, but a perpetuation of the cycle of problems. Fools turn to violence, but Wisdom prepares a feast.[10]

Notes

[1] Phyllis Trible, *God and the Rhetoric of Sexuality* (Philadelphia: Fortress, 1978).

[2] Ibid., 62.

[3] Ibid., 45.

[4] For further discussion of Wisdom in both Hebrew and Christian Scriptures see Susan Cady, Marian Ronan, and Hal Taussig, *Wisdom's Feast: Sophia in Study and Celebration* (San Francisco: Harper & Row, 1989) 15–46.

[5] For further development of these ideas see Martha Ann Kirk, "Come Dance Sophia's Circle," in Doug Adams and Michael E. Moynahan, eds., *Postmodern Worship and the Arts* (San Jose: Resource Publications, 2002) 108–15.

[6] Elizabeth A. Johnson, *She Who Is: The Mystery of God in Feminist Theological Discourse* (New York: Crossroad, 1996) 159.

[7] Raphael Patai, *The Hebrew Goddess* (3rd ed. Detroit: Wayne State University Press, 1990).

[8] Phyllis Bird, "Images of Women in the Old Testament," in Rosemary Radford Ruether, ed., *Religion and Sexism* (New York: Simon & Schuster, 1974) 65.

[9] For more on the suppression of female power through the suppression of female God imagery in the early development of Judaism see Rosemary Radford Ruether, "Male Monotheism and the Dualizing of Gender Metaphors," in *Sexism and God-Talk* (Boston: Beacon, 1983) 53–54.

[10] See the Appendix for "Wisdom Prepares A Feast," a celebration of Scripture, story, prayer, and ritual based on these ideas.

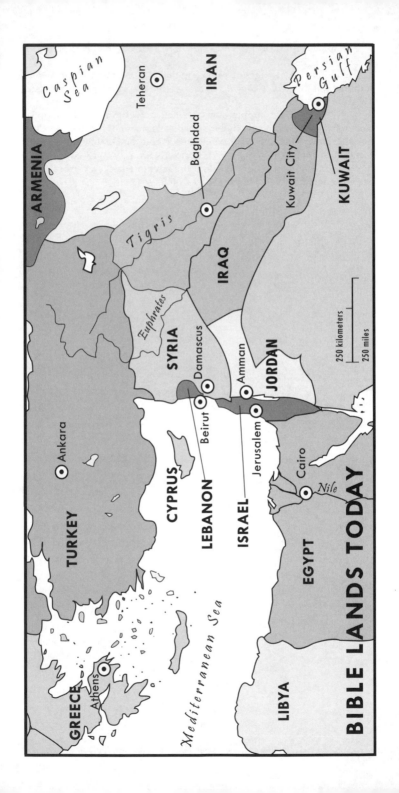

CHAPTER THREE

THE PILGRIMAGE
TO THE CENTER OF COMPASSION

Diary of Egeria, a Woman Pilgrim of the 380s C.E.

In the decade during which Christianity became the official religion of the Roman empire, the 380s C.E., Egeria, a nun from Spain or France, embarked on a three-year pilgrimage to learn of the places and people of the Bible and of the "living saints" there. In the course of her journey she visited the abbess of the monastery in Turkey founded where St. Thecla, according to legend, lived and died. Thecla, whose story was extremely popular among women and seems to have been spread by them, was a friend of Paul and, like him, boldly preached the gospel. From there, Egeria went on to Chalcedon to visit the shrine of the woman martyr "Euphemia, long known to me." About sixty-five years after Egeria's visit, churchmen met there for a council to define doctrines and turn to St. Euphemia for wisdom. Egeria, while on her journey, wrote to tell the nuns at home about the holy places, and that extraordinary account has survived.

> Leaving Tarsus, but still in Cilicia, I reached Pompeiopolis, a city by the sea, and from there I crossed into Isauria, and spent the night in a city called Corycus. On the third day I arrived at a city called Seleucia of Isauria, and, when I got there, I called on the bishop, a very godly man who had been a monk, and saw a very beautiful church in the city. Holy Thecla's is on a small hill about a mile and half from the city, so, as I had to stay somewhere, it was best to go straight on and spend the night there.

> Round the holy church there is a tremendous number of cells for men and women. And that was where I found one of my dearest friends, a holy deaconess called Marthana. I had come to know her in Jerusalem when she was up there on pilgrimage. She was the superior of some cells of *apotactites* or virgins, and I simply cannot tell you how pleased we were to see each other again. But I must get back to the point.

There are many cells on that hill, and in the middle a great wall round the *martyrium* itself, which is very beautiful. The wall was built to protect the church against the Isaurians, who are hostile, and always committing robberies, to prevent them trying to damage the monastery, which has been established there. In God's name I arrived at the *martyrium*, and we had a prayer there, and read the whole Acts of holy Thecla; and I gave heartfelt thanks to God for his mercy in letting me fulfill all my desires so completely, despite all my unworthiness. For two days I stayed there, visiting all the holy monks and *apotactites*, the men as well as the women; then, after praying and receiving Communion, I went back to Tarsus to rejoin my route.

I stayed there three days before setting off to continue my journey, and then after a day's traveling, arrived at a staging-post called Mansucrene below Mount Taurus. We stayed the night there, and the next day we climbed Mount Taurus, and continued along the road we already knew, since our outward journey had brought us along it. Passing through the same provinces of Cappadocia, Galatia, and Bithynia, I reached Chalcedon, and I stayed there because it contains the renowned martyrium of holy Euphemia, long known to me. Next day I crossed the sea and reached Constantinople, giving thanks to Christ our God for seeing fit, through no deserving of mine, to grant me the desire to go on this journey, and the strength to visit everything I wanted and now to return again to Constantinople.

And in all the churches at Constantinople, in the tombs of the apostles, and at many *martyria*, I never ceased to give thanks to Jesus our God for his grace in showing me such mercy.

So, loving ladies, light of my heart, this is where I am writing to you. My present plan is, in the name of Christ our God, to travel to Asia since I want to make a pilgrimage to Ephesus, and the *martyrium* of the holy and blessed Apostle John. If after that I am still alive, and able to visit further places, I will either tell you about them face to face (if God so wills), or at any rate write to you about them if my plans change. In any case, ladies, light of my heart, whether I am "in the body" or "out of the body," please do not forget me.[1]

One woman enjoys and gets strength from visiting another woman at a place made special by the memory of a holy woman who lived there. The visitor writes her friends, "loving ladies, light of my heart," to encourage them. This is a very simple scene, yet such a record is extraordinary. Hardly any words written by ancient Christian women have survived. Women were discouraged from traveling. Women church leaders are almost invisible in the huge pictures filled with churchmen. If women were to be remembered, it would be in relationship to men.

Though other first-person accounts like that of Egeria have not survived, some information on early Christian and Byzantine women pilgrims has. Several churchmen in developing their histories of the church and empire wrote of Helena, the mother of the emperor Constantine, who visited Palestine in 326 C.E. Jerome wrote of the Roman matron Paula traveling in Bible lands and then settling in Bethlehem in the 380s C.E. At about the same time Melania the Elder, described in the writings of Palladius, went on a pilgrimage, but then settled in Jerusalem. In the late 380s C.E. Poeminia, a member of the imperial family, with a retinue of bishops, priests, and eunuchs traveled to the east. In the 390s C.E. Sylvia of Aquitaine, the sister-in-law of a pretorian prefect, was a pilgrim. Melania the Younger, like her grandmother Melania the Elder, settled in Jerusalem. In 438–39 Eudocia Augusta, the consort of the eastern Roman Emperor, Theodosius II, encouraged by Melania, went to Jerusalem. After a number of years Eudoxia, the daughter of Eudocia and like her in an unpleasant marriage, went to Jerusalem. Why did these women go on pilgrimages? What are the origins of pilgrimage in the Jewish, Christian, and Islamic traditions?

Journey and Pilgrimage in the Bible

Sarah and Abraham journeyed from Ur of the Chaldees northwest along the Euphrates River and then down into the land of Canaan. Hebrew Scriptures also mention the journeys of Miriam and Moses and of the returning Babylonian exiles. Jews made pilgrimages to the Ark of the Covenant in Shiloh. From the time of Solomon's Temple, Jews went up to Jerusalem. After Herod's Temple had been built, at the time of Jewish festivals the population of Jerusalem tripled with all the pilgrims. Three festivals were celebrated with pilgrimages: Passover, Pentecost, and Booths, at all of which Jews were to appear before the Lord (Exod 23:14-17; Deut 16:16). Males, but not females, were obligated to go, but many women did attend.

In Christian Scriptures journeys are important. Mary and Joseph went to Bethlehem. The Magi seeking the Christ child were the archetypal pilgrims. Luke wrote of the pilgrimage to Jerusalem when the twelve-year-old Jesus was lost in the Temple. Jesus traveled to Egypt, Nazareth, the Sea of Galilee area, Jericho, and the Judean wilderness, around northern

Palestine, into what is now Lebanon, Syria, and Jordan, and repeatedly to Jerusalem for the feasts.

In Mark's gospel, the first to be written, Jesus gave the disciples directions for journeys to spread his good news: "He ordered them to take nothing for their journey except a staff; no
bread, no bag, no money in their belts; but to wear sandals and
not to put on two tunics. He said to them, "Wherever you enter
a house, stay there until you leave the place. If any place will
not welcome you and they refuse to hear you, as you leave,
shake off the dust that is on your feet as a testimony against
them" (Mark 6:8-12). His words may sound entirely impractical
for the modern traveler, but a light suitcase is much easier than
a heavy one and simple plans are better than complicated ones.
Tensions should be shaken off and forgotten and not stop one
from continuing or enjoying. Women disciples were among
those in the upper room at Pentecost, those commissioned to go
out to the ends of the earth. Were women among the early
groups sent out by Jesus? Did women like Mary Magdalene
have freedom to travel and to speak to strangers? Nomadic

women, like Bedouin women today, traveled, watching their flocks of sheep and goats and going to the wells.

Luke envisioned Jesus' active life as a journey toward Jerusalem (Luke 9:51). Jesus gave advice for traveling: "Whatever house you enter, first say, 'Peace to this house!' And if anyone is there who shares in peace, your peace will rest on that person; but if not, it will return to you" (Luke 10:5). He must have experienced peace at the home of Martha, Mary, and Lazarus because he frequently returned there. Luke used the journey motif to mean more than just the physical trip. On the journey toward Jerusalem, Jesus entered a village where Martha welcomed him to her home. The early followers of the way (of the Christ) on their journey toward Jerusalem (the place of *shalom* or *salaam*, of peace that is fullness of harmony and justice) were learning that women have a right to sit at the feet of a rabbi (to discuss and read Scripture as men do). The early followers were also learning about gathering to break bread, a ritual usually led by the head of the house whether female or male. The focus on the Christ among them was what really mattered. They did not need to be anxious about other things (Luke 10:38-42).

In John's gospel the journey of Jesus Christ is summarized: "I came from the Father and have come into the world; again, I am leaving the world and am going to the Father" (John 16:28). Jesus was God in self-exile, emptying himself, an itinerant preacher and healer with nowhere to lay his head, a challenge to all his followers who seek comfort, permanence, and security.

Jewish pilgrimages had been to the Temple, but for Jesus' followers the new temple is the Body of Christ. At the end of the gospels, in Acts, and in the epistles the journey is not to Jerusalem, but from Jerusalem to the ends of the earth. The journey is to go and share the good news and to feed the hungry, clothe the naked, shelter the homeless, heal the sick, and visit the imprisoned. The true Christian pilgrim begins to recognize Christ dying and rising in each face even to the ends of the earth.

Pilgrimage in Early Christianity

The tradition of Jerusalem as the spiritual navel of the world, the umbilical cord connecting the human with the divine, can be found in Judaism. Christians continued that idea of spiritual geography and also revered the tomb of Christ as a place of connection. Jerusalem was both the womb and the tomb where human life was connected with divine life. Within Christianity, unlike Judaism and Islam, there is no command to make a pilgrimage, but the practice appealed to Christ's followers. While the Christian idea of pilgrimage is related to the Jewish, there is a different emphasis. A Christian pilgrimage is an image of the inner journey toward the heavenly Jerusalem. A true Christian should be imbued with the spirit of Heb 13:14, "For here we have no lasting city, but we are looking for the city that is to come." The last book of the Bible, Revelation, poetically describes the new realm:

> Then I saw a new heaven and a new earth; for the first heaven and the first earth had passed away, and the sea was no more. And I saw the holy city, the new Jerusalem, coming down out of heaven from God, prepared as a bride adorned for her husband. And I heard a loud voice from the throne saying,
>
>> "See, the home of God is among mortals.
>> He will dwell with them as their God;
>> they will be his peoples,
>> and God himself will be with them;
>> he will wipe every tear from their eyes.
>> Death will be no more;
>> mourning and crying and pain will be no more,
>> for the first things have passed away." (Rev 21:1-4)

Melito of Sardis, the first identified Christian pilgrim, visited the Holy Land before 190 C.E.[2] Eusebius, who became bishop of Caesarea in about 313 C.E., wrote a biblical gazetteer. If any one person should be credited with attracting attention and making Roman Palestine into the "holy land, a place of pilgrimage" it should be Eusebius, because he both persuaded Constantine to invest in a building campaign there and wrote history to attract travelers. Helena, Constantine's mother, came to Palestine during Eusebius' lifetime and he probably welcomed and guided part of her journey. Not only in the Holy Land but along the way there, local people seem to have designated some of the "holy places" because they were conveniently located on roads. Pilgrims wanted to localize stories they had read.

During Constantine's era Christians' claiming of sites holy to them represented victory in a power struggle with pagans under whose domination they had lived. Constantine used the sites as a way of strengthening his own power since Christianity flourished in many parts of the empire and among many different cultural groups. After Christianity became a means of solidifying imperial power not only did pilgrimages to the Holy Land develop, but also desert spirituality. Ascetic life began and was centered in Egypt, but it soon spread to Palestine, especially the area around Jerusalem. Some ascetics—whether individually or in communities—had a calling to share their wisdom with pilgrims and/or to offer them hospitality. Some communities were specifically founded to care for pilgrims, and along the routes for European pilgrims could be found hospices hosted by religious communities. Maps of the Byzantine period are dotted with hundreds of *martyrium* shrines devoted to the martyrs. People have always made pilgrimages to the graves of loved ones, with these graves considered gates into the spiritual world.

After the Muslim conquest of the Holy Land it was possible for Christians to make pilgrimages, but it was more difficult and expensive. Consequently other places of pilgrimage developed in the West, such as the sites of Celtic saints in the British Isles and Santiago de Compostela in Spain. People might go to encounter saints, relics, or even living saints. In the Middle Ages cathedrals frequently had a labyrinth design on the floors. People who could not go to Jerusalem could walk and pray this path to the center. A tourist would be displeased with this cheap substitute, but being a tourist and being a pilgrim are different.

Pilgrimage in Islam

Muslims go to Jerusalem to pray because it is the third-holiest place in Islam, next to Mecca and Medina. However, when Muslims speak of "the pilgrimage," the *haj*, that means the trip to Mecca. Within Islam the definitive character of God is compassion. The call to prayer five times a day is a call to direct encounter with God. As one encounters God, one encounters compassion. For the daily practice of prayer the expectation for women is different from that for men, but for the pilgrimage both women and men perform the same rituals. In Islam one makes serious preparation before the pilgrimage, and with the homecoming one lives differently. One does not go on pilgrimage if one has unfulfilled family obligations. If children need to be provided for, if relations lack food or shelter, one serves God best by serving them first. One goes on the *haj* as a pilgrim, not as a tourist. One does not go to collect souvenirs, but with open hands for what touches the heart. Each should share the wisdom that has come from the experience; each should be a prophet. Those who have been on the *haj*, both women and men, take on more responsibility for the community. In the Muslim Quarter of the Old City of Jerusalem there are homes with painted images of the sacred place, the *Kaaba*, the shrine with the black stone in Mecca. The images proclaim to the neighborhood that the family living there has made the *haj*, the pilgrimage to Mecca, and that they will share because they have experienced this blessing.

Spirituality, Pilgrimage, and Women

Traditionally men have been associated with public spaces and women with private spaces. Men would go forth on journeys and adventures; women would remain at home caring for children and waiting for the men to return. The hero goes out to slay the dragon, conquer the other, kill or capture the prey. The pilgrimage is a heroic journey, but the goal is not the same. The pilgrim seeks the sacred. Destroying the other might be destroying a window to the sacred. Authentic pilgrims seek to understand the other, to find a common humanity, to learn from others and to share with others. The pilgrim does not conquer, claim, or put walls around the sacred destination of the pilgrimage, closing it off. The pilgrim hopes to find, to enjoy, and gently to pass through that sacred center open for all, awaiting all.

A pilgrimage is not just going to a particular holy place, but is a choice to leave the familiar, secure, comfortable, and convenient, believing that the gift of the divine that is to come will be greater than these. The pilgrim seeks the divine who is mystery and goes toward the unknown as an image of that. A pilgrim may be disoriented or at least surprised by the surroundings. One cannot control things as in familiar situations. A pilgrimage is as much an inner journey as an outer one. The main activity of a pilgrimage is not moving, not learning, not observing, not resting, though all of these are components, but prayer. Prayer is in the heart before leaving, along the way, at the destination, on the return, and in the homecoming. Pilgrimage is not the prayer of asking God for what "I" want, but the prayer of growing communion in which one comes to contemplate, praise, and thank the divine.

Pilgrimages seem to be particularly popular at times of transition in people's lives and at times of transition in a culture. Both types of transition may account for the recent popularity of pilgrimages. A major transition in the position of women in the world is taking place and the ancient tool of the pilgrimage is helpful in finding orientation in this transition. The pilgrim seeks to find the divine and in this to find herself or himself. Karen Armstrong has written:

> The cult of the holy place seems to have preceded any other form of reflection in the world: it was the axis for future cos-

mological speculation. Similarly pilgrimage, the first of our therapeutic quests, has remained an archetype of the later disciplines. The secret of its enduring success must surely be the dramatic simplicity with which it forces us to confront our need to root ourselves healthily and imaginatively in the past during our search for a spiritual centre of power.[3]

The search for women's past is more difficult than the search for men's past. The search for women's spiritual centers is more difficult because most of the signposts along the way show male images of the divine, who is beyond all the images.

Preparation

The physical preparation for a pilgrimage, the gathering of clothes, shoes, maps, resources for food and shelter, can be the outward sign of the spiritual preparation. One studies the route and the destination of the pilgrimage. Many possessions are a burden, not a boon, as one would be better off carrying less. A pilgrim does not go to shop, but to seek what is invisible to the eye. Clothes and shoes are the membranes to protect, but they must be flexible and light enough to facilitate movement. They help one to get close to the new, not be separated from it. Spiritually one needs to be covered so that he or she may not burn from the glory of the Son, or be drenched in waters of the rain, but the pilgrim must not be armored. Each of us lives in a particular cultural context that has given us certain assumptions. Sometimes these assumptions can harden into an armor of prejudice defining the other as bad rather than just recognizing the other as different. The efficient way we lead our lives with schedules can harden into an armor of control of time. A pilgrimage is not a crusade to defend my position and conquer the others'. The pilgrims' hearts should be softened as much as their shoes are worn. The maps are guides, but the right paths for glimpsing the sacred may be outside them.

Though only the saints attain perfect inner freedom, a pilgrim needs to examine her motivations. Does she go on a pilgrimage to please another? Is she on a pilgrimage to appease an angry or demanding god (not the God of the Jewish and Christian traditions)? Pilgrimages are not to prove goodness, stamina, or power; none of these reasons will do. Yet if these motives are mixed with one's yearning for the Holy One the discipline of the pilgrimage may be the fire that burns away the dross and leaves the gold.

Ancient pilgrimages were often so long and dangerous that a pilgrim could not be sure of return, so the journey took on the image of preparation to meet God. In the Middle Ages thousands of pilgrims died of sickness, exhaustion, and sometimes violence. People planning pilgrimages reviewed their lives, tried to settle accounts, to reconcile, and to be at peace. Many sought to confess and be absolved from their sins. Wealthy pilgrims often made donations to the needy before leaving. Some pilgrims left their possessions in trust with the church; if they returned safely they would continue to use their possessions, but if they did not return, the goods were to be for the needy. Before leaving for a pilgrimage to the Holy Land, Margery Kempe (1373–1439) asked the priest to make an announcement that if she owed debts to people they should come and make claims before she left. *The Book of Margery Kempe* was the first autobiography written in English and it describes, among other things, her pilgrimage.

Christian pilgrims often sought the prayers of their local communities to fortify them for their journeys. Pilgrimage was so elaborated by the Church that a liturgical ceremony was developed in which the pilgrims received not only blessings for their journeys but long, loose pilgrims' gowns, wide-brimmed hats with red crosses on them, staffs, pouches, and letters attesting that they were not profiteers.

Modern Orthodox pilgrims from Greece and Cyprus often save throughout their lives for a journey to Jerusalem. They make that pilgrimage near death, that they might touch the places where Jesus passed through death to life and that they may learn to make that transition peacefully. Going on a pilgrimage is entering the drama of the repeated life of Christ. A pilgrimage is more than just a Passion play; somewhat like the liturgy, a pilgrimage is entering into the timeless mysteries that one might enter into the grace of Christ's life and death.

Community and Interdependence

Some people in the ancient world felt called to be solitary pilgrims, but most traveled in groups for support and safety. Under the Emperor Jovinian in 364 C.E. a law was made that anyone who solicited consecrated virgins or widows was to be put to death. A number of the women included in this study—Helena, Melania the Elder, Melania the Younger, Eudocia, and Eudoxia—had retinues to accompany them. Egeria journeyed with monks, clerics, and at times bishops. Paula, her daughter Eustochium, Jerome, and probably some servants traveled together. Poimenia's entourage was splendid, with several ships carrying her eunuchs, Moorish slaves, and the bishop Diogenes.

Pilgrimages usually involve interdependence. Pilgrims do not have gardens to grow their foods, but are forced to eat from the gardens of others. Medieval pilgrims were urged to have their goods in common with the other pilgrims of their group, like the early Christian ideal in Acts 4:32. All was held in common and no one was needy among them. The forced proximity with other pilgrims and with strangers along the way can be a challenge for modern people used to independence, privacy, and control. Women pilgrims may have an advantage because they often have family skills of respecting, negotiating, and living interdependently. A disadvantage for women pilgrims is that women's needs are often trivialized in the public sphere.

While traveling with others can provide safety, or traveling with an organized tour can provide convenience, such protections can limit one's emotional and spiritual journey. One leaves home physically but keeps companions and comforts reminiscent of home. Even though one is in a group, planning periods or places of silence or solitude can open the wonders of the spiritual journey. Openness to the unexpected, the adventures, the serendipities is practice for openness to the divine who is not controllable or predictable.

The word "companion" comes from the Latin *cum panem*, with bread, the person with whom one shares bread. The Christ walked with a couple along the road to Emmaus. He seemed to be a stranger, but in that moment of sharing bread the couple's eyes were opened and their hearts were burning within them. Pilgrims, like that couple, begin to open their eyes more and more. They start to recognize many eucharistic bread-breakings along the way. The Eucharist was born on Jesus' pilgrimage to Jerusalem for the Passover. The Hebrew Passover was a kind of pilgrimage. Were women at the Last Supper table and was the wife that other person on the road to Emmaus? Was the bread made by women? Was the manna in the wilderness gathered by the women? The Christ is not the center of the all-male meal, but the center of an abundant table for children, old and young, females and males.

Modern pilgrims can encounter commercialism, theft, and the importuning poor. Discernment and prudence are needed. One should be careful, but travel with a basic conviction that there are infinitely more potential friends than enemies in the world. For me, being a woman has been more of an asset than a liability in travel. I neither try to dominate the others I encounter nor cower and let myself be dominated. At his last meal Jesus said that he did not call his companions servants, but friends (John 15:15). The hosts and strangers along the way should not be belittled as servants but respected as potential friends. Each step of the pilgrimage is learning to see. One is not in control, but that is all right. The journey is learning to choose simplicity, freedom, compassion, and wisdom. An authentic pilgrimage is an opportunity for the head to move the heart.

Challenges

The pilgrim's road is not always easy. The sights, smells, feels, and sounds are unfamiliar, sometimes even frightening. If a pilgrimage in no way calls for effort, for exertion or perseverance, will it really bring transformation? Making a pilgrimage can give one more compassion for the destitute, the homeless, immigrants, and refugees. Even though the insecurity felt by modern pilgrims is usually relatively small in comparison to that of ancient pilgrimages it can stretch one's heart to understand: "Foxes have holes, and birds of the air have nests; but the Son of Man has nowhere to lay his head" (Luke 9:58).

St. Paul uses the image of the athlete running as an image of the spiritual life. A pilgrimage has the dimension of discipline calling one beyond the ordinary daily effort of living. A pilgrimage takes strength. Many places of pilgrimage cannot be reached by plane, boat, train, bus, or car, or at the least the last stage of the journey must be on foot. Rushing can blind the pilgrim to the grace of each step. One does not rush in to get the holy; awareness, care, deliberation, and patience are needed. The God who shaped the mountains and carved out the valleys has enough time and invites the pilgrim into those moments beyond time. The holy is to be approached with care, as in this one may begin to recognize the holy in all of life.

Modern researchers have examined the idea that women are the weaker sex. What are the criteria for strength? Women live longer than men, and that might be called greater strength. Women carry and bear children, and this requires substantial physical endurance. This might be called greater strength. In dancing, running, and swimming women excel. What is strength? I am not an athlete, but I am a dancer. I know the exhilaration that comes when I have exerted what seems like all my strength, come to a threshold of pain, gone through it, and entered a new plateau of possibilities. Whether climbing Mount Sinai or moving through the interminable airport lines, pilgrims need strength.

Gregory of Nyssa and Jerome both wrote about the weakness of females with the idea that pilgrimages might just be too much for them. Helena was in her late seventies, but made the journey around the eastern section of the Roman empire. In writing of their visit to the ascetics of Egypt, Jerome demeaned women while extolling Paula, "With a zeal and courage unbelievable in a woman [Paula] forgot her sex and her physical weakness, and longed to make there, amongst those thousands of monks, a dwelling for herself and her daughters. All were welcoming her and she might have done so, if she had not been summoned away by a still greater longing for the holy places."[4] Paula was undaunted by the heat and discomfort of the desert and the travel. Gregory of Nyssa, who wrote such high praise of his sister Macrina's virtue and strength in founding and leading a monastic group, seems to question whether ordinary women should go on pilgrimage. Women need to be scrupulous to preserve their virtue.

> . . . the necessities of a journey are continually apt to reduce this scrupulousness to a very indifferent observation of such rules. For instance, it is impossible for a woman to accomplish so long a journey without a conductor; on account of her natural weakness she has to be put upon her horse and be lifted down again; she has to be supported in difficult situations . . . whether she leans on the help of a stranger, or on that of her servant she fails to keep the law of correct conduct; and as the inns and hostelries and cities of the East present many examples of license and of indifference to vice, how will it be possible for one passing through such smoke to escape without smarting eyes? Where the ear and the eye is defiled, the heart is too, by receiving all those foulnesses through eye and ear, how will it be possible to thread without infection such seats of contagion?[5]

This book examines women's stories as told by men and women's stories as told by themselves. In contrast to Gregory and Jerome's remarks about female weakness are Egeria's excited, energetic, and grateful comments day after day, month after month for three years. She in no way indicated that the rigors of a pilgrimage were beyond the strength of the female sex.

Destination, Return, and Homecoming

Not all was peaceful and happy at pilgrim places in Jerusalem. In 380 C.E. Gregory of Nyssa was sent there to settle a quarrel among the clergy and he wrote a letter expressing his frustration with the emphasis on pilgrim places: "If God's grace were more plentiful in the Jerusalem neighbourhood than elsewhere, then its inhabitants would not make sin so much the fashion. But as it is, there is no sort of filthy conduct they do not practice—cheating, adultery, theft, idolatry, poisoning, quarrelling and murder are commonplace. . . . Then what proof have you, in a place which allows things like that to go on, of the abundance of divine grace?"[6]

One arrives at the sacred place. Often the destination is full of noise and commercialism. There is disappointment after all the anticipation, and the thought that all that is left is a return home. The profound insight or the miraculous cure have not occurred. In the pilgrimage tradition the destination is the place where the veil or membrane separating the ordinary reality and the sacred are so thin. The tomb of Christ has always been a central place for pilgrims. Unless one can recognize and enter into the daily deaths that living in love brings, going to the tomb is of no value.

Women have traditionally been the people who have kept the home. A pilgrimage can be extending the boundaries of home, the boundaries of friendship, family, and who shares the nurture and the affection. On a pilgrimage people move out of themselves toward another center and finally through this are able to rediscover themselves. The Samaritan woman at the well learned that God is spirit and truth. This God is to be found and worshiped everywhere. The pilgrim can look not just on the mountain of Samaria or the Temple mount of Jerusalem, but into the faces of those at home. Awareness grows of the mystery in which one is living at all times.

One returns to life as normal, but it will never be the same again. The pilgrim searched for God, but even more, God searched for her. A pilgrim went to find God, but only because God first came to find him. The pilgrimage is learning to recognize the divine in the face of the children of Beirut and the children of Bethlehem and the children of Jerusalem, and being committed to the well-being of all the children in the world. A pilgrimage to the Holy Land is coming to understand that all lands are holy and all people are beloved of God.

Bible Lands: the Geographical Area Considered

Most of the stories in the Hebrew Scriptures take place in the small area between the eastern Mediterranean and the desert. This land of Palestine or Canaan is only about 150 miles long and stretches from "Dan to Beer Sheva." The Holy Land, a crossroads between Europe, Africa, and Asia, through the ages has been disputed territory and often a place of violence. Genesis tells of matriarchs and patriarchs settling in that land. Exodus and Joshua describe the Israelites' returning there and trying to take the land from the people who lived there. Much of the Bible describes constant struggles for that land. All the areas bordering it are part of the biblical stories, including what is now called Jordan, Lebanon, Syria, Sinai, and Egypt. The Jewish people were conquered by Babylon, which is now Iraq, which was then conquered by Persia (which is now Iran). Jesus' followers, especially Paul, spread his teachings around the Mediterranean to Turkey, Greece, Cyprus, Malta, and Rome. This book, while mostly focused on the area from "Dan to Beer Sheva," will also consider the other areas. While not actually mentioned in the Bible, the ancient cities of Carthage and Hippo in contemporary Tunisia have been included because they share cultural links with Bible lands.

Visiting the sites associated with women of antiquity and getting to know contemporary peoples of these countries can give one a sense of the connection between peoples that is often forgotten with the national borders of modern states and the politics of alliances and enemies. When one travels in Bible lands the modern distinctions that are made between Middle Eastern, European, and African begin to disappear. One can see ruins of baptismal fonts in North Africa similar to those in Palestine, similar to those in Italy. The Roman empire had the best system of roads until the modern period. The Mediterranean Sea served as a bridge of connection more than as a barrier, with regular trade voyages between Caesarea in Palestine, Tyre in Phoenicia, Antioch in Syria, Ephesus in Asia Minor, Athens and Corinth in Greece, and the cities of Rome, Carthage in North Africa, and Alexandria in Egypt.

The Time Periods Considered

In the history of forming their identity Jews, Christians, and Muslims, each of the peoples of the Religions of the Book, have displayed some violence, both physically and psychologically. As adolescents try to define themselves by opposing parents or others, so religions have attempted this. The writing of the Johannine author of the Fourth Gospel often stereotypes the Jews as blind and evil, confusing the issue that Jesus was a Jew and that among all groups there are some individuals who are open and some who are not. Women have participated in the violence of religions in different ways. Deborah, Jael, and Judith are remembered for destroying the "others." Um Sulaym Bint

Malhan tucked a dagger into her belt over her pregnant abdomen as she fought for the acceptance of the Muslims in Medina in the 620s C.E. Helena, the mother of Constantine, may have gone to Jerusalem and Bethlehem to honor the Christ, or her journey may have been political manipulation and psychological violence, imposing Christianity for the sake of political unity. Christian women certainly cheered on their Crusader husbands, who were killing thousands of Jews and Muslims. The Crusades were described as pilgrimages or as efforts to make ways safe for pilgrims, but they seem in fact to have come to contradict the heart of what a pilgrimage is, namely finding the sacred. Anyone, whether called Jew, Muslim, or Christian, who spills the blood of another does not reveal, but hides the face of the Compassionate One. All three religions of the Peoples of the Book have violated the heart of what a pilgrimage seeks. The violent imposition of Judaism in parts of the land of Canaan, the violent imposition of Christianity in parts of the Roman empire, and the violent imposition of Islam in Byzantium and some other areas are descriptive of history, but not prescriptive of divine will.

When adolescents become integrated, confident adults they do not have to define themselves by opposition to or destruction of the other. The Peoples of the Book are maturing, very slowly. The mystics and prophets lead the way. This book is an invitation to journey to the center where one may encounter the purifying fire, the tender embrace, and the infinite depths of compassion.

The issues of what in culture is important and what is lasting begin to shift. With whom is the divine blessing? Is it with peoples of Egypt whose religion lasted longer than Christianity has been in existence? Is it the kingdom of David that is destined by God? Is it the Babylonian empire, or the Assyrian, or the Persian? Perhaps the divine favor was with the Roman empire, which united such diverse peoples around the Mediterranean and developed a communication and travel network that helped spread Christianity? On the other hand, the intermeshing of the teachings of Jesus Christ with the political goals of the Constantinian and then Byzantine political empires may have been a profound distortion of authentic Christianity. Mohammed the prophet taught the sovereignty of God and the importance of complete submission to God's will. Is divine favor with those who follow the Islamic vision, which changed the boundaries and the connections of what had been Egyptian, Davidic, Babylonian, Assyrian, Persian, Roman, and Byzantine areas? The Crusaders conquered Jerusalem in 1099, slaying thousands of Muslim and Jewish children, women, and men as quickly as possible so that the soldiers could pray vespers together in the evening to thank God. Did the Holy One rejoice in this victory or weep? The traumatized Jewish survivors of the Nazi Holocaust seized land, homes, and businesses, and displaced 712,000 Palestinians.[7] Did the Holy One rejoice in the victory or weep? The United States, a nation so often identified with Christianity, in a few days bombed 50,000 children, women, and men of Iraq. Did the Holy One rejoice in the victory or weep?

On a modern journey one might begin to recognize the divine image reflected in the faces of the elderly. One might begin to hear God's voice five times a day as one hears the cry of the muezzin in the mosque inviting prayer. One tries to listen and to conform one's will to that of the Holy One. In the deep prayer and often tears at what is left of the Temple built by Herod, the Western or Wailing Wall, one might come to know the God who weeps with any who suffer. On a pilgrimage one might begin to learn that the Holy One weeps with any who have suffered and will be with those who give their lives trying to lessen suffering in the future. One might begin to listen to the growing voices of the women that have been so hard to discern in the five thousand years of written cultures in Egypt and Mesopotamia.

The Journey to Jerusalem, the Journey to the Center of Compassion

As was mentioned earlier, Jerusalem has significance as both a sacred womb and a sacred tomb. Medieval Christians, more interested in spiritual geography than physical geography, laid out maps with the Holy Land in the very center of the world. As was discussed in the last chapter, the Hebrew word for God's compassion, *rachămim*, is from the root word meaning womb. Phyllis Trible in *God and the Rhetoric of Sexuality* discusses the story given as an illustration of the wisdom of Solomon (1 Kgs 3:16-28). Two harlots have babies, but one dies during the night. Both harlots claim the living child as their own. While the two women argue, Solomon orders that the living child be cut in half and each woman given a part. The real mother feels compassion, *rachămim*, for her child and would rather give him up than see him killed. She has Godlike compassion. God's compassion for creatures is like the womb-love of a woman for her child.[8] The womb protects and nurtures, but then gives forth life. It does not permanently control, but selflessly gives. Out of the compassionate womb of Jerusalem people of faith are born. In

Jerusalem one may learn more of the sacred, that heartbeat of compassion at the center of all creation.

In Jerusalem one may learn more of the Wisdom tradition, one of the feminine faces of God mentioned in the last chapter. The story of the two mothers and Solomon manifests the Wisdom tradition. It involves the search for the true mother. The true Christian, the true Muslim, the true Jew all know that the true God would rather give than see life destroyed. To destroy is to betray Moses who carried God's tablets saying "Thou shalt not kill." To destroy is to betray Jesus who gave his life but would not take the life of another. And it is to betray Mohammed who said that God is essentially compassion.

Notes

[1] Egeria, *Egeria's Travels*. Newly translated with supporting documents and notes by John Wilkinson (London: S.P.C.K., 1971) 121–23.

[2] E. D. Hunt, *Holy Land Pilgrimage in the Late Roman Empire, 312–460* (Oxford: Oxford University Press, 1984) 81.

[3] Karen Armstrong, "A Passion for the Holy Places," *The Sunday Times Magazine* (April 15, 1990) 32.

[4] Martin Robinson, *Sacred Places, Pilgrim Paths* (London: Harper Collins, 1997) 175.

[5] Gregory of Nyssa, cited in Henry Wace and Philip Schaff, eds., *A Selected Library of Nicene and Post-Nicene Fathers of the Christian Church.* V: *Gregory of Nyssa* (New York: The Christian Literature Company, 1893) 382–83.

[6] *On Pilgrimages*, MPG 46.1009–16, as quoted by Wilkinson in *Egeria's Travels*, 21.

[7] Of the 712,000 Palestinians driven out of their homes by the Israelis in the late 1940s, about 50,000 were Christians. Thirty-five percent of all Palestinian Christians lost all their possessions, houses, businesses, and lands. Mitri Raheb, *I Am a Palestinian Christian*, translated by Ruth C. L. Gritsch. Foreword by Rosemary Radford Ruether (Minneapolis: Fortress, 1995) 16.

[8] Phyllis Trible, *God and the Rhetoric of Sexuality* (Philadelphia: Fortress, 1978) 31–59.

CHAPTER FOUR

SEEKING THE TRUE CROSS,
SEEKING THE TRUE HELENA

The 326 C.E. pilgrimage of Helena, the mother of the emperor Constantine, is significant for this study in two ways: her travels are the most glorified early Christian pilgrimage, and stories about her are examples of a woman's story being interpreted and reinterpreted by men. Legendary finder of the True Cross, Helena is a woman whose purposes, feelings, and spirituality remain unknown. Helena lived about 249 to 329 C.E., and she probably became a Christian in 312 C.E. after Constantine's acceptance of Christianity. In 324 C.E. he gave her the official title "Augusta," and from then on many coins were minted with her image.

In the first three hundred years of Christianity the symbol of the cross was unimportant. It was a tool of torture, an object of disgrace. Beginning in the fourth century, the symbol of the cross appears on houses, tombs, weapons, clothes, coins, and other objects, helping in the spread of Christianity. Great veneration for the cross began in Jerusalem in the fourth century and spread to other places where there were Christians. In the 320s C.E. a piece of wood believed to be the True Cross was found, greatly encouraging the cult of the cross.[1]

The foremost original source of information about Helena is the *Vita Constantini* by Eusebius, bishop of Caesarea, who was probably a part of her retinue during her visit to Palestine. His writings do not indicate that she was associated with the cross. In the late fourth and early fifth centuries three legends about the finding of the True Cross developed, one of which associated Helena with it. By 450 there were seven texts embellishing the legend of Helena finding the cross, those of Rufinus, Socrates (given below), Sozomen, Theodoret, Ambrose, Paulinus of Nola, and Sulpicius Severus.[2] The fifth-century Christian historian Socrates Scholasticus wrote this version:

> The mother of the emperor, Helena (after whom the emperor named the city, Helenopolis, formerly the town of Drepanes), enjoying [guidance] by God through dreams,

went to Jerusalem. Discovering that which formerly was Jerusalem to be "desolate as a crop-watcher's hut," according to the prophet (Is. 1:8 LXX), she diligently sought the tomb of Christ, the location of the grave from which he arose. And she found it with God's help, albeit with some trouble. What the cause of the trouble was, I shall briefly report. People who were inclined to Christianity honored the tomb after the time of Christ's Passion, but those who rejected Christianity heaped up earth upon the spot, built a temple of Aphrodite, and erected her statue, not preserving the memory of the place. This situation lasted a long time and the emperor's mother heard about it. Thus when she had the statue taken down, the soil that had been heaped up on the spot removed, and the area opened up, she found three crosses in the tomb. One was the blessed cross on which Christ had been outstretched and the others were those on which the two thieves were put to death by crucifixion. With these was also found the tablet of Pilate on which he had written that the crucified Christ was the King of the Jews, this title being proclaimed in various alphabets. The emperor's mother was in a state of some distress since it was unclear which cross they were seeking. The bishop of Jerusalem, named Macarius, soon alleviated her anxiety; by his faith he dismissed her doubt. For he asked God for a sign and received it. The sign was this: a certain woman of the area who suffered from a chronic disease had just come to the point of death. The bishop arranged for each of the crosses to be brought to the dying woman, believing that she would regain her strength if she touched the honored cross. Nor was he mistaken in his hope, for when the two crosses that were not the Lord's were brought near, she remained no less in her dying condition, but when the third, the genuine cross, was brought near her, the dying woman immediately was healed and regained her health. This, then was the way in which the wood of the cross was found. The emperor's mother built on the spot of the sepulchre a sumptuous church and named it the "New Jerusalem," placing it opposite that old and forsaken city. She left on the very spot a piece of the cross enclosed in a silver chest as a remembrance for those wanting to inquire after it. The other part she sent to the emperor, who, when he received it, believing that the city where it was kept would be made completely safe, concealed it in his own statue that was set on a great column of porphyry, placed in the forum that is called Constantine's Constantinople. Although I have written this from hearsay, nearly all the residents of the city of Constantinople say it is true. In addition, Constantine took the nails with which the hands of Christ were fixed to the cross (indeed, his mother had found them, too, in the tomb and had sent them) and made them into bridle-bits and a helmet that he used in his battles. The emperor defrayed the cost of all the supplies for the construction of the churches. He also wrote to Bishop Macarius to hasten the construction of these buildings. And when the emperor's mother had finished the "New Jerusalem," she constructed another church, not inferior, at the cave in Bethlehem where the birth of Christ according to the flesh took place. But this wasn't all: she built another church on the mountain of the Ascension. She was so pious in these matters that she prayed in the company of women. She invited the virgins who were listed on the rolls of the church to a banquet and served them herself, carrying the food to the tables. She also gave a great deal to the churches and to the poor. And when she had piously completed her life, she died at about eighty years of age. Her corpse was transported to the capital city, New Rome [Constantinople] and placed in the imperial tomb.[3]

The story as Socrates wrote it would hold up ideals for others to imitate: be a Christian to be one of the powerful elite of the empire; donate to churches, to the poor, and to groups of virgins dedicated to Christ; serve others; go on a pilgrimage to where Christ was; respect the emperor. Socrates' serious statement that the nails that hung Christ on the cross became part of the helmet and bridle that helped Constantine win military victories is sadly ironic. This early church historian points to a contradiction in the message of Christ's cross through the ages. Part of what nails Christ to the cross is ongoing violence, the destruction of others. Ambrose, in a sermon on February 25, 395 C.E. that was an obituary for the Emperor Theodosius speaks of Helena finding the cross and the nails while glorifying the empire inaugurated by Constantine. Ambrose also happens to be the theologian who developed the "just war" theory.

Though later generations lauded Constantine for the legacy of the Christian faith, his actual life was far from ideal. Constantine fought his father for the empire and won, telling his father that either he could drink poison or be dragged to death by a horse. The father chose poison. Later, on the night of October 27, 313, when Constantine was in the midst of another military struggle for power, he saw a cross and heard a voice, "In this sign you shall conquer." Constantine missed the meaning of the cross. Jesus died returning good for evil, refusing to return violence for violence. Christ conquered violence by refusing to return it and thus stopping the cycle of violence.

Constantine was superstitious; he had crosses painted on every shield, helmet, and trapping of his army by the morning of October 28. He won the Battle of the Milvian Bridge. This was the first time a Christian symbol had been used for violence, and Constantine wiped out his two rivals.

The Edict of Milan in 313 C.E. made Christianity legal. Early Christians depicted Christ as a teacher or a protecting shepherd. In the first two centuries Christians seemed to be learning and teaching the message and the example of nonviolence that Jesus Christ had given. When he was in the Garden of Olives praying and Judas brought guards to arrest him, Peter pulled out his sword and cut off the ear of the high priest. Jesus chose not to fight and not to flee. Those who live by the sword die by the sword. Jesus stopped Peter and he reached out and healed the man who had come to hurt him. The way of nonviolence is reaching out and healing the very ones who try to hurt. In the first two centuries those who followed Christ were beginning to understand that killing someone for one's own truth does nothing in settling differences. Dying for one's truth changes hearts. Christians were being persecuted and often killed, but their numbers grew. Nonviolence had not made Christians weaker. They had not been wiped out; instead, Christianity grew stronger.

Hippolytus of Rome, in his directions for church order written in 215 C.E., laid out the prerequisites for admission into the catechumenate, the many-year period of study, exploration, and discernment that would come before a person was allowed to be baptized and become a Christian. Section 14 said that if a person were a pimp he or she would have to give up "pimping" before entering the catechumenate. If one were not yet ready to do that, one was not ready to start studying Christianity. Section 16 said that if a man was in the military he must go to his superior and say that he would not kill another person in any circumstance. If the superior said that was impossible, the person must leave the military. Many sources before 313 show that followers of Christ knew he had taught nonviolence. No one could be a member of the Roman army and be a Christian.

In 313 Constantine started allying Church with empire, and the first "just war" theory was developed in 368. As Christians were profiting from the wealth of the empire they began to rationalize violence. By 416 *only* baptized Christians could be in the Roman army. Some bishops supported this, saying that it was a Christian's duty to be in the army.[4]

Constantine promoted and attended the Council of Nicea in 325 to increase his political power. Probably it was there that Macarius, bishop of Jerusalem, told Constantine about the temple of Aphrodite covering the area where Christians said Christ had been buried. Constantine initiated a grandiose building complex on the spot, with edifices adorned with gold, mosaics, and precious marble. The complex included the basilica, called the *Martyrium,* and the Rotunda, called the *Anastasis,* over the tomb. All were connected by an inner courtyard. In 1009 the basilica was destroyed, but the remodeled *Anastasis* still exists in the Church of the Holy Sepulchre.

Constantine had sought to make Christianity the official religion in the empire, though Christians were not the majority. He prohibited many cults and set up magnificent Christian churches that they might have appeal where there had been pagan shrines. The sudden change in religious policy in the empire caused unrest. Though Constantine had been executing this program somewhat prudently in the Western empire, once he had defeated Licinius in the Eastern empire he began hastily imposing Christianity and disturbing both pagans and Jews.[5]

In 326 Constantine had his son Crispus and his son's mother, Fausta, executed because he feared threats to his power. Helena had seen Constantine destroy his father years before, and this turmoil within the royal family was not a good image for the empire. Some scholars suggest that Helena journeyed to the eastern provinces of the Roman empire that year to spread a better image of their ruler. Eusebius wrote of her going to the holy places to pray for her son and her grandsons. The comment may have more to do with the piety of this bishop historian than hers, yet this grandmother in her seventies must have had some feelings about her grandson and son.

Eusebius, in his *Vita Constantini* II 42, indicated that Helena was not just going to Palestine to supervise the building of the churches, but also was motivated by faith in wanting to pray at the places where Christ's feet walked. Eusebius speaks of her generosity, good deeds, charity, humility, and piety. The bishop's edifying story of the religious pilgrimage in Palestine may be as important for motivations it excludes as for the devotion it includes. Helena was not traveling as a humble pilgrim; she was traveling as an Augusta, a representative of the emperor to all the eastern provinces.

Eusebius wrote of Helena helping prisoners and exiles, of her giving to the poor and to soldiers. In the Roman empire sometimes bonus gifts were given to soldiers for special occasions, but Helena was not there at a special time. Rebellious soldiers were given gifts to win their favor, and many of these soldiers had served under Licinius, whom Constantine defeated. Was she bribing to win their loyalty? In line with Constantine's policy of

Christianizing the empire by building churches, Helena in-
spected and brought gifts to the basilicas he initiated, but the stories of Helena as the founder of the churches at the holy places
spread extensively.[6] Across the empire she lavished gifts on
churches, gifts that could help attract converts. Helena seems to
have gone to the provinces of the Eastern empire as a political
ambassador to win favor for Constantine, but Eusebius describes
her as a pious pilgrim to the Holy Land. His story gives a model
for people to be pilgrims and to imitate the virtues he describes.

No texts of Helena's day suggest that she found the True
Cross, but she certainly carried her own cross. She seemed very
faithful to her son Constantine, but how did she feel about his
murdering his father, son, and wife? Did Helena visit Naim and
weep with the widow over spiritual and physical deaths? Or,
along the roads of Galilee, did Helena importune Christ as did
the mother of James and John, "May my son sit at your right
hand in the kingdom?" What did Helena understand of the
kingdom of God? The wooden fragment that was known as the
True Cross is lost today. Pilgrims visiting Helena's chapel below
the Church of the Holy Sepulchre in the legendary place where
the cross was found cannot venerate the wood. The challenge
for contemporary pilgrims is to recognize in their lives and in
the world the true crosses and what nails Christ there.

What did Helena believe, feel, and say? Her story was written and rewritten by churchmen at the service of developing
the patriarchal church. She is the supporting character in the
story of her powerful son. Women serve the church and women
support their sons. Yet what are women's stories as told by
themselves, not by men? What are women's lives in themselves, not as pieces of the lives of men? Can women's lives be
found? Where is the story of the nonviolent Christ in the story
of Christendom? Can he be found? Pilgrims are still seeking
and searching.

Notes

[1] Jan Willem Drijvers, *Helena Augusta: The Mother of Constantine the Great and the Legend of Her Finding of the True Cross* (Leiden: Brill, 1992) 93.

[2] Ibid., 79.

[3] Socrates Scholasticus, *Ecclesiastica Historia*, ed. Robert Hussey (Oxford, 1853) 1:104, as cited in Elizabeth Clark, *Women in the Early Church* (Wilmington: Michael Glazier, 1983) 184–86.

[4] Ideas from "The Non-Violent Jesus," a lecture presented by Emmanuel Charles McCarthy, September 1996, Our Lady of the Lake University, San Antonio, Texas.

[5] Drijvers, *Helena Augusta*, 67.

[6] Ibid., 65–67.

Black Sea

Constantinople

GOTI

Edessa

N
W ⊕ E
S

Shrine of St. Thecla in Seleucia

Antioch

SYRIA

CYPRUS

From Rome to Antioch is about 1400 miles

Nazareth

Mediterranean Sea

PALESTINA

Mount Nebo

Jerusalem
Gaza

Pelusium

Bethlehem

Alexandria

ARABIA

NITRIA

Memphis

AEGYPTUS

Mount Sinai

To Alexandria
and the Thebaid
returning by Goshen

Nile River

Red Sea

200 miles
322 km

Thebes

- - - EGERIA'S JOURNEYS - 381-384 C.E.

PAULA'S JOURNEYS - 385 C.E.

CHAPTER FIVE

ASCETIC LIFE, AN INNER JOURNEY

Paula and Egeria, Their Outer and Inner Journeys

Stories and words of women ascetics in Egypt, Palestine, Turkey, and Greece are a major part of the collection of words and accounts of early Christian monastics. Monastic structures, the community of Christians, and the politics of the church have contributed to the possibility of ascetic women's stories and words being preserved more than those of women in general. Female communities in the East had long existed before Melania in Jerusalem and Paula in Bethlehem, but the aristocratic background of these women gave their activities high profile. They had abundant resources and connections with notable churchmen and local civic leaders to get ongoing recognition of and support for their foundations. Through these means and the self-confidence that comes from being "called by God" these wellborn women exercised authority and power in ways that ordinary women usually could not. Melania, Paula, Macrina in Cappadocia, and Olympias in Constantinople had extensive control of their monastic institutions, and their lives were recorded by prominent churchmen.

The two ascetics most prominently represented are Paula and Egeria, and the accompanying map indicates the extent of their travels. Paula is significant not only as a founder of the women's monastic community in Bethlehem but as the patron of the male community there, a fine Scripture scholar, and a pilgrim whose travels were documented by Jerome. Though less is known of Egeria's background and her life as a nun, her own writing as a pilgrim reveals much about her interests, her outlook on life, and her relations with people and with God. More of her writings survive than those of any other ancient Christian woman, and they reveal a spiritual, intelligent, integrated, energetic, and courageous woman.

Beginnings of Christian Asceticism

Probably the earliest women and men choosing asceticism lived lives of devotion in their own homes. The *Didache*, a first- or second-century document of Church practices, mentions such a life. Paul, the first remembered Egyptian hermit, lived from 228 to 343 C.E. At the time of the Decian persecutions (ca. 250 C.E.) many Egyptian Christians fled to the deserts, especially to the Scetis area. Surprisingly, when Christianity became legal even more women and men fled to the desert than during the persecutions.

St. Anthony of Egypt left his sister with a women's community, probably in Alexandria, and went to the desert in 271 C.E. St. Hilarion, who was born in Gaza, went to study in Alexandria and then met Anthony. Hilarion returned to Gaza in 308 C.E. and contributed to the development of ascetic life in this area along the Mediterranean. A number of hermits lived near the coast. In Egypt Pachomius, known for the development of community life, lived from about 275 to 349 C.E. Egypt was the center of ascetic life but it also was developing in Sinai, Palestine, and Syria at about the same time. In Palestine there is a ten-mile-wide desert in a deep valley of the Jordan and the Dead Sea that is associated with Elijah and John the Baptist. By 200 C.E. Christian ascetics were living there. By 300 C.E. monasteries had developed in the region.

The life expectancy of people in the Roman empire was about 25 years. Only about one man in four lived to be 50, and even fewer women. For the population to remain steady, a woman needed to bear five children. Choosing virginity was considered antisocial, and families arranged marriages for daughters at any time after the age of puberty. Women sought a life of prayer in the desert, but some also may have wanted freedom from the expectations of husbands and family. A church gathering in Elvira, Spain in 306 C.E. discussed those who had made vows of virginity, noting that even more women than men had done this. In 314, two years after Constantine had accepted Christianity as a legal religion, bishops and priests gathered at Ancyra (Ankara, Turkey) to make plans for the growth of the Church. Those who had made vows of virginity were discussed as a significant group within the Church. After Christianity was legalized within the Roman empire the practice of this radical religion began to change. Many sincere followers believed that to authentically follow the poor and powerless Christ they needed to leave the comfort and power of institutionalized Roman Christianity as well as the growing compromises of Christianity with physical violence and militarism. People with these convictions fled to the desert, some metaphorically and some physically. The desert is a geographical term, but also a term for the experience a person has when going within. The desert is a place of beauty where one can focus on what matters, away from distractions. The Bible develops and then refers back to the Exodus as a desert time for God's people, a time for them to focus on what mattered. On the other hand, the desert is a barren place with wild beasts and devils. One must be brave to face these and survive.

From the 300s C.E. we have a number of written sources describing monasticism, though all appear to have been written by or edited by men.[1] Within them are words of the desert mothers, the "ammas," and lengthy stories of the lives of holy women, but apparently as reported by men. The criteria are usually what qualities or actions males consider significant. In the 330s Chariton and his monks had a monastery about six miles northeast of Jerusalem. Women ascetics, though not documented, probably lived in the area because Cyril of Jerusalem addresses them. His writing, the *Catechetical Lectures* from about 348, may be the earliest text on religious women and in it he encourages them in chastity because they are living angelic lives in the world. The Church is to pray for them as for bishops, priests, deacons, and solitaries, so they seem to have had some type of official recognition.[2] Knowledge of monasticism in the East spread to the West through Athanasius in the 330s and Jerome in the 370s. By the end of the fourth century there were women's *ceonobia* in Spain and Gaul. Egeria's record of her travels is not only significant for the stories of liturgy and life among Christians in Bible lands in the 380s, but also because it was written by a women religious for members of her community in Spain or Gaul.

A major source of information on women ascetics is *The Lausiac History*, a series of short stories of people and places seen by Palladius in about 379 C.E. He wrote that there were 20,000 nuns and 10,000 monks in the desert.[3] Palladius described a community of four hundred women in the Thebaid that was similar to Pachomius' monasteries for men. The monasteries involved routines of prayer with work such as farming, baking, basketweaving, shoemaking, manuscript-making, and learning the Bible by heart. In both the Greek and Latin collections of the *Apophthegmata patrum* there are sayings of Desert Mothers among those of the Desert Fathers, but the activities of these women are not recorded. Probably some of them lived alone in the desert as men did, since the women's writings are included with the men's. Palladius mentions Alexandra, who lived in a tomb as Anthony did.

Study was not as important to the desert monks as to the communities, but a few like Evagrius Ponticus were intellectuals. Amma Theodora may have been educated. She was consulted by many monks with problems and was in dialogue with Archbishop Theophilus. She faced difficulties frankly and encouraged humility.[4] Amma Syncletica seems to have been another counselor. She used the imagery of fire to signify purification.[5] Though we know nothing of the women's origins, both Theodora and Syncletica are Greek names. Amma Sarah, who bore a Jewish name, lived alone near the Nile for sixty years. She had to fight daily against the demons of lust for the first thirteen years. She was courageous, praying for strength but not fleeing her lifestyle. Though her culture had taught her that women are weak, she wrote: "According to nature, I am a woman, but not according to my thoughts."[6]

In ancient monastic popular literature most of the surviving stories are by men. Many describe women as seducers. In reality women are more often the victims of seduction and a few tales do describe women as such. One tells of a monk who left his *coenobium* on an errand and met a washerwoman. He was passionate for her and propositioned her. She answered him with wisdom and determination: "It is easy enough to think of, but I could cause you great suffering. . . . After performing the act you would be attacked by your conscience and you would either give yourself up to despair, or if not, you would still have to go through immense labors to reach again the point at which you are now: therefore, before you subject yourself to that pain, go on your way in peace."[7] Both Ammas of the desert and common washerwomen might have had more wisdom of holiness than men.

In 380 the Emperor Theodosius issued an edict defining orthodoxy, and the Roman empire became the Christian Roman empire. This context gave some support for monasticism. After 400 monasticism was an established movement and extensive human and financial resources developed around it. Monastic settlements proliferated around Jerusalem, and by the sixth century there were seven monasteries in the six miles between Jerusalem and Bethlehem. Traces of more than a hundred monasteries have been found in the Judean desert. In the fifteen miles from Jerusalem to Jericho and then on to the Dead Sea, the land drops from 800 meters above sea level to 400 meters below sea level, the lowest land in the world. Within a two-mile stretch there is a change from agricultural land to grazing land. Then near the sea habitation declines and sandy desert appears. Three types of monasticism developed in these three areas of agriculture, grazing land, and barren desert. Some of the monasteries, such as the *laura* of Saba where the hymn writer John Damascene lived, have been continuously occupied since their foundation in this period.

Some records exist of women solitaries, mostly in or near towns. Palladius mentions the deaconess of Antioch, Sabiniana, who was an aunt of John Chrysostom. Twice Melania spent periods in a hermitage on the Mount of Olives. Gregory the Great mentions women solitaries in Italy. *Coenobia* were founded by charismatic personalities rather than through a number of individuals coming together to form a cooperative. The earliest records of women's *coenobia* are on the east side of the Mediterranean.

John Cassian, from the region of the Danube, became a monk in Bethlehem and made an extensive tour of the Egyptian desert in the fifth century. He wrote some of the most complete descriptions of Eastern monasticism so that people of the West might understand it. He described the cenobites who lived in community and anchorites who lived alone but under the guidance of the abbot. Women followed similar patterns. Another form of ascetic life was the domestic monastery founded by family groups; some had males, some females, and some were dual monasteries with both sexes. The cenobites, who lived in community, were like the early Christians as described in Acts 4:32-35 and 2:44-45, who shared their goods.

While women ascetics are sometimes remembered in church history, patriarchal histories often gloss over the women's authority and self-determination. Stories of dependence on churchmen are emphasized. Melania the Elder, Melania the Younger, and Olympias were known for teaching women, converting them, and preparing them for baptism. The women also had influence on men. According to Palladius, Melania the Elder helped in reconciling an Antiochan schism involving four hundred monks. She did not hesitate to scold the deacon Jovinus, later a bishop, when he was pampering himself. When Evagrius Ponticus, an archdeacon of Constantinople, fell out of favor apparently for an illicit affair, Palladius wrote that Melania was not bashful in speaking to him:

> When the physicians were at a loss and could not find any cure, the blessed Melania said to him, "Son, your long illness displeases me. So tell me what is in your mind; for this sickness of yours perhaps comes from God." So he confessed the whole affair to her. Then she said to him: "Promise me before the Lord that you will keep to the standard of the monastic life, and sinner though I am, I will pray that you may be granted a longer life." So he agreed. And within a few days he became well, and got up and received from the hands of the lady herself a change of clothes [i.e., clericals, which he

had abandoned] and he went away and exiled himself in the mountains of Nitria, in Egypt.[8]

In Constantinople, Olympias defied the bishop Theophilus, with whom she disagreed, and kept her community in secession from communion with another bishop, Arsacius. Melania the Younger refused to be guided by the bishop of Hippo. Gillian Cloke, after extensive research on these early aristocratic monastic women, writes, "This top-lofty self confidence is manifestly one of the advantages of their possessive attitude towards the church: they evidently considered themselves comparable in terms of a God-given authority to any mere appointed functionary. The only men of God these women readily accorded respect as being more overtly directed by God than they (and they evidently thought little of men like Jovinus, Evagrius, Theodosius and Augustine in this respect) were the great hermits and ceonobites of the deserts, who themselves operated from outside the church hierarchy."[9] These men of the desert were not impressed by the wealth of the women. The women were more impressed by their spiritual authority than they were by the ecclesiastical authority of the other men.

Now that we have reviewed some general information on the ascetic life and on women's relationship to it, let us look in detail at the two most documented women ascetics who made pilgrimages in the early Christian centuries. The map indicates the extent of their travels.

Paula

Jerome returned to Italy from the East in 382 and wrote of people who were living ascetic lives there. In Rome's fashionable Aventine Hill neighborhood there were a number of women (Marcella, her mother Albina, and friends Lea and Asella; Paula and her daughters Blesilla, Paulina, Eustochium, and Rufina) who dedicated themselves to God and who fasted and prayed, lived and dressed simply, and avoided sexual activity. Both Marcella and Paula were serious students of the Bible and asked Jerome for information. After the death of Pope Damasus in 384 some of the Romans distorted the spiritual relationship of Jerome and Paula into a scandalous one. To avoid this criticism he left Rome.

Paula was a wealthy Roman woman, the mother of five children, generous to the poor of Rome, and devoted to her husband Toxotius. When he died, according to Jerome, Paula's grief was so great that she nearly died herself. Jerome speaks of her dedicating herself to God in her home in Rome for five years; she then felt a strong desire to go to the deserts where the Pauls and the Anthonys had encountered God. In a letter to Paula's daughter Eustochium praising Paula after she died in 404, Jerome writes: "No mother, it must be confessed, ever loved her children so dearly. Before setting out she gave them all that she had, disinheriting herself upon earth that she might find an inheritance in heaven."[10]

Paula left Rome in 385. Although Jerome had already left the city, he described her children sadly waving goodbye as she began her pilgrimage. She set sail from the mouth of the Tiber and went on to the island of Pontia to see the place where Domitilla had been banished for being a Christian. Paula went to Greece, Rhodes, Lycia, Cyprus, Seleucia in Cilicia, where the monastery of St. Thecla was, and Antioch. There she and her group met Jerome and they continued on pilgrimage together. Traveling on donkeys, they went to Berytus (Beirut), through Sidon, Zarephath, Tyre, Ptolemais, Dor, Caesarea (which was known as a place of many martyrs), Antipater, Diospolis (Lydda), Nicopolis (Emmaus), Jerusalem, Bethlehem, Gaza, Hebron, Jerusalem again, Jericho, the fountain of Elisha, the valley of Achor, Bethel, Mt. Ephraim, Shiloh, Neapolis or Schechem. They climbed Mt. Gerizim and visited Nazareth, Capernaum, the Lake of Tiberias, and Naim. Then Jerome wrote no more of Galilee, but continues with descriptions of places in Egypt, which probably indicates that they went from northern Palestine by ship. They stopped at Socoth as Egeria did, and then went to Alexandria and the nearby monastic centers of Nitria and Scete. Then they sailed from Pelusium in the northwest corner of Sinai to Maioma because of the intense heat. Paula seems to have traveled with a group of virgins including her daughter Eustochium. In the notes on biblical places, two having significant women are mentioned: Lydda, where Dorcas died, and Gibeah, where the concubine was cut into pieces by her husband. For both Egeria and Paula going to the monastery of St. Thecla was significant. The accounts of Paula's visits to these places are often related in this text.

Finally Paula settled in Bethlehem. She was very generous and used her wealth to support two communities: one of women and one of men, the latter including Jerome. In Paula's community parts of the Psalter were prayed five times a day and other times were devoted to Bible study, household chores, and sewing. She was known for denying herself and sleeping on a mat on the ground. Often she showed the gift of tears. While Jerome used flowery rhetoric in praising Paula's virtue, the radical and challenging nature of prophetic ascetics comes through in his comment that Paula was thought of as a fool:

. . . that owing to her great fervor in virtue some people thought her mad and declared that something should be done for her head. She replied in the words of the apostle, "we are made a spectacle unto the world and to angels and to men," and "we are fools for Christ's sake" but "the foolishness of God is wiser than men." It is for this reason she said that even the Saviour says to the Father, "Thou knowest my foolishness" and again "I am as a wonder unto many, but thou are my strong refuge." "I was a beast before thee; nevertheless, I am continually with thee." In the gospel we read that even His kinsfolk desired to bind Him as one of weak mind.

The transition from martyrdom to ascetic life as an ideal for the Christian can be seen in Jerome's subsequent comment that the "spotless service of a devout mind is itself a daily martyrdom."[11]

Paula died at 56 and was buried in a cave beside the cave of the Nativity of Christ. Jerome described her funeral as being attended by every monk and virgin in Palestine and the gathering was not just for a few days, but for a week. The poor who had benefited from her generosity were there. Many bishops, monks, and others chanted psalms in unison but in their own different languages. At the time she died in 404, when her daughter Eustochium took over leadership of the monastery, women of many nationalities were in the community.[12]

Egeria

In the late seventh century the monk Valerius wrote a letter to his brothers in northwestern Spain that speaks of the blessed nun Egeria. In the style of an inspiring sermon he wrote of her courage and the places she visited. Eighth- and ninth-century Spanish manuscripts briefly refer to Egeria. Finally, in 1884 a manuscript of about forty-eight pages on travels in the holy land was found in Italy, but both the beginning and the ending were missing. From internal evidence as well as fragments of other information scholars have speculated about the female author. Following the extensive scholarship of John Wilkinson, published in his *Egeria's Travels,* this manuscript was credited to Egeria, who visited the east between 381 and 384 C.E. and wrote her travel diary for her religious sisters at home, perhaps in Gaul or Spain.[13] Probably the surviving text is only a third of the original, but Peter the Deacon's *Book on the Holy Places* written in 1137 draws extensively on her writings. Careful study of his book gives some idea of the lost portions of her diary. His book was written forty years after the Latin Kingdom of Jerusalem had been established, when there was a growing interest in pilgrimage.

Egeria's writings are the first extensive accounts of Christian pilgrimage that still exist, with previous writings just briefly mentioning pilgrims and places visited. Paula's travels, chronicled by Jerome, happened more or less at the same time as Egeria's. Egeria had unbounded curiosity about the holy places and people. Travel in that period was not easy or comfortable, but she seemed to be full of energy stemming from her enthusiasm. She had a knowledge of Scripture, church classics, and prayers and liturgical practices. It appears from the quotations and names she cites that she used one of the Old Latin versions of the Bible translated from Greek. The Bible seems to be the only reference book she had with her, because she does not quote other writings. Egeria was interested in caves, houses, and buildings related to people in the Jewish and Christian Scriptures. She also sought to visit the *martyria*, places of the martyrs whether biblical or later Christian, and above all the places of Christ's ministry.

Her writings are the only extant detailed account of the liturgies in Jerusalem in the fourth century and they have been of great value in the modern liturgical movement. Within this century all major Christian denominations have tried to better understand the roots of Christian worship. Her descriptions, especially those of people preparing to be Christians during the Lenten season, and of the liturgies of Holy Week, Easter, and Pentecost have been extensively used by modern church scholars. The words of modern women are often overlooked or disregarded, but this ancient woman's writings are a major source of liturgical studies. Egeria, in describing the liturgies, also indicates the types of church leaders and their roles. She wrote of bishops, presbyters, archdeacons, and deacons, and she spoke of Marthana, the leader of the nuns at St. Thecla's, as a deaconess.

The following passage reveals something of her curiosity and enthusiasm. Egeria had been traveling for three years, but she still desired to go to a place that would involve twenty-five days of travel by stage.

> . . . and [when] I had seen all the places which were the object of my pilgrimage, I felt that the time had come to return in God's name to my own country. But God also moved me with a desire to go to Syrian Mesopotamia. The holy monks there are said to be numerous and of so indescribably excellent a life

that I wanted to pay them a visit; I also wanted to make a pilgrimage to the *martyrium* of the holy apostle Thomas. . . .
And, believe me, loving sisters, no Christian who has achieved
the journey to the holy places and Jerusalem misses going also
on the pilgrimage to Edessa. It is twenty-five staging-posts
away from Jerusalem . . . .

Fifteen miles after leaving Hierapolis I arrived in God's
name at the river Euphrates, and the Bible is right to call it
"the great river Euphrates." It is very big, and really rather
frightening since it flows very fast like the Rhone, but the Euphrates is much bigger. We had to cross in ships, big ones,
and that meant I spent maybe more than half a day there. So,
after crossing the river Euphrates, I went on in God's name
into the region of Syrian Mesopotamia . . . .

As soon as we arrived [in Edessa], we went straight to the
church and martyrium of holy Thomas; there we had our
usual prayers and everything which was our custom in holy
places. And we read also from the writing of holy Thomas
himself. The church there is large and beautiful, and built in
the new way—just right, in fact, to be a house of God. In this
city there was so much I wanted to see that I had to stay
there three days. I saw a great many *martyria* and visited the
holy monks, some of whom lived among the *martyria*, whilst
others had their cells further away from the city where it was
more private. The holy bishop of the city was a truly devout
man, both monk and confessor. He welcomed me and said,
"My daughter, I can see what a long journey this is on which
your faith has brought you—right from the other end of the
earth. So now please let us show you all the places Christians
should visit here." I gave thanks to God, and eagerly accepted the bishop's invitation.[14]

The bishop of Edessa was impressed by Egeria because she
had come "right from the other end of the earth," which is assumed to be the other side of the Roman empire, Spain or
France.[15] Many significant men including bishops, priests, and
monks had conversations with Egeria. Were they so willing to
spend time with a woman because she was from so far away,
because she obviously had monetary resources, because she
was so committed to learning about the Bible, or because she
seems to have had a warm, positive, enthusiastic, and charismatic personality? Probably all of these reasons contributed to
her being well received and getting extensive information.
Churchmen of that time, like most of those through the last two
thousand years, have not entered into dialogues with women

as mutually respected scholars, researchers, or companions. Egeria seems to have had great self-confidence, courage, a sense of adventure and independence, all rooted in a deep spirituality. She had spiritual freedom to try new paths and not be dependent on others' approval. Egeria was not a polished Latin scholar. She made mistakes in her syntax and she wrote in a conversational way, just as Mark was not a Greek scholar and has mistakes in his gospel. Fortunately their "poor writing" was saved nonetheless. Egeria seemed to have taken notes as she went along and then would occasionally take time to write the unified narrative.

John Wilkinson suggests this outline of Egeria's travels: (1) Jerusalem and the nearby area and Neapolis in Samaria in 381, (2) Alexandria, Nitria, and the Thebaid from 381 to 383, (3) Galilee including Nazareth, Capernaum, Scythopolis, Carmel, Sebastia, and returning to Jerusalem, where she wrote on the liturgy in 383, (4) Mount Sinai and Goshen from late November 383 through January 384, (5) Mount Nebo in January or February 384, (6) Carneas in February or March 384, (7) probably Easter in Jerusalem and on to Antioch in April, (8) Edessa and Carrae in April, (9) Tarsus and Seleucia to visit her friend Marthana at the shrine of St. Thecla in May 384, (10) Constantinople in June or July in 384, where she wrote of plans to go to Ephesus.[16] Egeria did not to hesitate to ask questions or go to any place that might give more insight. She recorded any details that might give her sisters more knowledge of the Bible. She must have had extensive financial resources, since she could travel for over three years and have an entourage and local guides. She never complained of the cost of things. While modern travelers seem to focus their interests on ancient buildings and places, she was extremely interested in the "living stones," the people of the local churches. Though the emperor Theodosius had just made Christianity the official religion of the empire in 380, the vast majority of the people were not Christians. Persecution for being a Christian was well remembered. Egeria met two bishops who had been exiled under Valens. Egeria concentrates on what is of interest for her religion and hardly mentions other tourist sites. Egeria, as a nun, wanted to learn about religious life from Egyptian nuns, monks, and hermits who were the chief founders of ascetic life. By the time of her visit a few different styles of ascetic life existed in Egypt. She may have described the different lifestyles, but those descriptions are not in the fragments of her manuscript that survive.

Egeria was a person of faith who respected the holy places and those who told her about them. At the same time she does not seem to be naïve or gullible. She does not repeat everything from the guides as facts. She writes with reservations that some things are "said to have been . . . ." Egeria wrote her sisters about the bishop of Zoar pointing out where Lot's wife turned into a pillar of salt, but adds that she really could not see anything at all.

Travel with its insecurities and inconveniences can bring out the worst in people, but Egeria is repeatedly grateful and positive. She thanks God for allowing her these wonderful experiences and she thanks her hosts and guides. Her description of the visit to Mount Nebo indicates her approach as a pilgrim:

> And it was where holy Moses the man of God blessed each of the children of Israel in order before his death. When we reached this plain, we went on to the very spot, and there we had a prayer, and from Deuteronomy we read not only the song, but also the blessings he pronounced over the children of Israel. At the end of the reading we had another prayer, and set off again, with thanksgiving to God. . . . And it was always our practice when we managed to reach one of the places we wanted to see to have first a prayer, then a reading from the book, then to say an appropriate psalm and another prayer. By God's grace we always followed this practice whenever we were able to reach a place that we wanted to see.[17]

Ritual patterns can help give people security and peace, and Egeria used her ritual pattern at each place. Egeria's pilgrimage led her to wisdom and compassion.

Notes

[1] For more information see Joan M. Petersen, *Handmaids of the Lord: Contemporary Descriptions of Feminine Asceticism in the First Six Centuries* (Kalamazoo: Cistercian Publications, 1996) 17–18.

[2] Cyril of Jerusalem, *Catechesis*, 4.24; 16.22. *MPG* 33:485, 949.

[3] Christopher Butler, *The Lausiac History of Palladius* (Cambridge: Texts and Studies, 1898) 212.

[4] *MPG* 65:201-204.

[5] *MPG* 65:421-428; *MPL* 73:862, 870, 890-91, 895-96, 909, 924-25, 937-38, 949-50, 993.

[6] *MPG* 65:420-21; *MPL* 73:876, 896-97, 925.

[7] Anon. 49 as quoted in Gillian Cloke, *This Female Man of God: Women and Spiritual Power in the Patristic Age* (London: Routledge, 1995) 204.

[8] *Lausiac History* 38, as quoted in Cloke, *This Female Man of God,* 176.

[9] Cloke, 177.

[10] "Letter 108, Jerome to Eustochium," in Ross S. Kraemer, *Maenads, Martyrs, Matrons, Monastics* (Philadelphia: Fortress, 1988) 142.

[11] Ibid., 156.

[12] "Letter 108, Jerome to Eustochium," in Ross S. Kraemer, 138–68.

[13] Egeria, *Egeria's Travels.* Newly translated with supporting documents and notes by John Wilkinson (London: S.P.C.K., 1971) 1–30.

[14] Ibid., 113–15.

[15] Ibid., 3.

[16] Ibid., 27–30.

[17] Ibid., 105–106.

PART TWO

STORIES, SITES, AND MAPS

CHAPTER SIX

GUIDES FOR READING

Part Two of the book follows a geographical order. The following guides could be used if one wishes to read the book chronologically, considering the unfolding of history, or thematically.

Timeline

Traditional Significant Events for the Lands of the Bible
Women Mentioned in Various Periods

Dates

Women Mentioned in the Text (~ indicates women who are legendary and/or time when the legend developed)

1900–1600 B.C.E. Patriarchs

Matriarchs Sarah, Hagar, Daughters of Sodom, Lot's Daughters, Rebecca, Leah, Rachel, Tamar who is daughter-in-law of Judah (Genesis), Wife of Potiphar (Exodus)

1250–1200 Exodus

Hebrew Midwives, Mother of Moses, Miriam, Egyptian princess. Rahab (Joshua)

1200–1030 Age of Judges

Deborah, Jael, daughter of Jephthah, Delilah, concubine of the Levite, dancing women who were abducted (Judges). Naomi and Ruth (Ruth)

1030–587 Age of Kings

Hannah (1 Sam 1–2), Abigail (1 Sam 25), Medium of Endor (1 Sam 28)

1004–965 David (Jerusalem conquered 1000)

Bathsheba (2 Sam 11), Tamar (David's daughter, 2 Sam 13), Wise Woman of Tekoa (2 Sam 14)

960 Solomon builds the Temple

Egyptian wife of Solomon (1 Kings 9:16), Queen of Sheba (1 Kings 10)

933 Kingdom divided (Israel and Judah)
Widow of Zarepthah (1 Kings 17), Shunammite woman (2 Kings 4), Huldah (2 Kings 22)

722 Israel, the northern kingdom, ends
Gomer, wife of Hosea (ca. 760s) (Hosea)

587 Babylonians conquer Judah
Susanna (Daniel 13)

586–333 Persian Period
God personified as female Wisdom: Woman who nurtures (Sir 15:1), Wisdom's beauty in nature (Sir 24:3), Wisdom, a hostess (Prov 9:1)

537 Return from the Babylonian exile

516 Dedication of the Second Temple
Esther (story associated with Xerxes, ca. 486)

445 Nehemiah rebuilds Jerusalem
Samaritan wife of Manasseh (4th c.)

350–167 Hellenistic Period

332 Alexander the Great in Palestine

301 Ptolemy (Egypt) and Seleucus (Syria)

167–37 Maccabaean-Hasmonean Period
Mother of the Maccabees (Maccabees), Queen Salome Alexandria of Jerusalem (ruled 79–68)

63 B.C.E.–627 C.E. Roman and Byzantine Period

63 Pompey conquers Jerusalem

37 B.C.E.–4 C.E. Herod the Great
Herod's daughter

6 or 7 B.C.E. Birth of Jesus
Women Associated with Jesus: Anne, Jesus' grandmother

In Mark's gospel: Peter's mother-in-law (Mark 1:29), daughter of Jairus (Mark 6:21), daughter in a broken marriage (Mark 6:19), woman with a hemorrhage (Mark 6:25 par. Luke 8:40), Syro-Phoenician or Canaanite woman (Mark 8:24 par. Matt 15:21), people bringing children (Mark 10:13 par. Matt 19:13), widow with her mite (Mark 12:41 par. Luke 21:1-4), woman at the house of Simon (Mark 14:3 parr. Luke 7:36; Matt 26:6-13), women going to the tomb (Mark 16:1).

In Luke's gospel: Elizabeth (Luke 1:26), Mary the mother of Jesus (Luke 1, 2), Anna the prophet (Luke 2:36), Widow of Naim (Luke 7:11), Mary Magdalene, Joanna, wife of Herod's steward Chuza, Susanna, and others who supported Jesus

(Luke 8:1), Martha and Mary (Luke 10:38), stooped woman (Luke 13:10), women with Jesus as he suffered (Luke 23:27; 23:50), women at the tomb (Luke 24:1), couple at Emmaus (Luke 24:13).

In Matthew's gospel: Genealogy of Jesus mentioning Rahab, Ruth, and the wife of Uriah (Matt 1:1), children massacred by Herod (Matt 2:16), the greatest in the reign of heaven (Matt 18:1-4), mother of James and John (Matt 20:20), women burying Jesus (Matt 27:54), women at the resurrection (Matt 28:1-10).

In John's gospel: Mary at Cana (John 2), Samaritan woman (John 4), adulteress (John 8), Martha, Mary, and Lazarus (John 11), Mary anointing Jesus (John 12), woman in labor (John 16:21), servant girl of the high priest (John 18:17), women at the cross (John 19:25), Mary Magdalene (John 20:11).

Female images of God in the Gospels and women in teaching stories used by Jesus: God like a seamstress (Luke 12:27), Jesus comparing himself to a mother hen (Luke 13:34, Matt 23:37), woman searching for the lost coin (Luke 15:8), woman and the corrupt judge (Luke 18:1), God like a bakerwoman (Matt 13:33), the wise and foolish virgins (Matt 25:1-13), woman in labor (John 16:20).

29 or 30 C.E. Death and resurrection of Christ
40 Queen Helena of Adiabene. Women in Acts and the Epistles: Gathered disciples receiving the Spirit (Acts 2), Ananias and Sapphira (Acts 5:1-11), Mary and Rhoda (Acts 12:11), daughters of Philip (Acts 21:8), Dorcas or Tabitha (Acts 9:36), Mary the mother of John Mark (Acts 12:12), mother of Timothy (Acts 16:1), Lydia (Acts 16:14), Damaris (Acts 17:32), Priscilla (Acts 18:2), Euodia and Syntyche (Phil 4:1), woman clothed with the sun (Rev. 12:1).

66–70 First revolt of the Jews against the Romans

70 Destruction of the Temple by Titus
Women of the Essene Community, Therapeutae women (first century). ~ Thecla

135 Second revolt of the Jews; Romans rebuild Jerusalem as "Aelia Capitolina" under Hadrian
Beruria. Maidservant of Rabbi Judah

Period of persecutions (2nd–4th c.)
Perpetua and Felicitas (d. 203), ~ Barbara (220–235), Zenobia (Septimia Bat Zabbai, ruled 266–70), Amma Sarah (second

half of the third century), Febronia (late third century), Euphemia (late third century), Agape, Irene, Chione (d. 304), ~ Catherine of Alexandria (d. 305), Amma Syncletica

313 Edict of Milan legalizing Christianity
Helena, Sister of Pachomius, Amma Theodora (late third and early fourth century)

324 Constantine by defeating Licinius becomes master of the East

325 Council of Nicea
Macrina (b. 327)

326 Golgotha begins to be reclaimed by Christians

335 Council of Jerusalem and dedication of the Church of the Holy Sepulchre
Martha, Martyr of Persia (350s), Faltonia Betitia Proba (c. 360), Olympias (ca. 364–408), Hypatia (370–415), Melania the Elder and Rufinus in Jerusalem (373)

337 Death of Constantine. Bishop Eusebius of Caesarea writes the *Life of Constantine*

381 Council of Constantinople
381–384 Egeria's travels, Abbess Marthana (Seleucia), Melania the Younger (383–440), 385 Paula and Eustochium settle in Bethlehem, Poimenia, Mother Tachom (late fourth century)

386–400 John Chrysostom's sermons

395 Division of the empire into East and West and beginning of the Byzantine Empire. Over 200 churches are built in Palestine
Amma Talis and Taor (Palladius wrote 420), Deaconess Athanasia (Delphi, 400s), Matrona of Perge (430–510)

431 Council of Ephesus
Empress Eudocia (Jerusalem trip 438), Bassa (444), Elizabeth the Wonderworker (fifth century), ~ Mary/Marinos of Tripoli (fifth century)

451 Council of Chalcedon
Empress Eudoxia, Empress Theodora (ca. 500–550), ~ Pelagia, ~ Maria, niece of Abraham, ~ Mary of Egypt (sixth-century story), ~ A Holy Fool and Anastasia the Deaconess (sixth-century story), ~ Thais the Harlot

614 Persians conquer Palestine
Khadija, Mohammed's first wife (d. 620), Fatima, daughter of Mohammed and Khadija

629 Peace settlement between Persia and Rome

637–1099 Arab Period. Jerusalem becomes El Kuds, a holy city for Muslims. Mohammed ascends from the Temple Mount to heaven

Al-Khansa, poet (ca. 600–670), Aʾisha bint Abi Bakr, Mohammed's beloved wife (613–678), Rabaʾi (712–801)

638 Persians surrender to the Sultan Omar

680 Council of Constantinople

691 Dome of the Rock built. Muslims allow Jews and Christians to live and worship in Jerusalem

730–787 First iconoclastic period, an era of controversy about the use of sacred images

787 Seventh Ecumenical Council held in Nicea

Kassiane (b. ca. 800), Theokite of Lesbos (800s), Theodora of Thessalonica (812–892), Athanasia of Aegina (800s)

815–892 Second iconoclastic period

834 Second Council of Constantinople

1054 Division between the Eastern and Western Christian churches; rivalry between the Patriarch of Constantinople and the Pope of Rome

1071 Muslims destroy some Christian shrines and bar pilgrims

1099–1291 Crusader Period

Queen Melisande of Jerusalem

1099 First Crusade captures Jerusalem and thousands of Jewish and Muslim children, women, and men are killed in one day

1187 Muslim forces led by Saladin of Egypt regain Jerusalem and reestablish it as a Muslim city

1219 Franciscans come to the Holy Land and gain the respect of the Muslim ruler

1291 Fall of Akko (Acre) and end of the Crusader Period

1187–1517 Mamaluk Period

1517–1917 Ottoman-Turkish Period

1517 Ottomans take Palestine. Rights of Muslims, Christians, and Jews respected

1538 Suleiman the Magnificent rebuilds the walls of Jerusalem

1917 Ottoman Turks are defeated in World War I and Palestine comes under British mandate through the League of Nations. As more Zionists move to Palestine, conflict grows between them and the Arab inhabitants

1947 United Nations recommends partition of Palestine; British prepare to leave

1948 State of Israel is proclaimed and Palestinians resist in the First Israeli-Arab War. Jerusalem divided between Israel and Jordan

1967 Israel wins control of the whole city of Jerusalem. Predominantly Palestinian population of East Jerusalem seeks civil rights and access to sacred sites for Muslims and Arab Christians. Parts of Palestine designated by the United Nations for the Palestinians remain under Israeli military occupation

The numbers below indicate the pages where the theme or person can be found.

Biblical Female Images of God

Hebrew Scriptures

Christian Scriptures and tradition

Types of Women

Women as Disciples, Scholars, or Teachers

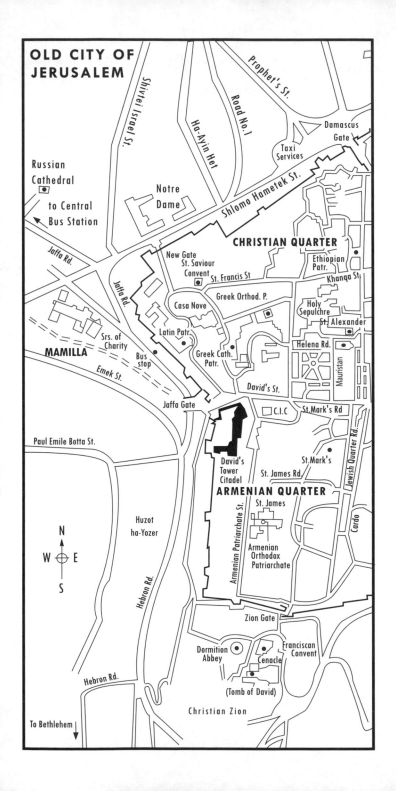

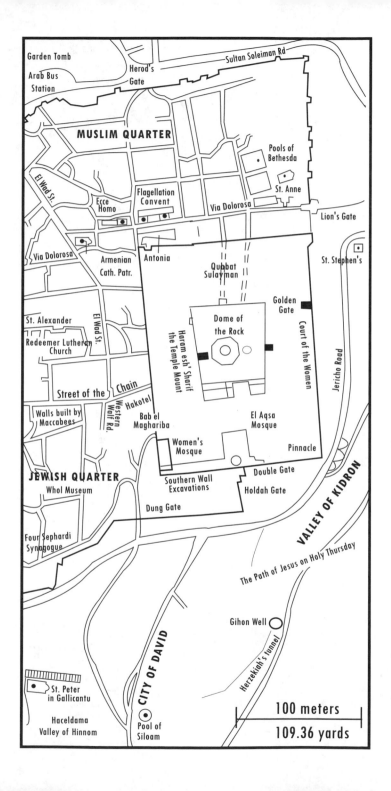

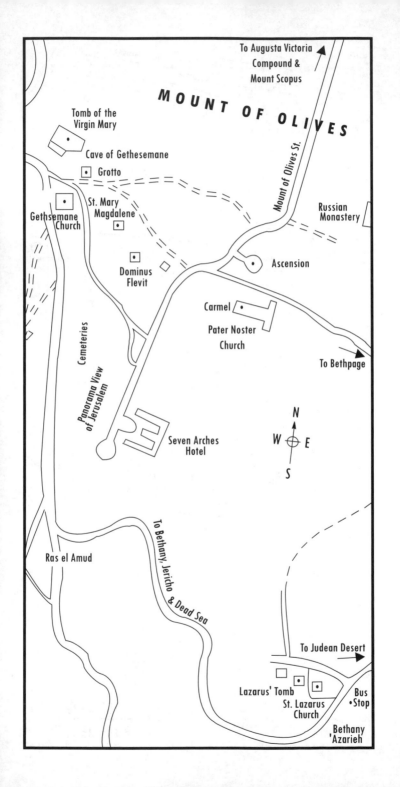

MOUNT OF OLIVES

To Augusta Victoria
Compound &
Mount Scopus

Tomb of the
Virgin Mary

Cave of Gethesemane

Grotto

St. Mary
Magdalene

Gethsemane
Church

Dominus
Flevit

Mount of Olives St.

Russian
Monastery

Ascension

Carmel

Pater Noster
Church

To Bethpage

Cemeteries

Panorama View
of Jerusalem

N
W ⊕ E
S

Seven Arches
Hotel

To Bethany, Jericho
& Dead Sea

Ras el Amud

To Judean Desert

Lazarus' Tomb

St. Lazarus
Church

Bus
• Stop

Bethany
'Azarieh

CHAPTER SEVEN

THE OLD CITY OF JERUSALEM

Introduction to the "Living Stones" of Jerusalem and to Women's Positions in the Religions of the Book

Jerusalem is not only a place of ancient stones but, as Paul described members of the Church, of "living stones." The large majority of Christians in the Holy Land are members of the Eastern Rites and Jerusalem has a rich variety of Eastern Christians who have established churches there. The Oriental Orthodox churches, including the Armenian Orthodox, Syrian Orthodox, Coptic Orthodox, and Ethiopian Orthodox, the "non-Chalcedonian" churches, hold to the teaching of the first three Ecumenical Councils. The Byzantine or Eastern Orthodox Churches, which include the Greek, Romanian, and Russian, accept the first seven Ecumenical Councils. The Greek Orthodox seem to be the oldest continuous group in Jerusalem. Accepting all the Ecumenical Councils are the Eastern Rites that are affiliated with the Roman Catholic Church including Melkite (Greek), Maronite, Armenian, Syrian, and Coptic. Western Christian groups include Roman Catholics, Lutherans, Anglicans, Presbyterians, Reformed, Methodists, Mennonites, Quakers, Baptists, Pentecostals, Brethren, Adventists, and some other small groups. Though there are many different groups of Christians in the Holy Land, the percentage of indigenous Christians has declined drastically. In 1840, twenty-five percent of Jerusalem was indigenous Christians. Now, due to political and economic pressures, less than three percent is Christian.[1]

While in the churches women are known for their service to those in need and women are at least half and sometimes more than half of those gathered for worship, very few have decision making or liturgical leadership positions in the churches of Jerusalem. Within Judaism women are known for service, but not for decision making in the synagogues. The government of Israel does not officially recognize the branches of Judaism in which there are ordained women rabbis. This means that women rabbis do not have official licensing for things such as witnessing weddings; nevertheless, some women rabbis do minister and are active in education. Among traditional Jews women's devotion to religion is often expressed in keeping a kosher kitchen and observing the religious rituals of the home such as the Sabbath and the Passover meal.

Muslim women do not go to the mosques as frequently as men. Women have the obligation to pray, but that is in relationship to their obligation to nurture and care for the family. Prayer is often in their homes rather than in the mosque.

The Old City

Damascus Gate

A Generous Businesswoman

The Damascus Gate is so named because it is the beginning of the road to that city, one of the oldest continuously occupied sites of the Middle East. While the walls and gate seen today only date back to Suleiman the Magnificent in the sixteenth century C.E., this is the location of a first-century C.E. gate. In the biblical world the city gates were main centers of political, social, and economic transactions, and the marketplace and social interchange today give an idea of that function. The woman of Proverbs, who appears at the end of a book probably edited in the early fifth century B.C.E. from older written and oral sources, was a good manager like many women who walk through this gate today. The text gives insight both into the virtues admired in a woman and the many tasks women performed. This woman worked with fabrics, food, farming, and finances. In the end:

> 30 Charm is deceitful, and beauty is vain,
>   but a woman who fears the LORD is to be praised.
> 31 Give her a share in the fruit of her hands,
>   and let her works praise her in the city gates.
>   (Read Proverbs 31:13-31)

Jaffa Gate

Tamar

Outside the walls and gate built by Suleiman the Magnificent would have been the road going toward Jaffa and also toward Timnah. The precise location of this very ancient story is unknown, but Tamar sat along the road going to Timnah, where her father-in-law would be going for the shearing of sheep. Widowed and neglected by him, she sought to seduce him. This story of seduction is more a story of the vulnerability of a woman in a culture where bearing children was all-important for having identity and worth. According to the genealogy of Jesus (Matt 1:1-17), in forty-two generations only four women, Tamar, Rahab, Ruth, and the wife of Uriah (Bathsheba), are mentioned and each woman was irregular in some way. In some poor countries today where there are no types of insurance or social security, women know that they need to bear about five children to have enough living children to take care of them in their old age. Tamar, the ancestor of Jesus, was a determined woman with a concern both for herself and for the perpetuation of the family. Finally Judah, her father-in-law, said,

> "She is more in the right than I, since I did not give her to my son Shelah." And he did not lie with her again.
>
> (Read Genesis 38:12-26)

The Muslim Quarter

St. Anne's Church, inside St. Stephen's gate

Remembering Anne, the Grandmother of Jesus

In this Gothic church, built by the Crusaders in 1140, one can recall the popular legend of the Apocryphal Gospel of Anne and Joachim, the parents of Mary. Next to the church is the pool of Bethsaida where Jesus healed a lame man (John 5). In 1104 Baldwin I had a convent built, and the Armenian Princess Arda was left there with the Benedictine nuns. Because of the royal visitor the convent received an endowment. Later a Romanesque church was built, followed by a Gothic structure. *Byzantine Daily Worship* elaborates on the legend of Jesus' grandparents:

> The story of the Nativity of Mary is told in an ancient manuscript written most probably at the beginning of the second century: the Proto-Gospel of James. The parents of Mary, Joachim and Anne, God-fearing and faithful observers of the Law, had not been blessed with children. Neither prayers nor tears helped relieve them from what was considered by the Israelites to be a curse, for to be without children meant to be excluded from the hope of giving birth to the Redeemer. One day, as Joachim entered the Temple to present an offering to the Lord, the High Priest drove him away, reviling him cruelly because he was without heirs.

Depressed and greatly grieved by these reproaches, Joachim wandered into the desert to hide his shame. In his solitude he opened his desolate heart to the Lord. At that very moment, his wife Anne was praying in her garden and pleading: "O Lord, look down with pity upon your servant and see her shame; to what shall I compare myself, O Lord? Shall I compare myself to the birds of the sky? No, they are better than I; You have blessed them with offspring, and I have none. Shall I compare myself to the beasts of the earth? No, they are also more fortunate than I; You have blessed them with offspring, and I have none. Shall I compare myself to the fishes in this pond? No, they have their young swimming about them, but I have no infant to fondle!" (The pond mentioned here exists to this day in Jerusalem; it is the pool of Bethsaida, near the house of Joachim and Anne, the same one where our Lord healed the paralytic.)

While Joachim prayed in the desert and Anne in her garden, an Angel of the Lord appeared to both and announced to them the conception of a daughter who would have a great destiny. Overwhelmed with joy, Joachim hurried home with the happy tidings. At the "Golden Gate" of the city, he met Anne, who was rising to tell him the same joyous news. In due time, Joachim and Anne had a baby girl, whom they called Mary, and they cared for her with the utmost tenderness until the day came for her presentation in the Temple.

At Vespers

At the Lamp-Lighting Psalms (Sixth Tone)

3. Indeed, some famous barren women have given birth by the will of God. But the nativity of Mary surpasses all nativities in honor and splendor, as it is worthy of the majesty of God, for she was born in a miraculous way of a barren mother and she herself gave birth in the flesh to the God of all, incarnate in her womb without human seed, against the laws of nature. She alone is the door through which the only-begotten Son of God has passed while leaving it sealed, as He had planned in his Eternal Wisdom. Thus did He bring salvation to all mankind.

Today the barren gates are opened and the Virgin, the Gate of God, comes forth. Today grace begins to bear fruit showing forth to the world the Mother of God, through whom earth is united to heaven for the salvation of our souls.[2]

Inside St. Stephen's Gate

Via Dolorosa, the Way of the Cross

The Women Who Suffered With Jesus

Byzantine pilgrims walked from the Eleona church on the Mount of Olives to Gethsemane on Holy Thursday night. They entered the old city through St. Stephen's Gate and walked the same route followed by Christians today on the Way of the Cross. The Byzantine pilgrims originally walked in a prayerful procession that did not make stops along the way. Over the centuries the custom of stopping and remembering the story of Jesus carrying his cross developed. After the crusades and political turmoil the followers of Francis of Assisi returned to be guardians of the holy places in Palestine in 1335. Not long afterward this group, which was particularly devoted to the suffering Christ, organized a prayerful walk through the streets. Although historical studies have revealed that Pilate stayed at what is now the Citadel inside the Jaffa Gate, Christians continue to walk and pray the same route hallowed by 1500 years of prayerful people. Franciscans lead the Stations of the Cross every Friday afternoon, starting near the Franciscan Monastery of the Flagellation down the street from St. Anne's Church.

Ecce Homo Convent of the Sisters of Sion

Pilate's Wife

The Sisters of Sion work for reconciliation among Jews, Christians, and Muslims and host many groups in their convent. The pavement in the museum below the convent was thought to be the place where Pilate judged Jesus. Marks in the pavement indicate a type of game that was played with dice by Roman soldiers. Contemporary studies indicate that Pilate and his wife stayed at what is now called the Citadel. This place where Christians have prayed through the centuries remembering the story of Pilate is appropriate to remember her.

> 19 While [Pilate] was sitting on the judgment seat, his wife sent word to him, "Have nothing to do with that innocent man, for today I have suffered a great deal because of a dream about him."
>
> (Read Matthew 27:16-26)

The Fourth Station at Armenian Catholic Church

Mary Meets Jesus

Pious tradition says that Mary and Jesus met as he was carrying the cross, and her grief was part of that prophesied by Simeon when Jesus was presented in the Temple as a baby.

> 34 Then Simeon blessed them and said to his mother Mary, "This child is destined for the falling and the rising of many in Israel, and to be a sign that will be opposed 35 so that the inner thoughts of many will be revealed—and a sword will pierce your own soul too."
>
> (Read Luke 2:28-35)

The Eighth Station at the Wall of the Orthodox Church on Aqabat el Khanga

The Daughters of Jerusalem

"Daughters of Jerusalem" was an expression frequently used in Hebrew Scriptures denoting not just the women of the city, but the people who through a history of almost a thousand years had experienced both the "glory of Jerusalem where God dwells in the Temple" and the repeated unfaithfulness, anguish, and destruction in Jerusalem. Jesus, in using that name for the women who sympathetically watched him carry his cross, evoked that history. He said to them,

> 28 "Daughters of Jerusalem, do not weep for me, but weep for yourselves and for your children. 29 For the days are surely coming when they will say, 'Blessed are the barren, and the wombs that never bore, and the breasts that never nursed.'"
>
> (Read Luke 23:27-31)

The Christian Quarter

The Church of the Holy Sepulchre

While Scripture speaks of being "one in Christ," this church reflects some of the sad realities of the divisions among Christians, with different areas for six different groups: Greek Orthodox, Catholics, Armenians, Copts, Ethiopians, and Syrians.

The Twelfth Station
in the Greek Orthodox Chapel
Upstairs in the Church of the Holy Sepulchre

Women at the Foot of the Cross

This chapel occupied by the oldest Christian group in Jerusalem is decorated with icons, mosaics, and a crucifix ornamented with silver over an opening to a rock. This is legendarily the rock at the foot of Jesus' cross and pilgrims, especially women with deep devotion, touch the rock and pray there. In John's gospel women have central roles, from the first miracle, which Jesus performs for a woman, and the first evangelist, who is a woman, to the end of Jesus' life at the cross. In the following passage the Gospel writer seems to imply more than concern for the welfare of Jesus' mother; the passage points toward women bringing wisdom and care to men in the Church and men bringing wisdom and care to women, a reciprocal relationship.

> 25 Meanwhile, standing near the cross of Jesus were his mother, and his mother's sister, Mary the wife of Clopas, and Mary Magdalene. 26 When Jesus saw his mother and the disciple whom he loved standing beside her, he said to his mother, "Woman, here is your son." 27 Then he said to the disciple, "Here is your mother." And from that hour the disciple took her into his own home.
>
> (John 19:25-27)

The Thirteenth Station
in the Church of the Holy Sepulchre

Women Who Took Down the Body of Jesus

Joseph of Arimathea wanted Jesus to be buried properly.

> 54 It was the day of Preparation, and the sabbath was beginning. 55 The women who had come with him from Galilee followed, and they saw the tomb and how his body was laid. 56 Then they returned, and prepared spices and ointments.
>
> (Read Luke 23:50-56)

The Stone of Unction

Paula's and Pilgrims' Devotion

Though there is no evidence that this stone is from the time of Jesus, this is the place where, since the late Middle Ages, pilgrims have remembered the anointing of his body. Greek Orthodox Christians often come to the stone to touch a mourning cloth to it, which is then to be placed over their bodies when they are buried. A pilgrimage to Jerusalem is often a preparation for death. (Read Matt 27: 54-60.)

Jerome wrote of Paula's emotion at the place where Jesus' body was said to have been. Though the wealthy invited her to luxury in Jerusalem, she was only interested in prayer.

> And although the proconsul of Palestine, who was an intimate friend of her house, sent forward his apparitors and gave orders to have his official residence placed at her disposal, she chose a humble cell in preference to it. Moreover, in visiting the holy places so great was the passion and the enthusiasm she exhibited for each, that she could never have torn herself away from one had she not been eager to visit the rest. Before the Cross she threw herself down in adoration as though she beheld the Lord hanging upon it; and when she entered the tomb which was the scene of the Resurrection she kissed the stone which the angel had rolled away from the door of the sepulchre. Indeed so ardent was her faith that she even licked with her mouth the very spot on which the Lord's body had lain, like one athirst for the river which he has longed for. What tears she shed there, what groans she uttered, and what grief she poured forth, all Jerusalem knows; the Lord also to whom she prayed knows.
>
> (PAULA, 143–44)

The Fourteenth Station, Tomb of Christ in the Church of the Holy Sepulchre

Women at the Tomb

This very elaborate marble structure was built over the cave discovered in the time of Constantine's building of the church at the site where first-century Christians had prayed. The design of the shrine is not the shape of a first-century tomb, but it is a place hallowed by the prayers of people for over 1600 years. The gospel resurrection stories and this tomb shrine should invite believers to stop trying to find the physical locations of the historical Jesus and start recognizing the omnipresence of the Risen Christ.

> 5 The women were terrified and bowed their faces to the ground, but the men said to them, "Why do you look for the living among the dead? He is not here, but has risen."
>
> (Read Luke 24:1-12)

The Chapel of St. Mary Magdalene

Mary Magdalene

In the eleventh century pilgrims began remembering Mary Magdalene in this area and dedicated a chapel to this apostle to the apostles. A contemporary bas-relief by Father Andrea Martini, O.F.M., depicts her encounter with Christ.

> 28 After the sabbath, as the first day of the week was dawning, Mary Magdalene and the other Mary went to see the tomb.
>
> (Read Matt 28:1-10)

The Ethiopian Chapel
to the Right of the Main Entrance to the Church
of the Holy Sepulchre

Queen of Sheba

The Queen of Sheba and King Solomon are pictured in an icon in the upstairs part of the chapel. A contemporary Ethiopian monastery is on the roof above the chapel and liturgical services are open to visitors. The Ethiopians are among the most ancient and continuous groups of Christians, claiming this queen as their ancestor. The Red Sea provided fairly easy travel between ancient Palestine and this East African region. Legends say that after the Queen of Sheba visited King Solomon she brought her people wisdom about God and also the Ark of the Covenant. The Quran has a story of the Queen, who was known for her leadership. Jesus praised the queen's wisdom (Matt 12:38-42; Luke 11:29-32).

> 1 When the queen of Sheba heard of the fame of Solomon, (fame due to the name of the LORD), she came to test him with hard questions. 2 She came to Jerusalem with a very great retinue, with camels bearing spices, and very much gold, and precious stones; and when she came to Solomon, she told him all that was on her mind.
>
> (Read 1 Kings 10:1-13)

The Crypt of St. Helena

Mother of Constantine

The lower chapel kept by the Armenians is covered with colorful mosaics, providing a dramatic environment for their liturgy which has a wealth of fine music kept alive through the ages. From the chapel one can enter the smaller, dark crypt. Devout persons have prayed here throughout the ages remembering the cross, the instrument of salvation. While the legend of Helena has inspired people, knowing more about her real story can help to clarify the way in which the goals of accumulating power in the empire were mingled with Christianity. (See Chapter Four for the stories of Helena.)

The Lutheran Church
of the Redeemer in the Mauristan

Women Pilgrims

In approximately 1070, in this area, St. Mary of the Latin Hospice for male pilgrims and St. John Hospice for the poor were built. By 1080 a hospice for women pilgrims, called St. Mary, was built and was cared for by Benedictine sisters. Within the modern Lutheran hospice near the church is a medieval cloister. Among the devout women who were pilgrims to the Holy Land at different times are Ortalano, the mother of Clare of Assisi, and Margery Kemp. (See Chapter Three for more on women pilgrims.)

The Armenian Quarter

Greek Catholic Patriarchate
and Museum of Eastern Rites

Egeria on Preparing People to be Christians

The Church of the Greek Catholic Patriarchate on the street of that name near Jaffa Gate has a living and very active community of indigenous Christians. The walls of the church are covered with icon murals of holy people including over twenty of the women mentioned in this book. The letter to the Hebrews speaks of being surrounded by a "cloud of witnesses," and this liturgical environment is reminiscent of that. The museum helps one to understand the rich variety of the worship traditions of Eastern Christians, which are more ancient than the Roman Catholic and Protestant traditions familiar in the West.

Egeria in the 380s C.E. was impressed with the care devoted to teaching and preparing people to be Christians in Jerusalem and she described this for her friends in Western Europe.

> I feel I should add something about the way they instruct those who are to be baptized at Easter. Names must be given in before the first day of Lent, which means that a presbyter takes down all the names before the start of the eight weeks for which Lent lasts here, as I have told you. Once the priest has all the names, on the second day of Lent at the start of the eight weeks, the bishop's chair is placed in the middle of the Great Church, the *Martyrium*, the presbyters sit in chairs on either side of him, and all the clergy stand. Then one by one

those seeking baptism are brought up, men coming with their fathers and women with their mothers. As they come in one by one, the bishop asks their neighbours questions about them: "Is this person leading a good life? Does he respect his parents? Is he a drunkard or a boaster?" He asks about all the serious human vices. And if his inquiries show him that someone has not committed any of these misdeeds, he himself puts down his name; but if someone is guilty he is told to go away, and the bishop tells him that he is to amend his ways before he may come to the font. He asks the men and the women the same questions. But it is not easy for a visitor to come to baptism if he has no witnesses who are acquainted with him.

Now, ladies and sisters, I want to write something which will save you from thinking all this is done without due explanation. They have here the custom that those who are preparing for baptism during the season of the Lenten fast go to be exorcised by the clergy first thing in the morning, directly after the morning dismissal in the *Anastasis*. As soon as that has taken place, the bishop's chair is placed in the Great Church, the *Martyrium*, and all those to be baptized, the men and the women, sit round him in a circle. There is a place where the fathers and mothers stand, and any of the people who want to listen (the faithful, of course) can come in and sit down, though not catechumens, who do not come in while the bishop is teaching.

His subject is God's Law; during the forty days he goes through the whole Bible, beginning with Genesis, and first relating the literal meaning of each passage, then interpreting its spiritual meaning. He also teaches them at this time all about the resurrection and the faith. And this is called catechesis. After five weeks' teaching they receive the Creed, whose content he explains article by article in the same way as he explained the Scriptures, first literally and then spiritually. Thus all the people in these parts are able to follow the Scriptures when they are read in church, since there has been teaching on all the Scriptures from six to nine in the morning all through Lent, three hours' catechesis a day. At ordinary services when the bishop sits and preaches, ladies and sisters, the faithful utter exclamations, but when they come and hear him explaining the catechesis, their exclamations are far louder, God is my witness; and when it is related and interpreted like this they ask questions on each point.

At nine o'clock they are dismissed from Catechesis, and the bishop is taken with singing straight to the *Anastasis*. So the dismissal is at nine, which makes three hours' teaching a day for seven weeks.

(EGERIA, 143–44)

Cathedral of St. James

Armenian Princesses and Refugees

In the fourth century C.E. Armenia was the first country to accept Christianity as its official religion, and there has been a constant stream of pilgrims since that time. In the 380s C.E. Egeria the pilgrim heard readings from the old Armenian lectionary in the liturgies in Jerusalem. In 444 a patrician woman named Bassa came to Jerusalem with the Empress Eudocia. At the site of the cathedral Bassa dedicated a chapel to Menas, an Egyptian saint. Bassa later became the leader of a nearby convent for women. From the eleventh to the fourteenth century the rulers of the Latin kingdom often married Armenian women, and as a result many of these women became queens of Jerusalem. In the early twentieth century the Turks killed almost two million Armenians. The Armenians and the Jews, both of whom have experienced painful genocides of their peoples, work zealously to keep their cultures alive.

The Citadel

This imposing fortress now houses a museum that reveals excavations of many levels of Jerusalem's history spanning the seventh century B.C.E. to the fourteenth century C.E. By the second century B.C.E. city walls surrounded this area. Pontius Pilate and his wife probably stayed here while in Jerusalem. (See **Ecce Homo Convent** for the story of Pilate's wife.)

St. Mark's Syrian Orthodox Church

Mary, the Mother of John Mark, and Rhoda

The language spoken in worship at this church is the language spoken by Jesus. A church was built in the fourth century on the spot said to be the residence of Mary, who gathered people at her home for prayer. When Peter was freed from prison he thought that people would be gathered with her. Apparently she was respected as a leader. Women led many early house churches where the foundations of the faith were laid for the first three hundred years before Christianity became legal and had public church buildings.

(Read Acts 12:11-14)

The Jewish Quarter

Wall Built by the Maccabees

Mother of the Maccabees

When the Seleucids controlled Palestine the Maccabees led the Jews in revolt and suffered brutal retaliation for this act. The seven sons of this mother were tortured and killed because they would not disobey Jewish law and eat pork as their captors wished them to do. While their mother is praised as a model of heroism, she also is said to have had "manly courage." Many authors cannot conceive of women as courageous in themselves.

> 20 The mother was especially admirable and worthy of honorable memory. Although she saw her seven sons perish within a single day, she bore it with good courage because of her hope in the Lord. 21 She encouraged each of them in the language of their ancestors.
>
> (Read 2 Macc 7:20-29)

Herodian Houses in the Wohl Archeological Museum

The High Priest's Servant

The architecture and luxurious possessions found in the Herodian houses indicate what life was like in Jerusalem for wealthy families in the first century C.E. Jesus was a prayerful Jew. He did not question the essence of the religion, but he did criticize those individuals and groups who became wealthy while neglecting the poor. The Palatial Mansion is thought to be the home of a high priest. How would it have felt to be a slave or a poor servant in such a home? Such a servant might have been attracted to Jesus' message of good news for the poor. Perhaps the young servant who spoke to Peter had previously seen him with Jesus.

> 66 While Peter was below in the courtyard, one of the servant-girls of the high priest came by. 67 When she saw Peter warming himself, she stared at him and said, "You also were with Jesus, the man from Nazareth."
>
> (Read Mark 14:66-72)

Wise and Foolish Virgins

The extensive collection of pottery and lamps gives one a sense of ancient Herodian households in this place. Jesus reflected on the importance of oil lamps.

> 1 "Then the kingdom of heaven will be like this. Ten bridesmaids took their lamps and went to meet the bridegroom. 2 Five of them were foolish, and five were wise."
>
> (Read Matt 25:1-13)

The Four Sephardi Synagogues

Prayerful Jewish Women

Jewish communities often have been the most highly literate groups of people because it has been important to them to learn how to read the Scriptures. However, women often did not have the same opportunities for study as men. Within Christianity and Islam there has been similar discrimination, with a preference for male leadership even in the midst of competent women. In spite of the prejudices, women have continued in their quest for the divine. The Central Synagogue was the women's section in a synagogue built in approximately 1610 C.E.

Haram esh-Sharif, the Temple Mount

Women of the Book

Jews, Christians, and Muslims are often referred to as the People of the Book, a term used in the Quran, because they believe in the one God revealed in the Scriptures. All three groups hold this area sacred. Jews remember that Solomon and Herod built temples here. Christians remember the Temple where Jesus was dedicated and often taught and prayed. Muslims remember Mohammed's night journey from Mecca to Jerusalem and his ascent into heaven. His "footprint" can still be seen in the Dome today, as can the "footprint" of Jesus on the Mount of Olives. Next to Mecca and Medina, this area is the holiest site for Muslims. At the Dome of the Rock, built in 691, pilgrims recall the story of Abraham preparing to sacrifice his son.

Qubbat Sulayman Monument

Mary Seeking Her Lost Child

Legends say that the twelve-year-old Jesus sat on this rock and taught the elders. Many groups of school children visit the Haram esh-Sharif area since it is one of the holiest places in Islamic tradition. Their mixture of piety, adventure, laughter, and play gives a glimpse of what ancient child pilgrims probably experienced there.

> 41 Now every year his parents went to Jerusalem for the festival of the Passover. 42 And when he was twelve years old, they went up as usual for the festival. 43 When the festival was ended and they started to return, the boy Jesus stayed behind in Jerusalem, but his parents did not know it.
>
> (Read Luke 2:41-52)

Dome of the Rock

Women Whose Children Are Sacrificed

Legends say that this rock was the place where Abraham prepared to sacrifice his son Isaac. Although the biblical text does not indicate whether Sarah knew that Isaac was to be sacrificed, a Jewish midrash says that Sarah had a vision of the event. Her loud scream was the voice of the angel that stopped Abraham from killing his son. Islamic legends say that it was Ishmael who was to be sacrificed. Can women scream together that the sacrifice of any child, another's or her own, is unacceptable? Can women scream loud enough to stop the senseless sacrifices of violence and war? Can the human family begin to realize that God has provided enough land, food, and resources for all?

> 14 So Abraham called that place "The LORD will provide"; as it is said to this day, "On the mount of the LORD it shall be provided."
>
> (Read Gen 22:1-14)

East Side of the Dome of the Rock

Court of the Women in Herod's Temple

There are often regulations about who can and cannot enter certain holy areas. In the ancient Temple there was a progression of holiness—areas for the Gentiles, Jewish women, Jewish men, clergy, and the high priests. In the El-Aksa mosque, as in others like it, one can see the area designated for women. Similarly, in traditional synagogues women are segregated from men. Furthermore, in traditional Orthodox and Catholic churches women cannot be ordained and by implication do not belong in the more sacred areas of the churches. Jesus recognized goodness in women such as the poor widow. Such women reveal some of the divine.

> 1 He looked up and saw rich people putting their gifts into the treasury; 2 he also saw a poor widow put in two small copper coins. 3 He said, "Truly I tell you, this poor widow has put in more than all of them; 4 for all of them have contributed out of their abundance, but she out of her poverty has put in all she had to live on."

(Luke 21:1-4)

El-Aksa Mosque

Rabiᵓa, the Mystic

The first mosque was built in this area between 709 and 719 C.E. The Women's Mosque and the Islamic Museum which are along the south wall of the Haram are good places to remember Rabiᵓa al-ᵓAdwiyya al-Qaysiyya of Basra, one of the greatest Muslim saints. She lived from 712 to 801 and, though she has no contemporaneous biographer, the many legends give some idea of her holiness and significance in the development of the Sufi mystical tradition. She was respected by men and many followed her wisdom. Sufi scholars, while giving preeminence to males, indicate that in holiness, in direct relationship with the divine, females and males are equal. The beauty and passion of her relationship with God can be seen in her prayers, such as:

> O my God, the best of Thy gifts within my heart is the hope of Thee and the sweetest word upon my tongue is Thy praise, and the hours which I love best are those in which I meet with Thee. O my God, I cannot endure without the remembrance of Thee in this world and how shall I be able to endure without the vision of Thee in the next world? O my Lord, my plaint to Thee is that I am but a stranger in Thy country, and lonely among Thy worshipers.[3]

Rabiᵓa's asceticism, prayer, and influence on disciples have led later writers to compare her with Christian mystics such as Catherine of Siena. Rabiᵓa refused to marry despite pressure, and used the imagery of relationship with the Divine Bridegroom, an image later used by Catherine. The following legend reflects Rabiᵓa's wit as well as her deep love of God. She had been urged to choose any husband she wanted from among the Sufis of Basra, which is in Iraq.

> She replied, "Yes, willingly. Who is the most learned of you, that I may marry him?" They said, "Hasan of Basra," so she said to him, "If you can give me the answer to four questions, I will be your wife." He said, "Ask, and if God permit, I will answer you."
>
> She said then, "What will the Judge of the world say when I die? That I have come out of the world a Muslim or an unbeliever?"
>
> Hasan answered, "This is among the hidden things, which are known only to God Most High."
>
> Then she said, "When I am put in the grave and Munkar and Nakir question me, shall I be able to answer them (satisfactorily) or not?" He replied, "This also is hidden."

She said next, "When the people are assembled at the Resurrection and the books are distributed, and some are given their book in the right hand and some in the left, shall I be given mine in my right hand or my left?" He could only say, "This also is among the hidden things."

Finally she asked, "When mankind is summoned (on the Day of Judgment), some to Paradise and some to Hell, in which of the two groups shall I be?" He answered as before, "This, too, is hidden, and none knows what is hidden save God, His is the glory and majesty."

Then she said to him, "Since this is so, and I have these four questions with which to concern myself, how should I need a husband with whom to be occupied?"

She is said to have emphasized her refusal with the following beautiful lines, but they cannot be attributed to her with any certainty:

> "My peace, O my brothers, is in solitude,
> And my Beloved is with me always,
> For His love is the test for me among mortal beings,
> When-e'er His Beauty I may contemplate,
> He is my 'mihrab,' towards Him is my 'qibla.'
> If I die of love, before completing satisfaction,
> Alas, for my anxiety in the world, alas for my distress,
> Healer (of souls), the heart feeds upon its desire,
> The striving after union with Thee has healed my soul,
> O my Joy and my Life abidingly,
> Thou wast the source of my life and from Thee also came
>   my ecstasy.
> I have separated myself from all created beings,
> My hope is for union with Thee, for that is the goal of
>   my desire."[4]

Like some of the Christian ammas, mothers of the desert, Rabi'a was known for her complete trust in God.

> Another friend of hers, Malik Dinar, once found her lying on an old rush mat, with a brick under her head to serve as a pillow and drinking and making her ablutions from a cracked jar and his heart was pained at the sight and he said, "I have rich friends and if you wish, I will take something from them for you." She said, "O Malik, you have made a great mistake. Is it not the same One Who gives daily bread to me and to them?" Malik said, "It is." She said, "Will He forget the poor because of their poverty or remember the rich because of their riches?" He said, "No." Then she said, "Since He knows my state, what have I to remind Him of? What He wills, we should also will."[5]

Parts of el-Aksa Mosque have been closed since the fire of 1969 when a Christian tourist tried to destroy the buildings on the Temple Mount, believing that it would bring about the return of the Messiah. In the closed area is a shrine dedicated to Jesus, whom Muslims respect as a prophet but do not believe to be divine.

Excavations at the Western Wall Plaza

The Western Wall

Huldah the Prophet

The third woman in the Bible given the title *nebiah,* that is, prophet (after Miriam and Deborah) is Huldah. King Josiah was zealous for religious reform in the late seventh century B.C.E. At the Temple the high priest Hilkiah had discovered a book of the Law and wondered about its authority. When it was shown to the king, who was eager to know and to observe God's Law, he said to go and consult God to ascertain its authenticity. They turned to a woman, Huldah, for wisdom. She was questioned and responded in the literary form standard for the Hebrew prophets, "Thus says the LORD . . . ." The text that was found is believed to have been an early form of the book of Deuteronomy.

Which books of sacred texts are to be in the canon with primary significance for the communities of believers and which are to considered of lesser importance, non-canonical, has been a central question for Jews and then for Christians. The Jewish council of Jamnia and a number of Christian gatherings have grappled with these questions. Protestant, Orthodox, and Roman Catholic Christians have slightly different collections of canonical books. The first time the question of the authenticity of a biblical text was raised, it was a woman who made the judgment. In that sense Huldah the prophet can be considered both the first biblical authority and a founder of biblical studies.[6]

> 14 So the priest Hilkiah, Ahikam, Achbor, Shaphan, and Asaiah went to the prophetess Huldah the wife of Shallum son of Tikvah, son of Harhas, keeper of the wardrobe; she resided in Jerusalem in the Second Quarter, where they consulted her. 15 She declared to them, "Thus says the LORD, the God of Israel . . . ."

(Read 2 Kings 22:8-16)

After Huldah, the respected woman prophet, had authenticated the text for the king, he and the religious authorities had all the people gather at the Temple and the text was read to them. When deaconesses were ordained in the early Church, Huldah was mentioned in the ceremony. The fourth-century *Apostolic Constitutions*, probably from Syria, which compiled liturgical and disciplinary writings from the first three centuries, had these directions and the following prayer for the ordination ceremony.

> And let the deaconess be honored by you as an image of the Holy Spirit. She should do or say nothing without the deacon, as the Comforter does not act or speak on its own, but glorified Christ and awaits his will. And as we do not believe in Christ apart from the teaching of the Spirit, so let no woman approach the deacon or the bishop without the deaconess. . . . Let your widows and orphans be reckoned by you as an image of a sacrificial altar. Let the virgins be honored as an image of the altar of incense and of the incense, in addition . . . .

At the ordination of a deaconess the bishop lays hands on her and says,

> "O eternal God, the Father of our Lord Jesus Christ, the Creator of man and of woman, who did fill with the Spirit Miriam, Deborah, Anna, and Huldah (Exod 15:20-21; Judges 5; Luke 2:36-38; 2 Kings 22:14-20), who did not deem unworthy that your only-begotten Son should be born of a woman, who also in the tent of witness and in the Temple ordained women as keepers of your holy gates, now look upon this your servant who is being ordained as a deaconess, and give her the Holy Spirit, and purify her from any defilement of the flesh and spirit (2 Cor 7:1), so that she may worthily accomplish the work entrusted to her and to your glory and the praise of your Christ, with whom to you and to the Holy Spirit be glory and adoration forever. Amen!"[7]

Excavations Outside the Double and Triple Gates Near the Western Wall Plaza

The Ritual Baths

Purification of Mary

To the east of the steps one can see a series of *mikvah,* or Jewish ritual baths. Jewish women were to be purified after their menstrual periods and after childbirth. Mary came here forty days after giving birth to Jesus. (See **Chorazin, Ritual Baths** for more background on women as unclean.)

> 2 Speak to the people of Israel, saying: If a woman conceives and bears a male child, she shall be ceremonially unclean seven days; as at the time of her menstruation, she shall be unclean. 3 On the eighth day the flesh of his foreskin shall be circumcised. 4 Her time of blood purification shall be thirty-three days; she shall not touch any holy thing, or come into the sanctuary, until the days of her purification are completed.
>
> (Read Lev 12:2-5)

Mary and Joseph fulfilled that ritual requirement:

> 22 When the time came for their purification according to the law of Moses, they brought him up to Jerusalem to present him to the Lord.
>
> (Read Luke 1:22-24)

The Huldah Gate (see also Tomb of Huldah)

Anna, the Prophet

While hundreds of babies were brought to the Temple daily to be presented to God, this older woman had the heart to recognize this special one, the Christ sent by God.

> 36 There was also a prophet, Anna the daughter of Phanuel, of the tribe of Asher. She was of a great age, having lived with her husband seven years after her marriage, 37 then as a widow to the age of eighty-four. She never left the temple but worshiped there with fasting and prayer night and day. 38 At that moment she came, and began to praise God and to speak about the child to all who were looking for the redemption of Jerusalem.
>
> (Read Luke 2:36-40)

Huldah and Anna, faithful women, were seen as role models for consecrated women deacons and widows in the church. The *Apostolic Constitutions*, a fourth-century document probably of Syrian origin, gives various Church laws, including these rules for widows:

> 1. Let widows assume their positions when they are not less than sixty years old (1 Tim 5:9), so that, to some extent, be-

cause of their age, there may be certainty not marred by sus-
picion about second marriages. But if you let a younger
woman be assumed into the order of widows, and if she
should marry, not being able to bear widowhood in her
youth, she will bring indecorum into people's estimation of
the order of widows. Moreover, she shall give an account to
God, not because she bound herself in a second marriage,
but because she did not keep her promise and behaved wan-
tonly toward Christ (1 Tim 5:11). Therefore it is necessary
when one makes a promise, to make it firmly, not recklessly.
"For it is better for her not to vow, than to vow and not pay"
(Eccl 5:5). But if a younger woman who lived with a husband
for a short time and lost him through death or by an occasion
of some other sort, and stays by herself, having the gift of
widowhood, she will be found blessed, resembling the
widow of Sarepta of Sidon, with whom the holy prophet
Elias stayed (1 Kings 17:9). A woman like this can be likened
to "Anna, the daughter of Phanuel of the tribe of Asher, who
did not leave the Temple, but continued in prayers and en-
treaties night and day, who being eighty years old, had lived
with a husband seven years from her virginity, who gloried
in the coming of Christ and gave thanks to the Lord and
spoke about him to all those who awaited redemption in Israel" (Luke 2:36, 37). Such a woman will be honored, since
she has been proved; she is both famed among men on earth
and has eternal praise with God in heaven.[8]

Notes

[1] Maria Thordson, *Christians 2000 A.D. Men and Women in the Land of Christ, A Living Church History* (Jerusalem: Emerezian Establishment, 1996) 110.

[2] Most Rev. Joseph Reya and Baron Jose de Vinck, *Byzantine Daily Worship* (Allendale, N.Y.: Alleluia Press, 1969) 437.

[3] Margaret Smith, *Rabiʾa the Mystic and Her Fellow-Saints in Islam* (Cambridge: Cambridge University Press, 1928, 1984) 30.

[4] Ibid., 11–12.

[5] Ibid., 25.

[6] Arlene Swidler, "In Search of Huldah," *The Bible Today* 98 (November 1978) 1780–85, at 1783.

[7] *Didascalia et Constitutiones Apostolorum*, ed. F. X. Funk (Paderborn, 1905) II, 26, 6, 105, as cited in Elizabeth Clark, *Women in the Early Church* (Wilmington: Michael Glazier, 1983) 177.

[8] Ibid., 177–78.

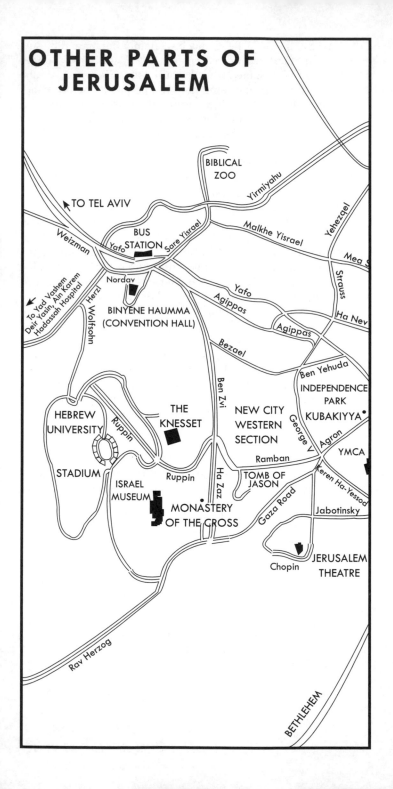

OTHER PARTS OF JERUSALEM

BIBLICAL ZOO

Yirmiyahu

TO TEL AVIV

Weizman

Malkhe Yisrael

Yehezqel

Mea S

BUS STATION

Yafo

Sare Yisrael

Strauss

Ha Nev

Nordav

Yafo

Agippas

Agippas

To Yad Vashem
Deir Yasin, Ain Karem
Hadassah Hospital

Herzl

Wolfsohn

BINYENE HAUMMA
(CONVENTION HALL)

Bezael

Ben Yehuda

INDEPENDENCE PARK

KUBAKIYYA

Ruppin

HEBREW UNIVERSITY

Ben Zvi

THE KNESSET

NEW CITY WESTERN SECTION

George V

Agron

YMCA

STADIUM

Ruppin

Ramban

TOMB OF JASON

Keren Ha-Yessod

ISRAEL MUSEUM

Ha Zaz

MONASTERY OF THE CROSS

Gaza Road

Jabotinsky

Chopin

JERUSALEM THEATRE

Rav Herzog

BETHLEHEM

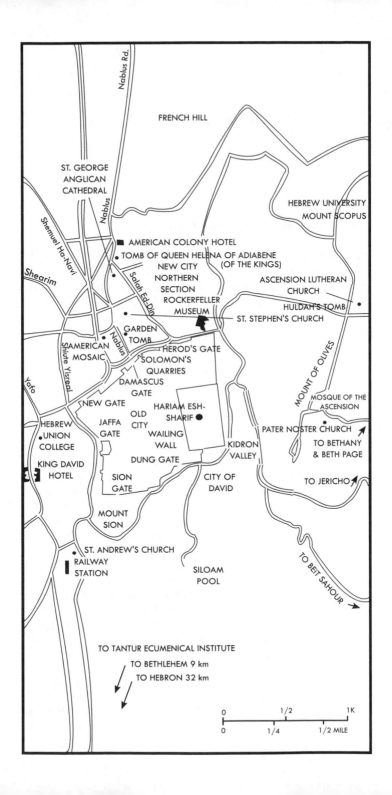

CHAPTER EIGHT

OTHER PARTS OF JERUSALEM

Mount Sion

Reflections by Egeria on Easter Liturgies

Between 444 and 460 the Empress Eudocia built the walls around Mount Sion, where in the 380s C.E. Egeria and pilgrims prayed. Egeria took careful notes on both the holy places and the ways Christians prayed, learned, and lived their faith. She left extensive descriptions of how Easter, the greatest Christian feast, was celebrated over an extended period of time and in a number of places:

> On each of the eight days of Easter the bishop, with all the clergy, the "infants" who have been baptized, all the *apotactites* both men and women, and any of the people who wish, go up to the Eleona after their meal (the Eleona contains the cave where Jesus used to teach his disciples) and in that church they have hymns and prayers, and also at the Imbomon (the place from which the Lord ascended into heaven). When the psalms and prayer are finished, they go down with singing to the Anastasis in time for the Lucernare. And this happens on each of the eight days: but on a Sunday at Easter time, after the people have been dismissed from the Lucernare at the Anastasis, they all lead the bishop with singing to Sion. When they get there, they have hymns suitable to the day and the place, a prayer, and the Gospel reading which describes the Lord coming to this place on this day, "when the doors were shut," for this happened in the very place where the church of Sion now stands. That was when one disciple, Thomas, was not present: and when he returned and the disciples told him that they had seen the Lord, he said, "unless I see I do not believe." After this reading and another prayer, the catechumens are blessed, and the faithful, and everyone goes home late, at about eight at night.
>
> In the morning the people all assemble in their usual way in the Great Church, the Martyrium, and have sermons for

the presbyters and then the bishop, and the offering is duly made in the way which is usual on a Sunday, except that the dismissal at the Martyrium is earlier, taking place before nine o'clock, and straight after the dismissal in the Martyrium all the people, every single one, take the bishop with singing to Sion, where they arrive in time for nine o'clock. When they arrive, they have a reading of the passage from the Acts of the Apostles about the descent of the spirit, and how all the languages spoken were understood, after which the service proceeds as usual.

The presbyters concern themselves with this reading because Sion (though it has now been altered into a church) is the very spot where what I have just mentioned was done by the multitude who were assembled with the apostles after the Lord's passion.

They have the reading there from the Acts of the Apostles, and afterwards the service proceeds as usual, and they make the Offering there. Then as the people are dismissed the archdeacon makes this announcement: "Let us be ready today on the Mount of Eleona at the Imbomon immediately after midday."

So all the people go home for a rest, and, as soon as they have had their meal, they go up Eleona, the Mount of Olives, each at his own pace, till there is not a Christian left in the city. Once they have climbed Eleona, the Mount of Olives, they go to the Imbomon (the place from which the Lord ascended into Heaven), where the bishop takes his seat, and also the presbyters and all the people. They have readings, and between them hymns and antiphons suited to this day and this place. Also the prayers which come between are concerned with subjects appropriate to the day and the place. They have the Gospel reading about the Lord's ascension, and then the reading from the Acts of the Apostles about the Lord ascending into heaven after the resurrection. When this is over, the catechumens are blessed, then the faithful.

(EGERIA, 139–40, 141–42)

Tomb of David

Tamar, Daughter of David

David was buried in the city of David on the eastern hill of Jerusalem, according to popular legends from the Byzantine era. The crowns placed on the tomb today are from Torah scrolls that were destroyed by the Nazis in Europe and hold memories of the tragedy.

While the stories of David show his unification of the Hebrew people, women are often overlooked or victimized as the stories of males unfold. David's daughter Tamar was raped by her half brother Amnon. David's sympathy was with his son, whom he loved, more than with his daughter, who had been incestuously violated.[1] Naming the evil of sexual violence, both ancient and modern, can begin to change people's consciousness about what is not acceptable.

> 20 Her brother Absalom said to her, "Has Amnon your brother been with you? Be quiet for now, my sister; he is your brother; do not take this to heart." So Tamar remained, a desolate woman, in her brother Absalom's house. 21 When King David heard of all these things, he became very angry, but he would not punish his son Amnon, because he loved him, for he was his firstborn. 22 But Absalom spoke to Amnon neither good nor bad; for Absalom hated Amnon, because he had raped his sister Tamar.
>
> (Read 2 Sam 13:1-22)

The Cenacle

God Who Nurtures

Here Christians remember the Last Supper. On one pillar is carved a mother pelican, which has frequently been used as a symbol of Christ's love present in the Eucharist. Ancient peoples thought that the female pelican gave her own flesh to her young as a human mother nourishes her child with her milk. The idea of God providing milk for the soul is a very ancient one that can be found in the *Odes of Solomon*, a second-century Christian document. While God is referred to as Father, he has milk-filled breasts to nourish the world:

> A cup of milk was offered to me:
> And I drank it in the sweetness of the delight of the Lord.
> The Son is the cup.
> And He who is milked is the Father;
> And He who milked Him is the Holy Spirit.
> Because His breasts were full;
> And it was not desirable that His milk should be spilt
>   to no purpose.
> And the Holy Spirit opened His bosom
> And mingled the milk of the two breasts of the Father,
> And gave the mixture to the world without their knowing:
> And they who take it are in the fullness of the right hand.[2]

Clement of Alexandria connected breast milk and blood to the image of Christ nursing through the wound in his side. Legends such as the lactation of St. Bernard and devotions focusing on the sacred heart of Christ and his wounded side mix images of blood and milk. The love and generosity of a mother who nurses her offspring with her very self is one of the most powerful images of the nourishment Christ gives through his body and blood. Medieval people understood maternal love as sacrificial; a mother might even die to give birth and certainly had to give generously to care for her child. The idea of the motherhood of God implied an accessible and tender God.

Daughters Shall Prophesy

At the time of Pentecost both women and men disciples gathered in the upper room. God's Spirit brings surprises.

> 17 "In the last days it will be, God declares,
> that I will pour out my Spirit upon all flesh,
> and your sons and your daughters shall prophesy,
> and your young men shall see visions,
> and your old men shall dream dreams.
> 18 Even upon my slaves, both men and women,
> in those days I will pour out my Spirit;
> and they shall prophesy."
>
> (Read Acts 2:14-18)

Dormition Abbey

Mary and Biblical Foremothers

This modern church built by the Benedictines in 1900 is on a site special to Christians since the first century C.E. The Madaba map of the sixth century showed the ancient Sion church in this area. Early legends described Mary "falling asleep" and in the Western Christian tradition this is celebrated on August 15 as the feast of the Assumption of Mary into heaven.

Upper Church

For the feast of the Assumption the last story of a woman in the Bible, Rev 12:14-17, is read. This dramatically symbolic story of the woman clothed with the sun is a part of apocalyptic literature, which has the purpose of assuring people that

good ultimately will prevail over evil. The woman cries out in labor pains as she gives birth. The dragon of evil stands near to destroy what is born of her. Christians have interpreted this as Mary giving birth to Christ, yet the story could be associated with women through the ages and in the present who give birth to literature, culture, heroic deeds, social service, wisdom, and children. Patriarchal dragons have swallowed and destroyed the memory of most of women's deeds and stories. Questioning the lack of women's stories and the lack of independent or heroic role models for women in those that do exist is confronting the dragon of sexism that has raged throughout five thousand years of literate culture. What makes a person heroic in a story has been analyzed extensively in works such as Joseph Campbell's *The Hero with a Thousand Faces*, yet the analysis of the heroic quests seems predominantly to apply to male heroes. The concept of the female hero needs to be explored more. Perhaps the female heroic quest is not going out to confront the dragons, but confronting the dragons of the patriarchally imposed limitations on their lives and abilities. Sometimes this involves external confrontation, but more often it means confronting the dragons within, the internalization of limits. Women questioning oppression are taking the first step on the heroic journey.

> 15 Then from his mouth the serpent poured water like a river after the woman, to sweep her away with the flood. 16 But the earth came to the help of the woman; it opened its mouth and swallowed the river that the dragon had poured from his mouth.

> (Read Rev 12:1-6, 13-18)

Lower Crypt Area

In the lower part of the church over a statue of Mary deceased is a mosaic of famous women of Scripture, including Eve. Mary is often referred to as the new Eve who brings into the world the Christ who redeems from the Fall. Stories of admiration for Mary, such as this third-century text, have developed over time:

> Now the apostles were in the place with Mary. And Bartholomew came to Peter and Andrew and John, and said to them: Let us ask Mary, her who is highly favoured, how she conceived the incomprehensible or how she carried him who cannot be carried or how she bore so much greatness. But they hesitated to ask her. Therefore Bartholomew said to

Peter: Father Peter, do you as the chief one go to her and ask her. But Peter said to John: You are a chaste youth and blameless; you must ask her. And as they all were doubtful and pondered the matter to and fro, Bartholomew came to her with a cheerful countenance and said: You who are highly favoured, tabernacle of the Most High, unblemished, we, all the apostles ask you, but they have sent me to you. Tell us how you conceived the incomprehensible, or how you carried him who cannot be carried or how you bore so much greatness. But Mary answered: Do not ask me concerning this mystery. If I begin to tell you, fire will come out of my mouth and consume the whole earth. But they asked her still more urgently. And since she did not wish to deny the apostles a hearing, she said: Let us stand up in prayer. And the apostles stood behind Mary. And she said to Peter: Peter, chief of the apostles, the greatest pillar, do you stand behind me? Did not our Lord say: *The head of the man is Christ, but the head of the woman is the man*? Therefore stand in front of me to pray. But they said to her: In you the Lord set his tabernacle and was pleased to [be] contained by you. Therefore you now have more right than we to lead in prayer. But she answered them: You are shining stars, as the prophet said: *I lifted up my eyes to the hills, from which comes my help* [Ps 120:1 LXX]. You, then, are the hills and you must pray. The apostles said to her: You ought to pray as the mother of the heavenly king. Mary said to them: In your likeness God formed the sparrows and sent them to the four corners of the world. But they answered her: He whom the seven heavens scarcely contain was pleased to be contained in you.

Then Mary stood up before them, and spread out her hands to heaven and began to pray thus: O God exceeding great and all-wise, king of the ages, indescribable, ineffable, who didst create the breadths of the heavens by thy word and arrange the vault of heaven in harmony, who didst give form to disorderly matter and didst bring together that which was separated, who didst part the gloom of the darkness from the light, who didst make the waters to flow from the same source, before whom the beings of the air tremble and the creatures of the earth fear, who didst give to the earth its place and didst not wish it to perish, in bestowing upon it abundant rain and caring for the nourishment of all things, the eternal Word (Logos) of the Father. The seven heavens could scarcely contain thee, but thou wast pleased to be contained in me, without causing me pain, thou who art the perfect Word (Logos) of the Father, through whom everything was created. Glorify thine exceedingly great name, and allow me to speak before thy holy apostles. And when she had ended the prayer, she began to say to them: Let us sit down on the ground . . . . (*The Questions of Bartholomew* II.1-14)[3]

City of David

Bathsheba

David built a palace on the summit of the hill where the Jebusites had had an acropolis. The fascinating excavations reveal history from the thirteenth century until the sixth century B.C.E. The hilly terrain of Jerusalem makes clearer the story of David's looking down and across the rooftops to spy a woman taking a bath. Bathsheba was purifying herself after her menstrual period. (See **Women Purifying Themselves in the Mikveh** [Chorazin] and **Purification of Mary** [Jerusalem].) Bathsheba has been portrayed as a seductive character in art and literature. More likely she was a vulnerable woman who could not escape the advances of a ruler. David not only had relations with her; he then killed her husband.

> 2 It happened, late one afternoon, when David rose from his couch and was walking about on the roof of the king's house, that he saw from the roof a woman bathing; the woman was very beautiful. 3 David sent someone to inquire about the woman.
>
> (Read 2 Sam 11:1-17)

St. Peter in Gallicantu

Repentant Women

After Peter denied Jesus three times, he heard a rooster crow. At this place of Peter's repentance stories of seeking God's mercy are remembered and the modern church has colorful mosaics of such stories, including stories of Mary of Egypt and Pelagia.

St. Pelagia

The Bible often portrays unfaithful Israel as a harlot, as in the book of Hosea. While some who study stories of women written by males say that the popularity of harlots reflects males' preoccupation with sexuality, Benedicta Ward believes that stories of harlots were popular because of the biblical imagery of the harlot as a metaphor for unfaithful people. Sexual infidelity then represented any type of unfaithfulness that separated people from God, the Great Lover. Among the stories are those of Mary of Egypt, Pelagia the actress of Antioch, Thais the Harlot, and Maria the niece of Abraham. Each of these harlots was transformed into a woman of great spiritual love. While faithful widows such as Paula, Melania, and Macrina gave a model of devotion, these prostitutes gave another model of responding to God.

In the decadence of the Roman empire Christians came to look upon actors, jesters, and prostitutes all as part of an immoral class. In the story of Pelagia the lively narrative describes a group of bishops holding a conference outside when Pelagia, beautifully and scantily dressed, rode by with joyful friends and servants. All the bishops hid their faces and would not look at her except Bishop Nonnus, a desert monk, who looked closely. Much to the shock of the other bishops, he said that her great beauty had delighted him. He was a man of deep prayer who could recognize her as a lovely creation of God and not be consumed by his own lust. Nonnus then used this as a teaching opportunity to contrast an indifferent Christian who takes little time to make the soul beautiful for Christ with the courtesan who spends much time working to please her lovers. The heavenly bridegroom has for the lover great gifts that eye has not seen, nor ear heard, the unimaginable treasures God has prepared for lovers (1 Cor 2:9). Nonnus prayed for Pelagia, and the next day she came to hear him preach, was converted, and Nonnus, assisted by deaconesses, baptized her.

> On the eighth day, when it is the custom for the baptized to take off their white robes, Pelagia rose in the night, though we did not know it, and took off her baptismal dress and put on a tunic and breeches belonging to the holy bishop Nonnus; and from that day she was never seen again in the city of Antioch. The holy lady Romana wept bitterly, but the holy bishop Nonnus said to her, "Do not weep, my daughter, but rejoice with great joy, for Pelagia has chosen the better part (Luke 10:42) like Mary whom the Lord preferred to Martha in the Gospel." Now Pelagia went to Jerusalem and built herself a cell on the mount of Olives and there she prayed to the Lord.
>
> After a little while the bishop of Antioch called the bishops together, so that they might all go back to their own homes. Three or four years later, I, James the deacon, wanted to go to Jerusalem to worship the resurrection of Christ and I asked the bishop to let me go. When he gave me his blessing he

said to me, "Brother deacon, when you reach the city of Jerusalem, ask the whereabouts of a certain brother Pelagius, a monk and a eunuch, who has lived there for some years shut up alone; go and visit him; truly I think you will be helped by him." I did not at all understand that he was talking about the handmaid of God, Pelagia.

So I reached Jerusalem, and when I had joined in the adoration of the Resurrection of our Lord Jesus Christ, on another day I made inquiries about the servant of God. I went and found him on the Mount of Olives where he used to pray to the Lord in a small cell which was closed on all sides, with one small window. I knocked on the window and at once she appeared and she recognized me, though I did not recognize her. How could I have known her again, with a face so emaciated by fasting? It seemed to me that her eyes had sunk inwards like a great pit. She said to me, "Where have you come from, brother?" And I replied, "I was sent to you by the order of the holy bishop Nonnus." At once she closed the little window on me, saying, "Tell him to pray for me, for he is a saint of God." At once she began the psalms of the third hour. I prayed beside the cell and then left, much helped by the sight of her angelic face. I returned to Jerusalem and began to visit the brothers in the monasteries there.

Throughout these monasteries, great indeed was the fame of the monk Pelagius. So I decided to make another journey to speak with her and receive some saving teaching. When I reached the cell and knocked, calling her name, there was no reply. I waited a second day and also a third, calling the name of Pelagius, but I could not hear anyone. Then I said to myself, "Either there is no one there or he who was a monk has left." But warned by a nudge from God, I said to myself, "I had better see if, in fact, he has died." So I broke open the little window; and I saw that he was dead. So I closed the opening and I was filled with sorrow. I ran all the way to Jerusalem and told whoever I met that the holy monk Pelagius who had wrought so many wonders was now at rest. Then the holy fathers came with monks from several monasteries and the door of the cell was broken in. They carried out his sacred little body as if it had been gold and silver they were carrying. When the fathers began to anoint the body with myrrh, they realized that it was a woman. They wanted to keep such a wonder hidden but they could not, because of the crowds of people thronging around, who cried out with a loud voice, "Glory to you, Lord Jesus Christ, for you have hidden away on earth such great treasures, women as well as men." So it was known to all the people, and monks came in from all the monasteries and also nuns, from Jericho and from the Jordan where the Lord was baptized, bearing candles and lamps and singing hymns; and the holy fathers bore her body to its burial.

May the life of this harlot, this account of total conversion, join us to her and bring us all to the mercy of the Lord on the day of judgment, to whom be glory and power and honour to the ages of ages. Amen.[4]

Cemeteries on the Mount of Olives

Sapphira

The Kidron Valley has been thought of as the valley of Jehoshaphat, supposed to be the place of final judgment. Jews, Christians, and Muslims have buried the dead there to be ready. As the valley has filled, the graves have been dug on the sides of the mount. Repeatedly religious traditions have invited persons to reflect on death as an invitation to value life and live righteously. Amid the thousands of tombs one might remember this story of sudden death, which was written to invite truthfulness and conversion from greed. The deaths of Sapphira and Ananias were a way of reminding the Christian community to live with integrity at every moment, for death can be imminent.

> 5 But a man named Ananias, with the consent of his wife Sapphira, sold a piece of property; 2 with his wife's knowledge, he kept back some of the proceeds, and brought only a part and laid it at the apostles' feet.
>
> (Read Acts 5:1-11)

Mosque of the Ascension

Reflections of Egeria on the Imbomon

In about 384 C.E. Egeria took part in worship where Christians remembered the ascension of Christ, but it was on the open hillock because no church had been built there yet.

> The next day, Sunday, is the beginning of the Easter week or, as they call it here, "The Great Week." At one o'clock all the people go up to the Eleona Church on the Mount of Olives. The bishop takes his seat, and they have hymns and antiphons suitable to the place and the day, and readings too. When three o'clock comes, they go up with hymns and sit down at the Imbomon, the place from which the Lord ascended into heaven.
>
> (EGERIA, 132–33)

The mosque is on the site of the early Church of the Ascension, which was built by Poimenia sometime between 384 and 390 C.E., though later popular legend said that Helena had built it. While devotion motivated Christian pilgrims to go to the holy places, some Christians seemed equally interested in the adventure of traveling. In a fragment of a Coptic *Life* of John of Lycopolis, in Palladius' story of visiting in Egypt, and in the *Life* of Peter the Iberian we find glimpses of Poimenia, a very wealthy woman of the Roman nobility. She approached the trip as had a long line of wealthy tourists to Egypt, including the Emperor Hadrian in 130 and others fascinated by Herodotus' descriptions. She had a few sailing vessels and a huge entourage with leisure and means to stop at many ports. She took a splendid voyage up the Nile supposedly to find the holy hermit John of Lycopolis in the Thebaiad and to get him to cure an ailment she had. The trip seems to have been more than prayerful devotion. Arriving in Alexandria in her own ships, she then hired a fleet of local boats to take her upriver. Her attendants included bishops, priests, eunuchs, and Moorish slaves. John, a holy hermit who had been in his cell for forty years and had not beheld a woman's face or handled money, did not entertain her, but Palladius related the following of the holy man:

> He did not entertain Poimenia, the servant of God, when she came to visit him, but he cleared up for her a number of secret things. He told her not to turn aside to Alexandria on her way down from the Thebaiad, "for there you must fall into temptation." Now she either deceived him outright or else forgot about that advice. She did turn aside to Alexandria to see the city for herself. On the journey she had her boats tied up near Nicopolis to wait for her. When her servant went ashore they had a fight with the natives, very desperate men, because of some kind of disorder. Some cut off the finger of a eunuch; another one they killed; not recognizing the saintly bishop Dionysius, they doused him in the river. After they had wounded all the other servants, they insulted and threatened her.[5]

Despite John's advice, she did spend time in Alexandria. Eventually she went on to Jerusalem to visit the holy places, but she acted like a Roman aristocratic tourist rather than a prayerful pilgrim. Eventually she had a church built on the Mount of Olives "around Christ's last footprints." She was also remembered for destroying an idol on Mount Gerizim in

Samaria. This kind of action would have been in keeping with the royal policy of trying to replace other cults with Christianity to strengthen the unity of the empire.

The Tomb of Huldah

Huldah the Prophet

The site of this tomb is popular lore. In the fourth century, when Christian pilgrimage was becoming very popular, many "tombs were found," including that of St. Stephen. During the Mamluk Period, 1250–1517, this tomb was said to belong to Mary the Egyptian. It is significant that since many of the male prophets had "tombs" where they could be remembered, people wanted a "tomb" to remember Huldah, who had lived in the seventh century B.C.E. (See **Western Wall of the Temple** for information on **Huldah**.)

Church of the Pater Noster or Eleona

Melania the Elder

In the late fourth century C.E. Melania the Elder lived and prayed on the Mount of Olives but, since the actual location is not known, the location of the ruins of the ancient Eleona church can be a peaceful place to remember her. Egeria wrote of the Eleona as the site of a cave first connected with the Ascension, but when the place for remembering the Ascension was moved further up the hill the cave was associated with Jesus' teaching. The modern church here takes its name from the Our Father and the prayer is inscribed in sixty-two languages.

Melania the Elder was a wealthy Roman aristocrat, born about 341 C.E., who married well and had three sons. Her husband and two of her sons died in one year. After that she went on a pilgrimage to the East, probably to Alexandria, and met monks who inspired her. Finally she established a monastic community on the Mount of Olives. Her friend Rufinus gathered a community of men nearby and she assisted him. Later Paula and Jerome were to follow this example in establishing a double monastery. Paula and Jerome probably visited these foundations, but because Jerome had arguments with Rufinus and was hostile toward him he does not mention their communities.

Melania lived on the Mount for about three decades. In 400 she went back to Nola, Italy, for a family gathering. She visited North Africa and then returned to Jerusalem, where she died about 410. Palladius wrote of her life there:

. . . Melania founded a monastery in Jerusalem, were she lived for twenty-seven years in the company of fifty virgins. A man called Rufinus, who came from Aquileia in Italy, lived there too. He was of very good family, of character similar to her own, and very energetic; later he was thought worthy to become a priest. During these twenty-seven years they welcomed people who visited Jerusalem for the sake of their vows—bishops, monks and deacons—and supported all their guests at their own expense. They settled the schism of Paulinus, which involved about four hundred monks, and together they won over all the heretics who denied the divinity of the Holy Spirit, and brought them into the Church. Thus they lived out their lives without causing scandal to anyone.

I have already given a superficial description of that wonderful saintly woman, Melania, in this book; nonetheless I should now like to reveal the rest of her story. It is not for me but for the inhabitants of Persia to describe how much of her wealth she spent with God-given generosity, as though she were burning it in a fire. No one—East, West, North, or South—has failed to enjoy her benefactions. During the thirty-seven years she lived apart from the world, she helped churches, monasteries, refugees, and prisoners with her private fortune; her family, her son himself and his personal guardians also furnished her with means. Because she persisted so long in her life of separation from the world, she did not possess so much as a square yard of land, nor was she distracted by desire for her son; her longing for her only son did not separate her from her love for Christ.

Through her prayers the young man achieved a high standard of education and character and made a distinguished marriage. He was to be found among the recipients of worldly honors and had two children. After a long time had passed, Melania heard about the situation of her granddaughter, how she was married and decided to separate herself from the world. As she was afraid that the couple might succumb to bad teaching or heresy or evil living, Melania, though an elderly lady of sixty, embarked on board ship, set sail from Caesaraea, and reached Rome twenty days later.

There she met Apronianus, a Greek, who was a very fortunate man and worthy of all possible respect. She gave him religious instruction and made him a Christian, having persuaded him to live in continence with his wife, who was her cousin and was called Avita. Then after having strengthened her granddaughter Melania and her husband Pinianus in their resolve, and after having instructed her daughter-in-law Albina, the wife of her son, she persuaded all of them to sell their possessions. She took them away from Rome and led them to the haven of a consecrated and peaceful life. Thus she "fought with beasts," that is, with the senators and their wives, who were preventing her from withdrawing the rest of her family from the world. She spoke to them this way: "Little children, it was written four hundred years ago that 'the last hour has come.' Why do you cling to your empty lives? Are you not afraid that the days of the Antichrist will overtake you and you may not enjoy your own or your inherited wealth?"

She set all these people free and brought them to monastic life. She gave religious instruction to her younger son Publicola and took him to Sicily. Having sold all her remaining property and received the money for it, she went to Jerusalem. After distributing all her worldly goods, she fell asleep forty days later, at a fine old age in the deepest peace. She left behind a monastery in Jerusalem and the money for its endowment.

Palladius also described the trauma people felt as the Roman empire, which had seemed so invulnerable, began to lose its power:

After all these people had left Rome, the barbarians stormed the city. The forecast of their invasion had long lain concealed in the prophetic books. They did not spare the bronze statues which stood in the Forum, but ravaged everything in their barbaric fury and consigned it to destruction. The result was that Rome, which had been adorned with beauty for twelve hundred years, became a ruin. Then those who had received religious training from Melania and those who had been opposed to such training from Melania both glorified God, who by overturning the accepted order of things, won over the unbelievers. Of all the people who had been taken prisoner, only those households were saved which had offered themselves as sacrifices to the Lord through the zeal of Melania.

She was a very learned lady, who loved the Word. She turned night into day and went carefully through all the works of the ancient commentators. Among these she read three million lines of Origen, two million five hundred thousand lines of Gregory, Stephen, Pierios, and Basil, and two million of other very erudite authors. She did not read them once only at random, but went laboriously through each book seven or eight times. She was therefore freed from pseudo-knowledge, and by the grace of their words she was able to be borne on wings. With the support of good hopes, she made herself into a bird of the Spirit and was able to soar away on her journey to Christ.[6]

Melania the Elder, Paula, and Melania the Younger are all examples of women who were serious scholars. It is unfortunate that their writings were not preserved.

Evangelical Lutheran Church of the Ascension
Melania the Younger

This modern church with its beautiful mosaics can be a quiet place to remember another of the wealthy famous women associated with the Mount of Olives, Melania the Younger. She was born in Rome in about 383 C.E. and was the granddaughter of Melania the Elder. Her family arranged that she marry Pinianus when she was about fourteen. Within five years she had borne and lost two children, and she urged her husband to consider letting her live her life in celibacy dedicated to God and that he do the same. Much to the displeasure of other family members, Melania and her husband began living simply at a country villa and giving their great wealth away. They spent some time in Sicily, then journeyed to Africa where they founded a monastery for women and one for men. They went as pilgrims to Jerusalem and then to Egypt to see the monasteries and hermitages in order to learn from the "living saints," as the ascetics were called. About 420 they went to Jerusalem. Melania began living as a recluse on the Mount of Olives, but she then founded a monastery for women there. She did not, however, want to be the leader of it but a community member ministering to the others. In 432, after Pinianus had died, Melania founded a men's monastery. She again spent time alone. She was very devoted to study; she read the whole Bible through three times a year and learned many of the psalms by heart. This is how the writer of the anonymous *Life of Melania,* who is presumed to be Gerontius, described her scholarship and dedication to prayer:

> She wrote elegantly and faultlessly in little notebooks. She mentally decided how much she should write each day, how much in the Canonical Books [of Scripture] she should read, and how much in the collections of homilies. After she had had her fill of these writings, she went through the lives of the Fathers as if she were eating a cake. Then she slept for an interval of about two hours. As soon as she awoke, she aroused her fellow ascetics, saying: Just as the blessed Abel

and each of the saints used to offer their first fruits to God, so we too will spend the first hours of the night in praise of God. We ought to spend every hour in watch and prayer, as it is written, because we do not know at what hour the thief will come.[7]

Melania was asked to go to the royal court in Constantinople to be with her uncle Volusian, the former prefect of Rome, who was negotiating a royal marriage alliance. **Eudoxia**, the daughter of the Eastern emperor Theodosius II (408–450) and **Eudocia**, was to marry Valentinian III, who was emperor of the West from 425 to 455. Melania was concerned about her uncle, who was not a Christian, and she thought she might minister to him, but the visit was challenging for her because she had had about twenty years of simple life and prayer and dreaded the pomp of the imperial court. Eudocia, who was a brilliant scholar and devout Christian, was very inspired by Melania and sought spiritual counsel from her. Melania urged the emperor to send Eudocia on pilgrimage to the holy places. (See **Seleucia** for the story of their meeting at Thecla's tomb, and see **St. Stephen's Church** for more on Eudocia.) After Melania had led her uncle to Christianity, given him "communion three times from her own hands" on his deathbed, and witnessed his peaceful death, she returned to Jerusalem. Gerontius' lengthy story of her life reveals a kind, tender person seeking an interior life and distancing herself from the wealth and power of the empire.

Dominus Flevit Church

Jesus Who Wept,
Jesus Who Compared Himself to a Mother Hen

In this church, with its wonderful view of Jerusalem, is a mosaic of a mother hen gathering her chicks. Some of the most frequently used female imagery of God in the Bible is that of mother birds: see Exod 19:4; Deut 32:11-13; Ruth 2:12; Pss 36:7-9; 57:1; 61:4; 63:7. (See Chapter 2 on female images of the divine.)

> 34 Jerusalem, Jerusalem, the city that kills the prophets and stones those who are sent to it! How often have I desired to gather your children together as a hen gathers her brood under her wings, and you were not willing! (Luke 13:34)

The Russian Orthodox Church of St. Mary Magdalene

Mary Magdalene

Czar Alexander III built this church in the nineteenth century in honor of his mother, who was named Magdalene. The Grand Duchess Elizabeth Teodronia, who was killed by the Bolsheviks in 1918, is buried here. Russian nuns care for the church. In John's gospel the designation of "apostle" for particular persons is never used, but "disciple" is. Women have clear roles of discipleship. Many of the non-canonical writings of the early Christian centuries indicate the importance of women as ministers of the gospel and the resulting jealousy of men:

> [The disciples] were grieved. They wept greatly, saying, "How shall we go to the gentiles and preach the gospel of the kingdom of the Son of Man? If they did not spare him, how will they spare us?" Then Mary stood up, greeted them all, and said to her brethren, "Do not weep and do not grieve nor be irresolute, for his grace will be entirely with you and will protect you. But rather let us praise his greatness, for he has prepared us and made us into men." When Mary said this, she turned their hearts to the Good, and they began to discuss the words of the [Savior].
>
> Peter said to Mary, "Sister, we know that the Savior loved you more than the rest of women. Tell us the words of the Savior which you remember—which you know (but) we do not, nor have we heard them." Mary answered and said, "What is hidden from you I will proclaim to you." And she began to speak to them these words: "I," she said, "saw the Lord in a vision and I said to him, 'Lord, I saw you today in a vision.' He answered and said to me, 'Blessed are you, that you did not waver at the sight of me. For where the mind is, there is the treasure.'"[8]

Gethsemane

Church of All Nations

Reflections of Egeria on the Mount of Olives

The modern church built around a rock is designed to be dark inside, with designs of olive branches on the ceiling. Even on bright days it creates an atmosphere of foreboding darkness in this garden where Jesus experienced spiritual darkness. Egeria wrote of the large church in which pilgrims remembered

Jesus' prayer at a certain large rock. Her description of the Holy Thursday night services continues:

When the cocks begin to crow, everyone leaves the Imbomon, and comes down with singing to the place where the Lord prayed. As the Gospels describe in the passage which begins, "And he was parted from them about a stone's cast, and prayed" (Luke 22:41). The bishop and all the people go into a graceful church which has been built there, and have a prayer appropriate to the place and the day, and one suitable hymn. Then the Gospel passage is read where he said to his disciples, "Watch, lest ye enter into temptation," (Matt 26:31-56) and, when the whole passage has been read, there is another prayer. From there all of them, including the smallest children, now go down with singing and conduct the bishop to Gethsemane. There are a great many people and they have been crowded together, tired by their vigil, and weakened by their daily fasting—and they have had a very big hill to come down—so they go very slowly on the way to Gethsemane. So that they can all see, they are provided with hundreds of church candles. When everyone arrives at Gethsemane, they have an appropriate prayer, a hymn, and then a reading from the Gospel about the Lord's arrest. By the time it has been read everyone is groaning and lamenting and weeping so loud that people even across the city can probably hear it all.

Next they go with singing to the city, and walking they reach the gate at the time when people can first recognize each other. And from there every single one of them, old and young, rich and poor, goes on through the centre of the city to be present at the next service—for this above all others is the day when no one leaves the vigil till morning comes. Thus the bishop is conducted from Gethsemane to the gate, and from there through the whole city as far as the Cross. By the time they arrive before the Cross it is pretty well full day, and they have another Gospel reading, the whole passage about the Lord being led away to Pilate, and all the recorded words of Pilate to the Lord or to the Jews.

Then the bishop speaks a word of encouragement to the people. They have been hard at it all night, and there is further effort in store for them in the day ahead. So he tells them not to be weary, but to put their hope in God, who will give them a reward out of all proportion to the effort they have made. When he has given them as much encouragement as he can, he speaks to them as follows: "Now off you go home till the next service, and sit down for a bit. Then all be back here at about eight o'clock so that till midday you can see the holy Wood of the Cross, that, as every one of us believes, helps us attain salvation. And from midday onwards we must assemble here before the Cross again, and give our minds to readings and prayers till nightfall."

(EGERIA, 135–36)

Tomb of the Virgin Mary
Legends of Christ's Mother

An anonymous writing of the second or third century known as the *Transitus Mariae* said that Mary was buried here. Queen Melisande († 1160), wife of a crusader king of Jerusalem, was also buried here. Mary, the mother of Jesus, is mentioned more often in the Quran than she is in Christian Scriptures, and Muslims consider this site holy because Mohammed saw a light over the tomb of his "sister Mary." Since the time of the construction of the church over the tomb in 1130 the Greeks, Armenians, Syrians, Copts, and Muslims alike have shared it.

The following description and prayer is for the Feast of the Dormition, August 15, which first became popular in the Byzantine empire between 588 and 602. Pope Theodore I (642–649), an easterner from Jerusalem, later introduced it to Rome and the West.

> According to a very early Christian legend, while the apostles were scattered all over the then-known world, preaching the Gospel, Mary remained in Jerusalem in the house of John. Her love of God, like an ardent flame, burned steadily in her body. Finally it was revealed to her that her life was about to end; she wished to see the Twelve once more before she died. Each one of them was miraculously carried away from where he happened to be and borne on a cloud to the house on Mount Sion in Jerusalem where Mary was approaching death; each one of them, that is, except Thomas. They saw Christ Himself come down from heaven and receive the soul of his Mother in his arms. They took her holy body and placed it in the tomb prepared for it in the valley of Cedron, near Gethsemane. Thomas arrived three days later, when all was over. He wished to see for the last time the face of the woman who had been the Temple of God. He went with the other apostles to the tomb, which they opened; they found it empty, but heard an angelic concert. Mary herself appeared to them and confirmed the fact of her Assumption into heaven.
>
> (First Tone) THE HOLY APOSTLES were taken up from every corner of the world and carried upon clouds by order of

God. (Fifth Tone) And they gathered around your pure remains, O Source of Life, and kissed them with reverence. (Second Tone) As for the most sublime Powers of heaven, they came with their own Leader. (Sixth Tone) To escort and to pay their last respects to the most honorable body that had contained Life Itself. Filled with awe, they marched together with the apostles in silent majesty, professing to the Princes of Heaven in a hushed voice: "Behold, the Queen of All, the divine maiden is coming!" (Third Tone) Lift up your gates and receive with becoming majesty the Mother of the Light that never fades. (Seventh Tone) Because through her, salvation was made possible for our human race. She is the one upon whom no one may gaze, and to whom no one is able to render sufficient glory. (Fourth Tone) For the special honor that made her sublime is beyond our understanding. (Eighth Tone) Wherefore, O most pure Mother of God, forever alive with your Son, the Source of Life, do not cease to intercede with Him that He may guard and save your people from every trouble, for you are our intercessor. (First Tone) To you we sing a hymn of glory with loud and joyful voices, now and forever.[9]

The Cave of Gethsemane

Legends of the Women Disciples

To the right of the tomb of Mary is a cave made into a chapel. Byzantine pilgrims said that the disciples rested here as Jesus prayed. In the Monastery of San Marco in Florence the Renaissance artist Fra Angelico painted the women disciples Martha and Mary resting in the garden along with the men.[10]

Bethphage

Martha's Profession of Faith

Here the Franciscan Church commemorates Jesus' ride into Jerusalem mounted on an ass. The stone here also records John 11:20, that Martha and Mary went out to meet Jesus before he arrived in Bethany. In 384 C.E. Egeria, while remembering that encounter, wrote of a church about a mile from Lazarus' tomb. In Matthew's gospel Peter recognizes Christ as the Messiah and Jesus responds, giving him a position of leadership, "You are Peter and on this rock . . . ." Within the community mentioned in John's gospel, women were leaders. Martha is the one who in the face of death still recognized Christ as the Messiah, the resurrection, and the life:

> 24 Martha said to him, "I know that he will rise again in the resurrection on the last day." 25 Jesus said to her, "I am the resurrection and the life. Those who believe in me, even though they die, will live, 26 and everyone who lives and believes in me will never die. Do you believe this?" 27 She said to him, "Yes, Lord, I believe that you are the Messiah, the Son of God, the one coming into the world."
>
> (Read John 11:20-37)

Bethany

Martha and Mary

The Franciscan Church of Lazarus, Mary, and Martha

Since at least the 300s C.E. pilgrims have prayed at the tomb here, and Jerome wrote of the church being built nearby. In 1138 Queen Melisande built a convent here for the Benedictine Sisters, including her own sister Iveta who in 1157 became abbess of the convent. Egeria described the observances in Bethany on the Saturday before Palm Sunday, which has come to be called Lazarus Saturday and is still observed by thousands of pilgrims:

> At dawn on the morning of Saturday the bishop makes the usual Saturday Offering. Then, for the dismissal, the archdeacon makes this announcement: "At one o'clock today let us all be ready at the Lazarium."
>
> Just at one o'clock everyone arrives at the Lazarium, which is Bethany, about two miles from the city. About half a mile before you get to the Lazarium from Jerusalem there is a church by the road. It is the spot where Lazarus' sister Mary met the Lord. All the monks meet the bishop when he arrives there, and the people go into the church. They have one hymn and an antiphon, and a reading from the gospel about Lazarus' sister meeting the Lord. Then, after a prayer, everyone is blessed, and they go on with singing to the Lazarium.
>
> By the time they arrive there so many people have collected that they fill not only the Lazarium itself, but all the fields around. They have hymns and antiphons which—like all the readings—are suitable to the day and the place. Then at the dismissal a presbyter announces Easter. He mounts a platform and reads the Gospel passage which begins "When Jesus came to Bethany six days before the Passover." After this reading, with its announcement of Easter, comes the dismissal.

They do it on this day because the Gospel describes what took place in Bethany "six days before the Passover," and it is six days from this Saturday to the Thursday night on which the Lord was arrested after the Supper. Thus they all return to the Anastasis and have Lucernare in the usual way.

The next day, Sunday, is the beginning of the Easter week or, as they call it here, "The Great Week."

(EGERIA, 131–32)

To the right of the entrance of the Franciscan Church is the pilgrims' dining room in what was once a medieval monastery. The table there is a good place to remember Jesus' visits. The population of Jerusalem tripled during the religious festivals, and food and lodging were very expensive. Perhaps that is why Jesus so often took advantage of the hospitality in Bethany at the home of Martha and Mary. While men would "sit at the feet of the Rabbi," that is, spend time discussing Torah with Jesus, that was not the women's place. Jesus invited Martha to join him nonetheless, and to study Scripture as men did. This story of table sharing in Luke's gospel could serve to remind the women who hosted house churches that the focus on Christ in their midst was more important then worrying about details of hospitality.

(Read Luke 10:38-42)

Hospitality at the Supper Before the Last Supper

Inside the Church are mosaics depicting the many gospel stories that took place in Bethany. The woman who was a sinner, the one who anointed Jesus at the home of Simon the leper, has been confused with Martha's sister Mary and also with Mary Magdalene. (For the woman at Simon's home see **Mount Tabor**.) Martha's sister Mary also anointed Jesus. Her profuse generosity and love were not understood.

> 2 There they gave a dinner for him. Martha served, and Lazarus was one of those at the table with him. 3 Mary took a pound of costly perfume made of pure nard, anointed Jesus' feet, and wiped them with her hair.
>
> (Read John 12:1-8)

The Tomb of Lazarus

Lamentation

Jesus had seen the deep emotions of women, and perhaps that freed him to show his own emotion and weep. The women begged that there might be life where there was death. Jesus called Lazarus to life but invited the community to unbind him. People are invited to free each other to enjoy God's fullness of life.

> 38 Then Jesus, again greatly disturbed, came to the tomb. It was a cave, and a stone was lying against it. 39 Jesus said, "Take away the stone." Martha, the sister of the dead man, said to him, "Lord, already there is a stench because he has been dead four days." 40 Jesus said to her, "Did I not tell you that if you believed, you would see the glory of God?"
>
> (Read John 11: 38-44)

The New City: Northern Section

Tomb of Queen Helena of Adiabene (Tomb of the Kings)

A Convert to Judaism

Helena of Adiabene and her son were converted by Jewish merchants and came to Jerusalem on pilgrimage during the famine in 44–46 C.E. Helena lived in Jerusalem for the next twenty years. Although she returned to her own country, she requested that she be buried in Jerusalem. Her tomb was so elaborate that ancient writers thought it belonged to the kings of Judah.

Josephus, the famous Jewish historian of the first century C.E., described Helena's goodness:

> Helena, the mother of the king, saw that peace prevailed in the kingdom and that her son was prosperous and the object of admiration in all men's eyes, even those of foreigners, thanks to the prudence that God gave him. Now she had conceived a desire to go to the city of Jerusalem and to worship at the temple of God, which was famous throughout the world, and to make thank-offerings there. She consequently asked her son to give her leave. Izates was most enthusiastic in granting his mother's request, made great preparations for her journey, and gave her a large sum of money. He even escorted her for a considerable distance, and she completed her journey to the city of Jerusalem. Her arrival was very advantageous for the people of Jerusalem, for at that time the city was hard pressed by famine and many were perishing from want of money to purchase what they needed. Queen Helena sent some of her attendants to Alexandria to buy grain for

large sums and others to Cyprus to bring back a cargo of dried figs. Her attendants speedily returned with these provisions, which she thereupon distributed among the needy. She has thus left a very great name that will be famous forever among our whole people for her benefaction. When her son Izates learned of the famine, he likewise sent a great sum of money to leaders of the Jerusalemites. The distribution of this fund to the needy delivered many from the extremely severe pressure of famine. But I shall leave to a later time the further tale of good deeds performed for our city by this royal pair.

Not long afterwards Izates passed away, having completed fifty-five years of his life and having been monarch for twenty-four; he left twenty-four sons and twenty-four daughters. His orders were that his brother Monobazus should succeed to the throne. Thus Monobazus was rewarded for faithfully keeping the throne for his brother during the latter's absence from home after his father's death. His mother Helena was sorely distressed by the news of her son's death, as was to be expected of a mother bereft of a son so very religious. She was, however, consoled on hearing that the succession had passed to her eldest son and hastened to join him. She arrived in Adiabene but did not long survive her son Izates, for, weighted down with age and with the pain of her sorrow, she quickly breathed out her last. Monobazus sent her bones and those of his brother to Jerusalem with instructions that they should be buried in the three pyramids that his mother had erected at a distance of three furlongs from the city of Jerusalem.[11]

St. Stephen's Church

Empress Eudocia

The contemporary church is built over the fifth-century church founded by Eudocia. Portions of the ancient mosaic floor can be seen in the modern structure. Though Stephen was the first Christian martyr (Acts 7), it was only in 415 C.E. that his relics appeared. A Palestinian priest had a vision to dig for them in a certain place, and the story relates that instantly seventy-three people were healed, demons fled, and other miracles occurred. As more pilgrims came to the Holy Land there was increasing interest in going to places with biblical stories and other legends. Some of these relics had surfaced in the court of Constantinople. When Eudocia came on pilgrimage in 438 C.E. she put some of the relics in the church of St. Lawrence, which had been sponsored by her sister-in-law Pulcheria. In 460 Eudocia built a church in honor of St. Stephen and moved relics there.

The empress was a brilliant woman, the daughter of Leontius, the chair of rhetoric in Athens. By the time she married the emperor she had been baptized a Christian by the bishop of Constantinople. She wrote verse paraphrases of the biblical books, Homeric centos on Christ, and three books of hexameters on the martyrs Cyprian and Justina. All the texts seem to be lost except that on Cyprian. While in Antioch on the way to Jerusalem she gave a speech in praise of the city and adapted verses from Homer. She was a great success; a bronze statue of her commemorated her achievements. So few public monuments commemorate women!

After her daughter Eudoxia was married to the emperor of the West, Eudocia made a pilgrimage to thank God. The journey was also to see Melania the Younger, who had inspired Eudocia when she visited Constantinople, and to bestow gifts on churches along the way to strengthen the empire as Helena, the mother of Constantine, had done. (See **Mount of Olives** and **Seleucia.**) When Eudocia returned to Constantinople there was some family tension. Was she in conflict with Pulcheria, who was very strong and often advised her emperor brother? Rumors said that Eudocia had committed adultery and the emperor wanted to banish her. Some scholars say that the picture of a good, pious emperor was a fabrication of his biographers who wished to support the empire. He was insecure with his very brilliant wife and just wanted to get rid of her, so he exiled her to Palestine. Melania the Younger met her at St. Thecla Shrine in Seleucia. Did these two women get strength and comfort from the heroic woman Thecla, who refused to marry?

For a few years her entourage was supported by the emperor, but when in 444 he sent Saturninus to murder two clergymen who attended her she had Saturninus murdered. Then she got no more support from Constantinople, but she had family funds of her own. Theological debates were raging about how to define Christ's humanity and divinity. St. Stephen's was large, so it was chosen for a gathering of 10,000 monks from the surrounding area to discuss Christ's nature. They opposed saying that Christ had two natures, and they told Bishop Juvenal to express their position at the Council of Chalcedon. Juvenal went, but after listening to others who wanted the "two natures in one person" theory, and in order to curry favor for his wish that Jerusalem be declared a patriarchate, he agreed to the Council's decision. At first both the monks and Eudocia stood in opposition to the proclamation of Chalcedon, but they eventually came to accept it.

The argument that the bishop of Rome, Leo, used to try to change her mind was that looking at the holy places themselves could help one accept that Christ had a human life, a human nature. He did not persuade her. After the emperor was killed in Rome in 455 by the Vandals who were invading, and Eudocia's daughter and grandchildren were captured, she sought spiritual counsel. At that time she came to accept the decision of Chalcedon and returned to communion with Bishop Juvenal. Many monks and people followed her example.

Elizabeth Clark in *Ascetic Piety and Women's Faith* analyzes the stories of Eudocia and of Melania the Younger. The male authors use the stories to defend their own theological positions in the midst of controversies as much as they actually try to describe the women.[12]

The Garden Tomb

Mary Magdalene, Apostle to the Apostles

Outside the Damascus Gate on Nablus Road is a garden where one can pray. Historical evidence for this being Christ's tomb does not exist, but the garden can give one an idea of how the place of Mary's encounter with the risen Christ might have looked. This suffering woman was the one sent to proclaim the resurrection.

> 18 Mary Magdalene went and announced to the disciples, "I have seen the Lord"; and she told them that he had said these things to her.
>
> (Read John 20: 11-18)

St. George Anglican Cathedral and the Benshoff Museum

Created in God's Own Image

St. George's complex has a place of worship, a museum with displays from Tel Dothan, an educational center, and a garden with some of the plants mentioned in the Bible. The garden is a pleasant place to ponder the mystery of creation, the great variety God has made, and the idea that both females and males image God.

> 27 So God created humankind in his image, in the image of God he created them; male and female he created them. 28

God blessed them, and God said to them, "Be fruitful and multiply, and fill the earth and subdue it; and have dominion over the fish of the sea and over the birds of the air and over every living thing that moves upon the earth." 29 God said, "See, I have given you every plant yielding seed that is upon the face of all the earth, and every tree with seed in its fruit; you shall have them for food."

(Read Gen 1:11-12, 24-29)

The New City: Western Section

Yad Vashem Museum and Deir Yasin

God Who Weeps

Yad Vashem Museum, a place commemorating the Holocaust of 1939–1945, during which approximately six million Jews (then over two-thirds of all the Jews in the world) were killed by the Nazis, can be a place to reflect on the fact that trying to destroy "the other" is never good. God weeps with suffering people. The land where Yad Vashem was built was farmland of the Palestinian people of the village of Deir Yasin. In 1948 Zionists went into the village and massacred 254 of the men, women, and children and threw their bodies in a well. Menachem Begin boastfully described this in his book *The Revolt*.[13] News of the massacre spread and caused many Palestinians in other places to try to flee or hide. The Jews suffered greatly as victims of the Nazis. Then some Jews, as traumatized victims, made the Palestinians their victims. More than five hundred Palestinian towns and villages were destroyed, sealed, or taken by Israel and 800,000 Palestinian people were expelled from their land from 1947 to 1949.[14]

A number of biblical women heroes are praised because they destroyed enemies just as did Joshua, David, and other "good" kings. Deborah successfully directed the battle at Mount Tabor (Judg 4:4-16); Jael drove a tent peg through the head of the enemy Sisera (Judg 4:17-22); Judith beheaded Holofernes (Judith 13). While the courage of these women can be admired, wisdom reveals the foolishness and inadequacy of violence as a way of dealing with differences. In earlier eras violent destruction of the other was considered a solution, but the dangerous myth of redemptive violence is today being unmasked. Violence never stops violence. Mahatma Gandhi said that he would be willing to die for what he believed in, but he would never be willing to kill for it.

The Wisdom tradition of the Peoples of the Book invites people to question the human image of the Divine as a warrior.

While slavery and monarchy were accepted conventions in past eras, human intelligence calls for human rights and democracy for the future. War was accepted, but it is both ineffective and inadequate for the future. The Holy One is nurturing and compassionate. The Holy One weeps with those who suffer. The Holy One invites true believers to work toward the alleviation of all suffering in the world. This wisdom is at the center of Judaism, Christianity, and Islam. The history of the twentieth-century Jewish Holocaust and of biblical lands for the last four thousand years indicates that humankind is slow to learn divine wisdom.

> 17 You shall say to them this word:
> Let my eyes run down with tears night and day,
> and let them not cease,
> for the virgin daughter—my people—is struck down with a
>   crushing blow,
> with a very grievous wound.
> 18 If I go out into the field,
> look—those killed by the sword!
> And if I enter the city,
> look—those sick with famine!
> For both prophet and priest ply their trade throughout
>   the land,
> and have no knowledge.

(Jer 14:17-18)

Monastery of the Cross

Orthodox Women Hymn Writers

In the sixth century a church was built on this site because an ancient legend said that here grew the tree from which Christ's cross was fashioned. In 1039 the king of Georgia began building a monastery here. In 1685 it was purchased by the Greek Orthodox Church. They welcome visitors to see the art and architecture and to spend time on retreat with the nuns and monks. In this place, where the praises of God are sung daily, it is appropriate to remember that Byzantine women in many places have contributed to the rich collection of Orthodox hymns.

Hymnody is a rich source for understanding theology and spirituality. In biblical times women were recognized as the singers of songs and ballads, both religious and secular. Did the early Christian women who hosted house churches lead the singing? Did they begin to make up songs about the Christ who was transforming their lives? Documents speak of the mothers of the desert, the women forming monastic communities, and other ascetics spending large parts of their time singing the praises of God. Did they make up melodies to the psalms? Did they begin to compose the poetry of canticles and ballads? Eva Catafygiotu Topping in *Sacred Songs: Studies in Byzantine Hymnography* discusses some of the women who have used their gifts to create liturgical music, including Kassiane.

> In about 800 C.E. Kassiane was born in Constantinople and she was a daughter of an official at the imperial court. Though most women did not have this opportunity, she received a good education. While she was still young, Theodore, the important abbot of Studios Monastery of St. John, praised her writing and her zeal for Orthodoxy and its liturgical traditions. One story of Kassiane says that she was among the group of women from whom the emperor Theophilos would choose a wife and he indicated his favor of her by handing her a golden apple. "Kassia was Theophilos's first choice. But in the awkwardness of a first declaration, the prince could only observe that, in this world, women had been the cause of much evil: 'And surely, Sir,' she pertly replied, 'they have likewise been the occasion of much good.' Displeased by Kassia's 'unseasonable wit' in the defense of her unjustly maligned sex, Theophilos then gave the golden apple to Theodora, who appreciated the value of womanly silence."[15]

Theodora became empress, but Kassiane became a nun and then abbess. Despite the imperial law against icons she stood with those who affirmed them as building up people's faith. She encouraged those in prison and in exile for holding this belief. Because of her resistance she suffered persecution. Once she was beaten for her position. This did not lessen her convictions. She was impatient with people lacking courage and once she wrote, "I hate silence when it is time to speak." Empress Theodora, like Kassiane, believed that the use of icons was good. After her husband died in 842 she ended the iconoclastic controversy that had raged in church and state for over a century.

The Byzantine liturgy is dramatic, rich in sacred poetry, and much of that is conveyed through music. In lists of Byzantine hymn writers Thekla, Theodosia, and Palaiologina are mentioned, but none of their hymns have survived. Fortunately twenty-three hymns by Kassiane are in the liturgical books of the Eastern Orthodox Church. Her hymn "Woman Fallen into Many Sins" is used within the Holy Week services. The hymn survives in many manuscripts from the eleventh to the sixteenth centuries and is lauded as a masterpiece of Greek religious poetry:

Lord, she who fell into many sins has recognized your God-
head and has joined the myrrh-bearing women;
    weeping she brings myrrh for you before your
        entombment.
"Alas," she cries, "what night is upon me, what a dark and
moonless madness of unrestraint, a lust for sin.
Accept my welling tears, you who procure the water of the
sea through the clouds;
    incline to the grievings of my heart,
You who made the sky bow down by the unutterable abase-
ment [of your incarnation].
Many times will I kiss your undefiled feet, and then dry
them with the hair of my head;
those feet whose footfall Eve heard at dusk in Paradise and
    hid in terror.
Who will trace out the multitude of my transgressions,
    or the abysses [unpredictability] of your judgments,
        Saviour of souls?
Do not overlook me, your servant, in your boundless
    compassion."[16]

Knesset

Queen Salome Alexandra

This parliament building was inaugurated in 1966 for the
state of Israel, which was founded in 1948. When Salome's husband, the king of Judah, was dying he wished for his wife to
rule. She had a reign of prosperity and peace for nine years
from 78 to 69 B.C.E. and was called the "Good Queen Alexandra."
When she died her sons fought for power; then Pompey inter-
vened and took the land for the Roman empire. Until 1948, the
last Jewish ruler independent of other states was this woman.

Israel Museum

The Vulnerability of Divorced Women

Extensive collections document the rich history of this area.
The Shrine of the Book contains the Dead Sea Scrolls and other artifacts found in the area of Qumran. In the desert the purse of an
ancient Jewish woman was found with her divorce papers.
Under Jewish law a woman could only get a divorce if the man
agreed. If he did not agree, she was bound to him. In biblical
times women who were not associated with fathers, brothers, or
husbands were economically very vulnerable.

Suppose a man enters into marriage with a woman, but she does not please him because he finds something objectionable about her, and so he writes her a certificate of divorce, puts it in her hand, and sends her out of his house; she then leaves his house 2 and goes off to become another man's wife.

(Read Deut 24: 1-4)

Hebrew Union College and Museum

Beruriah, the Unordained Rabbi

Beruriah was a brilliant woman who lived in Palestine in the second century C.E. She beheld the intense Roman opposition to the Jews that climaxed in the suppression of the Jewish state in 135 C.E. Her father, Rabbi Hananya, was killed in the persecution under Hadrian. She had gone through the three-year intensive study of the Torah that those preparing to be rabbis do, and she is praised for her exceptional knowledge. She is the only woman in the Talmudic literature whose views on religious laws became part of the official texts. A number of stories of her discussing or debating with men have been written down and she is always shown as the wiser person. Her opinion on Torah became law, *halacha.* Beruriah also clearly indicated that she did not like the way women were put down or were referred to as light-minded. A number of stories indicate that she was also a good teacher, knowing how to encourage and challenge students. She was married to the very respected Rabbi Meir. The Talmud has this story of them:

> Certain ruffians lived near Rabbi Meir; they bullied him, and Meir prayed that they would die. His wife Beruriah said to him: "You are relying on the verse, 'Let the sinners be consumed from the earth' (Ps 104:35). But in fact it says 'sins,' not 'sinners.' And consider the end of the verse: 'and let the wicked be no more.' If sin is destroyed, there will be no more sinners left. You should instead pray for mercy for them, so that they may do penance." So he asked mercy for them, and they did penance.[17]

This reveals her analysis and application of Scripture, but it especially shows her compassion and concern for people. Her husband took her advice. To understand the next story of the two of them one should keep in mind that the Sabbath is observed as something very special and very precious by devout Jews.

> When two of their sons died on the Sabbath, Beruriah did not inform Meir of their children's death upon his return from the

academy in order not to grieve him on the Sabbath! Only after the Havdalah prayer did she broach the matter, saying: Some time ago a certain man came and left something in my trust; now he has called for it. Shall I return it to him or not? Naturally Meir replied in the affirmative, whereupon Beruriah showed him their dead children. When Meir began to weep, she asked: Did you not tell me that we must give back what is given on trust? The Lord gave, and the Lord has taken away.[18]

A thousand years after she lived, a malicious story was written that Beruriah gave in to adultery and committed suicide. Perhaps this developed because men were uncomfortable with such a brilliant woman, as stories of Mary Magdalene as a sexual sinner developed about the woman Christ had sent as the apostle to the apostles.

Y.M.C.A. on King David Street

Dancing Daughters and a Dancing God

Dancing and singing are images of joy in the Bible, and dance was frequently a part of religious expression. Zephaniah not only spoke of the people dancing, but his description of God (Zeph 3:17) can be translated "God will dance with joy over you and renew you with love." Programs of folk dance and song are regularly held at the Y.M.C.A., a building with a tower that provides a fine view of the city.

> 14 Sing aloud, O daughter Zion;
> shout, O Israel!
> Rejoice and exult with all your heart,
> O daughter Jerusalem!

(Read Zeph 3:14-18)

The prophet Jeremiah described the exile as not dancing, while the restoration of the people was celebrated with dance. "Then shall the young women rejoice in the dance, and the young men and the old shall be merry. I will turn their mourning into joy, I will comfort them, and give them gladness for sorrow" (Jer 31:13). When Jesus was trying to describe people's unwillingness to follow God's invitation he described them as not dancing to the piper, in Matt 11:17.

Ain Karim

Elizabeth

Church of the Visitation

In the second century there was a legend that Elizabeth and Zechariah had brought John the Baptist here as a baby to hide him from Herod's soldiers, who were killing baby boys. Eventually Christians began to localize the story of Mary's visit to Elizabeth in this area. Mary sang a canticle of joy proclaiming God as the savior of the vulnerable.

> 52 He has brought down the powerful from their thrones,
> and lifted up the lowly;
> 53 he has filled the hungry with good things,
> and sent the rich away empty.
>
> (Read Luke 1:39-56)

Church of St. John the Baptist

In the fifth century a church was built here in remembrance of the Nativity of John. People would not believe Elizabeth's words about what their son should be named, but wanted the authority of her husband.

> 57 Now the time came for Elizabeth to give birth, and she bore a son. 58 Her neighbors and relatives heard that the Lord had shown his great mercy to her, and they rejoiced with her.
>
> (Read Luke 1:57-66)

Hadassah Hospital

Women's Names and Families

The beautiful stained glass windows by Marc Chagall commemorate the twelve tribes of Israel, named for the sons of Jacob. Jacob had wanted the younger sister Rachel as his bride, but her father tricked him into marrying Leah. Both women suffered; both women were jealous of the other. In cultures where women's worth is based primarily on bearing children, especially sons, women often do not realize their intrinsic worth.

> 30 When Rachel saw that she bore Jacob no children, she envied her sister; and she said to Jacob, "Give me children, or I shall die!"
>
> (Read Gen 29:28–30:26)

The New City: The Southern Section

St. Andrew's Scottish Presbyterian Church

Rizpah

Near Hebron Road a couple of miles southwest of the Old City, St. Andrew's sits on a hillside, and near the entrance road a first-century tomb was excavated. It is not enclosed and one can explore it and consider the care and concern that have traditionally gone into preparing a site and burying the dead. A major insult in the ancient world was refusing a dead person the dignity of a decent burial. The Gibeonites wanted revenge on Saul, who mistreated them, so they asked David for seven of the descendants of Saul. David took Saul's sons, and the Gibeonites dismembered them and left their bodies exposed. Rizpah, the mother of some of the sons, faithfully watched over their bodies.

> 10 Then Rizpah the daughter of Aiah took sackcloth, and spread it on a rock for herself, from the beginning of harvest until rain fell on them from the heavens; she did not allow the birds of the air to come on the bodies by day, or the wild animals by night.
>
> (Read 2 Sam 21:8-10)

Finally, seeing Rizpah's courage and compassion in the face of the violence of the men, David had the bones gathered and buried. The Greek tragedy *Antigone* is also a story of a woman determined to protect the remains of the dead.

Tantur Ecumenical Institute

Women in Labor

Legends say that Mary had her first labor pains on this hill encircled by olive trees on the outskirts of Jerusalem, immediately before entering Bethlehem! One can see ruins of a Byzantine monastery and stones from the Crusader hospice. Today the Tantur Center encourages interfaith dialogue among Christians, Jews, and Muslims as well as ecumenical dialogues between the Eastern Orthodox, Western Catholic, and Protestant traditions. A little farther down the road toward Bethlehem is Rachel's tomb, where she was buried after dying from a difficult labor in giving birth to Benjamin. Between Tantur and Rachel's tomb is a contemporary residence for women studying to be midwives at Bethlehem University.

In the discourse at the Last Supper, Jesus used the imagery of labor pains, inviting patience and perseverance in difficult times. Contemporary theological dialogue will be stillborn if women's voices are not a part of it.

> 21 When a woman is in labor, she has pain, because her hour has come. But when her child is born, she no longer remembers the anguish because of the joy of having brought a human being into the world.
>
> (Read John 16:20-22)

Notes

[1] For a careful analysis of this story see Phyllis Trible, *Texts of Terror: Literary-Feminist Readings of Biblical Narratives* (Philadelphia: Fortress, 1984) 37–63.

[2] Rendel Harris and Alphonse Mingana, eds., *The Odes of and Psalms of Solomon* (Manchester: The University Press; New York: Longmans, Green & Co., 1916–20) 2: 298ff. (Ode 19:1-5), as quoted in Leonard Swidler, *Biblical Affirmations of Women* (Philadelphia: Westminister, 1979) 71.

[3] *The Gospel of Bartholomew* 2:1-14, trans. Felix Scheidweiler and Wilhelm Schneemelcher, in Wilhelm Schneemelcher, ed., *New Testament Apocrypha* (English translation ed. R. McL. Wilson; rev. ed. Louisville: Westminster, 1991) Vol. 1: *Gospels and Related Writings* (Philadelphia: Westminster, 1963) 537–53, at 543–44.

[4] *The Life of Saint Pelagia the Harlot written by the Deacon James and translated into Latin by Eustochius*, from *Vita Sanctae Pelagiae, Meretricis*, MPL 73, cols. 663-72. English translation from Benedicta Ward, *Harlots of the Desert, A Study of Repentance in Early Monastic Sources* (London: Mowbray, 1987) 73–75.

[5] *Palladius: The Lausiac History*, trans. and annotated by Robert T. Meyer. ACW 34 (Westminster, Md.: Newman Press, 1965) 103.

[6] *The Lausiac History of Palladius*, as translated in Joan M. Petersen, *Handmaids of the Lord: Contemporary Descriptions of Feminine Asceticism in the First Six Centuries* (Kalamazoo: Cistercian Publications, 1996) 303–306.

[7] "Melania the Younger" by Gerontius, as translated in Joan M. Petersen, *Handmaids of the Lord*, 327.

[8] *The Gospel of Mary [Magdalene]* (BG 8502, 1) 9.6–10.16, trans. George MacRae and R. McL. Wilson, intro. Karen L. King, and ed. Douglas M. Parrott, in James M. Robinson, ed., *Nag Hammadi Library in English* (3rd rev. ed. San Francisco: Harper & Row, 1988) 525.

[9] Most Rev. Joseph Reya and Baron José de Vinck, *Byzantine Daily Worship* (Allendale, N.Y.: Alleluia Press, 1969) 755–56.

[10] Elisabeth Moltman-Wendel, *The Women Around Jesus* (New York: Crossroad, 1982) 30.

[11] Flavius Josephus, *Jewish Antiquities* XX. 53, 92–96, trans. Louis H. Feldman, Loeb Classical Library, vol. 9 (Cambridge: Harvard University Press, 1965) 419, 437–39.

[12] Elizabeth A. Clark, *Ascetic Piety and Women's Faith: Essays on Late Ancient Christianity* (Lewiston, N.Y.: Edwin Mellen, 1986) passim.

[13] See Naim Stifan Ateek, *Justice and Only Justice: A Palestinian Theology of Liberation* (Maryknoll, N. Y.: Orbis, 1989) 8, 30.

[14] Naim Stifan Ateek, Hilary Rantisi, and Kent Williams, *"Our Story": The Palestinians* (Jerusalem: Sabeel Ecumenical Liberation Theology Center, 1999) 11, 13.

[15] Eve Catafygioru Topping, *Sacred Songs: Studies in Byzantine Hymnography* (Minneapolis: Light and Life, 1997) 195.

[16] Kassiane's hymn is translated by Eva Catafygiotu Topping in ibid., 197.

[17] *b.Berakhot* 10a. For an imaginative modern treatment of Rabbi Beruriah, see Stefanie Müller, "Living With the Torah: A Conversation with Rabbi Beruriah," in Claudia Janssen, Ute Ochtendung, and Beate Wehn, eds., *Transgressors: Toward a Feminist Biblical Theology* (Collegeville: The Liturgical Press, 2002) 9–17. The passage from *b.Ber.* is on p. 14.

[18] *m.Prov.* 30.10, as translated in Leonard J. Swidler, *Biblical Affirmations of Woman* (Philadelphia: Westminster, 1979) 103–04.

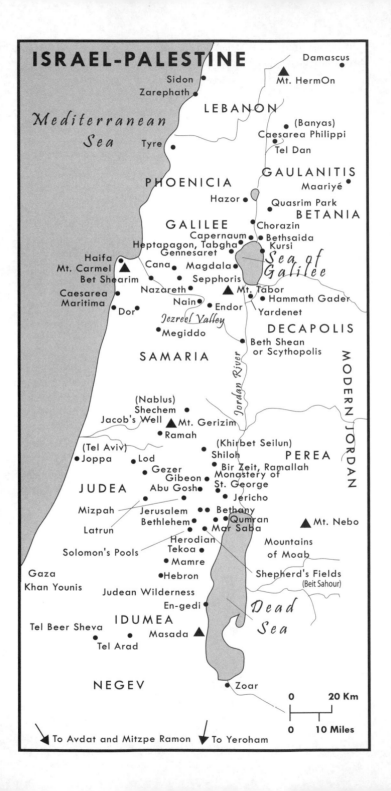

ISRAEL-PALESTINE

Mediterranean Sea

Damascus
Mt. HermOn
Sidon
Zarephath
LEBANON
Tyre
(Banyas)
Caesarea Philippi
Tel Dan
PHOENICIA
GAULANITIS
Maariyé
Hazor
Quasrim Park
BETANIA
GALILEE
Chorazin
Capernaum
Bethsaida
Heptapagon, Tabgha
Kursi
Gennesaret
Sea of Galilee
Haifa
Cana
Magdala
Mt. Carmel
Sepphoris
Bet Shearim
Nazareth
Mt. Tabor
Caesarea Maritima
Hammath Gader
Nain
Endor
Dor
Yardenet
Jezreel Valley
DECAPOLIS
Megiddo
Beth Shean or Scythopolis
SAMARIA
Jordan River
MODERN JORDAN
(Nablus)
Shechem
Jacob's Well
Mt. Gerizim
Ramah
(Khirbet Seilun)
PEREA
(Tel Aviv)
Shiloh
Joppa
Lod
Bir Zeit, Ramallah
Gezer
Monastery of
Gibeon
St. George
JUDEA
Abu Gosh
Jericho
Mizpah
Jerusalem
Bethany
Mt. Nebo
Latrun
Bethlehem
Qumran
Mar Saba
Herodian
Solomon's Pools
Mountains of Moab
Tekoa
Mamre
Shepherd's Fields
Gaza
Hebron
(Beit Sahour)
Khan Younis
Judean Wilderness
En-gedi
Dead Sea
Tel Beer Sheva
IDUMEA
Tel Arad
Masada

NEGEV
Zoar

0   20 Km

0   10 Miles

To Avdat and Mitzpe Ramon   To Yeroham

CHAPTER NINE

ISRAEL AND PALESTINE

Abu Gosh

Couple on the Road to Emmaus

Christians have localized the story of Emmaus in a number of different places, including Abu Gosh. The Hospitallers built a Gothic church here in 1140. Since the two persons walking along the road from Jerusalem to Emmaus seem to be going home together there is good reason to believe that they were a married couple. It was not until the breaking of the bread that they recognized Christ. Today a Benedictine double community of nuns and priests carries on worship in the church and offers hospitality to retreatants, echoing the hospitality of the couple to the stranger they met on the road. Can the life of the Risen Christ be recognized in women as well as men?

> 28 As they came near the village to which they were going, he walked ahead as if he were going on. 29 But they urged him strongly, saying, "Stay with us, because it is almost evening and the day is now nearly over." So he went in to stay with them. 30 When he was at the table with them, he took bread, blessed and broke it, and gave it to them. 31 Then their eyes were opened, and they recognized him; and he vanished from their sight.
>
> (Read Luke 24:13-35)

Avdat, Yeroham

Hagar

The ruins of Avdat, a first-century Nabatean city on a trade route, can be seen in the midst of the barren Negev wilderness. The harshness of the huge desert might call one to reflection on the similar harshness of Sarah and Abraham's directive to Hagar to leave their home, take the son Abraham sired, and go the wilderness. Avdat is about 20 kilometers south of the twentieth-century settlement of Yeroham, a name that was chosen as sounding something like "Bir Rahma." That name was based on the root word for womb, which in both Hebrew and Arabic sounds like "r-h-m"; the root word for womb is also the root word for mercy. A favored Arabic name today is Rahim, which means benevolent or merciful. Hagar found the "well of mercy." The Bedouins of the El Azazme tribe who reside between Hebron and Beer Sheva and beyond call this ancient well about 50 kilometers south of Beer Sheva the "well of mercy." Wells are the focal point in nomadic cultures; herds return to them, people are buried near them, and communication takes place. The well is in the middle of the Negev, which is why it was chosen for a new settlement of the Jewish Agency in 1951 for settlers from Romania. Since then other settlers have come from Morocco, Iran, India, the Soviet Union, and elsewhere. They and the Bedouins dispute the water rights and ownership of the "well of mercy."

> 1 Now Sarai, Abram's wife, bore him no children. She had an Egyptian slave-girl whose name was Hagar, 2 and Sarai said to Abram, "You see that the LORD has prevented me from bearing children; go in to my slave-girl; it may be that I shall obtain children by her."

> (Read Gen 16:1-6)

Banyas, or Caesarea Philippi

God, the Rock Who Bore You

This park, with springs and a majestic rock mountain, is the place where Jesus said to Peter "On this rock I will build my church." When Jesus used images in his teaching he was often in areas where he could have pointed to them. Pointing to this strong, beautiful rock face would certainly be an effective teaching device. In Deuteronomy people are urged to remember God, secure like a rock and lifegiving like a mother giving birth.

> You were unmindful of the Rock that bore you;
> you forgot the God who gave you birth. (Deut 32:18)

Eusebius in the early fourth century C.E. wrote that there were statues of Christ and the woman with the hemorrhage here, but no traces of these are left today.

Bet Shean, or Scythopolis

Maria, the Niece of Abraham the Hermit

The extensive excavations reveal that people have lived here for almost six thousand years. This Roman city was famous for its production of linen. Cyril of Scythopolis, a sixth-century historian, wrote biographies of seven religious leaders in Palestine that reveal much about the Christianity of the times.

In the heart of this flourishing city, in the Odion area, was a much-visited house of prostitution. The original story of Maria comes from the deserts of Egypt, but a discouraged woman such as Maria, who had been seduced, could have worked in the house of prostitution here. Occasionally there are stories of children among the desert ascetics. Cassian wrote of Patermucius, who came to be a monk with his eight-year-old son. Paula the Younger, while still a teenager, joined her grandmother in Bethlehem, but she does not seem to have been the challenge that some boys were. "Do not bring young boys here; four churches in Scetis have been destroyed because of boys," said a monk, as recorded by Isaac of the Cells.

Many legends surround Abba Abraham, a desert hermit. In one story his brother died and the people brought the brother's daughter, the seven-year-old Maria, to the desert hermit. She lived in a cell near his and daily they would pray the Psalms together. A visiting monk seduced her and she was so ashamed that she fled to the city, where she became a prostitute. In this story, as in the story of the woman caught in adultery in John's gospel, no more is said about the man involved. Abba Abraham seeking to save his niece is compared to Abraham seeking to save Lot. Abba Abraham was deeply concerned about her, and when he found out where she was he dressed as a soldier and went to rescue her. The monks who told the story obviously thought a soldier could easily get into a brothel, but a monk could not. The story seems to focus on trusting the mercy of God. Abraham never judged Maria. She was seduced into intercourse, but the real problem was that she despaired and did not realize the greatness of God's forgiveness. "It is not new to fall, my daughter; what is wrong is to lie down when you have fallen." In this story, as in a number of others, a member of the Christian community starts to reveal the merciful face of God to another who does not yet recognize it.

The narrative of Abraham's deception in the brothel is quite vivid and humorous. The following part of the story is the turning point after the keeper of the brothel has been very controlling and the Abba has had to work hard to get privacy with Maria.

When he had seated himself on the bed, Maria said to him, "Come, sir, let me unfasten your trousers for you." And he said, "First close the door carefully and lock it." The girl wanted to unfasten him first but he would not let her. When she had locked the door, she came towards him and the old man said to her, "Mistress Maria, come close to me." And when she had come close he held her firmly with one hand, as if about to kiss her, but snatching the hat from his head, in a voice breaking with tears, he said to her, "Don't you know me, Maria my child? Dear heart, am I not he who took care of you? What happened, my dear? Who hurt you, my daughter? What has become of the dress of angels that you used to wear? What has become of your virginity, your tears, your vigils, all your prayers? From what a height you have fallen, my child, into such a pit as this! Why, when you sinned, did you not tell me? Why could you not come and speak of it with me? For of course I would have done penance for you, I and our dearest Ephraim. Why did you not do that? Why instead did you hurt me, and give me this unbearable weight of grief? For who is without sin, save God alone?" While he was saying this and much besides, Maria sat like a stone between his hands, overcome both by shame and fear. In tears, the old man said to her, "Why do you not speak to me, my heart? Have I not come to take you home, my child? On me be your sin, my daughter, and on the day of judgment I will render an account of it for you to the Lord; it is I who will be responsible for this to God." And so until the middle of the night Abraham consoled Maria with words of this kind and covered her with tears. After a while she plucked up courage and, weeping, she said to him, "I could not come to you; I was so very much ashamed. How can I pray again to God when I am defiled with sin which is as filthy as this?" The holy man said to her, "Upon me be your sin, Maria, and let God lay it to my account. Only listen to me and come, let us go back where we belong. See, our dearest Ephraim is grieving so much for you and he is praying all the time for you to the Lord. My dear, do not draw back from the mercy of God. To you, your sins seem like mountains, but God has spread his mercy over all He has made. So we once read together how an unclean woman came to the Lord and he did not send her away but cleansed her, and she washed his feet with her tears and wiped them with the hairs of her head. If sparks could set fire to the ocean, then indeed your sins could defile the purity of God! It is not new to fall, my daughter; what is wrong is to lie down when you have fallen. Remember where you stood before you fell. The Devil once mocked you, but now he will know that you can rise more strong than ever before. I beg you, take pity on my old age and do not make me grieve any more. Get up and come with me to our cell. Do not be afraid; sin is only part of being human; it happened to you very quickly and now by the help of God you are coming out of it even more quickly, for he does not will the death of sinners, but rather that they may live." Then she said to him, "If you know of any penance I can do which God will receive from me, command me and lo, I will do it. Go first, and I will follow and I will kiss your footprints as I go. For you have so grieved for me that you came down even into this pit of filth in order to bring me out." So she laid her head on his feet and wept away the rest of the night saying, "What can I give to You, O Lord, to repay all that you have done for me?"

When morning came, blessed Abraham said to her, "Get up, my daughter, and let us go home." She said to him, "I have this small amount of gold and these clothes, what do you want me to do with them?" And Abraham said, "Leave it all here, Maria, for it came from evil." So they got up and went out. He placed her on the horse and he went first leading it, like a shepherd with the lost sheep he had found, bearing it home upon his shoulders with joy. So with a glad heart Abraham made the journey home with his niece. When they arrived he put her into the inner cell, and he himself stayed in the outside one. So she put on the hair shirt and in humility of soul and body she wore out her eyes with weeping, with vigils, with the most strict asceticism, praying constantly to the Lord in modesty and stillness, lamenting her sins in firm hope of forgiveness. She prayed so movingly that no one who heard her lamentation could refrain from weeping. Who would not give thanks for her to God? For her repentance was greater than all measure of grief. While she prayed to the Lord to forgive what she had done, she asked God also for a sign that this was accomplished. The most merciful God, who does not will that anyone should perish but that all should repent, having seen such repentance rewarded her prayers after three years by giving her the gift of healing. Crowds of people came to her daily and she would heal them all by her prayers for their salvation.[1]

Bet Shearim

The Maidservant of Rabbi Judah

Bet Shearim, ruins with a large necropolis and some unique art and architecture, was a central town of the estate of

Berenice, the great-granddaughter of Herod the Great. After the Roman retaliation against the Jews' revolt in Judah in 132–135, Torah study was concentrated in the north. Rabbi Judah ha-Nassi (135–217) was recognized as the leader of the remaining Jews. He was probably given some land in Bet Shearim, where he developed the Sanhedrin and was a wise teacher in Torah study. He compiled the oral code of the Law that is called the Mishnah. He had a maidservant whose name is never given, but she is mentioned five or six times in the Babylonian Talmud. She knew some Hebrew and the style of symbolic speaking among rabbis and their students. One incident speaks of her cleaning the room while the rabbi and students were studying Torah. She mumbled the answers they were not getting as she moved around. She was able to comment on difficult Bible passages. A curse that she placed on a rough man was described in the Talmud and used as an example.

> Then R. Samuel b. Nahmani got up on his feet and said: Why even a "separation" imposed by one of the domestics in Rabbi's house was not treated lightly by the Rabbis for three years; how much more so one imposed by our colleague, Rabbi Judah! . . . What (was the incident) of the domestic in Rabbi's house? It was one of the maidservants in Rabbi's house that had noticed a man beating his grown-up son and said, Let that fellow be under a *shammetha!* Because he sinned against the words (of Holy Writ): *Put not a stumbling-block before the blind.* For it is taught: *and not put a stumbling-block before the blind;* that text applies to the one who beats his grown-up son (and caused him to rebel).[2]

This woman's authority was respected and she knew how to use Scripture to back up what she said. The last story of the maidservant shows her compassion and her wisdom.

> On the day when Rabbi died the Rabbis decreed a public fast and offered prayers for heavenly mercy. They, furthermore, announced that whoever said that Rabbi was dead would be stabbed with a sword. Rabbi's handmaid ascended the roof and prayed: the immortals desire Rabbi (to join them) and the mortals desire Rabbi (to remain with them); may it be the will (of God) that the mortals may overpower the immortals. When, however, she saw how often he resorted to the privy, painfully taking off his *tefillin* and putting them on again, she prayed: May it be the will (of the Almighty) that the immortals may overpower the mortals. As the Rabbis incessantly continued their prayers for (heavenly) mercy she took up a

jar and threw it down from the roof to the ground. (For a moment) they ceased praying and the soul of the Rabbi departed to its eternal rest.[3]

Anyone who has watched the dying in pain knows that there is a time when they need to be psychologically and spiritually given permission to be free.

Bethlehem

Bethlehem Streets

Bakerwoman

Bethlehem means "house of bread." Jesus compares the mysterious and pervasive power of God's reign to leaven. God is like a bakerwoman who leavens and waits. Small bakeries can be seen on the streets near the Nativity Church.

> 33 He told them another parable: "The kingdom of heaven is like yeast that a woman took and mixed in with three measures of flour until all of it was leavened." (Matt 13:33)

Rachel's Tomb

Rachel's Giving Birth and Dying

Scripture says that Jacob built a memorial where they buried his wife, reportedly the present site. Muslims, part of the family of Abraham, respect the Jewish patriarchs, matriarchs, and prophets as important in their tradition. The tombs of saints in Palestine are venerated by both Jews and Muslims. An Arabic shrine was built over Rachel's tomb during the Ottoman Empire. Jewish, Christian, and Muslim women liked to pray there. In more recent times veneration of the places has led to competition, efforts to control, and displays of nationalism.[4] Today Rachel's tomb has been defined as Jewish and not for Muslims. Jewish women come here to pray for fertility and for the children they already have. Rachel can be translated as "mother love," "womb," or "compassion." The symbol of Rachel is the Divine Ewe, the mother of the Holy Lamb in the early Hebrew matrilineal tribes. Women often use a Hebrew prayer at the tomb asking that on the merits of their mother Rachel and other deserving women God may fulfill their wish for children.

> 16 Then they journeyed from Bethel; and when they were still some distance from Ephrath, Rachel was in childbirth, and she had hard labor. 17 When she was in her hard labor, the midwife said to her, "Do not be afraid; for now you will have another son." 18 As her soul was departing (for she died), she named him Ben-oni; but his father called him Benjamin. 19 So Rachel died, and she was buried on the way to Ephrath (that is, Bethlehem), 20 and Jacob set up a pillar at her grave; it is the pillar of Rachel's tomb, which is there to this day. 21 Israel journeyed on, and pitched his tent beyond the tower of Eder. (Gen 35:16-21)

Emmanuel Convent

St. Anne

From the hillside retreat rooms of the convent one can see the Judean wilderness, and on a clear day the mountains of Moab on the other side of the Dead Sea. Although this convent of Melkite Sisters is modern, there is a display map of some of the ancient monastic foundations in the area. Six such foundations are known to be located between Jerusalem and Bethlehem, and over seventy in the Judean wilderness. The Sisters carry on the ancient traditions of chanting the Psalms, hospitality, and simple labor and lifestyle. They welcome guests to pray with them in a chapel covered with icons of biblical women and many women saints such as St. Anne, who is commemorated in their liturgical books in the following text for the "Feast of the Maternity of Anne" on December 9. (See **St. Anne's Church, Jerusalem.**)

At Vespers

At the Lamp-Lighting Psalms (Fourth Tone)

The barren Anne leaped for joy when she gave birth to Mary the Virgin, who in turn will give birth in the flesh to God the Word. Overflowing with happiness, she cried out; "Rejoice for me, O all tribes of Israel, for I have given birth according to the will of God, my Benefactor, who answered my prayer and wiped out my shame. According to his promise, He has healed the pains of my heart through the pains of birthgiving" (Twice).

At the Apostichon (Fifth Tone)

Anne (this name means divine grace), cried out once in her prayer, asking for a child, and said to the God of us all and our Creator; "O Adonai Sabaoth, you know what shame it is to be barren. Heal the pain of my heart, open the flow of my womb and make the fruitless one fruitful, so that we may offer you the child as a gift, blessing, praising, glorifying and singing a hymn to your love, through which the world obtains great mercy."

Stichon: The Lord swore to David a sure oath from which He will not turn back.

Once upon a time Anne was in prayer, beseeching the Lord with great fervor for a child. She heard the voice of the angel who told her that God had granted her wish, saying in plain words; "Do not grieve, for your prayer has reached the Lord. Wipe out your tears, for you shall be an olive tree sprouting a magnificent branch, the Virgin from whom will spring the Flower, Christ-in-the-flesh, who will grant great mercy to the world."

Stichon: From your very Self, I will set up a Son on your throne.

The honorable couple Joachim and Anne have given birth to a lamb, who in turn will give birth in a manner beyond understanding to the Lamb of God who is to be sacrificed for all mankind. They offer to the Lord an unceasing and humble praise. Let us, therefore, glorify them with fervor and overflow with happiness at the birth of the one who was born of them in a miraculous way; Mary, the Mother of our God, through whom great mercy is granted to us all.

Glory be to the Father and to the Son and to the Holy Spirit, now and always and for ever and ever. Amen.[5]

Church of the Nativity with the Cave of the Nativity of Christ

Paula at the Cave

The church used by both Greek Orthodox and Armenians is located over a cave where Christians have remembered the birth of Christ since at least the second century. Paula, a wealthy Roman woman, used her fortune and her talents to make Bethlehem a monastic center. Jerome began living there in 384 C.E. and Paula and her daughter Eustochium joined him in 386 C.E. Paula supported Jerome as he translated the Bible into Latin and did other writings. The following is Jerome's description of the first time Paula experienced the Cave of the Nativity:

> Then, after distributing money to the poor and her fellow-servants (sic) so far as her means allowed, she proceeded to Bethlehem stopping only on the right side of the road to visit Rachel's tomb. (Here it was that she gave birth to her son destined to be not what his dying mother called him, Benoni, that is the "Son of my pangs" but as his father in the spirit prophetically named him Benjamin, that is "the Son of the right hand.") After this she came to Bethlehem and entered into the cave where the Saviour was born. Here, when she looked upon the inn made sacred by the virgin and the stall where the ox knew his owner and the ass his master's crib, and where the words of the same prophet had been fulfilled "Blessed is he that soweth beside the waters where the ox and the ass trample the seed under their feet." When she looked upon these things I say, she protested in my hearing that she could behold with the eyes of faith the infant Lord wrapped in swaddling clothes and crying in the manger, the wise men worshipping Him, the star shining overhead, the virgin mother, the attentive foster-father, the shepherds coming by night to see "the word that was come to pass" and thus even then to consecrate those opening phrases of the evangelist John "In the beginning was the word" and "the word was made flesh." She declared that she could see the slaughtered innocents, the raging Herod, Joseph and Mary fleeing into Egypt; and with a mixture of tears and joy she cried: "Hail

Bethlehem, house of bread, wherein was born that Bread that came down from heaven. Hail Ephratah, land of fruitfulness and fertility, whose fruit is the Lord Himself. Concerning thee has Micah prophesied of old, 'Thou Bethlehem Ephratah art not the least among the thousands of Judah, for out of thee shall he come forth unto me that is to be ruler in Israel; whose goings forth have been from of old, from everlasting. Therefore wilt thou give them up, until the time that she which travaileth hath brought forth: then the remnant of his brethren shall return unto the children of Israel.'"

(PAULA, 144–45)

St. Catherine's Church and the Cave of Paula and Jerome

The Church of the Nativity is joined to St. Catherine's Catholic Church. Downstairs, below St. Catherine's, is a cave in which is said to be the tomb of Paula and where Jerome studied and wrote. Paula and her daughter were serious students and this is how Jerome described them.

She asked leave that she and her daughter might read over the old and new testament under my guidance. Out of modesty I at first refused compliance, but as she persisted in her demand and frequently urged me to consent to it, I at last did so and taught her what I had learned not from myself—for self-confidence is the worst of teachers—but from the church's most famous writers. Wherever I stuck fast and honestly confessed myself at fault she would by no means rest content but would force me by fresh questions to point out to her which of many different solutions seemed to me the most probable. I will mention here another fact which to those who are envious may well seem incredible. While I myself beginning as a young man have with much toil and effort partially acquired the Hebrew tongue and study it now unceasingly lest if I leave it, it also may leave me; Paula, on making up her mind that she too would learn it, succeeded so well that she could chant the psalms in Hebrew and could speak the language without a trace of the pronunciation peculiar to Latin. The same accomplishment can be seen to this day in her daughter Eustochium, who always kept close to her mother's side, obeyed all her commands, never slept apart from her, never walked abroad or took a meal without her, never had a penny that she could call her own, rejoiced when her mother gave to the poor her little patrimony, and fully believed that in filial affection she had the best heritage and truest riches.

(PAULA, 164)

Jerome's Cave

Jerome recognized that Paula was a kind and generous woman and also a very strong and determined one—more ready to convince a pope than to let a pope convince her.

> How shall I describe her kindness and attention toward the sick or the wonderful care and devotion with which she nursed them? Yet, although when others were sick she freely gave them every indulgence, and even allowed them to eat meat; when she fell ill herself, she made no concessions to her own weakness, and seemed unfairly to change in her own case to harshness the kindness which she was always ready to show to others. In the extreme heat of the month of July she was once attacked by a violent fever and we despaired of her life. However by God's mercy she rallied, and the doctors urged upon her the necessity of taking a little light wine to accelerate her recovery; saying that if she continued to drink water they feared that she might become dropsical. I on my side secretly appealed to the blessed Pope Epiphanius to admonish, nay even to compel her, to take the wine. But she with her usual sagacity and quickness at once perceived the stratagem, and with a smile let him see that the advice he was giving her was after all not his but mine. Not to waste more words, the blessed prelate after many exhortations left her chamber; and when I asked him what he had accomplished, replied, "Only this: that old as I am I have been almost persuaded to drink no more wine."
>
> (PAULA, 158–59)

Paula's Tomb

This is Jerome's description of Paula's funeral. It indicates his and others' great esteem for her as a leader in fourth-century Bethlehem.

> The bishops lifted up the dead woman with their own hands, placed her upon a bier, and carrying her on their shoulders to the church in the cave of the Saviour, laid her down in the centre of it. Other bishops meantime carried torches and tapers in the procession, and yet others led the singing of the choirs. The whole population of the cities of Palestine came to her funeral. Not a single monk lurked in the desert or lingered in his cell. Not a single virgin remained shut up in the seclusion of her chamber. To each and all it would have seemed sacrilege to have withheld the last tokens of respect from a woman so saintly. As in the case of Dorcas, the widows and the poor showed the garments

Paula had given them, while the destitute cried aloud that they had lost in her a mother and a nurse. Strange to say, the paleness of death had not altered her expression; only a certain solemnity and seriousness had overspread her features. You would have thought her not dead but asleep.

One after another they chanted the psalms, now in Greek, now in Latin, now in Syriac; and this not merely for the three days which elapsed before she was buried beneath the church and close to the cave of the Lord, but throughout the remainder of the week.

(PAULA, 166)

Milk Grotto Church

Nursing Women

Legends say that when Joseph, Mary, and Jesus had to flee Bethlehem in haste to escape Herod's soldiers, who were killing baby boys, Mary was nursing Jesus here. Some of her milk spilled on the rock and it became white. Nursing Christian and Muslim mothers come here to pray for their babies and to take some of the powdered rock to drink because they believe the rock will provide them with good milk for their babies. Some years ago a group of skeptical scientists tested the rock and found that it contained calcium, which does indeed have healing properties. In the cave of the chapel, where the smoke of candles has darkened most of the white rock, one can see copies of famous paintings of Mary nursing Jesus. Early peoples had a sense of the divine blessing them through the nourishment of the earth. Although men lead most Jewish, Christian, and Muslim services, women have their own ways of relating to the divine. Like Rachel's tomb, this shrine is a place where local women come to pray for the well-being of their children.

Even though very few ancient women's writings have been preserved, a poem by the Roman aristocratic woman Faltonia Betitia Proba from about 360 expresses her faith and her extensive knowledge. The poem is in cento form, meaning that it is composed of verses chosen from earlier poetry. Faltonia was integrating the works of Virgil, which she obviously knew very well. This poem, while written in Rome, is a meditation on Mary, Herod, and the massacre of the innocents.

Events early divined his schemes and dire
Wickedness realized the gathering storm,
She first. And knowing what would come to pass,

She had commissioned that the babe be reared
In secret, while the king's concern was
Indecisive, while his mind was boiling
Hot with wrath. But overwrought, the ruler
Gave the command to cast the scion down
And all his future race, to burn him up
With flames banked underneath; he ordered men
Dispatched who would report the facts.
They did as told, and on the double went
And terrorized the city, filled it full
Of panic. Then shouts and strident squalling,
The sobbing breath of babes in arms crescendoed.
Corpses of sons lay strewn before their parents'
Eyes, flung at the doorway. But the mother,
With good reason spurred to terror at
Such plaintive sobs, ferrying her child
Upon her breast, escaped the violent mob,
And made her way again to the full mangers.
And here, beneath the pitching, lowly roof,
She began to nurse her son, her full paps
Milking to his tender lips. Here, child,
Your cradle will be the first to pour
Out blossoms in profusion, just for you;
And mixed with cheerful sow's bread everywhere
Will be the earth; and bit by bit the Egyptian bean
Will overflow with delicate acanthus.[6]

Christmas Lutheran Church Women's Center

Women Who Care for Each Other

In Moab the widowed Ruth told her widowed mother-in-law Naomi that she wished to go with her to Bethlehem. In a culture where one's relationship to a male is essential for economic and physical security, Ruth's choice to stay with an older woman is quite remarkable. This women's center encourages analysis of women's challenges and potentials and bonding among women to bring a better future.

> 15 So [Naomi] said, "See, your sister-in-law has gone back to her people and to her gods; return after your sister-in-law." 16 But Ruth said,
>
> "Do not press me to leave you or to turn back from following you!
>   Where you go, I will go;

where you lodge, I will lodge;
your people shall be my people,
and your God my God.
17 Where you die, I will die—
there will I be buried."

(Read Ruth 1:8-18)

Carmelite Convent

Paula, a Good Leader

This cloistered convent on a hillside of Bethlehem, where the type of monastic traditions developed by Paula continue, is a good place to remember the simple and joyful lifestyle of nuns. A nineteenth-century Palestinian woman whom many considered a saint lived here. Sister Mary is called the "little Arab" and she is being considered for canonization.

Jerome wrote about what Paula had organized; considering the rigid class distinctions in the ancient world, Christianity was a challenge.

> Besides establishing a monastery for men, the charge of which she left to men, she divided into three companies and monasteries the numerous virgins whom she had gathered out of different provinces, some of whom are of noble birth while others belonged to the middle or lower classes. But, although they worked and had their meal separately from each other, these three companies met together for psalm-singing and prayer. After the chanting of the Alleluia—the signal by which they were summoned to the Collect—no one was permitted to remain behind. But either first or among the first Paula used to await the arrival of the others, urging them to diligence rather by her own modest example than by motives of fear. At dawn, at the third, sixth and ninth hours, at evening, and at midnight they recited the psalter each in turn. No sister was allowed to be ignorant of the psalms, and all had every day to learn a certain portion of the holy scriptures. On the Lord's day only they proceeded to the church beside which they lived, each company following its own mother-superior. Returning home in the same order, they then devoted themselves to their allotted tasks, and made garments either for themselves or else for others. . . . When a sister was backward in coming to the recitation of the psalms or showed herself remiss in her work, Paula used to approach her in different ways. Was she quick tempered? Paula coaxed her. Was she phlegmatic?

Paula chided her, copying the example of the apostle who said; "What will ye? Shall I come to you with a rod or in love and in the spirit of meekness?" Apart from food and raiment she allowed no one to have anything she could call her own, for Paul had said, "Having food and raiment let us be therewith content." She was afraid lest the custom of having more should breed covetousness in them; or appetite which no wealth can satisfy, for the more it has the more it requires, and neither opulence nor indigence is able to diminish it. When the sisters quarreled one with another she reconciled them with soothing words.

(PAULA, 157)

The Herodion, Har Hordos

Mothers of Massacred Children

The fortified Palace of Herod, built between 24 and 15 B.C.E. and located about 6 kilometers southeast of Bethlehem, appears as a conical hill against the horizon. Herod funded his numerous palaces through a heavy taxation of the people. This, coupled with the severity and cruelty he displayed toward his subjects, made him a very unpopular ruler. Just as the Pharaoh in the book of Exodus tried to kill all the male babies, so did Herod attempt to do the same. Matthew develops the idea that Christ is like Moses, the prophet sent by God. The evangelist also compares the grief to that at the time of the Babylonian siege of Jerusalem.

> 17 Then was fulfilled what had been spoken through the prophet Jeremiah:
> 18 "A voice was heard in Ramah,
> wailing and loud lamentation,
> Rachel weeping for her children;
> she refused to be consoled, because they are no more."
> (Read Matt 2:13-17)

Bir Zeit University Women's Center

Women Who Demand Justice

This university, with Muslim and Christian students, provides many families their first opportunities for daughters to get university educations. A Women's Center with resources and activities encourages research and analysis of contemporary issues that will hopefully bring more justice. In Luke's gospel Jesus compares a woman who speaks adamantly for justice with one who has faith in prayer. The judge finally gives in to her.

> 4 . . . "Though I have no fear of God and no respect for anyone, 5 yet because this widow keeps bothering me, I will grant her justice, so that she may not wear me out by continually coming."

(Read Luke 18:1-8)

Caesarea Maritima

This Mediterranean port was the capital of Palestine for almost six hundred years, and fascinating ruins from many periods have been excavated. It was here that the ruler Pontius Pilate lived, and today there is still an inscription of his name on the theater. Eusebius became bishop of Caesarea in 314, and he wrote extensively on the history and geography of biblical lands. It is in his *Life of Constantine* that we learn of the Emperor Constantine's mother Helena. (See Chapter 4 on **Helena.**)

The Theater (Caesarea)

The Daughters of Philip

Here there is an inscription that has lasted for almost two thousand years with the name of the man who condemned Jesus to death. Yet the names of many women prophets who spread the gospel of Jesus are unknown.

> 8 The next day we left and came to Caesarea; and we went into the house of Philip the evangelist, one of the seven, and stayed with him. 9 He had four unmarried daughters who had the gift of prophecy. (Acts 21:8-9)

Cana

Wedding Feast

The current town of Cana does not date back to the time of Jesus, but it is in the general area of Galilee where he taught and performed miracles. Modern Christians localize the story of Jesus' first miracle at the modern town, where one can buy and enjoy local wine. Women seem to have been leaders in the community of the Johannine writer, and they have pivotal roles in John's gospel. The mother of Jesus calls forth the first miracle. The Samaritan woman is the first evangelist. Martha believes in Jesus as the "resurrection and the life." The women remain at the cross. Mary Magdalene is the apostle to the apostles after the resurrection. From the beginning to the end of the gospel women have faith and women share the faith.

> 1 On the third day there was a wedding in Cana of Galilee, and the mother of Jesus was there. 2 Jesus and his disciples had also been invited to the wedding. 3 When the wine gave out, the mother of Jesus said to him, "They have no wine."
>
> (Read John 2:1-11)

Capernaum

Although Nazareth and Bethlehem are associated with Jesus, Capernaum is referred to in the gospel as "his own town," where Jesus centered his ministry.

The House of Peter's Mother-in-Law (Capernaum)

Women Eager to Serve

From what is known of the teaching practices of itinerant rabbis and from archaeological evidence, there is reason to believe that the home of Peter's mother-in-law became a base where Jesus and his disciples repeatedly came, rested, dialogued, and studied. The home became a simple house church, then an octagonal building was added. Egeria wrote, "The house of the prince of the apostles has been made into a church, with its original walls still standing . . . . There also is the synagogue where the Lord cured a man possessed of a devil (Mark 1:23). The way in is up many stairs, and it is made of dressed stone."

> 29 As soon as they left the synagogue, they entered the house of Simon and Andrew, with James and John. 30 Now Simon's mother-in-law was in bed with a fever, and they told him about her at once. 31 He came and took her by the hand and lifted her up. Then the fever left her, and she began to serve them. (Mark 1:29-31)

The Ruins of the House Between the Synagogue and the House of Peter's Mother-in-Law (Capernaum)

The Daughter of Jairus

Though there is no specific information, one who cared for the synagogue often lived beside it. Perhaps this is the home of Jairus who begged Jesus to save the daughter that he loved. A child of twelve and a woman who had bled for twelve years were both restored.

> 40 . . . Then he put them all outside, and took the child's father and mother and those who were with him, and went in where the child was. 41 He took her by the hand and said to her, *"Talitha cum,"* which means, "Little girl, get up!" 42 And immediately the girl got up and began to walk about (she was twelve years of age). At this they were overcome with amazement. 43 He strictly ordered them that no one should know this, and told them to give her something to eat.
>
> (Read Mark 5:21-43)

The Mill Stones (Capernaum)

Women Grinding Grain

Bread was a staple food in the ancient Near East. Some theorists believe that women developed agriculture. Today women perform two-thirds of the work hours of the world, caring for home and family as well as working outside the home. Was this imbalance of work hours also present in the ancient world? Clear evidence is lacking, but women who were not wealthy often performed hard physical labor. For example, two women would work together in order to turn a heavy mill stone like those seen here. In an apocalyptic passage that indicates how unpredictable and quick the end could be, Jesus used the image of women working together grinding grain as an analogy.

> 33 "Those who try to make their life secure will lose it, but those who lose their life will keep it. 34 I tell you, on that night there will be two in one bed; one will be taken and the other left. 35 There will be two women grinding meal together; one will be taken and the other left." (Luke 17:33-35)

Chorazin (Korazim)

Here the excavations provide an idea of what life was like in biblical times. One can view the well-preserved *mikveh* (ritual bath), synagogue, and many homes.

The Mikveh (Chorazin)

Women Purifying Themselves After Their Menstrual Periods and Childbirth

The ritual bath has the required seven steps down and seven up. Jewish society considered blood the seat of life; when women had shed blood in some way, its power and holiness was feared. All societies have trouble with both what is "too good" and "too bad," that is, the liminal. Jewish ritual law defined the leper as unclean and not to be touched, and women while they were shedding blood as unclean and not to be touched. While the original meaning of this ritual law may have been based on high regard for women and their function, the law brought about isolation from others. It excluded women from participation in the priesthood, from entering the sanctuary, and from offering sacrifices. Not only Jews, but many groups such as Hindus, Zoroastrians, Buddhists, and Muslims have such taboos. Classical civilizations also feared women's blood; for instance, Pliny said that women in their periods would turn wine sour, make crops wither, kill grafts, dry seeds in gardens, cause the fruit of trees to fall off, dim the bright surface of mirrors, dull the edge of steel and the gleam of ivory, kill bees, rust iron and bronze, and cause a horrible smell to fill the air. Dogs who taste the blood become mad, and their bite becomes poisonous, as in rabies.

When King David spied on Bathsheba, Uriah's wife, who was bathing, she was taking a ritual bath to purify herself after her menstrual period (2 Sam 11:1-5). (See **Bathsheba** in the **City of David, Jerusalem**) While Christianity has not had ritual baths for women after their periods, many of the ideas from the classical world of excluding women from public worship because of menstruation and pregnancy were carried over into Christian thought and practice. Legislation on these matters is still in effect in the Eastern, Russian, and Ethiopian Orthodox Churches. Such prohibitions remained in canon law in the Roman Catholic Church until the sixteenth century, and vestiges of the attitudes shaped by those laws still persist.

Women seem to have been freed from blood taboos by Christ, but slowly social pressures returned them to subjugation. In the Council of Jerusalem the apostles tried to emphasize that sanctity was spiritual, and Paul did this repeatedly. The *Didascalia* and the *Constitutiones Apostolorum* say that women shall not have any imputation of sin against them during their periods. The document cites the woman with a hemorrhage who touched the fringe of Christ's garment and says that she was not blamed for this, but cured. Despite the attitude expressed in the *Didascalia,* Jerome wrote that nothing is so unclean as a woman in her periods: what she touches she makes unclean; other writers have had similar comments. In the early centuries the clerical ministry of deaconess was not allowed until women were over sixty, as this would mean that they had passed menopause.

In 601 Pope Gregory the Great wrote to Augustine of Canterbury, answering his questions. The Pope said that women should not be kept out of the church or away from communion during menstruation and pregnancy. Yet despite Gregory's letter, when Theodore of Tarsus became Bishop of Canterbury in 668 he issued penitentiary regulations and among them was the Eastern custom, "women during the time of menstruation shall not enter a church nor shall they communicate, neither nuns nor laity shall presume to do so. If they do they are to be given the penance of three day fasting." In Europe as well as England such rules were imposed, though there was some mitigation of them during the time of Gratian.

Penitentiaries from the eighth to the eleventh century continued to forbid women access to a church and communion during their periods. In France at the Synod of Meaux it was decided that women were not to be denied entry to a church, but it was considered better if they did not come during their periods. As late as 1684 there are records of women being told to remain outside the door of the church and not come in. In 1572 a canon forbade women receiving communion for some time after the birth of a child. An English book of penitential law, *Liber Legum Ecclesiasticarum,* told women that they must stay in their places and not approach the altar during Mass because they "must be careful not to render impure any of the things that pertain to the ministry of the church." The priest would come down to them to receive what offering they would like to give. Apparently the clerics had no qualms about receiving money from these persons considered too "unclean" to get near the altar.

Primitive ideas of women's ritual impurity have continued in both a feastday focusing on the "purifying" of a woman and in the ritual before the baptism of a child. Until the recent revision of the liturgical calendar the Catholic Church celebrated February 2 as the "Purification of the Blessed Virgin Mary" and remembered Luke 2:22-24, which concerns the ritual of purifying a woman after childbirth. (See the **Purification of Mary** at the **Ritual Baths** in the **Old City of Jerusalem.**) Now the feast is called "The Presentation of the Lord." Until the recent reforms there was a ritual of "churching" a woman before the baptism of her infant. The form of the ritual was from the period of Pope Paul V (1605–1621). Outside the church the priests prayed over the woman that she might be purified after giving birth. Only after this purification did she enter the church. The 1928 *Book of Common Prayer* used in the Episcopal Church until 1979 had a "Service of Thanksgiving for Women after Childbirth," which was subtitled "The Churching of Women." Some English women who gave birth during the 1950s speak of being unwelcome in relatives' and friends' homes until they had gone to the clergy to be "churched."[7]

Family Homes (Chorazin)

God Like the Woman Who Searched for Her Coin

Looking at the floors of the houses, one can see how coins could easily get lost in the irregular stone surfaces. While art and literature often portray and celebrate God as a good shepherd looking for the lost sheep, the parallel image of the woman searching for a lost coin is not one that is typically used in stained glass windows or paintings imaging God.

> 8 "Or what woman having ten silver coins, if she loses one of them, does not light a lamp, sweep the house, and search carefully until she finds it? 9 When she has found it, she calls together her friends and neighbors, saying, 'Rejoice with me, for I have found the coin that I had lost.' 10 Just so, I tell you, there is joy in the presence of the angels of God over one sinner who repents."
>
> (Read Luke 15:1-10)

The Synagogue (Chorazin)

The Bent-over Woman

The gospel text does not indicate the town where this miracle occurred; perhaps it was here. Authorities are not always pleased when God has freed someone from fear or limitations.

15 The Lord answered him and said, "You hypocrites! Does not each of you on the sabbath untie his ox or his donkey from the manger, and lead it away to give it water? 16 And ought not this woman, a daughter of Abraham whom Satan bound for eighteen long years, be set free from this bondage on the sabbath day?"

(Read Luke 13:10-17)

Dead Sea

Lot's Daughters

In a desert environment hospitality is a very important virtue, yet this painful story raises the question whether it is acceptable to mistreat one's own daughters, offering them for rape, in order that one can be hospitable to male strangers. Is the sexual violation of women acceptable?

4 But before they lay down, the men of the city, the men of Sodom, both young and old, all the people to the last man, surrounded the house; 5 and they called to Lot, "Where are the men who came to you tonight? Bring them out to us, so that we may know them." 6 Lot went out of the door to the men, shut the door after him, 7 and said, "I beg you, my brothers, do not act so wickedly. 8 Look, I have two daughters who have not known a man; let me bring them out to you, and do to them as you please; only do nothing to these men, for they have come under the shelter of my roof." (Gen 19:4-8)

Reflections by Egeria on the Dead Sea

South of the Dead Sea would be En Boqeq and the area of Zohar to which Egeria refers. Though Egeria was open to the stories she was told and the places that she was shown, apparently the bishop's story was more than she could take.

To our left was the whole country of the Sodomites, including Zoar, the only one of the five cities which remains today. There is still something left of it, but all that is left of the others is heaps of ruins, because they were burned to ashes. We were also shown the place were Lot's wife had her memorial, as you read in the Bible. But what we saw, reverend ladies, was not the actual pillar, but only the place where it had once been. The pillar itself, they say has been submerged in the Dead Sea—at any rate we did not see it, and I cannot pretend we did. In fact it was the bishop there, the Bishop of

Zoar, who told us that it was now a good many years since the pillar had been visible.

(EGERIA, 107)

Dor

Reflections on Paula's Journey by the Coast

This place, with its fine harbor, has been occupied since the fifteenth century B.C.E. The excavations of the ancient city are within walking distance of the bathing beach near Nahsholim-Dor. Jerome wrote of Paula's journey in this area:

> Here she could not fail to admire the ruins of Dor, once a most powerful city; the Strato's Tower, which though at one time insignificant was rebuilt by Herod king of Judea and named Caesarea in honour of Caesar Augustus. Here she saw the house of Cornelius now turned into a Christian church; and the humble abode of Philip; and the chambers of his daughters the four virgins "which did prophesy." She arrived next at Antipatris, a small town half in ruins, named by Herod after his father Antipater, and at Lydda, now become Diospolis, a place made famous by the raising again of Dorcas and the restoration to health of Aeneas. Not far from this are Arimathea, the village of Joseph who buried the Lord, and Nob, once a city of priests but now the tomb in which their slain bodies rest. Joppa too is hard by, the port of Jonah's flight; which also—if I may introduce a poetic fable—saw Andromeda bound to the rock.

(PAULA, 143)

Purple Dye Factory (Dor)

Lydia of Philippi

By the edge of the sea tanks were cut into the rock and filled with water in order to cultivate the murex sea snail, which is the source of purple dye. It took 12,000 murex to make one-and-a-half grams of dye, which would be worth about $200. Purple was the color of those in authority. When Lydia, who lived in Philippi, a major trading city across the Mediterranean in Greece, was described as a seller of purple this meant more than simply being a cloth seller. Rather, she worked in a very prosperous trade. After hearing of Christ, Lydia used her talents to help build the Christian community of Philippi.

14 A certain woman named Lydia, a worshiper of God, was listening to us; she was from the city of Thyatira and a dealer in purple cloth. The Lord opened her heart to listen eagerly to what was said by Paul. 15 When she and her household were baptized, she urged us, saying, "If you have judged me to be faithful to the Lord, come and stay at my home." And she prevailed upon us.

(Read Acts 16:11-15)

Endor (Horvat)

The Medium Whom Saul Consulted

Saul disguised himself and went to this village a little south-west of Mount Tabor to consult a woman who was known for her psychic powers. He had banished such people from the land, and yet, when frightened, he wanted one. Since women have not always had equal access to education and to official recognition, they sometimes have clandestine ways of working or exercising power.

> 8 So Saul disguised himself and put on other clothes and went there, he and two men with him. They came to the woman by night. And he said, "Consult a spirit for me, and bring up for me the one whom I name to you." 9 The woman said to him, "Surely you know what Saul has done, how he has cut off the mediums and the wizards from the land. Why then are you laying a snare for my life to bring about my death?" 10 But Saul swore to her by the LORD, "As the LORD lives, no punishment shall come upon you for this thing."

(Read 1 Sam 28:5-25)

En Gedi (Zafzafot)

Lovers Who Relate Mutually

En Gedi was a fertile place with vineyards and medicinal plants that made it an image of good. The garden of the Song of Songs is a restoration of the loss of the Garden of Eden. Woman and man were meant to dwell together in intimacy and mutu-ality, "flesh of my flesh and bone of my bone." Genesis de-scribes God's intention gone awry, so that the male dominates the female. However, the Song of Songs, probably written as poetry to celebrate love between women and men, was in-cluded along with other sacred texts that associated love with God. This poetry reveals a mutually loving relationship, that

between female and male. Here the woman is active, expressive, and often initiates lovemaking. The poetry goes back and forth between the voice of the man and that of the woman. (Also see **Solomon's Pools**.)

> 13 My beloved is to me a bag of myrrh
> that lies between my breasts.
> 14 My beloved is to me a cluster of henna blossoms
> in the vineyards of En-gedi.
> 15 Ah, you are beautiful, my love;
> ah, you are beautiful;
> your eyes are doves.
> 16 Ah, you are beautiful, my beloved,
> truly lovely.
> Our couch is green;
> 17 the beams of our house are cedar,
> our rafters are pine.

(Read Song 1:1–2:17)

Gaza

Wisdom Personified

This seaside area, full of beautiful beaches, is a crossroads between Asia and Africa and thus has repeatedly been at the center of claims from rival groups seeking control of it. Gaza also has been a creative center for early monastic tradition with its proximity to the Egyptian monastics and connections with the north and with the sea. Hilarion of Palestine went to learn about monasticism from Antony in Egypt; then, in 310 C.E., he built a monastery in Gaza that was said to have attracted three thousand monks.

The majesty of the sea and the beauty of creation manifest some of the splendor and mystery of the divine. The Wisdom literature often personifies God's wisdom incarnate as feminine. The Holy One even delights to play with humankind.

> 27 When he established the heavens, I was there,
> when he drew a circle on the face of the deep,
> 28 when he made firm the skies above,
> when he established the fountains of the deep,
> 29 when he assigned to the sea its limit,
> so that the waters might not transgress his command,
> when he marked out the foundations of the earth,
> 30 then I was beside him, like a master worker;
> and I was daily his delight,
> rejoicing before him always,
> 31 rejoicing in his inhabited world
> and delighting in the human race.
>
> (Read Prov 8:22-31)

The Great Mosque (Gaza)

Al-Khansaʾ, the Poet

This location first contained a Roman temple. Later it was the site of a Byzantine Greek Church. Finally, the Norman Crusaders built a large church, which was later converted into the present mosque. No matter which group has prayed there, each has earnestly sought the divine and grappled with the mysteries of life and death.

Tumadir bint ʿAmru al-Harith bin al-Sharid, who was called Al-Khansaʾ, was of the Madar nomadic tribe of Arabia who were known for both courage in battle and talent in poetry. She was born in 600 and died in 670, spanning the time period in which

Mohammed's revelations came to be known and accepted. As a child she was considered intelligent and lovely, sharing her poetry at births, weddings, and funerals. Al-Khansaʾ would not marry until she found the husband she wanted. She was married three times, outliving all her husbands.

Al-Khansaʾ took part in the poetry contests in which poets would recite for an audience and a judge.

> On one such occasion, after two men poets had recited, the judgment angered the losing competitor. The judge is supposed to have turned to al-Khansaʾ and said, "what do you think: Recite some of your poetry for us." She replied with a line still considered a classic, which has achieved the status of a proverb in Arabic.
>
> > Among desert guides, Sakhar was peerless
> > Like a beacon on the peak of a high mountain.
>
> After hearing the line, the annoyed competitor is alleged to have said, "We've never seen a better woman poet than you." To this al-Khansaʾ replied, "Don't you want to say that I am the best poet, male or female?"[8]

Her poems are considered great examples of early Arabic literature. Mohammed admired her poetry and would have her recite it for him. Considering that two of her brothers and later four of her sons were killed in battles, this poem called "Lament for a Brother" is particularly poignant.

> What have we done to you, death
> that you treat us so,
> with always another catch
> one day a warrior
> the next a head of state;
> charmed by the loyal
> you choose the best.
> Iniquitous, unequaling death
> I would not complain
> if you were just but you take the worthy
> leaving fools for us.
>
> Fifty years among us
> upholding rights
> annulling wrongs,
> impatient death
> could you not wait a little longer
> He still would be here
> and mine, a brother

without a flaw. Peace
be upon him and spring
rains water his tomb but
could you not wait
    a little longer
    a little longer,
you came too soon.[9]

Napoleon's Citadel (Gaza)

Delilah

This large stone building in which Napoleon stayed for a few days is now a girls' school. The massive stone walls provide a good setting for remembering Delilah and Samson, who was imprisoned in the Gaza area. Many biblical stories describe women as manipulative or seductive. Because women often lacked financial resources and education, charm and beauty were their only means of gaining power and influence. Such women have been classified as either "good" (Judith, Jael, Esther) or "bad" (Delilah) depending on whether or not they used their power for the Hebrew people. However, even the women using their power for their people are often viewed as questionable or manipulative. Can women see beyond tribal divisions and use their influence for the good of the whole human community? Can men and women respect each other's influence instead of relating with dominance or manipulation? Can a balance of power be created through education and opportunities?

> 4 After this he fell in love with a woman in the valley of Sorek, whose name was Delilah. 5 The lords of the Philistines came to her and said to her, "Coax him, and find out what makes his strength so great, and how we may overpower him, so that we may bind him in order to subdue him; and we will each give you eleven hundred pieces of silver." 6 So Delilah said to Samson, "Please tell me what makes your strength so great, and how you could be bound, so that one could subdue you."
>
> (Read Judg 16:1-22)

In the end of the story we read how Samson pulled down the supporting pillars of the Temple of Dagon. At Tell Qasileh on the north bank of the Yarkon River, about a mile before it enters into the Mediterranean, a Philistine temple has been excavated. Though there is no specific way to connect it with Samson, it does reveal architecture with two massive pillars and indicates a style of building used by the Philistines.

Gezer

Women Valued by the Wealth of their Dowries

This Tel near Kibbutz Gezer has excavations going back to the Middle Bronze Age. Near the Solomonic Gate one can remember Solomon's wife. The Pharaoh Siamun took over Gezer in the early part of Solomon's rule, angering Solomon. To try to placate him the Pharaoh gave his daughter as a wife for Solomon and the city of Gezer as her dowry. The gates of Solomon's rebuilt city still can be seen today.

Dowries remain a significant issue in parts of the modern world. In Muslim countries today women's dowries are protected under Islamic law and women retain control of their family property even when married. In some parts of India women are mistreated or killed if they do not have large enough dowries.

> 16 (Pharaoh king of Egypt had gone up and captured Gezer and burned it down, had killed the Canaanites who lived in the city, and had given it as dowry to his daughter, Solomon's wife; 17 so Solomon rebuilt Gezer), Lower Beth-horon, 18 Baalath, Tamar in the wilderness, within the land, 19 as well as all of Solomon's storage cities, the cities for his chariots, the cities for his cavalry, and whatever Solomon desired to build, in Jerusalem, in Lebanon, and in all the land of his dominion.
>
> (1 Kings 9:16-19)

Hammat Gezer

The Empress Eudokia

In Jesus' time many sick people went to the Sea of Galilee to enjoy the therapeutic effects of the hot springs. Those in need of healing also may have heard of the itinerant rabbi from Nazareth who healed. In the mid-sixth century the baths at the hot springs were further developed by Empress Eudokia, who had twenty-six fountains built there. A poem she is said to have written is engraved on a marble slab on the floor. Eudokia was the granddaughter of Empress Eudocia, who had come to Jerusalem on pilgrimage to thank God for her daughter's marriage, and died there in forced exile in 460. (See **St. Stephen's Church, Jerusalem**.) The younger Eudokia came to Jerusalem to flee her Vandal husband, Hunneric, to pray at the holy places, and to visit her grandmother's tomb. She also died in Jerusalem. Did both of these women who had been in painful marriages find healing in touching the land of Jesus, as the hemorrhaging women had found in touching the hem of his cloak?

Hazor

Deborah

Deborah, the wife of Lappidoth (the phrase translated "wife of Lappidoth" may instead mean "a woman gifted with spirit"), was respected as a prophet and a judge during a period when the judges exercised overall leadership in Israel. Deborah showed courage when the men were afraid, encouraging Barak to defeat an army at Hazor in about 1125 B.C.E. This unified the tribes of Issachar, Zebulun, and Naphtali from the north and the tribes of Ephraim, Benjamin, and Manasseh from the south and led to forty years of peace.

> 4 At that time Deborah, a prophetess, wife of Lappidoth, was judging Israel. 5 She used to sit under the palm of Deborah between Ramah and Bethel in the hill country of Ephraim; and the Israelites came up to her for judgment. 6 She sent and summoned Barak son of Abinoam from Kedesh in Naphtali, and said to him, "The LORD, the God of Israel, commands you, 'Go, take position at Mount Tabor, bringing ten thousand from the tribe of Naphtali and the tribe of Zebulun. 7 I will draw out Sisera, the general of Jabin's army, to meet you by the Wadi Kishon with his chariots and his troops; and I will give him into your hand.'" 8 Barak said to her, "If you will go with me, I will go; but if you will not go with me, I will not go."
>
> (Read Judg 4:4-8)

Hebron

The Matriarchs

The Arabic name of Hebron is Al-Khalil, the title given to Abraham, which means "friend of God." Abraham's descendants, Jews, Christians, and Muslims, all of whom consider this place sacred, again and again forget how to be friends to each other. This place has been continuously occupied for over 5000 years.

The Tombs of the Matriarchs and Patriarchs

Sarah died near Hebron, and Abraham bought a field in which to bury her. Abraham, Isaac and Rebecca, Jacob and Leah are said to be buried near Sarah (Gen 13:18; 25:8-10; 35:27). The massive mosque Al-haram al-Ibrahimi includes part of the Crusader church built over the Christian Byzantine basilica, which was at the site of the tombs. Jews, Christians, and Muslims have all had sacred buildings here. Now Jews have a synagogue inside the structure on one side and Muslims pray on the other. One can walk through the mosque of the women to the tomb of Abraham. Some persons hold that the Jewish descendants of Abraham (and not the Muslim descendants of Abraham) have exclusive rights to own all the land of Israel/Palestine because God gave the land to Abraham. Yet many contemporary rabbis say that this ancient passage indicates Abraham's respect for different persons who owned the land. He did not indicate that God had given him exclusive property rights.

When Jacob was dying in Egypt he gave these instructions:

> 29 Then he charged them, saying to them, "I am about to be gathered to my people. Bury me with my ancestors—in the cave in the field of Ephron the Hittite, 30 in the cave in the field at Machpelah, near Mamre, in the land of Canaan, in the field that Abraham bought from Ephron the Hittite as a burial site. 31 There Abraham and his wife Sarah were buried; there Isaac and his wife Rebekah were buried; and there I buried Leah— 32 the field and the cave that is in it were purchased from the Hittites." 33 When Jacob ended his charge to his sons, he drew up his feet into the bed, breathed his last, and was gathered to his people.
>
> (Read Gen 49:29-33)

The Souq

In the old town of Hebron is a colorful souq, or marketplace, where one can find foods and crafts that reveal both the similarities and the differences in lifestyles of the present-day women and their ancestors who once lived here.

Heptapegon or Tabgha

Egeria's Reflections

This lovely place where seven springs flow into the Sea of Galilee has been popular with pilgrims since the early centuries. In the 380s Egeria described it thus:

> Not far away from there [Capernaum] are some stone steps where the Lord stood. And in the same place by this sea is a grassy field with plenty of hay and many palm trees. By them are seven springs, each flowing strongly. And this is the field where the Lord fed the people with the five loaves and the two fishes. In fact the stone on which the Lord placed the bread has now been made into an altar. People who go there take away small pieces of the stone to bring them prosperity, and they are very effective. Past the walls of this church goes the public highway on which the Apostle Matthew had his place of custom. Near there on a mountain is the cave to which the Savior climbed and spoke the Beatitudes.
>
> (EGERIA, 196, 200)

Church of the Primacy of Peter

Egeria spoke of two stones and a cave where Christians prayed. This church built over the stone that stretches out into the sea is where pilgrims remember the Risen Christ making breakfast for his disciples and asking Peter if he really loved him.

Church of the Multiplication of the Loaves and Fishes

Benedictines have a retreat house by the church, a modern replica of the fifth-century building, which includes many of the ancient mosaics including that of loaves and fishes by the stone of which Egeria wrote.

Church of the Sermon on the Mount

Near the top of the mount with the little cave of which Egeria wrote, an eight-sided church with the words of the eight beatitudes has been built. Sisters from Italy have a hospice for pilgrims here with a beautiful view of the Sea of Galilee.

Stone Along the Road on the Way From Heptapegon to Capernaum

The woman with the hemorrhage

Modern pilgrims have erected a stone by the eucalyptus trees on the right of the highway, in the general area where early pilgrims had a stone remembering the woman who was so desperate for healing. Jesus praised her faith.

> 47 When the woman saw that she could not remain hidden, she came trembling; and falling down before him, she declared in the presence of all the people why she had touched him, and how she had been immediately healed. 48 He said to her, "Daughter, your faith has made you well; go in peace."
>
> (Read Luke 8:40-48)

The Herodion, or Har Hordos (See Bethlehem)

Jericho

Paula in Jericho

By the fourth century, when Paula and Jerome traveled to Jericho, there were already many sites designated to show pilgrims its history.

> After this Paula visited the tomb of Lazarus and beheld the hospitable roof of Mary and Martha, as well as Bethphage, 'the town of the priestly jaws.' Here it was that a restive foal typical of the Gentiles received the bridle of God, and covered with the garments of the apostles offered its lowly back for Him to sit on. From this she went straight on down the hill to Jericho thinking of the wounded man in the gospel, of the savagery of the priests and Levites who passed him by, and of the kindness of the Samaritan, that is, the guardian, who placed the half-dead man upon his own beast and brought him down to the inn of the church. She noticed the place called Adomim or the Place of Blood, so-called because much blood was shed there in the frequent incursions of marauders. She beheld also the sycamore tree of Zacchaeus, by which is signified the good works of repentance whereby he trod under foot his former sins of bloodshed and rapine, and from which he saw the Most High as from a pinnacle of virtue. She was shewn too the spot by the wayside where the blind men

sat who, receiving their sight from the Lord, became types of the two peoples who should believe upon Him . . . .

Scarcely had the night passed away when burning with eagerness she hastened to the Jordan, stood by the brink of the river, and as the sun rose recalled to mind the rising of the sun of righteousness; how the priest's feet stood firm in the middle of the riverbed; how afterwards at the command of Elijah and Elisha the waters were divided hither and thither and made way for them to pass; and again how the Lord had cleansed by His baptism waters which the deluge had polluted and the destruction of mankind had defiled.

(PAULA, 147–48)

Tel es-Sultan, or Ancient Jericho

Rahab

In the 1950s Dame Kathleen Kenyon excavated this place, which has been continuously occupied for over 10,000 years. Early inhabitants began to produce food rather than merely gathering it; some scholars believe that women developed agriculture while men were hunting. Though the ancient walls predate biblical times, Rahab the prostitute who lived by the wall of the city can be remembered here. She helped and hid Joshua and his men. Many ancient stories including those of the Bible describe one group violently taking the land and possessions of another. Such stories are descriptive, not prescriptive of how persons should relate to each other.

> 12 Now then, since I have dealt kindly with you, swear to me by the LORD that you in turn will deal kindly with my family. Give me a sign of good faith 13 that you will spare my father and mother, my brothers and sisters, and all who belong to them, and deliver our lives from death."
>
> (Read Josh 2:1-21)

Herod's Palace in Jericho (See **Tulul Abu el Aliaq**)

Jordan River near Jericho

Transformation of Baptism

Though John the Baptist was preaching in the Judean wilderness near Jericho and baptized Jesus near where the Jordan goes into the Dead Sea, Yardenit is a popular place for pilgrims to reflect on baptism. The site is near where the Jordan leaves the Sea of Galilee near Kibbutz Kegania Aleph. This passage in Paul's writings may be part of an early hymn used at baptisms:

> 27 As many of you as were baptized into Christ have clothed yourselves with Christ. 28 There is no longer Jew or Greek, there is no longer slave or free, there is no longer male and female; for all of you are one in Christ Jesus.
>
> (Read Gal 3:27-28)

Jezreel Valley (Northern Kingdom)

Hosea's Unfaithful Wife

In the Northern Kingdom of Judah the prophet Hosea spoke in the last years of Jeroboam II (786–746 B.C.E.), calling the people to turn from idolatry and the ruthless oppression of the poor. Hosea presents his call to conversion with the metaphor of his invitation to his unfaithful wife Gomer to return to him. He also weaves in the imagery surrounding Baal, a fertility god who gave his worshipers needed food from the earth. Hosea's passionate and tender words describe how God uses punishment in medicinal ways to turn people from false love so that they may return to true love. Thus Hosea establishes the covenant imagery of God as husband and the people as spouse, a familiar theme used in Hebrew Scripture as well as in the Christian writings of John and Paul, who portray Christ as the bridegroom.

Hosea's words are tender and beautiful, yet all metaphors have limits and disadvantages. Unfaithful men in both ancient and modern times are just as numerous (if not more so) than unfaithful women, yet Scripture repeatedly dwells on the image of unfaithful women. Would Christianity be different if texts and preaching throughout the ages offered images of unfaithful men as a balance? Would Christianity be different if God's pain and longing for sinners was depicted by women's pain at their straying husbands?

> 13 I will punish her for the festival days of the Baals,
> when she offered incense to them
> and decked herself with her ring and jewelry,
> and went after her lovers,
> and forgot me, says the LORD.
> 14 Therefore, I will now allure her,
> and bring her into the wilderness,
> and speak tenderly to her.
>
> (Read Hos 2:8-23)

Jib, or the biblical Gibeon
(See *St. Andrew's Church, Jerusalem*)

Khan Younis in the Gaza Region

Khadija and Fatima

This second-largest city in Gaza is an agricultural center and has a Bedouin market every Wednesday. It is only a few miles from the sea. The many industrious women of the market can serve as a reminder of Mohammed's wife, Khadija, a fine businesswoman, and their daughter, Fatima. Muslim tradition says that there are four perfect women, and Khadija and Fatima are two of them. Khadija lived in Saudi Arabia in the sixth century C.E. and was a successful trader with much property. She hired the younger Mohammed to take care of her goods and manage some of her business. She liked him and they married and lived happily for twenty years. She is considered the first Muslim, for she was the first to hear the revelations that Mohammed was receiving in the mountains. She supported him not only materially, but also spiritually and this helped him lay the basis for the Islamic movement. As long as she was alive, she was his only wife. Perhaps respect for her as a good manager of resources influenced the provisions for women in Islamic law. Within contemporary Sharia, Islamic law, women keep the property they have when they are married; it is not merged with that of the husband. Before they are married, Sharia allows women to make contracts that will protect them and their property if the marriage is not successful.

Fatima was born in Mecca and grew up in a household with her elder sisters and boy cousin, Ali, who was to become her husband and a leader in Islam after her father's death. Fatima died when she was twenty, only a few months after her father's death. She had already born a daughter, Zainab, two sons, Hassan and Hussein, and another daughter. Fatima was known as a devoted wife and mother, a good manager of her home and one who was generous toward the poor. Her family would often fast for a day and use the money to help those in need. In Islam fasting is respected as a way of growing in compassion for the needy and in self-discipline.

Kursi

Deaconesses Who Baptized

Kursi is where ancient pilgrims remembered the exorcism of the Gerasene demoniac (Mark 5:1), although now there are indications that it took place elsewhere. Excavations reveal the largest Byzantine monastic complex in Galilee. In the baptistry on the right side of altar area the cross-shaped baptismal font symbolizes Paul's words that in baptism we die with Christ so that we may live with him.

> Wherefore, O bishop, appoint workers of righteousness as helpers who may cooperate with you unto salvation. Those that please you out of all the people you shall choose and appoint as deacons, a man for the performance of most things that are required, but a woman for the ministry of women. For there are houses where you cannot send a deacon to the women, on account of the heathen, but you may send a deaconess. Also, because in many other matters that office of a woman deacon is required. In the first place, when women go down into the water those who go down into the water ought to be anointed by a deaconess with the oil of anointing; and where there is no woman at hand, and especially no deaconess, he who baptizes must of necessity anoint her who is being baptized. But where there are women, and especially a deaconess, it is not fitting that women should be seen by men; but with imposition of the hand you anoint the head only. As of old the priests and kings were anointed in Israel, do you in like manner, with imposition of the hand, anoint the head of those who receive baptism, whether of men or of women; and afterwards—whether you yourself baptize, or command the deacons or presbyters to baptize— let a woman deacon, as we have already said, anoint the women.
>
> But let a man pronounce over them the invocation of the divine Names in the water. And when she who is being baptized has come up from the water, let the deaconess receive her, and teach and instruct her how the seal of baptism ought to be kept unbroken in purity and holiness. For this cause we say that the ministry of a woman deacon is especially needful and important. For our Lord and Savior also was ministered unto by women ministers, Mary Magdalene, and Mary the daughter of James and mother of Joses, and the mother of the sons of Zebedee, with other women besides (Matt 27:56; Mark 15:40; Luke 8:2-3). And you also have need of the ministry of a deaconess for many things; for a deaconess is required to go into the houses of the heathen where there are believing women, and to visit those who are sick, and to minister to them in that of which they have need, and to bathe those who have begun to recover from sickness.
>
> Let the deacons imitate the bishops in their conversation: nay let them even be laboring more than he. Let them not

love filthy lucre; but let them be diligent in the ministry. And in proportion to the number of the congregation of the people of the Church, so let deacons be, that they may be able to take knowledge of each severally and refresh all; so that for the aged women who are infirm, and for the brethren and sisters who are in sickness—for every one they may provide the ministry which is proper for each.

But let a woman rather be devoted to the ministry of women, and a male deacon to the ministry of men. And let them be ready to obey and to submit to the command of the bishops. And let them labor and toil in every place where they are sent to minister or to speak of some matter to any one.[10]

Latrun

Paula Remembered the Concubine

Aijalon Park covers the Arab village of Imwas (Emmaus), which was destroyed when the Palestinians were driven out in 1967. The village was one of the places where pilgrims remembered the story of Emmaus. A modern Cistercian monastery, which continues the ancient art of wine making, is in the area. Ruins of the Emmaus-Nicopolis site, containing both churches and Roman baths, can serve as a place to remember the sad story of the concubine who was dismembered by her husband. The pilgrim Paula recalled that very event in this area.

> Again resuming her journey, she came to Nicopolis, once called Emmaus, where the Lord became known in the breaking of bread, an action by which He dedicated the house of Cleopas as a church. Starting thence she made her way up lower and higher Bethhoran, cities founded by Solomon but subsequently destroyed by several devastating wars; seeing on her right Ajalon and Gibeon where Joshua the son of Nun when fighting against the five kings gave commandments to the sun and moon, where also he condemned the Gibeonites (who by a craftier stratagem had obtained a treaty) to be hewers of wood and drawers of water. At Gibeah also, now a complete ruin, she stopped for a little while remembering its sin, and the cutting of the concubine into pieces, and how in spite of this three hundred men of the tribe of Benjamin were saved that in after days Paul might be called a Benjamite.
>
> (PAULA, 143)

As in the story of Lot, who was willing to throw out his daughters to be raped, in the following story the men are willing to sacrifice a daughter and a concubine. A Levite who is traveling home with his concubine has been offered hospitality by an old man.

> 22 While they were enjoying themselves, the men of the city, a perverse lot, surrounded the house, and started pounding on the door. They said to the old man, the master of the house, "Bring out the man who came into your house, so that we may have intercourse with him." 23 And the man, the master of the house, went out to them and said to them, "No, my brothers, do not act so wickedly. Since this man is my guest, do not do this vile thing."
>
> (Read Judg 19:22–20:6)

After the concubine had been raped (the text does not indicate whether she was dead or not), her husband cut her in twelve pieces and sent the pieces to the twelve tribes of Israel to generate anger so that they would join him in taking revenge. Often revenge is worse than the original evil. The pieces of the concubine so angered the other tribes that they began a battle in which 25,000 of the tribe of Benjamin were killed. Violence as a solution only leads to more violence. When the other tribes realized that one of the tribes of Israel might be wiped out, they kidnapped women to be wives for the surviving men. (See **Shiloh.**)

Lod

Martha, George, and the Dragon

The story of St. George slaying a dragon to save a maiden whom it would devour is associated with Lod. St. George is the patron saint of the Palestinian Christians. His name is often used for Christian churches and artistic depictions of George and the dragon can be seen in many churches and monasteries in Bible lands. In the Bible and in mythology there are images of sea monsters, dragons, and beasts that imply chaos and evil. Often the symbolic stories have reason personified as male destroying the unconscious or chaos personified as female. Destroying the other is central in these legends. Alternative legends describe St. Martha bravely facing and taming a dragon. Martha of Bethany, who has often been stereotyped as the anxious domestic, was understood as Martha who recognizes Jesus as the resurrection, the Christ, the Messiah. The dragon of the evil of death has been transformed. Story and art both shape people's consciousness and horizons and have the power to transform them.

Artistic portrayals of Martha and the dragon developed especially in Europe, from the twelfth century onward, in areas where women were active in ministry. Elisabeth Moltmann-Wendel in *The Women Around Jesus* reproduces and discusses many of these depictions, such as the paintings in the Church of St. Laurence, Nuremberg, Germany and in Main, Switzerland, the works of Bernardino Luini and Antonio Corregio in Italy, and the sculpture in the Church of the Madonna d'Onero in Carona, near Lugano. Moltmann-Wendel further discusses the value of recognizing and befriending the unconscious rather than trying to suppress or destroy it. The barefoot Martha in flowing dresses is a contrast to the armored George. Any religious tradition, whether it be Christianity, Islam, or Judaism, set on destroying rather than respecting the other needs to be examined. The history of the Holy Land seems to be dominated by George's approach rather than that of Martha.

Magdala, Midgal

Mary Magdalene and the Other Women Who Supported Jesus

A walled-in area containing some unexcavated ruins next to a seaside park in modern Magdala is the only hint of the flourishing fishing town that, according to Josephus, had 40,000 residents. The risen Christ sent Mary of Magdala to proclaim to his brothers that he was alive. She was the apostle to the apostles. While two churches and extensive excavations commemorate Peter on the north side of the water, nothing commemorates Mary Magdalene in her city. Why aren't there as many monuments to women as to men?

> 1 Soon afterwards he went on through cities and villages, proclaiming and bringing the good news of the kingdom of God. The twelve were with him, 2 as well as some women who had been cured of evil spirits and infirmities: Mary, called Magdalene, from whom seven demons had gone out, 3 and Joanna, the wife of Herod's steward Chuza, and Susanna, and many others, who provided for them out of their resources.
>
> (Read Luke 8:1-3)

Mamre, or Ramat el-Khalil

Sarah Laughed

About 1.6 kilometers from Hebron the Russian Orthodox Church keeps watch over the "Oak of Abraham," which in legends is known as Mamre. Here Sarah and Abraham offered hospitality to the three strangers who said that God would give the elderly couple a child. In 325 Constantine's mother-in-law, Eutropia, built a church here in order to focus devotion to Christ in a place of popular superstitions.

> 9 They said to him, "Where is your wife Sarah?" And he said, "There, in the tent." 10 Then one said, "I will surely return to you in due season, and your wife Sarah shall have a son." And Sarah was listening at the tent entrance behind him. 11 Now Abraham and Sarah were old, advanced in age; it had ceased to be with Sarah after the manner of women. 12 So Sarah laughed to herself, saying, "After I have grown old, and my husband is old, shall I have pleasure?"
>
> (Read Gen 18:1-15)

Mar Saba

Unwelcomed Women

This monastery, about 14 kilometers east of Bethlehem, contains over a hundred cells, although only about ten Greek Orthodox monks live there today. The monastery looks quite dramatic, built as it is into the rock above the Kidron River in the middle of the desert. St. Sabas came from the Cappodocian area of Turkey to be a monk in the Judean wilderness. He lived in solitude in the cave for five years but subsequently allowed others to join him. In 491, with money from his mother, he built a hospice. While hospitality was a respected virtue among ascetics of the desert, unfortunately fear of women and misogyny were also common. Women have never been allowed to enter Mar Saba. They may only look at the monastery from the nearby "women's tower."

Celibacy for the reign of God is a gift that can lead to a deep prayer life, but unintegrated sexuality and sexual drives can lead to fear of and projection of evil onto members of the other sex. Many stories of ancient desert monks portray women as evil temptresses. Early Irish monastic communities had cultural connections with those of the Middle East. In Ireland there is the story of St. Kevin, who had a little home high on a precipice. A woman came and he pushed her off the edge; his celibacy was more important than her life. For such a mentality, the only way to stay celibate is to stop women, who want to rape men.

> In Lower Egypt there was an anchorite who was well-known because he dwelt in a solitary cell in the desert. Now by the

power of Satan, a shameless woman who had heard of him said to some young men, "What would you give me if I could cause your anchorite to fall?" They agreed to give her something of value. In the evening she went out and came to his cell as though she had lost her way, and when she knocked, the anchorite came out. When he saw her he was troubled and said, "How have you come here?" Weeping, she said, "I came her because I have lost my way." Filled with compassion, he made her come into the entry, and he returned to his cell and shut it, but the unfortunate creature began to cry out, "Abba, the wild animals are eating me." He was uneasy again, but fearing the judgment of God, he said, "What is the source of this hardness of mine?" and he opened the door and made her come inside. Then the devil attempted to attack him with his arrows. Pondering the warfare of the enemy, he said, "The ways of the enemy are darkness, whereas the Son of God is light," and he rose and lit the lamp. Burning with desire, he said, "Those who commit such acts go to the punishment; try then, and see if you can bear the everlasting fire," and he put his finger into the lamp and burnt it without feeling, so extreme was the sensual flame. He went on doing this until morning, burning all his fingers. The unfortunate woman, seeing what he was doing, was petrified with fear. In the morning the young men came to see the anchorite and said to him, "Did a woman come here last night?" He said, "Yes, she is inside asleep." They entered and found her dead, and they said to him, "Abba, she is dead." Then, uncovering his hands, he showed them to them, saying, "Look what the daughter of the devil has done to me: she has destroyed my fingers," and he told them what had happened and said, "It is written, 'Do not render evil for evil,'" and he prayed and awoke her, and she went away and lived wisely the rest of her life.[11]

Masada

Women Victims of War

When Herod the Great was trying to gain control of Palestine in 40 B.C.E. and needed to escape the Parthians he hid his mother, sisters, fiancée, and her mother in the mountain fortress of Masada. In 66 C.E. some of the Jewish rebels took refuge here and raided nearby people for their needs. They killed over seven hundred women and children at En Gedi during Passover. The Jewish historian Josephus wrote of Jews who had fled here after the fall of Jerusalem in 70 C.E. When the

Romans besieged them and it was obvious they would take Masada the next day, the Jews preferred suicide to becoming captives. The story, as Josephus developed it, says that when the Roman soldiers entered Masada they found two women and five children who had hidden, and all the rest were dead. Josephus may have created the story in this dramatic way in order to focus the blame for the war on the Sicarii, a small group of revolutionaries, rather than on the Jewish people.

History is always developed within systems of values and presuppositions. Much of the patriarchal history of the world has glorified war and warriors and has defined one side, "our side," as all right while the other side is all wrong. Do memorials of violence and war actually glorify and encourage more violence? Should they instead unmask this addiction? Is killing the enemy a better solution than mediating and negotiating? Early founders of the state of Israel, which was born in the trauma of the Holocaust, have used the story of Masada to build the identity of Israelis as those who would rather die than surrender. Israel has won five wars since the founding of the nation, but it has never won peace. Stories glorifying war do not bring cultures of peace.

Megiddo

Judith

Megiddo is located at the pass through the Carmel mountains, a very important route connecting the continents of Europe, Africa, and Asia for both traders and armies. The excavations reveal fortified cities over 5000 years old. Because so many battles have been fought here, this place is symbolic of the final battle portrayed in Revelation 16:6.

Megiddo is also an appropriate place for remembering Judith. The story of Judith, contained in the Septuagint, or Greek Scripture, is not historical. Hence the places in the story cannot be found. However, it is a very well developed tale of the rescue of Israel's people, and it also resembles the story of David and Goliath. Like David, Judith is much smaller than the leader of the opposition, but she possesses unique skills and, most importantly, God's strength. Like David she carries home the head of the general in order to assure her people not to fear. Below is Judith's prayer that men who have raped women might be punished. This seems to be the only such prayer in the Bible. There are innumerable prayers for military victories as well as a multitude of records of raped women, augmented by imagery of the nation of Israel both as a violated woman and as a harlot. Women's voices crying out against rape are seldom heard in either religious or legal texts.

> 1 Then Judith prostrated herself, put ashes on her head, and uncovered the sackcloth she was wearing. At the very time when the evening incense was being offered in the house of God in Jerusalem, Judith cried out to the Lord with a loud voice, and said, 2 "O Lord God of my ancestor Simeon, to whom you gave a sword to take revenge on those strangers who had torn off a virgin's clothing to defile her, and exposed her thighs to put her to shame, and polluted her womb to disgrace her; for you said, 'It shall not be done'—yet they did it."

> (Read Jdt 9:1-2)

Mizpah, Tel en-Nasbeh
Jephthah's Daughter

In the area of Ramallah, a little north of Gibeon, the ancient city of Mizpah has been excavated by Howard Bade of Pacific School of Religion. Jephthah prayed that God would give him a military victory, promising to sacrifice to God the first person who came out of his house when he returned home. Interpretations of the story of Jephthah's daughter have traditionally centered on the importance of keeping one's vows, as well as on the daughter's support of her father in keeping his vow. Perhaps the story is not an ideal for us to imitate, but is rather a reflection on human imprudence and the willingness to sacrifice anything and anyone for the sake of victory. In the modern world nations pour billions of dollars into the production of weapons while sacrificing the needs of their own children. The daughter in this story went away to grieve, but returned to be sacrificed. Perhaps daughters need to go away and not return, for the unreasonable sacrifices seem to go on and on.

(Read Judg 11:29-40)

Monastery of St. George of Koziba
Wealthy Women and Mary's Intervention

This remote desert place, located on a steep cliff on the Wadi Qilt in the Judean desert, is where Elijah is said to have rested on his way to Sinai. The apocryphal text says that Joachim came here and wept because his wife Anne was sterile. Then an angel announced that they would have a child, who was to be Mary, the mother of Jesus. Hermits began living here in the 420s, and eventually a monastery was founded in 480. The monastery has been known for its hospitality—even to women.

> A wealthy Byzantine noblewoman, suffering from an incurable disease, decided to go to Jerusalem to pray for a cure. Having visited the Holy City she went to the Jordan, and made a tour of the monasteries, offering gifts and asking prayer of the monks for healing. As her litter was being carried up the Ascent of Saint Zaccheus, she had a vision of the Mother of God, who said to her, "Why, noble lady, do you go about everywhere and yet do not enter my house?" She replied, "Where is your house, my Lady, that I may enter it?" The Mother of God said, "When you reach the place called Pepingia, my house is below the valley." "I have heard," replied the noblewoman, "that women may not go there." "Go down," said the Blessed One, "I will introduce you." When the noblewoman arrived at the monastery, although monks were at prayer, the door was open. When the monks emerged, they were enraged to find a woman in the inner court. After she explained the circumstances, the superior went to counsel with the senior monks, and concluded, "This is from the Mother of God. We can do nothing!" He had her litter placed in the sacristy. At the sound of the night office she rose, completely cured, and gave thanks to Our Lady.[12]

Mount Carmel and Haifa

Abigail, a Mediator

Ancient Phoenicians and Romans considered this lovely area near the Bay of Haifa to be a sacred place. In this century the people of the Baha'i faith, who believe in the unity of all people and try to foster peace, have built their main center in Haifa.

Abigail (Mount Carmel and Haifa Area)

Scripture does not mention where Abigail and Nabal, her first husband, lived, but their flocks pastured in the Carmel area. The story of her first marriage echoes that of many people in marriages where drinking and abuse abounds. This woman, who shared her food in order to prevent violence, needs to be studied not just as the wife of David, but as one who offers an enduring model of wisdom. Dorothee Sölle writes, "Her speech practically disables David legally. She cleverly points at the presents that she has brought along for David's soldiers, but her religious argument is even more eloquent: so far God has saved David from staining his hands with blood and he will continue to establish and strengthen his rule without David having to resert to evil or vengeful acts."[13]

> 32 David said to Abigail, "Blessed be the LORD, the God of Israel, who sent you to meet me today! 33 Blessed be your good sense, and blessed be you, who have kept me today from bloodguilt and from avenging myself by my own hand! 34 For as surely as the LORD the God of Israel lives, who has restrained me from hurting you, unless you had hurried and come to meet me, truly by morning there would not have been left to Nabal so much as one male." 35 Then David received from her hand what she had brought him; he said to her, "Go up to your house in peace; see, I have heeded your voice, and I have granted your petition."
>
> (Read 1 Sam 25:2-42)

(See the Appendix for more on Abigail as a figure of wisdom.)

Cave of el-Khader, the School of the Prophets

The Widow of the Guild Prophet

At this place where Elijah has been remembered since the third century C.E., the mosque was made into a synagogue in 1948. Another cave associated with Elijah is located near the Carmelite monastery. Druzes, Muslims, and Christians gather there July 19–20 for prayer. Elisha, who followed in Elijah's footsteps, is also remembered in the Carmel area. After she shared her food with the prophet Elisha, the widow's generosity was rewarded in turn by God's generosity, which never runs out.

> 1 Now the wife of a member of the company of prophets cried to Elisha, "Your servant my husband is dead; and you know that your servant feared the LORD, but a creditor has come to take my two children as slaves."
>
> (Read 2 Kings 4:1-7)

Mount Gerizim near Nablus

A Beloved Daughter and Wife

The Samaritan woman who spoke to Jesus at the well referred to the temple of her people. Some of the ruins of the temple as well as those of a church can be seen on Mount Gerizim. Josephus wrote of both a father's and a husband's care for a Samaritan woman. In cultures in which political alliances were usually more important than love in marriages this is a touching story of a cross-cultural marriage that held together in spite of social pressure.

In the late fourth century B.C.E. Manasseh was the priest of the Temple in Jerusalem, the brother of the high priest. He accepted as his wife Nicaso, the daughter of Sanballat, the leader of the Samaritans, who hoped thereby to forge an alliance between his people and the Jews. The authorities in Jerusalem were scandalized, and demanded that Manasseh choose between his foreign wife and his priestly office. If he retained her as wife, he could no longer officiate at the altar. Although deeply in love, Manasseh seriously considered divorce. Emotionally he could not surrender the priestly office that was the hereditary dignity of his family. When Sanballat became aware that his daughter might be repudiated, he promised Manasseh that if he followed his heart he would make him high priest of the Samaritans, and would build for him on Mount Gerizim a temple like that in Jerusalem. Many of the priests in Jerusalem whose marital situations paralleled that of Manasseh followed him to Samaria.[14]

Mount Hermon or Mount Tabor

Woman Who Recognizes the Christ

Associating the story of the Transfiguration with Mount Tabor seems to be a mistake, since the other events of Mark's gospel would place it farther north in the area of Mount Hermon. Mark's gospel does have a geographical pattern, while Luke's has a pattern of ideas, but not accurate geography. However, Tabor is a place where pilgrims have remembered the story since the fourth century. Both Greek Orthodox and Latin Catholics have sanctuaries on the mountain, which has a spectacular view.

While pilgrims seem to have mistaken the place of the Transfiguration, the disciples appear to have mistaken what Jesus' mission as the Christ, the anointed one of God, really was. Immediately before the Transfiguration and twice after, Jesus kept explaining that he was to serve, to suffer, and to die (Mark 8:27-38; 9:30-32; 10:32-45). In Mark's gospel it was a woman who understood the identity of Christ and he praised her, saying that wherever the gospel would be preached, what she had done would be told in memory of her. Unfortunately, as Elisabeth Schüssler Fiorenza has pointed out in *In Memory of Her,* the woman's name was not even recorded; so also, women's history has been neglected.

> 3 While he was at Bethany in the house of Simon the leper, as he sat at the table, a woman came with an alabaster jar of very costly ointment of nard, and she broke open the jar and poured the ointment on his head.
>
> (Read Mark 14:3-9)

Nablus, or Shechem

Paula's Experiences at Shechem

Sarah and Abraham came to this area in about 1850 B.C.E. Sixteen centuries later, the Samaritans built their own temple on Mount Gerizim. This is Jerome's description of Paula's visit in the 380s C.E.:

What shall I say about Shiloh where a ruined altar is still shewn to-day (sic), and where the tribe of Benjamin antici-pated Romulus in the rape of the Sabine women? Passing by Shechem (not Sychar as many wrongly read) or as it is now called Neapolis, she entered the church built upon the side of Mount Gerizim around Jacob's well; that well where the Lord was sitting when hungry and thirsty. He was refreshed by the faith of the woman of Samaria. Forsaking her five hus-bands by whom are intended the five books of Moses, and that sixth not a husband of whom she boasted, to wit the false teacher Dositheus, she found the true Messiah and the true Saviour. Turning away thence Paula saw the tombs of the twelve patriarchs, and Samaria which in honour of Au-gustus Herod renamed Augusta or in Greek Sebaste. There lie the prophets Elisha and Obadiah and John the Baptist than whom there is not a greater among those that are born of women. And here she was filled with terror by the mar-vels she beheld; for she saw demons screaming under differ-ent tortures before the tombs of the saints, and men howling like wolves, baying like dogs, roaring like lions, hissing like serpents and bellowing like bulls. They twisted their heads and bent them backwards until they touched the ground; women too were suspended head downward and their clothes did not fall off. Paula pitied them all, and shedding tears over them prayed Christ to have mercy on them. And weak as she was she climbed the mountain on foot; for in two of its caves Obadiah in a time of persecution and famine had fed a hundred prophets with bread and water.

(PAULA, 148–49)

Jacob's Well

Rachel, Leah, and the Samaritan Woman

On the outskirts of Nablus is an ancient well, now in a Greek Orthodox shrine. It was here that Jacob met Rachel, who tended her father's sheep. Shepherdesses like Rachel can be seen in the area today. The story of Rachel and her sister Leah indicates the pain that can come when women are valued more for child bearing then for themselves.

> 9 While he was still speaking with them, Rachel came with her father's sheep; for she kept them. 10 Now when Jacob saw Rachel, the daughter of his mother's brother Laban, and the sheep of his mother's brother Laban, Jacob went up and rolled the stone from the well's mouth, and watered the flock

of his mother's brother Laban. 11 Then Jacob kissed Rachel, and wept aloud. 12 And Jacob told Rachel that he was her father's kinsman, and that he was Rebekah's son; and she ran and told her father.   (Read Gen 29:9-32)

John's gospel has women in central roles. For example, he tells us that the Samaritan woman goes to proclaim the man who had revealed himself to her as the Messiah. In about 380 a church with a baptistry was built here. Crusaders wrote of Benedictine sisters taking care of the well in 1175. Perhaps Queen Melisande, who was exiled to Nablus in 1152, had supported them:

> 39 Many Samaritans from that city believed in him because of the woman's testimony, "He told me everything I have ever done." 40 So when the Samaritans came to him, they asked him to stay with them; and he stayed there two days. 41 And many more believed because of his word. 42 They said to the woman, "It is no longer because of what you said that we believe, for we have heard for ourselves, and we know that this is truly the Savior of the world."
>   (Read John 4:19-42)

Nain

The Shunammite Woman

Jesus' gift of life to the son of the widow of Nain mirrors the miracle of Elisha in Shumen, which is across from Nain. The Shunammite woman was kind to the prophet. When her son died, she begged Elisha's help.

> 8 One day Elisha was passing through Shunem, where a wealthy woman lived, who urged him to have a meal. So whenever he passed that way, he would stop there for a meal. 9 She said to her husband, "Look, I am sure that this man who regularly passes our way is a holy man of God. 10 Let us make a small roof chamber with walls, and put there for him a bed, a table, a chair, and a lamp, so that he can stay there whenever he comes to us."   (Read 2 Kings 4:8-37)

The Widow of Nain

The people of Nain were taking the only son of a widow to be buried

> 13 When the Lord saw her, he had compassion for her and said to her, "Do not weep." 14 Then he came forward and

touched the bier, and the bearers stood still. And he said, "Young man, I say to you, rise!" 15 The dead man sat up and began to speak, and Jesus gave him to his mother. 16 Fear seized all of them; and they glorified God, saying, "A great prophet has risen among us!" and "God has looked favorably on his people!"

(Read Luke 7:11-17)

Nazareth

The Annunciation

St. Gabriel's Greek Orthodox Church, where the Annunciation is remembered, is at the site of a well. Since getting water was a main part of the workday of ancient women, many legends have placed Mary's meeting with the angel Gabriel near a well. As in Jerusalem, the largest and most continuous Christian group in the area is the Greek Orthodox.

Egeria the pilgrim as well as Paula and Jerome visited Nazareth and were impressed with the cave where Mary was said to have lived. Over this cave is built the modern Franciscan Church, with extensive art work from all over the world depicting Mary. This is Jerome's description of Paula's visit in Galilee:

> Then she passed quickly through Nazareth the nursery of the Lord; Cana and Capernaum familiar with the signs wrought by Him; the lake of Tiberias sanctified by His voyages upon it; the wilderness where countless Gentiles were satisfied with a few loaves while the twelve baskets of the tribes of Israel were filled with the fragments left by them that had eaten. She made the ascent of mount Tabor whereon the Lord was transfigured. In the distance she beheld the range of Hermon; and the wide stretching plains of Galilee where Sisera and all his host had once been overcome by Barak; and the torrent Kishon separating the level ground into two parts. Near by also the town of Nain was pointed out to her, where the widow's son was raised. Time would fail me sooner than speech were I to recount all the places to which the revered Paula was carried by her incredible faith.

(PAULA, 149)

The Qu'ran, the collection of the sacred texts of Islam, mentions Mary over thirty times, more often than the Bible does. Submission to God's will is central to the Islamic faith, and Mary is the paragon of such obedience. The Qu'ran tells of

Zechariah and Elizabeth, the parents of John the Baptist (compare Luke 1:5-25) and Mary (compare Luke 2:26).

There did Zacharius pray to his Lord. He said: My Lord grant me from Thee goodly offspring; surely Thou art the Hearer of prayer.

So the angels called to him as he stood praying in the sanctuary: Allah gives Thee the good news of John, verifying a word from Allah, and honorable and chaste and a prophet from among the good ones.

He said: My lord how can I have a son when old age has already come upon me, and my wife is barren? He said: Even thus does Allah do what he pleases.

He said: My Lord appoint a sign for me. Said He: Thy sign is that thou speak not to men for three days except by signs. And remember thy Lord much and glorify (Him) in the evening and early morning.

Section 5 : Birth of Jesus and His Ministry

And when the angels said: O Mary, surely Allah has chosen thee and purified thee and chosen thee above the women of the world.

O Mary, be obedient to thy Lord and humble thyself and bow down with those who bow.

This is of the tidings of things unseen which We reveal to thee. And thou was not with them when they cast their pens (to decide) which of them should have Mary in his charge, and thou was not with them when they contended one with another.

When the angels said: O Mary, surely Allah gives you good news with a word from Him (of one) whose name is the Messiah, Jesus, son of Mary, worthy of regard in this world and the Hereafter, and of those who are drawn nigh (to Allah).

And he will speak to the people when in the cradle and when of old age, and (he will be) one of the good ones.

She said: My Lord, how can I have a son and man has not yet touched me? He said: Even so; Allah creates what He pleases. When He decrees a matter, He only says to it, Be, and it is.

And He will teach him the Book of Wisdom and the Torah and the Gospel:

And (make him) a messenger to the children of Israel (saying): I have come to you with a sign from your Lord, that I determine for you out of dust the form of a bird, then I breathe into it and it becomes a bird with Allah's permission, and I heal the blind and the leprous, and bring the dead to life with Allah's permission; and I inform you of what you should eat and what you should store in your houses. Surely there is a sign in this for you, if you are believers.[15]

Melkite Church

This church has in its complex a building that has been a synagogue. Pilgrims commemorate Luke 4:16-30, the story of Jesus in the synagogue of Nazareth, there but the structure is not actually that old. The Byzantine liturgy of the church has this very poetic reflection, which is used for the Feast of the Presentation of the Lord:

At Vespers

At the Lamp-lighting Psalms (Sixth Tone)

1 and 2: Gabriel came to you, O Maiden, and disclosed God's plan which was from all eternity. He joyfully offered you his greetings and cried out: "Hail, O land without human seed! Hail, O bush untouched by fire! Hail, O depth no human eye can fathom! Hail, O bridge that leads up to heaven! Hail, O fleece receiving the heavenly manna! Hail, O dissolution of the curse! Hail, O Maiden who returned Adam to grace! The Lord is with you." (Twice)

3 and 4: The virginal Maiden replied to the Captain of the heavenly hosts and said: "You come to me in human form; why then do you speak in words beyond human understanding, saying, 'The Lord is with you,' and 'The Lord will dwell in your womb'? Explain to me how I am to become a spacious vessel, a dwelling place of holiness for the One who is above the Cherubim. Mislead me not, for I know no pleasure of the body nor do I know man: How then shall I give birth to a Son?" (Twice)

5 and 6: The Bodiless One answered the Maiden and said: "Whenever God so desires, He can overcome the laws of nature: what is impossible to man may be accomplished by Him. Wherefore, O Woman most holy and pure, believe the truth of my word." She answered and said: "Be it done to me according to your word, and I will give birth to the Bodiless One who will take flesh from me, so that by his union with a body, man may be raised to the original state of grace, for He is almighty." (Twice)[16]

Negev

Hagar

The Makhtest Ramon Visitors' Center, with its displays on the natural history of the Negev, includes exhibits on the wilderness. The biblical narrative again and again mentions the wilderness. When Hagar was thrown out by Abraham and Sarah, who were near Hebron, she went south toward her country and toward Param. Muslim women sometimes describe Hagar as the woman cared for by God when people mistreated her. God was speaking to Abraham:

> 13 "As for the son of the slave woman, I will make a nation of him also, because he is your offspring." 14 So Abraham rose early in the morning, and took bread and a skin of

water, and gave it to Hagar, putting it on her shoulder, along with the child, and sent her away. And she departed, and wandered about in the wilderness of Beer-sheba. 15 When the water in the skin was gone, she cast the child under one of the bushes. 16 Then she went and sat down opposite him a good way off, about the distance of a bowshot; for she said, "Do not let me look on the death of the child." And as she sat opposite him, she lifted up her voice and wept.

(Read Gen 21:8-21)

Qasrin Park

Wisdom, a Woman Who Nurtures

In the Golan area, ancient Qasrin Park contains both excavations of a well-preserved synagogue and reconstructions of a Jewish village from the late fourth to the eighth centuries C.E. The home and its furnishings, particularly those of the kitchen, reveal the places where ordinary women of the time worked and lived. Orthodox Jewish women who keep kosher are "ritual experts." Preparing food and keeping the home are sacred actions through which women can know the presence of God. The synagogue and the home, the so-called male and female spheres respectively, can help one to reflect on the ways women experience intimacy with the divine.

In some Wisdom literature God is personified as a woman. The wise woman generously nourishes all. (See the Appendix on Abigail as a wise woman.)

> 1 Whoever fears the Lord will do this,
> and whoever holds to the law will obtain wisdom.
> 2 She will come to meet him like a mother,
> and like a young bride she will welcome him.
> 3 She will feed him with the bread of learning,
> and give him the water of wisdom to drink.
>
> (Read Sir 15:1-10)

Qumran

God Like a Loving Mother

In approximately 150 B.C.E. the Teacher of Righteousness and fifty Essenes seeking a more devout life settled here. They shared work and goods, had common prayers and meals, and made papyrus near the Dead Sea. One can still see the site of the scriptorium where they worked. It is not clear to what extent women participated in the reading, writing, and around-the-clock study of the Torah, which was an important part of the Essene lifestyle. Women do not necessarily have equal opportunities, and ancient stereotyping still persists. In the modern world two-thirds of the illiterate are females.

The isolated desert environment, with its dry climate, preserved many of the scrolls made by the Essenes until they were found in 1947. Among them was the oldest known text of Isaiah, which contained the poignant words, "Comfort my people, O comfort them." The community of Essenes, which was to be democratic in decision making, settled problems through discussion in a counsel chamber that still can be seen today. Were women allowed to be a part of the democratic process or, as in Greece, was democracy only for the men? Women and children were about a fourth of the population, according to the evidence of the tombs that have been excavated. Some of the literature of Qumran is negative toward women and sexuality. In the first century B.C.E., however, someone at Qumran wrote this prayer, which addresses God as both father and mother:

> . . . my mother did not know me,
> and my father abandoned me to you.
> Because you are father to all the sons of your truth.
> In them you rejoice,
> like one full of gentleness for her child,
> and like a wet-nurse,
> you clutch to your chest all your creatures.[17]

Ramallah Women's Center

God the Seamstress

The Society of Inash El-Usra, which means "The Revival of the Family," has a center in El Bireh in the Ramallah area. This contemporary center has a museum displaying Palestinian arts and crafts, a library, and the women's cooperative, offering sewing, canning, and other work opportunities. Women continue to have unequal economic opportunities globally. In the twenty-first century women perform two-thirds of the work hours of the world, but receive only about ten percent of the world's income. In societies where there have been political upheavals or displacements women often carry extra burdens.

Sewing women are like God, the God of creation who clothed Adam and Eve (Gen 3:21). They are like the God of the

Exodus who saw that the wandering people in the wilderness did not go without clothes (Neh 9:20-21). They are like the God of celebration who clothes creation in beauty.

> 27 Consider the lilies, how they grow: they neither toil nor spin; yet I tell you, even Solomon in all his glory was not clothed like one of these. 28 But if God so clothes the grass of the field, which is alive today and tomorrow is thrown into the oven, how much more will he clothe you—you of little faith!
>
> (Read Luke 12:27-28)

Ramat el-Khalil (see **Mamre**)

Samaria (Shomeron)

The Daughter in a Broken Marriage

Extensive ruins reveal the prominence of this city that Herod the Great renamed Sebaste. The head of John the Baptist is said to be buried in a church here. John the Baptist was baptizing at Aenon near Salim, about five kilometers from Nablus. Herod Antipas, son of Herod the Great, married Herodias, the wife of his brother, and John the Baptist told him that this was not right. Herod resented this remark and imprisoned John.

When parents separate, divorce, or have extramarital affairs, children sometimes suffer in complicated social situations. Although Western patriarchal literature, painting, and dance have portrayed the daughter of Herodias as an evil, seductive woman, the biblical story itself needs to be re-examined.[18] Did the daughter miss her real father? How did she feel about Herod, her mother's new lover? How did she feel about dancing at a party for him? How did the girl feel about her mother exploiting her talent to bring about this brutal murder?

> 24 She went out and said to her mother, "What should I ask for?" She replied, "The head of John the baptizer." 25 Immediately she rushed back to the king and requested, "I want you to give me at once the head of John the Baptist on a platter."
>
> (Read Mark 6:19-29)

Tel Balata or Shechem

Dinah

The ruins of the tel indicate a sixteenth-century B.C.E. city state that was one of the main centers of population in the area.

There Jacob and his family settled. Dinah, the daughter of Leah and Jacob, was raped by the son of the chief of the region of Shechem. Her father was afraid of the people of the locality. Her brothers Simeon and Levi pretended that they would live peacefully with the inhabitants if the men would be circumcised as the people of the covenant were. Then, when the men were in pain from the circumcision, Simeon and Levi attacked them, killed them all, and seized their wives and property. As with other stories of rape in the Bible, it is not clear if the brothers are concerned about the feelings and well-being of their sister, or just about the disgrace of their property being used without their permission. Dinah is never again mentioned in Scripture. Some scholars believe that when the aged Jacob spoke of Simeon and Levi as violent he was alluding to this episode (Gen 49:5-7).

> 1 Now Dinah the daughter of Leah, whom she had borne to Jacob, went out to visit the women of the region. 2 When Shechem son of Hamor the Hivite, prince of the region, saw her, he seized her and lay with her by force.
>
> (Read Gen 34:1-13)

Sea of Galilee

Wisdom, a Creator

The lake, which is about 21 by 12 kilometers, is both a lovely spot and an image for the ministry of Jesus. Christian Scriptures connect Christ with the figure of Wisdom sent by God. While the historical Jesus was a male, the resurrected Christ transcends genders and includes all. Christ Sophia is an all-embracing image of the wisdom of the Holy One touching and transforming creation. John's gospel uses many of the images from this poetic passage from Wisdom literature, written in Jerusalem about two hundred years before Jesus lived:

> 3 I came forth from the mouth of the Most High,
>   and covered the earth like a mist.
> 4 I dwelt in the highest heavens,
>   and my throne was in a pillar of cloud.
> 5 Alone I compassed the vault of heaven
>   and traversed the depths of the abyss.
> 6 Over waves of the sea, over all the earth,
>   and over every people and nation I have held sway.
>
> (Read Sir 24:3-22)

Sepphoris (Zippori)

Women Who Host Banquets

When Herod Antipas had this city rebuilt he needed many artisans. Perhaps the opportunity for work drew Joseph and Mary to the area. While some scholars believe that Joseph and Jesus did construction work here, others believe that good Jews would not have mixed with the Hellenized population. The excavations reveal a theater with a wonderful view and a home with a magnificent mosaic in the dining room. The triclinium, or U-shaped arrangement in which diners reclined on the floor, reveals eating customs of the period. It is probable that Jesus and his disciples had this arrangement at the Last Supper. The mosaic contains images of Dionysus, the god of celebration and life, and other mythological figures. At the place where a hostess would normally sit is a well-preserved mosaic of a lovely woman. The atmosphere of beauty and joy in this dining room invites reflection on the centrality of meals in human experience and the image of the divine as the lady Wisdom who nourishes others.

> 1 Wisdom has built her house,
>   she has hewn her seven pillars.
> 2 She has slaughtered her animals, she has mixed her wine,
>   she has also set her table.
> 3 She has sent out her servant-girls, she calls
>   from the highest places in the town,
> 4 "You that are simple, turn in here!"
>   To those without sense she says,
> 5 "Come, eat of my bread
>   and drink of the wine I have mixed.
> 6 Lay aside immaturity, and live,
>   and walk in the way of insight."

(Read Prov 9:1-6)

Shepherds' Fields in Beit Sahour near Bethlehem

Mary, the Mother of the Lamb and the Shepherd

The Greek Orthodox community has the only fifth-century church outside of Jerusalem that has survived in good condition. It was built so that pilgrims would remember what was said to be the place where the angels appeared to the shepherds, announcing the birth of Christ. The church is over a cave that was used for worship in the fourth century. The shepherds are said to be buried here. Egeria wrote of being shown a cave that contained an altar for worship located near where the shepherds lived. A monastery of nuns was founded here, but in 614 the Persians killed the hundred nuns. These prayers are used for December 31, "The Leave-taking of the Nativity of the Lord," in the Byzantine rite. The prayer book explains the image of Mary used.

> The Byzantine-Greek expression "Parrēsia" designates the right free citizens had to speak in the legislative assembly and before a court of justice, where they could defend themselves against an accusation or appeal to a higher authority for revision of a sentence imposed upon them. In parliament and before the courts, free men wore the "stole": a sleeveless robe, open on both sides. Slaves and young boys were not allowed to wear it: they were naked *(gymnoi),* stripped of the right to speak in public. Before the throne of God, the Virgin acts as a "stole" for men enslaved by sin: for mankind is "naked" since original sin (cf. Gen 3:7).
>
> THE SHEPHERDS heard the angels singing hymns of praise to the coming of Christ in the flesh. And running to Him as to a shepherd, they saw him as a spotless Lamb grazing at Mary's breast. They sang a hymn to her and said:
>
> Hail, O Mother of Lamb and Shepherd;
>> hail, O Fold of rational sheep!
> Hail, O Protection against unseen foes;
>> hail, O Key to the doors of Paradise!
> Hail, for the heavenly rejoice with the earth;
>> hail, for the earthly meet the heavens in song!
> Hail, the unsilenced Voice of Apostles!
>> hail, the undaunted Might of Martyrs!
> Hail, O steadfast Foundation of faith;
>> hail, O shining Emblem of grace!
> Hail, O you through whom Hades was despoiled;
>> hail, O you through whom we were clothed with glory!
> V. Hail, O Bride and Maiden ever-pure!
> R. Hail, O Bride and Maiden ever-pure![19]

Nearby, the Franciscans have a Roman Catholic church with ruins of a fourth-century monastery marking where nomadic shepherds stayed in the first century.

> 8 In that region there were shepherds living in the fields, keeping watch over their flock by night. 9 Then an angel of the Lord stood before them, and the glory of the Lord shone around them, and they were terrified.
>
> (Read Luke 2:8-19)

Shiloh (Khirbet Seilûn)

Women as Property

In the time of the Judges, maidens went to dance at Shiloh to celebrate the harvest. The other eleven tribes of Israel who had killed the women of the tribe of Benjamin told the Benjaminite men to abduct these dancing maidens to be their wives so that the tribe would continue. Six hundred women were raped as part of the cycle of violence following the raping of the concubine. (See **Latrun** for more of the story.)

Throughout history men have raped women during and after battles, and it is often viewed as a "natural" act, namely as a way of further demeaning the opponent. Three thousand years have passed since this story was first recorded, and only now is there a movement to define rape as a "war crime" and unacceptable as part of "fair war."

> 20 And they instructed the Benjaminites, saying, "Go and lie in wait in the vineyards, 21 and watch; when the young women of Shiloh come out to dance in the dances, then come out of the vineyards and each of you carry off a wife for himself from the young women of Shiloh, and go to the land of Benjamin."

(Read Judg 21:15-23)

Hannah

Hannah longed and prayed for a child at Shiloh. Her deep faith and desire for a child burst forth in her canticle. Her prayer is a prototype for the canticle of Mary, the Magnificat, in Luke's gospel. God lifts up the poor and the needy.

> 3 Talk no more so very proudly,
>   let not arrogance come from your mouth;
> for the LORD is a God of knowledge,
>   and by him actions are weighed.
> 4 The bows of the mighty are broken,
>   but the feeble gird on strength.
> 5 Those who were full have hired themselves out for bread,
>   but those who were hungry are fat with spoil.
> The barren has borne seven,
>   but she who has many children is forlorn.

(Read 1 Sam 1:9–2:1)

The first temple built for the Ark of the Covenant was here before David centralized worship in Jerusalem. People made pilgrimages to Shiloh until the Philistines took the Ark.

Solomon's Pools
The Delights of Love

These ancient reservoirs near Bethlehem, which once supplied water for it and Jerusalem, do not date back to Solomon, but they do create an atmosphere fit for a king and a queen. This area is a fitting place to reflect on the love poetry of Scripture known as the Song of Solomon or Song of Songs.

The text repeatedly addresses the "daughters of Jerusalem" and is in the form of a collection of love poems with lines labeled for the bride, the groom, or the daughters of Jerusalem. The woman speaks eighty-one verses in comparison to the forty-nine attributed to the man. The woman initiates in work and in love-making. She describes the mutuality of the love, "My lover is mine, and I am his," a challenging statement in a culture in which men had the right to divorce, but women had no corresponding right because women were to belong to men. The mother is mentioned seven times, the father not at all. This probably indicates a matriarchal or matrilineal sense even in the midst of a tradition focused on fathers and sons. Were these songs first used at gatherings of women where they sang and danced, looking forward to the coming wedding? Other ancient Middle Eastern love poetry, such as a text from Sumer in about 1920 B.C.E., has active, passionate women celebrating the goodness of love.

> 1 Where has your beloved gone,
>   O fairest among women?
> Which way has your beloved turned,
>   that we may seek him with you?
> 2 My beloved has gone down to his garden,
>   to the beds of spices,
> to pasture his flock in the gardens,
>   and to gather lilies.
> 3 I am my beloved's and my beloved is mine;
>   he pastures his flock among the lilies.
>
> (Read Song 6:1-12)

Tabgha (see **Heptapegon**)

Tekoa

The Wise Woman of Tekoa

This village, only a few miles from the Herodion, was the home of a woman who challenged David. This wise woman, like the prophet Nathan, told David a story to try to teach him. Like the woman who spoke to King Solomon to save the life of her child, this wise woman spoke to David in an effort to save the life of Absalom.

> 4 When the woman of Tekoa came to the king, she fell on her face to the ground and did obeisance, and said, "Help, O king!" 5 The king asked her, "What is your trouble?" She answered, "Alas, I am a widow; my husband is dead. 6 Your servant had two sons, and they fought with one another in the field; there was no one to part them, and one struck the other and killed him. 7 Now the whole family has risen against your servant. They say, 'Give up the man who struck his brother, so that we may kill him for the life of his brother whom he murdered, even if we destroy the heir as well.' Thus they would quench my one remaining ember, and leave to my husband neither name nor remnant on the face of the earth."
>
> (Read 2 Sam 14:4-21)

Tel Arad

People Whose Sacred Space Has Been Closed

Extensive excavations reveal this city that flourished in 2900 B.C.E. The layout of the houses, temples, city walls, and well reveals a plan for conserving the water supply in this very hot area. People raised animals, traded, and eventually developed a prosperous trade, producing pitch with chemicals from the nearby Dead Sea. Later, when the Israelites lived here, they built a Holy of Holies with an altar of sacrifice, the reconstruction of which can be seen today. King Hezekiah wanted to centralize worship in Jerusalem and had the sanctuary closed. While centralizing a religion may be good, organizational and institutional aspects of a religious system should not be confused with a personal or community relationship with the divine. The worship place of believers is sometimes closed by external authorities. Rafael Patai in *The Hebrew Goddess* analyzes some of the political domination interwoven with Hebrew relationships with the divine. Spaces where women initiate worship are often closed or disparaged.

Tel Aviv-Jaffa (Yafo)

Dorcas, or Tabitha

Antiquities Museum of Tel Aviv and the Excavations at St. Peter's Church

This area near the Mediterranean has been inhabited since about 5000 B.C.E., and the seaport has attracted many invaders, including the Egyptians, who wrote of it in 1468 B.C.E.

Peter was staying in Lydda, about 18 kilometers inland from Joppa, when grieving friends of Dorcas asked him to come to where she had died. She was known for her assistance to the poor and her fine needlework. Peter came and said "Tabitha, arise," and she got up to continue serving others.

This book is an attempt to invite ancient women to arise so that their spirits of generosity and wisdom may touch and empower people today.

> 38 Since Lydda was near Joppa, the disciples, who heard that Peter was there, sent two men to him with the request, "Please come to us without delay." 39 So Peter got up and went with them; and when he arrived, they took him to the room upstairs. All the widows stood beside him, weeping and showing tunics and other clothing that Dorcas had made while she was with them.
>
> (Read Acts 9:36-43)

Tel Beer Sheva

Sarah, Who Is Repeatedly Used by Abraham

The Museum of the Negev, the reconstructed horned altar, the excavated tel and its well give much information about ancient life. Such wells were important for pastoral nomads. Abraham made a treaty with Abimelech, negotiating water rights. Bedouin people who dwell in the Middle East today have customs and laws similar to those of the nomadic people of biblical times. They are known for their hospitality, and continue to raise sheep, goats, and camels.

Genesis tells a story twice of Abraham (and once of Isaac) in which the patriarch, fearing that a ruler or chieftain will kill

him because the rival covets his beautiful wife, protects himself by saying that his wife is really his sister. In one of the stories Sarah is taken into the harem of the Pharaoh in Egypt and must be rescued by divine intervention. The next story concerns Abimelech:

> 1 From there Abraham journeyed toward the region of the Negeb, and settled between Kadesh and Shur. While residing in Gerar as an alien, 2 Abraham said of his wife Sarah, "She is my sister." And King Abimelech of Gerar sent and took Sarah. 3 But God came to Abimelech in a dream by night, and said to him, "You are about to die because of the woman whom you have taken; for she is a married woman."
> (Read Gen 20:1-18)

The Bible often deals with stories of God working through the wombs of women. God closed the wombs of all those in the house of Abimelech until Sarah was released (Gen 20:1-18). God also took care of another mistreated woman, Leah. Her father had deceptively passed her off to Jacob, who loved her sister, Rachel. "When the LORD saw that Leah was unloved, he opened her womb," and she had four children (Gen 29:31). Hannah, though loved by her husband, suffered from barrenness and taunting by another wife. God remembers Hannah and she conceives (1 Sam. 1:1-20). Job, Jeremiah, and the psalmist all speak of God molding people in the wombs (Job 3:1-3, 11 and 31:13-15; Jer 20:14-18; Pss 22:9-10; 139:13-16).

Tel Dan

Ruth and Naomi

The beautiful nature preserve of Tel Dan includes one of the headstreams of the Jordan river. The tel clearly reveals two ancient gates. One is the only Middle Bronze Age gate to remain intact, and the other is from the ninth-century Israelite city. Gates were main places for settling legal matters, trading, and socializing. Sometimes Scripture uses "gate" to mean the town council. Though the story of Ruth took place in the Bethlehem area, the complex of the gates with openings and benches here gives one an idea of the scene of Boaz at the city gate getting a decision about who had rights or obligations to Ruth, the widow and Moabite.

> 1 No sooner had Boaz gone up to the gate and sat down there than the next-of-kin, of whom Boaz had spoken, came passing by. So Boaz said, "Come over, friend; sit down here." And he went over and sat down. 2 Then Boaz took ten men of the elders of the city, and said, "Sit down here"; so they sat down.
>
> (Read Ruth 1:1-12)

Tulul Abu el Aliaq, Herod's Palace

Herod's Daughter

Cleopatra, to whom Mark Antony gave the important oasis of Jericho, leased this area to Herod the Great, who built another palace here. Once when Herod fainted in the bath here he heard his servants rejoicing that their cruel master was dead.

He had a hundred respected Jewish leaders imprisoned and ordered that when he did actually die, all of them were to be killed. This would assure that there would be some mourning at the time of his death. He did die at this palace, five days after killing his eldest son and heir. His daughter stopped Herod's soldiers from executing the hundred people.

Notes

[1] *The Life of Maria the Harlot, niece of Abraham the Hermit,* written by the Archdeacon Ephraim, translated into Latin by an anonymous translator. *MPL* 73, cols. 651-60 (BHL 12). English translation in Benedicta Ward, *Harlots of the Desert. A Study of Repentance in Early Monastic Sources* (London: Mowbray, 1987) 97–99.

[2] *b.Moʿed Qaṭ* 17a, as cited in Leonard Swidler, *Biblical Affirmations of Women* (Philadelphia: Westminister, 1979) 109.

[3] *b.Ketub.* 104a as cited in ibid., 109.

[4] Rivka Gonen. *To the Tombs of the Righteous: Pilgrimage in Contemporary Israel* (Jerusalem: The Israel Museum, 1998) 77.

[5] Most Rev. Joseph Reyna and Baron José de Vinck, *Byzantine Daily Worship* (Allendale, N.Y.: Alleluia Press, 1969) 538–39.

[6] "A Cento" by Faltonia Betitia Proba (*CSEL* 16. 576), in Elizabeth Clark, *Women in the Early Church* (Wilmington: Michael Glazier, 1983) 167–68.

[7] For more information see Martha Ann Kirk, *The Prophetess Led Them in Praise: Women's Stories in Ritual.* Ph.D. dissertation, Graduate Theological Union, Berkeley, California, 1986, 124–28.

[8] Elizabeth Warnock Fernea and Basima Qattan Bezergan, *Middle Eastern Muslim Women Speak* (Austin: University of Texas Press, 1977) 4.

[9] Omar S. Pound, *Arabic and Persian Poems in English* (New York: New Directions, 1970) as cited in Fernea and Bezergan, *Middle Eastern Muslim Women Speak,* 5.

[10] *Didascalia Apostolorum* 3.12.1-13.1, as cited in Barbara Bowe, et al., eds., *Silent Voices, Sacred Lives* (Mahwah, N.J.: Paulist) 156–57.

[11] Benedicta Ward, *The Wisdom of the Desert Fathers: Apophthegmata Patrum from the Anonymous Series* (Oxford: S.L.G. Press, 1975) 18–19.

[12] Anthony of Koziba, *Miracles of the Mother of God at Koziba* 1, as cited in Jerome Murphy-O'Connor, *The Holy Land* (Oxford: Oxford University Press, 1998) 352.

[13] Dorothee Sölle, *Great Women of the Bible in Art and Literature* (Grand Rapids: Eerdmans, 1994) 170.

[14] Josephus, *Antiquities* 11:302-12, as cited in Murphy-O'Connor, *The Holy Land,* 363.

[15] *The Holy Qurʾan* (Columbus: Ahamadiyyah Anjuman Isha at Islam, 1991) 140–41.

[16] Reya and de Vinck, *Byzantine Daily Worship,* 658–59

[17] 1QH XVII 35-36, in Florentino García-Martínez, *The Dead Sea Scrolls Translated: The Qumran Texts in English.* Trans. Wilfred G. E. Watson (2nd ed. Leiden, et al.: Brill; Grand Rapids: Eerdmans, 1996) 350.

[18] For more on biblical women and dance see Martha Ann Kirk, "Biblical Women and Feminist Exegesis: Women Dancing Men's Ideas or Women Dancing Women," 134–50, and Diane Apostolos-Cappadona, "Scriptural Women Who Danced," 95–108 in Doug Adams and Diane Apostolos-Cappadona, eds., *Dance as Religious Studies* (New York: Crossroad, 1990).

[19] Reya and de Vinck, *Byzantine Daily Worship,* 971.

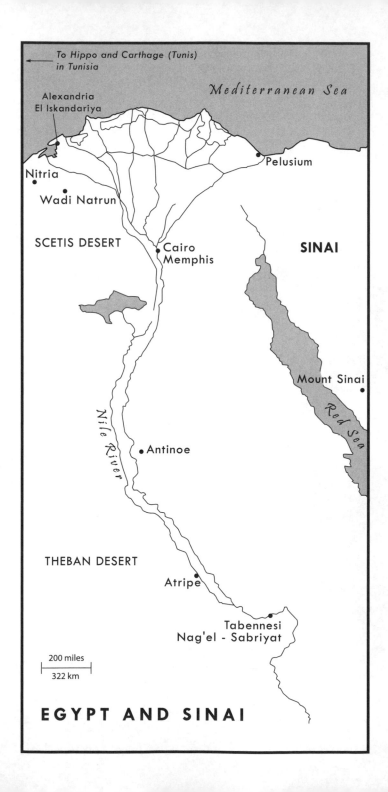

To Hippo and Carthage (Tunis)
in Tunisia

Mediterranean Sea

Alexandria
El Iskandariya

Pelusium

Nitria

Wadi Natrun

SCETIS DESERT

SINAI

Cairo
Memphis

Mount Sinai

Nile River

Red Sea

Antinoe

THEBAN DESERT

Atripe

Tabennesi
Nag'el - Sabriyat

200 miles
322 km

EGYPT AND SINAI

CHAPTER TEN

SINAI, EGYPT, AND TUNISIA

Alexandria, El Iskandariya

Modern Alexandria has been built so that little of the ancient city, established by Alexander the Great in 332 B.C.E., can be seen. The Greco-Roman Museum with 40,000 artifacts helps one imagine its history. Ancient Alexandria was an educational center with a huge library of over 500,000 volumes. It was the greatest center of philosophy in the ancient world, so it is not surprising that much early Christian theology developed there.

The Coptic Church dates its calendar from 284 C.E., when a period of severe persecution began. In the early fourth century Diocletian destroyed churches and, according to Coptic tradition, killed over sixty Christians a day for about five years in a vain attempt to stop the spread of the religion. Monasticism originated in Egypt, spreading across the Middle East and then to Europe. Among the nuns commemorated in Egypt are St. Demiana and the forty virgins who gave their lives for their faith. Though there were many ancient nuns' monasteries, only five of these remain today and all are in Cairo. They include Prince Tadros Monastery in Harit el Rome, the Virgin's Monastery and St. George's Monastery in Harit Zewaila, and Abu Sifan Monastery and St. George Monastery in Masr el Adima. St. Anthony was said to have left his sister with nuns in Alexandria before going to lead a life of prayer in the desert.

Therapeutae and Therapeutrides, Jewish Contemplatives

In the first century C.E. much of the population of Alexandria was Jewish. Near the city lived a community of Jewish ascetic contemplatives. Philo described their monastic lifestyle, somewhat similar to that of the Essenes in Palestine. Though the main teachers were men, women were respected in the community. Dance was an important part of their prayer and Eusebius, the bishop of Caesarea, associated early Christian liturgical dance with the Therapeutae and Therapeutrides.[1] Dance in prayer can be a healing experience helping to integrate body and spirit. Women have often been leaders in religious dance.[2]

> This common sanctuary in which they meet every seventh day is a double enclosure, one portion set apart for the use of the men, the other for the women. For the women too regularly make part of the audience with the same ardour and the same sense of their calling. The wall between the two chambers rises up from the ground to three or four cubits [four and a half to over six feet] built in the form of a breast work, while the space above up to the roof is left open. This arrangement serves two purposes; the modesty becoming to the female sex is preserved, while the women sitting within ear-shot can easily follow what is said since there is nothing to obstruct the voice of the speaker.[3]

> . . .

> The feast is shared by women also, most of them aged virgins, who have kept their chastity not under compulsion, like some of the Greek priestesses, but of their own free will in their ardent yearning for wisdom. Eager to have her for their life mate they have spurned the pleasures of the body and desire no mortal offspring but those immortal children which only the soul that is dear to God can bring to birth unaided because the Father has sown in her spiritual rays enabling her to hold the verities of wisdom.

> The order of reclining is so apportioned that the men sit by themselves on the right and the women by themselves on the left.[4]

> . . .

> After the supper they hold the sacred vigil which is conducted in the following way. They rise up all together and standing in the middle of the refectory form themselves first into two choirs, one of men and one of women, the leader and precentor chosen for each being the most honored amongst them and also the most musical. Then they sing hymns to God composed of many measures and set to many melodies, sometimes chanting together, sometimes taking up the harmony antiphonally, hands and feet keeping time in accompaniment, and rapt with enthusiasm reproduce sometimes the lyrics of the procession,

sometimes of the halt and of the wheeling and counter-wheeling of a choric dance. Then when each choir has separately done its own part in the feast, having drunk as in the Bacchic rites of the strong wine of God's love they mix and both together become a single choir, a copy of the choir set up of old beside the Red Sea in honor of the wonders there wrought . . . . This wonderful sight and experience, an act transcending word and thought and hope, so filled with ecstasy both men and women that forming a single choir they sang hymns of thanksgiving to God their savior, the men led by the prophet Moses and the women by the prophetess Miriam.

It is on this model above all that the choir of the Therapeutae and Therapeutrides, note in response to note, the treble of the women blending with the bass of the men, create an harmonious concert, music in the truest sense.[5]

St. Mark's Coptic Cathedral (Alexandria)

Potamiaena and Basilides

This account from the third century in Alexandria describes the martyrdom of Potamiaena, her mother, and a soldier who was converted by the good example of the heroic women. The description of tortures and a defense of chastity are common themes in martyrdom stories of the period. (See Chapter 1 on the "epic passion" style of writing used.) Eusebius wrote that the soldier between his conversion and his execution was a catechetical student of the famous teacher Origen.

The Martyrdom of Potamiaena and Basilides

Seventh among these [disciples of Origen] should be numbered Basilides, who had led the famous Potamiaena to execution. Even today she is much in honor among her own people. Boundless was the struggle she endured against her lovers in defense of her bodily purity and chastity (in which she was pre-eminent), for the perfection of her body as well as her soul was in full flower. Boundless too were her sufferings, until at last after tortures terrible and horrifying to describe she was consumed by fire with her mother Marcella.

The story goes that her judge, a man named Aquilla, subjected her entire body to cruel torments, and then threatened to hand her over to his gladiators to assault her physically. For a moment the girl reflected, and then when asked what her decision was, she gave some answer which impressed them as being contrary to their religion.

No sooner had she uttered the word and received the sentence of condemnation, when a man named Basilides, who was one of those in the armed services, seized the condemned girl and led her off to execution. The crowd then tried to annoy her and to insult her with vulgar remarks; but Basilides, showing her the utmost pity and kindness, prevented them and drove them off. The girl welcomed the sympathy shown her and urged the man to be of good heart; when she went to her Lord she would pay him back for all he had done for her. After she had said this she nobly endured the end: boiling pitch was slowly poured drop by drop over different parts of her body, from her toes to the top of her head. Such was the struggle that this magnificent young woman endured.

Not long afterwards Basilides for one reason or another was asked by his fellow soldiers to take an oath; but he insisted that he was not at all allowed to do so, since he was a Christian and made no secret of it. For a while they thought at first he was joking; but then when he persistently assured them it was so, he was brought before the magistrate, and when he admitted the situation he was put into prison. His brothers in the Lord came to visit him, and when they questioned him about this strange and sudden turn, he is said to have replied that three days after her martyrdom Potamiaena appeared to him at night and put a crown on his head; she said that she had requested his grace from the Lord and had obtained her prayer, and that she would welcome him before long.

At this his Christian brothers shared with him the Seal of the Lord, and on the next day he was beheaded, eminent in his witness for the Lord. Indeed, in accordance with what has been said many others in Alexandria are reported to have gone over to the word of Christ in a body, after Potamiaena had appeared to them in sleep and called their names. But this must now suffice.[6]

Roman Amphitheater

The Legend of St. Catherine of Alexandria and the History of Hypatia

The legend of St. Catherine says that she was a beautiful and brilliant Christian woman whose learning attracted the educated and important men of the city, even the Emperor Maximianus. When her intelligent arguments prevailed over those of the male pagan philosophers they wanted her killed for her faith. In 305 C.E. they had her tortured on a wheel, but miraculously it broke. Finally she was beheaded and the angels carried her body to Mount Sinai where she is buried. (See **Mount Sinai.**) Eastern Christians celebrate her feast on November 25. The story of Catherine, like that of Thecla, has been extremely popular among women. Educated women, like Catherine, often feel that they have to hide their knowledge because men might be threatened by them. St. Catherine's body at Mount Sinai was said to exude an oil that cured the sick. A crusader took back oil and cured the bishop of Nantes, whereupon Catherine's fame spread in Europe.

The legend of St. Catherine seems to have been developed to overshadow the story of a real woman, Hypatia, who was born about 370 in Alexandria. The main source for information is Synesius of Cyrene (370–413), who was her student. After his studies in Alexandria he was ambassador to Constantinople. Eventually he became a Christian and then bishop of Cyrene. This is how Hypatia is described in the *Church History* of Socrates Scholasticus (380–450).

> The daughter of the mathematician Theon was so learned that she surpassed all the philosophers of her age. She continued the Platonic tradition as this had been mediated by Plotinus, and she introduced into all the philosophical disciplines those who were willing to learn. Those who desired to work with philosophy thronged together and gathered around her because of her learning and authority. She had connections to the leading men in the city. She was not ashamed to spend her time in the company of men, for all held her in great respect and revered her for her purity.[7]

Hypatia was taught by her father and soon surpassed him in mathematics, astronomy, mechanics, and the desire to engage in all areas of philosophy. She was a popular and respected teacher for about twenty years, from when she was about twenty-five until she was killed in her forties. The Byzantine lexicon *Studias* described her in this way.

> She, a woman, put on the philosopher's cloak and held lectures at public expense on Plato and the writings of Aristotle or on any other philosopher out in the city for all who were interested. She was practiced in speaking and schooled in dialectics, she possessed insight into practical activities and showed a sense of the duties as a citizen. Accordingly, the whole city looked on her with favour and she was held in high esteem. On occasion, holders of municipal office paid a call on her when they took office.[8]

Hypatia wrote studies in mathematics and science and many letters, none of which have been preserved, though writings of her male contemporaries are extant. While the contemporary sources emphasize her intelligence, later sources seem to dwell on her physical attractiveness. This story from the *Life of Isidore* describes what one of her contemporaries thought was a good example of her virtue. This is how an intelligent woman of antiquity handled sexual harassment in the workplace.

> One of the pupils fell in love with her. He had no mastery over his feelings, and gave expression to his passion. Ill-informed sources claim that Hypatia used music to heal him, but this is not in keeping with the truth: knowledge of music had been lost a long time before this. On the contrary, what she did was to take out a bloody piece of cloth such as women use. She showed him this sign of women's impurity and said: "It is only this that you love, young man, not the real beauty."[9]

When Synesius, her former student who became a bishop, lost his sons, he wrote her seeking consolation, saying, "I am dictating this letter as I lie in bed. May it reach you in good health, you who are my mother, sister, teacher and benefactress . . . ." All of his letters reveal great respect for her goodness and a warm sense of friendship. Seven of his letters to her and five other letters that talk about her are extant. In his last letter he describes how he has written two books, one inspired by God and another in response to people's criticisms of him because he integrates philosophy and theology. He seeks her philosophical and literary opinion of whether they are good enough to publish.

Cyril, who became patriarch of Alexandria in 412, was power-hungry and rigid and surrounded himself with a band of monks known as *parabolani*, "daredevils." They were known to provoke street fights and riots, harassing the large Jewish population of Alexandria. Cyril expelled the Jews and allowed others to plunder their property. The imperial prefect of the city, Orestes, though he was a Christian, challenged Cyril's unjust actions. Hypatia was a friend of Orestes and Cyril feared that she would support him. Socrates Scholaticus described what happened to Hypatia:

> One of the bishop's lectors, called Peter, led *parabolani* around with him. They lay in waiting at a place they knew the noble lady would pass by, then they pulled her out of the coach and dragged her with them to the Kessarian church.

Here they stripped her naked and mocked her. They killed her by throwing bricks at her. They cut her body into small pieces, and the remains were burnt in an orgy. Cyril and the Alexandrian church were harshly criticized for this. For those who take Christ's path have nothing to do with murder and strife and all violence. This took place in Cyril's fourth year as bishop, while Honorius was consul for the tenth time and Theodosius for the seventh time, in the month of March, in Lent.[10]

No one punished the guilty, because the officials were bribed. As time passed the legend of Catherine developed and spread. In the nineteenth century Cyril was honored by Pope Leo XIII as a doctor of the church.

Dier Abu Mina (outside Alexandria)

Amma Syncletica

This contemporary Coptic monastery is where St. Mina, an important fourth-century Egyptian saint, was buried. He chose to live in the wilderness and was known as a friend of the animals there. The ancient monastery of St. Mina was built by St. Athanasius, the pope of Alexandria. St. Mark's Coptic Cathedral in Alexandria regularly has transportation for pilgrims' trips to this shrine. This area is an appropriate place to remember Amma Syncletica, who is believed to have lived in the desert, or more exactly in a tomb, near Alexandria, probably in the third century. Eventually other women gathered around her. Her sayings were teachings for them. Her words, like those of Theodora and Sarah, are found in a collection of short sayings of holy people of the desert that developed over a period of about two hundred years. In this edited and re-edited collection it is difficult to know exact words or facts, but clearly the wisdom and holiness of some of the women in the desert was impressive enough to merit recording their words and calling them *ammai*, mothers. Amma Syncletica has received more attention than the other Desert Mothers because of a fifth-century "Life of Amma Syncletica," wrongly attributed to Athanasius.

1. Amma Syncletica said, "In the beginning there are a great many battles and a good deal of suffering for those who are advancing towards God and afterwards, ineffable joy. It is like those who wish to light a fire; at first they are choked by the smoke and cry, and by this means obtain what they seek (as it is said: 'our God is a consuming fire' [Heb 12.24]): so

we also must kindle the divine fire in ourselves through tears and hard work."

. . .

3. She also said, "We who have chosen this way of life must obtain perfect temperance. It is true that among seculars, also, temperance has the freedom of the city, but intemperance co-habits with it, because they sin with all the other senses. Their gaze is shameless and they laugh immoderately."

. . .

5. Blessed Syncletica was asked if poverty is a perfect good. She said, "For those who are capable of it, it is a perfect good. Those who can sustain it receive suffering in the body but rest in the soul, for just as one washes coarse clothes by tram-pling them underfoot and turning them about in all direc-tions, even so the strong soul becomes much more stable thanks to voluntary poverty."
6. She also said, "If you find yourself in a monastery do not go to another place, for that will harm you a great deal. Just as the bird who abandons the eggs she was sitting on prevents them from hatching, so the monk or the nun grows cold and their faith dies, when they go from one place to another."

. . .

8. She also said, "If illness weighs us down, let us not be sor-rowful as though because of the illness and the prostration of our bodies we could not sing, for all these things are for our good, for the purification of our desires. Truly fasting and sleeping on the ground are set before us because of our sen-suality. If illness then weakens this sensuality the reason for these practices is superfluous. For this is the great asceticism: to control oneself in illness and to sing hymns of thanks-giving to God."
9. She also said, "When you have to fast, do not pretend ill-ness. For those who do not fast often fall into real sicknesses. If you have begun to act well, do not turn back through con-straint of the enemy, for through your endurance, the enemy is destroyed. Those who put out to sea at first sail with a favourable wind; then the sails spread, but later the winds become adverse. Then the ship is tossed by the waves and is no longer controlled by the rudder. But when in a little while there is a calm, and the tempest dies down, then the ship sails on again. So it is with us; when we are driven by the spirits who are against us, we hold on to the cross as our sail and so we can set a safe course."

. . .

12. She also said, "It is dangerous for anyone to teach who has not first been trained in the 'practical' life. For if someone who owns a ruined house receives guests there, he does them harm because of the dilapidation of his dwelling. It is the same in the case of someone who has not first built an interior dwelling; he causes loss to those who come. By words one may convert them to salvation, but by evil behavior, one injures them."

13. She also said, "It is good not to get angry, but if this should happen, the Apostle does not allow you a whole day for this passion, for he says: 'Let not the sun go down' (Eph 4.25). Will you wait till all your time is ended? Why hate the man who has grieved you? It is not he who has done the wrong, but the devil. Hate sickness but not the sick person."

. . .

15. She also said, "There is an asceticism which is determined by the enemy and his disciples practice it. So how are we to distinguish between the divine and royal asceticism and the demonic tyranny? Clearly through its quality of balance. Always use a single rule of fasting. Do not fast four or five days and break it the following day with any amount of food. In truth lack of proportion always corrupts. While you are young and healthy, fast, for old age with its weakness will come. As long as you can, lay up treasure, so that when you cannot, you will be at peace."

. . .

19. Amma Syncletica said, "There are many who live in the mountains and behave as if they were in the town, and they are wasting their time. It is possible to be a solitary in one's mind while living in a crowd, and it is possible for one who is a solitary to live in the crowd of his own thoughts."

. . .

21. She also said, "Just as a treasure that is exposed loses its value, so a virtue which is known vanishes; just as wax melts when it is near fire, so the soul is destroyed by praise and loses all the results of its labour."

22. She also said, "Just as it is impossible to be at the same moment both a plant and a seed, so it is impossible for us to be surrounded by worldly honour and at the same time to bear heavenly fruit."

. . .

27. She also said, "There is grief that is useful, and there is grief that is destructive. The first sort consists in weeping over one's faults and weeping over the weakness of one's

neighbors, in order not to destroy one's purpose, and attach oneself to the perfect good. But there is also a grief that comes from the enemy, full of mockery, which some call *accidie*. This spirit must be cast out, mainly by prayer and psalmody."[11]

Antinoe

Amma Talis and Taor

Palladius' *Lausiac History,* written in 419 and 420 and a major source for early monasticism in Egypt, Palestine, Syria, and Asia Minor, is organized as a record of his travels and who and what interested him. The following passage indicates that Amma Talis was respected as a fine monastic leader and that Taor was a virtuous ascetic. The passage also reveals Palladius' surprise that Talis, a woman, should be comfortable enough in her celibacy to touch a man quite spontaneously and unselfconsciously. The passage reveals Palladius' interest in a beautiful woman as well.

> In the town of Antinoë are twelve monasteries of women. Here I met Amma Talis, a woman eighty years old in the ascetic life, as her neighbors affirmed. Sixty young women lived with her. They loved her so much that no lock was placed in the hall of the monastery, as in others, but they were held in check by their love for her. The old woman had such a high degree of self-control that when I had entered and taken a seat, she came and sat with me and placed her hands on my shoulders in a burst of frankness.
>
> In this monastery was a maiden, a disciple of hers named Taor, who had spent thirty years there. She was never willing to take a new garment, hood, or shoes, but said: "I have no need for them unless I must go out." The others all go out every Sunday to church for Communion, but she stays behind in her cell dressed in rags, ever sitting at her work. She is so graceful in appearance that even a well-controlled person might be led astray by her beauty were not chastity her defense and did not her decorum turn sinful eyes to fear and shame.[12]

Cairo (Coptic Section)

In this area of Cairo one finds the Coptic Museum, with the best collection of Coptic art in the world. Many ancient churches, a synagogue, and a library containing portions of the Nag Hammadi codices are in the area. Copts have a rich liturgical tradition going back to the first centuries of Christianity; they assert that it was St. Mark who first brought Christianity to Egypt. The pope of the Coptic Church three times a year reenacts Jesus' ritual at the Last Supper of washing feet and also encourages a spirit of hospitality.

Al-Muallaqa Church or the Church of the Virgin (Coptic Cairo)

St. Sergius and St. Bacchus Church

Mary, Jesus, and Joseph in Egypt

Al-Muallaqa is probably the oldest extant Christian church in Egypt, with wooden beams from the third century and a number of ancient icons. The nearby St. Sergius and St. Bacchus was built over a cave where the Holy Family is said to have rested. They are also said to have rested at El-Meharrak Monastery in Kiskam Mountain in Assyout in upper Egypt.

> 13 Now after they had left, an angel of the Lord appeared to Joseph in a dream and said, "Get up, take the child and his mother, and flee to Egypt, and remain there until I tell you; for Herod is about to search for the child, to destroy him." 14 Then Joseph got up, took the child and his mother by night, and went to Egypt, 15 and remained there until the death of Herod. This was to fulfill what had been spoken by the Lord through the prophet, "Out of Egypt I have called my son."
>
> (Matt 2:13-15)

St. Barbara Church (Coptic Cairo)

Determined Women

Legend says when Barbara tried to bring her father to Christianity, he killed her. Many stories of women saints describe opposition from family members. Yet the women courageously hold their beliefs. Some of the relics of Barbara and of Catherine are enshrined in the church. As contemporary families might treasure photos of deceased great grandparents, so Christians have treasured relics as tangible reminders of ancestors in faith. Barbara, as on the cover, is often shown holding a chalice. She is a patron of the dying and brings the Eucharist.

Ben Ezra Synagogue (Coptic Cairo)

The Midwives, Miriam, and Pharaoh's Daughter

This beautifully decorated synagogue, the oldest in Egypt, was built on the site of a fourth-century Christian church that had been closed by Hakim the Mad. After he died the Jewish community bought it. Many legends are associated with it. Mary is said to have drawn water to wash Jesus here. This is also where Moses' sister hid him to save his life. The first two chapters of Exodus may be an oral tradition of women that was later incorporated into the larger patriarchal text. Imagine women telling each other that the most powerful ruler in the world had just been outwitted by two slave women. Then slave women and a princess, even women of different nations, worked together to fool the powerful because the women thought the life of a child was more important than protecting a power system. These delightful and subversive stories invite contemporary courageous, compassionate actions.

> 15 The king of Egypt said to the Hebrew midwives, one of whom was named Shiphrah and the other Puah, 16 "When you act as midwives to the Hebrew women, and see them on the birthstool, if it is a boy, kill him; but if it is a girl, she shall live." 17 But the midwives feared God; they did not do as the king of Egypt commanded them, but they let the boys live. 18 So the king of Egypt summoned the midwives and said to them, "Why have you done this, and allowed the boys to live?" 19 The midwives said to Pharaoh, "Because the Hebrew women are not like the Egyptian women; for they are vigorous and give birth before the midwife comes to them." 20 So God dealt well with the midwives; and the people multiplied and became very strong.
>
> (Read Exod 1:15–2:10)

Memphis Ruins (South of Cairo)

Potiphar's Wife

The ruins of Memphis and a museum are 20 kilometers south of Cairo near Saqqara, where the wealthy people of Memphis were buried. In the Papyrus D'Orbiney of about 1225 B.C.E. a folk tale describes a young man who tries to seduce his elder brother's wife. Did such popular lore influence the story of Joseph? He may have gone to Egypt during the Hyksos dynasty, 1720–1500 B.C.E., which had its capital in Memphis. The

Hyksos, of Semitic origin, had gained power in Egypt. During their reign many other Semites were brought as slaves to Egypt and some achieved high office.

In the biblical story Potiphar left Joseph completely in charge of his home. The theme of the seductive woman has been popular throughout history, although women are more often the victims of seduction and violence than the perpetrators. Statistics of contemporary rapes document this. Nevertheless, the seductive woman is a major theme in literature and art, most of which has been created by males.

> 6 So he left all that he had in Joseph's charge; and, with him there, he had no concern for anything but the food that he ate. Now Joseph was handsome and good-looking. 7 And after a time his master's wife cast her eyes on Joseph and said, "Lie with me." 8 But he refused and said to his master's wife, "Look, with me here, my master has no concern about anything in the house, and he has put everything that he has in my hand. 9 He is not greater in this house than I am, nor has he kept back anything from me except yourself, because you are his wife. How then could I do this great wickedness, and sin against God?" 10 And although she spoke to Joseph day after day, he would not consent to lie beside her or to be with her.
>
> (Read Gen 39:6-20)

Nitria (Southwest of Alexandria)

Amma Theodora

Near the end of the third century Amma Theodora lived in the desert of Nitria or Scetis and was respected by many of the desert ascetics who sought her wisdom. She was a friend of Bishop Theophilus of Alexandria who lived c. 345 to 412 C.E. Her sayings focus especially on "knowing how to profit in times of conflict," that is, having the self-discipline to continue though things may seem unbearable. Hers was sound teaching for both men and women, and those who edited the collection of sayings describe her as having the qualities of an ideal teacher.

Amma Theodora praised living in "peace with oneself," but often depression or restlessness may come and torment or discourage a person.

> 2. Amma Theodora said, "Let us strive to enter by the narrow gate. Just as the trees, if they have not stood before the winter's storms, cannot bear fruit, so it is with us; this present age

is a storm and it is only through many trials and temptations that we can obtain an inheritance in the kingdom of heaven."

3. She also said, "It is good to live in peace, for the wise man practices perpetual prayer. It is truly a great thing for a virgin or a monk to live in peace, especially for the younger ones. However, you should realize that as soon as you intend to live in peace, at once evil comes and weighs down your soul through *accidie,* faintheartedness, and evil thoughts. It also attacks your body through sickness, debility, weakening of the knees, and all the members. It dissipates the strength of soul and body, so that one believes one is ill and no longer able to pray. But if we are vigilant, all these temptations fall away. There was, in fact a monk who was seized by cold and fever every time he began to pray, and he suffered from headaches too. In this condition, he said to himself, 'I am ill, and near to death; so now I will get up before I die and pray.' By reasoning in this way, he did violence to himself and prayed. When he had finished, the fever abated also. So, by reasoning in this way, the brother resisted, and prayed and was able to conquer his thoughts."

. . .

7. Amma Theodora also said, "There was a monk, who, because of the great number of his temptations said, 'I will go away from here.' As he was putting on his sandals, he saw another man who was also putting on his sandals and this other monk said to him, 'Is it on my account that you are going away? Because I go before you wherever you are going.'"

. . .

10. Another of the old men questioned Amma Theodora saying, "At the resurrection of the dead, how shall we rise?" She said, "As pledge, example, and as prototype we have him who died for us and is risen, Christ our God."[13]

Paula's Reflections on Nitria

In the late fourth century Paula and Jerome visited the Nitria area famous for holy people. Jerome described their visit and Paula's growing sense that she was called to live an ascetic life.

. . . No sooner did Paula come in sight of [Nitria] than there came to meet her the reverend and estimable bishop, the confessor Isidore, accompanied by countless multitudes of monks many of whom were of priestly or of Levitical rank. On seeing these Paula rejoiced to behold the Lord's glory manifested in them, but protested that she had no claim to be received with such honour. Need I speak of the Macarii, Arsenius, Serapion, or other pillars of Christ! Was there any cell that she did not enter? Or any man at whose feet she did not throw herself? In each of His saints she believed that she saw Christ Himself; and whatever she bestowed upon them she rejoiced to feel that she had bestowed it upon the Lord. Her enthusiasm was wonderful and her endurance scarcely credible in a woman. Forgetful of her sex and of her weakness she even desired to make her abode, together with the girls who accompanied her, among these thousands of monks. And, as they were all willing to welcome her, she might perhaps have sought and obtained permission to do so; had she not been drawn away by still greater passion for the holy places. . . . Not long afterwards, making up her mind to dwell permanently in holy Bethlehem, she took up her abode for three years in a miserable hostelry; till she could build the requisite cells and monastic buildings, to say nothing of a guest house for passing travelers where they might find the welcome which Mary and Joseph had missed.

(PAULA, 150)

Mount Sinai, Gebel or Jebel Musa

Egeria Climbing Mount Sinai

The 7,490-foot-high Mount Sinai, or Jebel Musa, has been regarded for over 1700 years as the place where God gave Moses the ten commandments. Monks settled in the area and during Constantine's era a small chapel was built, according to legend by Helena, at the base of the mountain where the burning bush was said to have been. Modern pilgrims awake about two or three in the morning and climb the mountain to praise God on top as the sun rises. Egeria, with her usual determination and enthusiasm, traveled across the desolate Sinai wilderness and recounted what the climb was like.

> They are hard to climb. You do not go round and round them, spiraling up gently, but straight at each one as if you were going up a wall, and then straight down to the foot, till you reach the foot of the central mountain, Sinai itself. Here then, impelled by Christ our God and assisted by the prayers of the holy men who accompanied us, we made the great effort of the climb. It was quite impossible to ride up, but though I had to go on foot I was not conscious of the effort—in fact I hardly noticed it because, by God's will, I was seeing my hopes coming true.

So at ten o'clock we arrived on the summit of Sinai, the Mount of God where the Law was given, and the place where God's glory came down on the day when the mountain was smoking. The church that is now there is not impressive for its size (there is too little room on the summit), but it has a grace all its own. And when with God's help we had climbed right to the top and reached the door of this church, there was the presbyter, the one who is appointed to the church, coming to meet us from his cell. He was a healthy old man, a monk from his boyhood and an "ascetic" as they call it here—in fact just the man for the place. Several other presbyters met us too, and all the monks who lived near the mountain, or at least all who were not prevented from coming by their age or their health.

All there is on the actual summit of the central mountain is the church and the cave of holy Moses. No one lives there. So when the whole passage had been read to us from the Book of Moses (on the very spot!) we made the offering in the usual way and received communion. As we were coming out of church the presbyters of the place gave us "blessings," some fruits which grow on the mountain itself. For although Sinai, the holy Mount, is too stony even for bushes to grow on it, there is a little soil round the foot of the mountains, the central one and those around it, and in this the holy monks are always busy planting shrubs, and setting out orchards or vegetable-beds round their cells. It may look as if they gather fruit which is growing in the mountain soil, but in fact everything is the result of their own hard work.

We had received communion and the holy men had given us the "blessings." Now we were outside the church door, and at once I asked them if they would point out to us all the different places. The holy men willingly agreed. They showed us the cave where holy Moses was when for the second time he went up into the Mount of God and a second time received the tables of stone after breaking the first ones when the people sinned. They showed us all other places we wanted to see, and also the ones they knew about themselves. I want you to be quite clear about these mountains, reverend ladies my sisters, which surrounded us as we stood beside the church looking down from the summit of the mountain in the middle. They had been almost too much for us to climb, and I really do not think there were any that were higher (apart from the central one which is higher still) even though they looked like little hillocks to us as we stood on the central mountain. From there we were able to see Egypt and Palestine, the Red Sea and the Parthinian Sea (the part that takes you to Alexandria), as well as the vast lands of the Saracens—all unbelievably far below us. All this was pointed out to us by the holy men.

We had been looking forward to all this so much that we had been eager to make the climb. Now that we had done all we wanted and climbed to the summit of the Mount of God, we began to descend. We passed on to another mountain next to it which from the church there is called "On Horeb." This is the Horeb to which the holy Prophet Elijah fled from the presence of King Ahab, and it was there that God spoke to him with the words "What does thou here Elijah?" as is written in the Books of the Kingdoms. Indeed whenever we arrived, I always wanted the Bible passage to be read to us.

(EGERIA, 93–95)

Pelusium (East Corner of the Nile Delta)

Amma Sarah

Pelusium was in the desert between contemporary Ismailia and Port Said. In the second half of the third century C.E. Amma Sarah lived for about sixty years near the Nile in the area of Pelusium. For the first thirteen years she struggled with lust. She did not pray that it would go away, but she prayed that God would help her. She felt no need to dress as a man, though some women in the desert did. One of her comments displays both her self-confidence and the way women were disdained. She told some visiting monks that she was like a man and they were like women. Life in the desert, like the essence of Christianity, offered women freedom from the limitations of the stereotypical gender roles and the materialism of their societies. In the area of Pelusium there were many people, both men and women, who sought to live prayerful, ascetic lives. Sarah's sayings reveal that she encountered some hostility toward women, but she does not let this hold her back in her quest for holiness.

> 4. . . . two old men, great anchorites, came to the district of Pelusia to visit her. When they arrived one said to the other, "Let us humiliate this old woman." So they said to her, "Be careful not to become conceited thinking to yourself: 'Look how anchorites are coming to see me, a mere woman.'" But Amma Sarah said to them, "According to nature I am a woman, but not according to my thoughts."

> 5. Amma Sarah said, "If I prayed God that all men should approve of my conduct, I should find myself a penitent at the door of each one, but I shall rather pray that my heart may be pure towards all."

> . . .

7. She also said, "It is good to give alms for men's sake. Even if it is only done to please men, through it one can begin to seek to please God."

8. Some monks of Scetis came one day to visit Amma Sarah. She offered them a small basket of fruit. They left the good fruit and ate the bad. So she said to them, "You are true monks of Scetis."

9. She also said to the brothers, "It is I who am a man, you who are women."[14]

Red Sea

Miriam Leading a Liturgy of Praise

A number of routes have been proposed for the Exodus. Did the people cross at the Red Sea or the Sea of Reeds? Was there one exodus or a number of migrations? One of the suggestions is that they crossed around the city of Suez where the canal meets the Red Sea.

One of the oldest fragments of Scripture from the Yahwist source is the story of Miriam leading song and dance to celebrate freedom from bondage. She is described as a *nebiah,* which is the feminine form of the Hebrew word for prophet, *nabi.* The prophet Micah of the eighth century B.C.E. seems to reflect an early tradition that not just Moses, but also Miriam and Aaron were leaders of the Exodus (Mic 6:3-4). The story of Miriam leading the people in praising God may reflect Egyptian traditions of priestesses who led rituals. While gratitude when one has found freedom is appropriate, the wish for the destruction of the oppressors is not. Many contemporary Jews use a version of the Seder, the Passover service commemorating the Exodus, in which a drop of wine is poured out for each of the ten ways that the Egyptians suffered. It is not fitting to have a full cup of wine, symbolic of a full cup of joy, if someone else has had to suffer. God desires good for each human being. Part of the Passover journey is moving to be more God-like, that is, more compassionate. God calls humans to lessen or alleviate the suffering of others, never to inflict greater suffering. The Exodus dance started with Miriam, but as long as some are drowning or suffering the dance is not complete. Hebrew and Egyptian, male and female, and all God's family are called into a circle dance of unity and joy.

20 Then the prophet Miriam, Aaron's sister, took a tambourine in her hand; and all the women went out after her with tambourines and with dancing. 21 And Miriam sang to them: "Sing to the LORD, for he has triumphed gloriously; horse and rider he has thrown into the sea." (Exod 15:20)

Tabennesi (Nag³el-Sabriyat)

The Sister of Pachomius

Some sources say the sister of Pachomius was "probably called Maria," acknowledging her, but also the reality of women's history and names not being considered important. Pachomius, born of non-Christian parents, was drafted into the army and sent down the Nile to Thebes. While living in the rather squalid conditions set aside for young conscripts Pachomius experienced the kindness of local Christians. After he was released from the army in 313 he began a simple life of growing food in a small village and he wanted to learn of Christianity. He chose to be baptized. Remembering the Christians who had been kind to him, he began sharing his food with the poor and with passing strangers, but soon more and more came and he felt overwhelmed. After three years of serving those in need he felt that he was called to be a solitary monk like many men in the region. In about 323, after seven years as an anchorite, Pachomius came across a deserted village called Tabennesi and he had a vision to found a community there. He had a sense that the ascetic life as led by some Christians in the desert was not adequately responsive to a central concept of the Gospel, the call to active charity. A few men began living around him and following his ideas, and within half a dozen years this grew to a community of over a hundred, mostly Coptic-speaking peasants but also some men from the Greco-Roman elite. Pachomius' living model of *koinonia* spread through the writings of Athanasius, the bishop of Alexandria, who visited him in 329, and also through the writings and translations done by Jerome. This model of eastern monastic life thus became known in the West and grew in popularity.

Pachomius had been away from his family for about fifteen years when his sister came to Tabennesi in 329. He did not go to greet her, but sent the doorkeeper to tell her, "Do not be distressed . . . because you have not seen me. But if you wish to share in this holy life so that you may find mercy before God, examine yourself on every point. The brothers will build a place for you to retire to. And doubtless, for your sake the Lord will call others to you. . . ."[15] Apparently Maria had an authentic call to this lifestyle and soon the monks built a women's monastery not far from theirs. Pachomius considered the Gospel the primary rule of life for his followers, but he had begun to compile practical regulations for the men and also shared these with the women. As Basil and his sister Macrina each had communities with similar organizational principles, so Pachomius and his sister each had followers. For a period Maria exercised leadership in the community, but as it grew Pachomius sent an older, respected monk named Apa Peter to live among the women, preaching to them on Scripture and advising and supervising them. Maria's community grew and another for women was started in Tsmine.

Economically the women's communities were united with those of the men, which produced food, flax, and other raw materials. The women processed these raw materials, making all the textiles and garments for both the men and the women. The women seem to have produced more than the monasteries needed, and the surplus was sold. The routine of praying psalms, learning Scripture, and doing manual labor in a context of celibacy and community sharing was a most appealing life for many women. The women seemed to have had relative independence in their day-to-day affairs, but overall the women's foundations were under the leadership of the central male foundation and its economic system. No history of the women from their points of view exist, they are only known through the male histories which describe this system as satisfactory.

A Holy Fool and Anastasia, the Deaconess

This delightful tale from the Abba Daniel story cycle is full of humor and surprise, and is part of a collection of sixth-century Syriac stories. Syriac monasticism had close links with Egyptian. God's wisdom is like foolishness, and "holy fools" frequently appear in the Byzantine tradition, especially in the Russian branch. This version of the story identifies Anastasia with the deaconess with whom the Patriarch Severos of Antioch corresponded. Holiness gives a woman so much courage that she can even flee the advances of an emperor.

Abba Daniel and a disciple were traveling and stopped at a monastery of nuns in Tabennesi. The abbess has invited them in and washed their feet, a gesture of hospitality.

> . . . She made a great occasion for the whole monastery and set up a table before the blessed man, placing just soaked crusts in front of Daniel, and boiled lentils in front of his disciple, together with a little bread, while for all the sisters she had cooked food with oil and a little wine and some other things. When they had enjoyed themselves, the blessed man said, "What was this that you did, bringing us the inferior and yourselves the better food?" The abbess replied, "My Lord, you are a solitary, and I gave you the food of solitaries, and I gave your disciple food suitable for a solitary's disciple, because that is what he is; whereas we ate something better because we are weak women." The blessed man said to her, "So be it."
>
> It was a matter of wonder and amazement with these sisters that they lived in deep silence, and in everything they carried out their ministrations and seeing to all their needs either by means of signs or using the *semantron*. Now there were more than three hundred of them. The blessed man said to the abbess, "Are the sisters always like this, or is this something put on for our sakes?" The abbess replied, "Your handmaids are always like this."
>
> 4. He prayed over them and gave praise to God. Then he got up from the colonnade and went into the courtyard, where he caught sight of a sister sprawling on the ground in the middle of the courtyard. He asked the abbess, "Who is this,

mother?" The abbess told him, "My Lord, this is a poor simpleton, who has gone out of her mind; she throws herself about wherever she happens to be." He told his disciple to take some water that was in a pail and throw it over her, at which she got up as though from a drunken sleep, stood up, and went off to some other place. Then the old man said to his disciple, "Do me a favor, my son, and go and see where the poor mad girl is sleeping." The disciple went off and found her sleeping by the monastery latrines. He came back and told his master, at which the blessed man said to the disciple, "Do me a favor, my son, and keep vigil with me tonight."

When everyone else had gone off to sleep, the blessed man went off with his disciple and stood somewhere where they could see the mad girl, without her being aware of them. She, on seeing that all the sisters had gone off to sleep, stood up in prayer, stretching out her hands to heaven. From her hands there issued as it were sparks and flames of fire as she knelt down and stood up throughout the entire night, with tears streaming down onto the ground like rivulets of water. She used to do this every day.

The blessed man told his disciple, "Go quietly, my son, and call the abbess and her assistant to me." When they arrived, the blessed man showed her to them saying, "You see this mad girl? Truly God loves people who are mad like this." At that point the *semantron* sounded for midnight service, and the news spread among the sisters; there was a great commotion amongst them, as they wailed and wept over all the evils they had inflicted on the mad girl, supposing that she really was a simpleton and crazy.

Then, because they had stayed awake, the blessed man and his disciple laid themselves down for a little and rested. The blessed girl, once she had learnt that her secret had been disclosed, got up that same night and went to the place where the blessed man was sleeping, took his cowl and staff, wrote down a message on a tablet, hung it on the monastery gate, and left: where she went, and where she died no one ever knew. On the tablet the following was written, "Farewell, my sisters in Christ, and pray for me for our Lord's sake. Forgive me for causing you such disturbance."

The blessed man at once assembled all the sisters and spoke with them the word of salvation, comforting them and telling them, "You have seen this mad girl; in truth God loves mad people such as these, who are drunkenly mad with ardent love for him." He then sealed them with the sign of the cross and departed from there with his disciple.

5. Once they had arrived at Skete, the old man said to his disciple, "My son, go and visit the old man who lives further

into the desert than we do." For there was an old man, a eunuch, who lived eighteen miles into the desert from Skete. The way that brother used to visit this old man was as follows: he used to bring one jar full of water and place it in front of the entrance to the cell; he would knock and then return without uttering any word. With him he would bring back an empty jar. This took place once a week.

One day the old man said to the disciple, "My son, look and see if there is anything beside that old man's cave; when you find an ostracon with something written on it, bring it with you."

When the disciple obeyed Abba Daniel, he found a message to bring tools to bury the old man. Both of them went and were blessed by praying with the holy old man who asked Abba Daniel for the Sacrament. After sharing the Sacrament, the old man released his spirit to God and died. The disciple prepared the man's body for burial.

When they had buried him and performed the service and prayers, the blessed Daniel said to his disciple, "My son, let us today break our fast, and break bread over the old man." Having partaken of the Sacrament, they found a few bits of flat bread and some soaked crusts; then, once they had eaten and had something to drink, they took the old man's girdle and returned to their cell, praising and giving thanks to God.

8. As they were journeying, the disciple asked the old man, "Father, did you know that the eunuch we buried was a woman? As I was putting on the burial garment, I felt and noticed that she had breasts hanging down like two withered leaves." The old man said, "Yes, my son, I know he was really a woman. If you would like I will tell you her story; listen. She was a patrician lady of the highest rank in the kingdom of the Emperor Justinian. Now the Emperor Justinian wanted to introduce her into the palace because of her beauty and great virtue, but when the empress Theodora learnt of this she was put out and wanted to have her sent into exile. On discovering this, Anastasia got up one night, hired a boat, took various of her possessions, and came to Alexandria where she resided at the Ennatron, building there a monastery that is called the Monastery of the Patrician to this day. When she learnt that Theodora was dead and that the Emperor Justinian wanted to send for her and introduce her into his royal court, she fled from Alexandria by night and came here. She asked me to give her a cell outside Skete, revealing to me her whole story, I gave her this cave, and she changed her clothes for a man's. She has been here twenty-eight years today, without anyone knowing apart from you and me and one other man—even though the *magistrianoi* were sent by

the emperor in search for her, and not just by the emperor, but also by the patriarch and all of Alexandria. Yet no one has found her to this day. See, my son, now how many people have been brought up at court, yet have performed battle against the adversary, battering their bodies, and living like angels on Earth. As for us, when we were in the world, how many times did we not even have any bread to eat our fill, yet when we turned to the monastic garb we have had abundance of food and drink but were unable to acquire any such way of virtue. Let us pray then, my son, that the Lord may hold us worthy of the same course and way of life, and may we find, along with this holy father, mercy on that day; and together with this father and brother Anastosios the eunuch, may we be worthy of the kingdom that does not pass away." Now Anastasia was her name.

9. The blessed disciple then went to his cell, sat down and wrote all this that he had heard and seen. This patrician Anastasia was a deaconess in the time of the holy Severos, he wrote her many letters, full of explanations of the things she used to ask him about, when she lived in a monastery with sisters, before she arrived in the desert of Skete.[16]

Tgeban Desert Village of Atripe

Mother Tachom

Only fragments of the story of Tachom, the leader of the women's monastery that was a part of Shenoute of Atripe's foundation, have been preserved. Shenoute proposed a theory of the equality of women and men, rich and poor, educated and uneducated in Christian monastic life. When Mother Tachom attempted to implement the described structure of equality of women and men she was strongly reprimanded by Shenoute for disrupting necessary order.

In the middle of the fourth century C.E. two anchorites founded monastic communities near modern Sohag and another about an hour south in the desert near the village of Atripe, which came to be called the White Monastery from the color of its walls. The present church of Sohag is within the area of the original sanctuary of the White Monastery. In about 383 C.E. Shenoute, the nephew of Pgol, the founder of the White Monastery, became the leader of the group of about thirty men and of the nearby women's group following their lifestyle. Shenoute was a charismatic and strong leader who made this foundation one of the largest and most influential in Egypt. He was a central founder of monophysite monasticism, yet western documents that come out of the tradition of Hellenized Christianity hardly mention him. This reflects the tension between Coptic Christians and other Christians that followed the arguments at the Council of Chalcedon about how to describe the nature of Christ. Ancient sources say that 1,800 nuns and 2,200 monks were a part of his foundation, which included about ten square kilometers of settlements.

The following is from Shenoute's rule, *De pietate feminum*, which describes the equality of persons.

> Or has the kingdom of heaven solely been prepared for men? So that it has not been prepared for women to enter as well? . . . Indeed, just as there are many men who are at times strong and many women who are weak, there are on the other hand many women who are at times strong and victorious, and many men, too, who are inferior to them and weaker [than they are]. The same battle has been assigned to men and women, and the same crown stands before those men and women who together will have persevered.[17]

Some of Shenoute's writings seem to reflect women's equality; for instance, the mother of a woman's monastery was to supervise it as Shenoute did the men's. Women who felt called could go to the desert for a while to be hermits, as did men. Shenoute had extensive regulations to assure that each member received equal food and clothing. However, as the women's monasteries developed Shenoute directed the mothers to reveal everything that happened in their monasteries to Shenoute, through an "elder brother" whom he had appointed to live among them. In this way Shenoute could be sure that all the rules were being properly observed. The women did not want to give the men news of everything. For infringements of the rule the elder brother was to beat the disobedient sister on the soles of her feet a prescribed number of times while the mother and her assistant held the sister.

When Mother Tachom became the leader of a monastery, after spending some years as the assistant and observing how rigid the rules were and how much corporal punishment was used to ensure obedience, she questioned the elder brother's competence. Shenoute wrote Mother Tachom, reminding her of when he had come personally to punish the nuns there, "so that the entire village in which you live was filled with your imbecile voice."[18] He continued to talk about her failing to obey the elder brother, "And if he, whom we sent to you, is not your father—and according to the order and the laws of God he is—then you are also for your part not mother."[19] In other words, she would be tearing apart the very structure to which she belonged. Shenoute said that she was a proud fool, like those who built the tower of Babel. She was stupid and would bring confusion. Tachom's writings no longer exist, and one wonders how she would have explained the situation.

A main concept of Shenoute's foundations was equality—of the rich and the poor, the educated and the uneducated, the slaves and the free born, and of females and males. Yet Tachom was not given the freedom to lead her nuns as males had the freedom to lead local groups; an elder brother had to be there to control. Shenoute's successor Besa frequently wrote of the women's rebellion, lack of obedience, and failure to disclose everything. If the women's writings still existed, would a different picture be given of male interference in their lives? In Pachomius' model of religious life, from the very beginning female communities were described as being subservient to males. The Western Church chose to follow Pachomius' model and ignore Shenoute's, which described equality. Within the modern world could some of the wisdom of Shenoute's model without the weaknesses of his practice be reclaimed?

Wadi Natru (Scetis Desert Area)

Thaïs, the Harlot

Modern Wadi Natru is about 100 kilometers west of Cairo. During the Roman persecutions thousands of Christians fled to this area. Some began to live the ascetic life as hermits, and others began to form monastic groups. The region is called the Sketis Desert and in Coptic that word means "the balance of hearts." A few kilometers from the town are four monasteries established in the fourth century called Abba Makar, Baramous, El-Sourian, and St. Bishoy. Deir al-Anba Bishoi, as this last monastery is called, welcomes pilgrims for prayer.

The active monasteries in the desert of Wadi Natru are fascinating places to reflect on ancient monastic life. There the monks prayed to know about Thaïs' salvation as described in the following legend. Prostitution was popular in ancient cities, where women were often desperate to support themselves. Alexander the Great and his general Ptolemy were fascinated by a prostitute called Thaïs. Legend said that she provoked Alexander to burn the Great Hall in Persepolis. The monks of Egypt had stories about a prostitute called Thaïs, perhaps from Alexandria. The story is a dramatic teaching device to show that God's forgiveness is not won by one's actions, but is a gracious gift. Thaïs wanted to know God's gift and she was isolated to do so. The story is harsh, but it holds the spiritual wisdom to focus on what really matters.

Hrotswitha, a tenth-century canoness of the abbey of Gandersheim, wrote Christian plays using the style of Terence. During this period when drama had waned and most women did not have the opportunity to learn to write, this intelligent woman not only wrote, but chose to develop the ancient stories about women. Hrotswitha used the stories of Thaïs and of Maria, the niece of Abraham, as bases of her dramas, giving dramatic development to Thaïs' beauty of spirit.

> I. There was a certain harlot called Thaïs and she was so beautiful that many for her sake sold all that they had and reduced themselves to utter poverty; quarrels arose among her lovers and often the doorstep of this girl's house was soaked in the blood of young men. When Abba Paphnutius heard about it, he put on secular clothes and went to see her in a certain city in Egypt. He handed her a silver piece as the price and said, "Let us go inside." When he went in, he sat down on the bed which was draped with precious covers and he invited her, saying, "If there is a more private chamber, let us go in there." She said, "There is one, but if it is people you are afraid of, no one ever enters this room; except, of course, for God, for there is no place that is hidden from the eyes of divinity." When the old man heard this, he said to her, "So you know there is a God?" She answered him, "I know about God and about the eternal kingdom and also about the future torments of sinners." "But if you know this," he said, "why are you causing the loss of so many souls so that you will be condemned to render an account not only of your own sins but of theirs as well?" When Thaïs heard this, she threw herself at the feet of Paphnutius and begged him with tears, "Give me a penance, Father, for I trust to find forgiveness by your prayers. I beg you to wait for just three hours, and after that, wherever you tell me to go, I will go, and whatever you tell me to do, I will do it." So Paphnutius arranged a meeting place with her and she went out and collected together all the goods that she had received by her sins and piled them all together in the middle of the city, while all the people watched, saying, "Come here, all of you who have sinned with me, and see how I am burning whatever you gave me." The value of it was forty pounds.
>
> II. When it was all consumed, she went to the place that the father had arranged with her. Then he sought out a monastery of virgins and took her into a small cell, sealing the door with lead and leaving only a small opening through

which food could be passed to her, and he ordered her to be given daily a little bread and a little water by the sisters of the monastery. When Thaïs realized that the door was sealed with lead, she said to him, "Father, where do you want me to urinate?" and he replied, "In the cell, as you deserve." Then she asked him how she should pray to God, and he said to her, "You are not worthy to name God, or to take his divine name upon your lips, or to lift up your hands to heaven, for your lips are full of sin and you hands are stained with iniquity; only stand facing towards the east and repeat often only this: 'You who made me, have mercy upon me.'"

III. When she had been enclosed in this way for three years, Paphnutius began to be anxious, and so he went to see Abba Antony, to ask him if her sins had been forgiven by the Lord or not. When he arrived, he recounted the affair to him in detail, and Abba Antony called together all his disciples and they agreed to keep vigil all night and each of them to persist in prayer so that God might reveal to one of them the truth of the matter about which Paphnutius had come. Each retired to his cell and took up continuous prayer. Then Paul, the great disciple of St. Antony, suddenly saw in the sky a bed adorned with precious cloths and guarded by three virgins whose faces shone with brightness. Then Paul said to them; "Surely so great a glory can only be for my father Antony?" but a voice spoke to him saying, "This is not for your father Antony, but for the harlot Thaïs." Paul went quickly and reported what he had heard and seen and Paphnutius recognized the will of God and set off for the monastery where the girl was enclosed. He began to open the door for her which he had sealed up, but she begged to be left shut up in there. When the door was open he said to her, "Come out, for God has forgiven you your sins." She replied, "I call God to witness that since I came in here my sins have always been before my eyes as a burden; they have never been out of my sight and I have always wept to see them." Abba Paphnutius said to her, "God has forgiven your sins not because of your penance but because you have always had the remembrance of your sins in your soul." When he had taken Thaïs out, she lived for fifteen days and then passed away in peace.[20]

Tunisia

Carthage or Tunis

Saints Perpetua and Felicitas

Carthage, though not visited by Paul, was part of the circle of trade cities around the Mediterranean that were continually linked by a flow of goods and ideas. He visited a number of the other cities. The Roman Empire provided the best system of communication and travel in the areas around the Mediterranean until modern times, and this facilitated the spread of Christianity. Since almost all the written records of the words of Christian women of antiquity have been lost or destroyed, it seems important to include the following words of Perpetua, which may be the earliest extant example. The ruins of Carthage have Roman baths, villas, and the amphitheater. This amphitheater is one of the oldest in the empire and can give a sense of the context of the bloody entertainment put on there, with gladiators, wild beasts, and prisoners like Perpetua and Felicitas being tortured to death.

In a Roman persecution of 203 C.E. a young mother named Perpetua, who was nursing her baby, and a slave, Felicitas, were arrested with others preparing to become Christians. These are Perpetua's thoughts.

> A number of young catechumens were arrested, Revocatus and his fellow slave Felicitas, Saturninus and Secundulus, and with them Vivia Perpetua, a newly married woman of good family and upbringing. Her mother and father were still alive and one of her two brothers was a catechumen like herself. She was about twenty-two years old and had an infant son at the breast. (Now from this point on the entire account of her ordeal is her own, according to her own ideas and in the way that she herself wrote it down.)
>
> While we were still under arrest (she said), my father out of love for me was trying to persuade me and shake my resolution. "Father," said I, "do you see this vase here, for example, or waterpot or whatever?"
>
> "Yes, I do," said he.
>
> And I told him: "Could it be called by any other name than what it is?"
>
> And he said: "No."
>
> "Well, so, too, I cannot be called anything other than what I am, a Christian."
>
> At this my father was so angered by the word "Christian" that he moved towards me as though he would pluck my

eyes out. But he left it at that and departed, vanquished along with his diabolical arguments.

For a few days afterwards I gave thanks to the Lord that I was separated from my father, and I was comforted by his absence. During these few days I was baptized, and I was inspired by the spirit not to ask for any other favour after the water but simply the perseverance of the flesh. A few days later we were lodged in the prison; and I was terrified as I had never before been in such a dark hole. What a difficult time it was! With the crowd, the heat was stifling; then there was the extortion of the soldiers; and to crown all, I was tortured with worry for my baby there.

Then Tertius and Pomponius, those blessed deacons who tried to take care of us, bribed the soldiers to allow us to go to a better part of the prison to refresh ourselves for a few hours. All then left that dungeon and shifted for themselves. I nursed my baby, who was faint from hunger. In my anxiety I spoke to my mother about the child, tried to comfort my brother, and I gave the child into their charge. I was in pain because I saw them suffering out of pity for me. These were the trials I had to endure for many days. Then I got permission for my baby to stay with me in prison. At once I recovered my health, relieved as I was of my worry and anxiety over the child. My prison had suddenly become a palace, so that I wanted to be there rather than anywhere else.[21]

While in prison Perpetua has a number of dreams of triumphing over evil, and these bring her comfort. Dreams are often a revelation of deep inner truth, in this case probably her response to her father's anger. She and her companions were sentenced to be thrown to the beasts. Perpetua was concerned about her baby who was nursing, but then the baby stopped wanting breast milk and her breasts no longer gave her discomfort.

In Roman culture, with its significant class distinctions, Christians were an exception. Slaves and free people had a common bond, their faith. Felicitas the slave woman suffered alongside her noble companion.

As for Felicitas, she too enjoyed the Lord's favour in this wise. She had been pregnant when she was arrested, and was now in her eighth month. As the day of the spectacle drew near she was very distressed that her martyrdom would be postponed because of her pregnancy; for it is against the law for women with child to be executed. Thus she might have to shed her holy, innocent blood afterwards along with others who were criminals. Her comrades in martyrdom were also saddened; for they were afraid that they would have to leave behind so fine a companion to travel alone on the same road to hope. And so, two days before the contest, they poured forth a prayer to the Lord in one torrent of common grief. And immediately after their prayer the birth pains came upon her. She suffered a good deal in her labour because of the natural difficulty of an eight months' delivery.

Hence one of the assistants of the prison guards said to her: "You suffer so much now—what will you do when you are tossed to the beasts? Little did you think of them when you refused to sacrifice."

"What I am suffering now," she replied, "I suffer by myself. But then another will be inside me who will suffer for me, just as I shall be suffering for him." And she gave birth to a girl; and one of the sisters brought her up as her own daughter.[22]

Hippo

Monica, the Mother of Augustine

As Augustine, his brother, and his mother Monica were sailing down the Tiber River in Italy on their way back to Hippo, their home in North Africa, Monica became ill and died suddenly. Like Jerome after his supporter Paula's death and Gregory of Nyssa after the loss of his sister Macrina, Augustine wrote a beautiful tribute to his mother as a woman of faith who had helped shape his own faith. Unfortunately the writings of the women themselves no longer exist.

Augustine could recognize that Monica had suffered from the abuse of his father, but he believed in the customs of the day, which kept women with their husbands even when they were psychologically or physically abused. Such patriarchal definitions of women's virtue could be questioned. On the other hand Monica's wisdom as a peacemaker and as one who extinguished anger by speaking kindly is to be praised.

> My mother was educated, therefore, in a modest sober way, being rather made obedient to her parents by you than to you by her parents. And when she reached marriageable age, she was given to a husband whom she served "as her lord." She tried to win him to you, preaching you to him by her behavior in which you had made her beautiful to her husband, reverently lovable and admirable in his sight. So she tolerated his infidelities and never had a jealous scene with her husband about them. She awaited your mercy upon

him, that he might grow chaste through faith in you. Although an extremely kind man by nature, he was, in fact, also very hot-tempered. Only when he had calmed down and had become quiet, when she saw an opportunity, she would explain her actions, if perchance he had been aroused to anger unreasonably. Indeed there were many wives with much milder husbands who bore the marks of beatings, even in the form of facial disfigurement, and coming together to talk, they would complain of their husbands' behavior. Yet my mother, speaking lightly but seriously, warned them that the fault was in their tongues. And they were often amazed, knowing how violent a husband she had to live with, that it had never been heard of, nor had there been any evidence to show that Patricius had ever beaten his wife or that there had been a family quarrel that had lasted as much as a single day.

This great gift also, O my God, my mercy, you gave to your good servant, in whose womb you created me, that she showed herself, wherever possible, a peacemaker between people quarreling and minds at discord. But my mother would never report to one woman what had been said about her by another except insofar as what had been said might help to reconcile the two. . . . you were the master who, deep in the school of her heart, taught her this lesson.

Finally, toward the end of his earthly life, she won her husband over to you, and now that he was a believer, she no longer had to lament the things she had to tolerate when he was not yet a believer. She was also the servant of your servants. Whoever knew her praised many things in her, and honored and loved you, because they felt your presence in her heart, through the fruitful evidence of her saintly manner of life. She had been the wife of one husband, had requited her parents, had governed her house piously, was well reported of for good works; she had "brought up her children" as often "travailing in birth of them" as she saw them straying away from you (1 Tim 5:9; Gal 4:19).

Finally, Lord, of all of us—since by your gift we are allowed to speak—who before her death were living together after receiving the grace of baptism, she took as much care as though she were the mother of us all, and served us as though she were the daughter of us all.[23]

Notes

[1] "Therapeutae" is the masculine form of the word and "Therapeutrides" the feminine.

[2] For more information on this see Doug Adams, "Communal Dance Forms and Consequences in Biblical Worship," p. 40, and Martha Ann Kirk, "Biblical Women and Feminist Exegesis: Women Dancing Men's Ideas or Women Dancing Women," p. 134 in Doug Adams and Diane Apostolos-Cappadona, eds., *Dance as Religious Studies* (New York: Crossroad, 1990).

[3] Philo, *On the Contemplative Life*, 32–33. Trans. F. H. Colson, G. H. Whitaker, W. Earp, and R. Marcus, *Philo*. Vol. 9, Loeb Classical Library (Cambridge, Mass.: Harvard University Press, 1929–53) 131–33.

[4] Philo, *On the Contemplative Life*, 68–69, in ibid., 155.

[5] Philo, *On the Contemplative Life*, 83–88, in ibid., 165–67.

[6] Eusebius, "Martyrdom of Potamiaena and Basilides," *Ecclesiastical History* 6:5, in *The Acts of the Christian Martyrs*, trans. Hubert Musurillo (Oxford: Clarendon Press, 1972) 33–35.

[7] Socrates Scholasticus, as cited in Kari Vogt, "The Hierophant of Philosophy: Hypatia of Alexandria," in Kari Elisabeth Børresen and Kari Vogt, *Women's Studies of the Christian and Islamic Traditions: Ancient, Medieval, and Renaissance Foremothers* (Boston: Kluwer Academic, 1993) 156–57.

[8] From Rudolf Asmus, ed., *Das Leben des Philosophen Isidoros von Damaskios aus Damaskos* (Leipzig: Meiner, 1911) 31, as quoted in Vogt, "Hierophant," 157–58.

[9] *Das Leben des Philosophen Isidoros*, 32, quoted in Vogt, "Hierophant," 159–60.

[10] Socrates Scholasticus as quoted in Vogt, "Hierophant," 165.

[11] Benedicta Ward, *The Desert Christian: Sayings of the Desert Fathers*, trans. Benedicta Ward, S.L.G. (Kalamazoo: Cistercian Publications, revised edition, 1984, copyright © Benedicta Ward, 1975) 230–35.

[12] Palladius, *The Lausiac History*. English Translation by Robert T. Meyer. ACW 34 (Westminster, Md.: Newman Press, 1965).

[13] Ward, *The Desert Christian*, 82–84.

[14] Ibid., 229–30.

[15] Susanna Elm, *Virgins of God: The Making of Asceticism in Late Antiquity* (Oxford: Clarendon Press, 1994) 290.

[16] "Anastasia" in Paulus Peeters, ed., *Bibliotheca Hagiographica Orientalis* 242 (Brussels: Bollandist Society, 1910), translated from François Nau's edition of the Syriac in *Revue de l'Orient Chretien* 5 (1900) 391–401, in *Holy Women of the Syrian Orient*, intro. and trans. Sebastian P. Brock and Susan Ashbrook Harvery (Berkeley: University of California Press, 1987) 144-49.

[17] *CSEL* 108.23, 5-21, as quoted in Elm, *Virgins of God,* 303.

[18] Ibid.

[19] Ibid.

[20] *Life of St. Thaïs the Harlot,* from a Latin translation of a Greek text by an anonymous author from *MPL* 73, cols. 661-62. English translation in Benedicta Ward, *Harlots of the Desert: A Study of Repentance in Early Monastic Sources*. Latin translation of a Greek text by an anonymous author (London: Mowbray, 1987) 83–84.

[21] "The Acts of Perpetua and Felicitas," in *The Acts of the Christian Martyrs*, trans. Herbert Musurillo (Oxford: Clarendon Press, 1972) 107–108.

[22] Ibid., 123.

[23] Aurelius Augustinus, *Confessions* 9.9, in Mary T. Clark, trans., *Augustine of Hippo: Selected Writings* (New York: Paulist, 1984) 110–21.

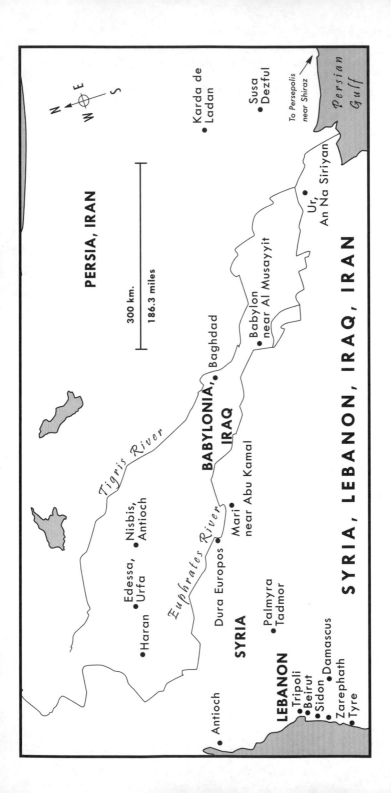

CHAPTER ELEVEN

IRAN, IRAQ, AND JORDAN

Iran

Karda de Ledan in Khuzistan

Martha, Martyr of Persia

In the Persian Empire by the middle of the third century C.E. there were many Christian communities of Syriac-speaking peoples. After Shapur I's military campaigns in 256 C.E. many Greek-speaking Christians were seized to work for the empire; where they went, they shared their faith with others. Though the Persian authorities, who practiced Zoroastrian religion, were hostile toward Christians, widespread persecution only broke out in the 340s when there was conflict with the Roman Empire, which had recently legitimized Christianity. In 341 Bishop Simeon from the country south of Baghdad was executed because he would not levy taxes on the Christians to support the war effort. One of the king's craftsmen, Posi, a Christian who had been brought from Roman territory to a new city built by Shapur, held fast to his faith and was martyred. The following account, originally in Syriac, is from the story of his daughter, Martha, who took a vow of virginity. Zoroastrians found the concept of virginity abhorrent. Martha had been arrested and the king had told the chief Mobed that if she would renounce Christianity or consent to marriage she would be freed. As she got stronger and feistier, the chief got angrier.

> So the chief Mobed went out and started to interrogate the glorious Martha as follows: "What are you?" To which the blessed Martha replied derisively, "I am a woman, as you can see." Those who happened to be there in the presence of the chief Mobed blushed and bent down their heads when they heard the wise Martha's reply to his question. The Mobed's face bacame green with anger and shame, but he controlled his feelings and said, "Reply to my question." To which the wise Martha said, "I did reply to the question I was asked."

"I asked you what is your religion," said the Mobed. The glorious Martha replied,

"I am a Christian, as my clothing shows."

The Mobed went on, "Tell me the truth, are you the daughter of that crazy Posi who went out of his mind and opposed the king, with the result that he was put to an evil death?" To this the blessed girl replied, "Humanly speaking, I am his daughter, but also by faith I am the daughter of the Posi who is wise in his God and sane in the firm stand he took on behalf of the King of kings, the King of truth, the Posi who yesterday acquired everlasting life by means of his dying for his God. If only God would hold me worthy to be a true daughter of this blessed Posi, who is now with the saints in light and eternal rest, while I am still among sinners in this world of sorrows."

The Mobed then said, "Listen to me, and I will advise you what is your best course: the king of kings is merciful and he does not desire anyone's death, but in his goodness he wishes all his friends to become fellow-religionists of his and so be honored by him. So it was the case of your father: because the king liked him, he honored him and gave him advancement; but your father acted foolishly and said things that were quite out of place, whereupon the king of kings urged him not to be stubborn, but to no effect. This was the reason why he was put to death. And now in your case, do not act stubbornly as your father did, but do the will of Shapur, king of kings and lord of the regions. As a result you will be greatly honored, and whatever you ask for your own comfort will be granted by the king."

The glorious Martha replied, "May king Shapur live, may his graciousness never leave him, may his compassion continue; may his graciousness be preserved by his children and his compassion redound to himself and on the people who deserve it. May the life that he loves be accorded to all his brethren and friends, but let all who imitate my father meet the evil death you said my father died. As for me, a wretched handmaid, the dregs of the handmaids of God and of the king, why should any transient honor come to me? I have decided to become the object of abuse like my father for the sake of my father's God, and I will die like him because of my faith in God."

The Mobed said, "I am aware of the hardness of heart you Christians have—a people guilty of death. Furthermore, no obedient offspring is likely to come from a rebellious man like Posi. Nevertheless, simply so that I shall not be held guilty before God of not having done my best to warn you, I am taking all this trouble over you in order to bring you over to the religion of the excellent gods who care for the world."

The holy Martha replied, "You have said your part, and I have said mine—unless you are quite blind and are paying no attention to the true state of affairs that I have described. Otherwise you have both heard and seen which exhortation is profitable and which harmful; which leads to the kingdom of heaven, which leads to the fire of Gehenna, which provides life, and which engenders death."

The Mobed went on: "Listen to me and don't be stubborn and obstinate, following your own perverted wishes in everything. Instead, seeing that you are set on not giving up your religion, act as you like, but do this one thing only, and you shall live and not die: you are a young girl, and a very pretty one—find a husband and get married, have sons and daughters, and don't hold on to the disgusting pretext of the 'covenant.'"

The wise virgin Martha replied, "If a virgin is betrothed to a man, does the natural law order that someone else should come along, attack her fiancé, and snatch away this girl who has already been betrothed? Or does it say that such a virgin should give herself up to marry a man who is not her fiancé?"

"No," answered the Mobed.

The betrothed of Christ, Martha, said, "So how can your authority order me to marry a man to whom I am not betrothed when I am already betrothed to someone else?"

To which the Mobed said, "Are you really betrothed, then?" And the blessed Martha replied, "I am in truth betrothed." "To whom?" asked the Mobed. "Is not your honor aware of him?" said the glorious Martha. "Where is he?" asked the Mobed. Wise in our Lord, she replied, "He has set out on a long journey on business; but he is close by and is on the point of coming back." "What is his name?" inquired the Mobed. "Jesus," replied the blessed Martha.

Still not understanding, the Mobed went on, "What country has he gone to? In which city is he now?" The splendid Martha replied, "He has gone off to heaven, and he is now in Jerusalem on high."

At this point the Mobed realized that she was speaking of our Lord Jesus Christ, whereupon he said, "Didn't I say at the very beginning that this was a stubborn people, not open to persuasion? I will spatter you from head to toe with blood, and then your fiancé can come along to find you turned into dust and rubbish: let him marry you then."

The courageous Martha replied, "He will indeed come in glory, riding on the chariot of the clouds, accompanied by the angels and powers of heaven, and all that is appropriate for his wedding feast; he will shake the dust off the bodies of all those who are betrothed to him, wash them in the dew of heaven, anoint them with the oil of gladness, and clothe them in the garment of righteousness, which consists of glorious light; he will place on their fingers rings as the surety of his grace, while on their heads he will put a crown of splendor, that is to say, unfading glory. He will allow them to sit on his chariot—the glorious cloud—and will raise them up into the air, bringing them into the heavenly bridal chamber that has been set up in a place not made by hands, but built in Jerusalem the free city on high."

When the chief Mobed heard this, he left her in his palace and went in to inform the king of everything. The king then gave orders for the impudent girl and daughter of an impudent father to be taken outside the city and immolated on the very spot where her father had been killed.[1]

Persepolis (near Sh‹r‹z)

The strength of women

Ruins of this impressive ancient palace and a museum are about forty miles from Shiraz in southern Iran. Cyrus the Great and Darius ruled here. When Cyrus the Great conquered the Babylonian empire he allowed the Jews to return to Israel, and so he is praised in the biblical text.

When the Jews were in exile here during the reign of Darius, legend says that Jewish pages at the court were having a dispute over what in the world was the strongest force. The first said wine, for it brings all down, the second said the king, and the third, Zerubbabel, who became the leader of the Jews, said women. This incident is in Esdras in the Septuagint Greek Bible, but not in the Masoretic Hebrew text. Since the Council of Trent, Esdras has been assigned to the biblical "apocrypha."

> 13 Then the third, who had spoken of women and truth (and this was Zerubbabel), began to speak: 14 "Gentlemen, is not the king great, and are not men many, and is not wine strong? Who is it, then, that rules them, or has the mastery over them? Is it not women? 15 Women gave birth to the king and to every people that rules over sea and land. 16 From women they came; and women brought up the very men who plant the vineyards from which comes wine. 17 Women make men's clothes; they bring men glory; men cannot exist without women. 18 If men gather gold and silver or any other beautiful thing, and then see a woman lovely in appearance and beauty, 19 they let all those things go, and gape at her, and with open mouths stare at her, and all prefer

her to gold or silver or any other beautiful thing. 20 A man leaves his own father, who brought him up, and his own country, and clings to his wife. 21 With his wife he ends his days, with no thought of his father or his mother or his country. 22 Therefore you must realize that women rule over you!

"Do you not labor and toil, and bring everything and give it to women? 23 A man takes his sword, and goes out to travel and rob and steal and to sail the sea and rivers; 24 he faces lions, and he walks in darkness, and when he steals and robs and plunders, he brings it back to the woman he loves. 25 A man loves his wife more than his father or his mother. 26 Many men have lost their minds because of women, and have become slaves because of them. 27 Many have perished, or stumbled, or sinned because of women. 28 And now do you not believe me?

"Is not the king great in his power? Do not all lands fear to touch him? 29 Yet I have seen him with Apame, the king's concubine, the daughter of the illustrious Bartacus; she would sit at the king's right hand 30 and take the crown from the king's head and put it on her own, and slap the king with her left hand. 31 At this the king would gaze at her with mouth agape. If she smiles at him, he laughs; if she loses her temper with him, he flatters her, so that she may be reconciled to him. 32 Gentlemen, why are not women strong, since they do such things?" (1 Esdr 4:13-32)[2]

Susa (or Shush), Dezful

Esther

Although Susa was a major city dating back to about 4000 B.C.E., in comparison to Persepolis not many ruins remain. The fictionalized story of Esther cannot be located, but the narrative associates her with Xerxes (Ahasuerus), who had a winter palace at Susa. Xerxes ruled about 485 to 464 B.C.E. The Persian empire conquered the Babylonian empire in the sixth and fifth centuries B.C.E. Esther was probably written at the close of the fourth century as the Persian empire was ending, in order to teach that God would continually watch over the people of Israel and would never abandon them. The story was also written to explain the origin of the feast of Purim and began to be read in Jewish worship on that feastday, a practice continuing today. The reading is dramatic and festive and is meant to delight children. As the story is read aloud, the people yell "boo" when they hear the name of Haman, and they cheer when they hear the name of Mordecai. On the feast of Purim, Jewish children often dress up in costumes representing the characters of the book.

Esther serves as a paradigm of a courageous woman willing to risk her own life to try to save others. The ending of the book, however, is vindictive. Vengeance is never a good solution, as it only perpetuates the cycle of violence. In the Hebrew text of Esther, God is never mentioned; however, in the expanded Greek text Esther says a prayer.

> 12 When they told Mordecai what Esther had said, 13 Mordecai told them to reply to Esther, "Do not think that in the king's palace you will escape any more than all the other Jews. 14 For if you keep silence at such a time as this, relief and deliverance will rise for the Jews from another quarter, but you and your father's family will perish. Who knows? Perhaps you have come to royal dignity for just such a time as this." 15 Then Esther said in reply to Mordecai, 16 "Go, gather all the Jews to be found in Susa, and hold a fast on my behalf, and neither eat nor drink for three days, night or day. I and my maids will also fast as you do. After that I will go to the king, though it is against the law; and if I perish, I perish." 17 Mordecai then went away and did everything as Esther had ordered him. (Esth 4:12-17)

Iraq

Babylon (near Al Musayyit)

Susanna

The Chaldean Church, also called the Assyrian Church, a Catholic Uniate, has its patriarch in Baghdad. The ruins of Babylon on the Euphrates River about 50 miles south of Baghdad have been excavated and partially restored by the Iraqi Department of Antiquities. They include the remains of the Temple of Marduk and a replica of the Ishtar Gate. (The original Ishtar Gate is in the Pergamon Museum in Berlin.) The Babylonian goddess Ishtar was the Mesopotamian form of the Semitic goddess Astarte, who is associated with both erotic love and war. Hammurabi (1792–1750 B.C.E.) developed Babylon and built the first ziggurat, the kind of structure that underlies the biblical story of the Tower of Babel. Hammurabi is remembered for his Code of Laws, actually legal precedents in 282 cases, inscribed on a stone stele that was in the Temple of Marduk. In 1902 large pieces of this were found in Susa. The cases include family law, economic law, and criminal cases, and some are similar to the Mosaic Law.

Biblical authors often used female images in trying to describe evil. They looked on Babylon as the great enemy and wrote very pejorative comments about "her." The author of Revelation, searching for terrible images to describe Rome, called it "Babylon the great, mother of harlots and all the world's abominations." Modern readers need to sift through the political and religious polemic and come to understand more of the literary, legal, and artistic accomplishments of the people of Babylon, the largest city in the world, at the time of Nebuchadnezzar II. For instance, the final form of the Epic of Gilgamesh was written here. Israel, a small, poor country astride a trade route between the continents, hated the big powers that took and controlled it. Small countries colonized or economically used by powerful countries often demonize them, but relationships of domination will not exist forever. When will the dominant countries of the world today be in ruins like Babylon, the largest and greatest city? When will modern weapons systems, "security," crumble like the walls around the ancient cities? In the story of Susanna the powerful and dominant crumble under the truth.

The book of Daniel supposedly describes events at the court of Nebuchadnezzar II, who rebuilt the city and made it the largest in the world. He conquered Jerusalem and brought many of the people of Judah there as captives (2 Kgs 25:1-21; Psalm 137; Isaiah 13, 14, 21). The story of Susanna is in the Greek text of Daniel, but not in the Hebrew book. The story is not historically based, but is apocalyptic literature designed to teach that ultimately good will overcome evil.

> 42 Then Susanna cried out with a loud voice, and said, "O eternal God, you know what is secret and are aware of all things before they come to be; 43 you know that these men have given false evidence against me. And now I am to die, though I have done none of the wicked things that they have charged against me!" 44 The Lord heard her cry.
>
> (Read Dan 13:1-63)

The story of Susanna describes an innocent woman whom two elders want to rape. Victims of sexual violence often feel confusion and think that they may be responsible for taking part in sexual activities. This confusion is rooted in patriarchal scriptural texts and is still an extensive problem for women today. Scripture in at least one place makes a distinction between rape and consenting sex, saying the woman is not guilty (Deut 22:25-27), but then Scripture and ethics through the centuries have continued to confuse the issues. In the story of

Susanna, after the elders have threatened to rape her she says that it is better to fall into their power without guilt "than to sin before the Lord" (Dan 13:22). One could argue that she was going to enjoy being raped, and therefore it would be a sin; this is highly unlikely and an unacceptable excuse for distorted patriarchal ethics. If she allowed the elders to rape her (rather than being killed), she would not have committed the sin of adultery. One sins if one knowingly and willingly does or wishes to do an evil action. The *Anchor Bible* commentary on Susanna continues such warped ethics: "Unwilling to sin against her God by committing adultery, Susanna started screaming . . . ."[3] The notion that a woman enjoys being raped could be a male egotistical fantasy or a misguided rationalization for a terrible kind of violence.

Ur of the Chaldees, An Na Siriyan

Sarah

Ur dates to 4000 B.C.E., with ziggurat and royal tombs, and is one of the most impressive ancient sites in Iraq. The biblical narrative of Sarah and Abraham begins here.

> 28 Haran died before his father Terah in the land of his birth, in Ur of the Chaldeans. 29 Abram and Nahor took wives; the name of Abram's wife was Sarai, and the name of Nahor's wife was Milcah. She was the daughter of Haran the father of Milcah and Iscah. 30 Now Sarai was barren; she had no child.

> (Read Gen 11:28–12:3)

The text refers to Sarah as barren. Savina J. Teubal in her book *Sarah the Priestess, the First Matriarch of Genesis* theorizes that the biblical word for being childless has been translated with the pejorative word "barren" for Sarah, Rebecca, and Rachel, and that these narratives come from older stories of priestesses who remained childless for certain portions or all of their lives because that was their role. Patriarchal retelling and writing of these women's stories has misunderstood and twisted many of the meanings. Proper sexual alliances of priestesses brought blessings and improper ones brought curses. The stories of Sarah with the Pharoah, with Abimelech, and with Abraham at the sacred grove of Mamre may be associated with this idea of proper and improper alliances.[4]

Jordan (See map on p. 142.)

Mountains of Moab

Lot's Daughters

The mountains of Moab are near Naur and northeast of Mount Nebo. Scripture contains many jokes that modern readers do not understand as such. Oral humor is hard to capture in written texts, and when the texts are translated to other languages and cultures, the joke is often lost. Moreover, though humor is a great gift, it can also be used to demean, and this is true in some cases where humor appears in the Bible. One such instance is a bawdy joke in Genesis that simultaneously demeans women and characterizes Israel's neighbors and rivals as "incestuous bastards." The daughters of Lot, bereft of their husbands through the destruction of Sodom, get their father drunk and then lie with him.

> 36 Thus both the daughters of Lot became pregnant by their father. 37 The firstborn bore a son, and named him Moab; he is the ancestor of the Moabites to this day. 38 The younger also bore a son and named him Ben-ammi; he is the ancestor of the Ammonites to this day. (Gen 19:36-38)

God blessed and made a part of salvation history one of those people who had been demeaned in that joke. The Moabite woman Ruth cared for her mother-in-law Naomi and also became an ancestor of Christ.

Mount Nebo

Reflections by Egeria on Mount Nebo

About 30 kilometers south of Amman is Madaba, with a famous mosaic map of Palestine including Jerusalem from about 560. West of Madaba is Mount Nebo, known as the place were Moses saw the promised land, but then died. Franciscans have excavated a sixth-century church there. About fifty kilometers southwest of Madaba is Machaerus, Herod's fortress where John the Baptist was imprisoned and beheaded. When Egeria traveled in the 380s C.E. this area was already important for pilgrims. While modern day pilgrims may rightly be skeptical of Egeria's guides' "precise knowledge" of where events had taken place over a thousand years before, pilgrims can learn from her consistently taking time to pray, read Scripture, and integrate the inner meaning of her outer journey:

And it was always our practice when we managed to reach one of the places we wanted to see to have first a prayer, then a reading from the book, then to say an appropriate psalm and another prayer. By God's grace we always followed this practice whenever we were able to reach a place we wanted to see.

Now we had to hurry to carry out our intention of reaching Mount Nebo. As we travelled along, the local presbyter from Livias (we had asked him to leave his home and accompany us because he knew the area so well) asked us, "Would you like to see the water that falls from the rock, which Moses gave to the children of Israel when they were thirsty? You can if you have the energy to turn off the road at about the sixth milestone." At this we were eager to go. We turned off at once, the presbyter led the way, and we followed him. It is a place with a tiny church under a mountain—not Nebo, but another one not very far from Nebo but further in. A great many monks lived there, truly holy men of the kind known here as ascetics.

The holy monks were good enough to receive us very hospitably, and welcomed us indoors. Going in with them we joined them in prayer, and they then very kindly gave us the "blessings" which it is normal for them to give for those whom they entertain. Between the church and the cells was a plentiful spring which flowed from the rock, beautifully clear and with an excellent taste, and we asked the holy monks who lived there about the water which tasted so remarkably good. "This," they told us, "is the water which the holy Moses gave the children of Israel in this desert." As usual we had there a prayer, a reading from the Books of Moses, and one psalm.

Then we set off for the mountain, and with us came the holy clergy and monks who had accompanied us, and many of the holy monks who lived near the spring were kind enough to come too, or at least the ones who had the energy to ascend Mount Nebo. So we set out and came to the foot of Mount Nebo; it was very high, but mostly possible to ascend on the donkeys, though there were some steeper parts where we had to dismount, and it was hard going.

On reaching the mountain-top we came to a church, not a very big one, right on the summit of Mount Nebo, and inside, in the position of the pulpit, I saw a slightly raised place about the size of a normal tomb. I asked about it, and the holy men replied, " Holy Moses was buried here—by angels, since the Bible tells us no human being knoweth his burial. And there is no doubt that it was angels who buried him, since the actual tomb where he was buried can be seen today.

Our predecessors pointed out this place to us, and now we point it out to you. They told us that this tradition came from their predecessors."

Soon we had had the prayer and the other things which were usual in a holy place, and we were about to leave the church. Then the presbyters and holy monks who were familiar with the place asked us, "Would you like to see the places which are described in the Books of Moses? If so, go out of the church door to the actual summit, the place which has the view, and spend a little time looking at it. We will tell you which places you can see." This delighted us, and we went straight out. From the church door itself we saw where the Jordan runs into the Dead Sea, and the place was down below where we were standing. Then, facing us, we saw Livias on our side of the Jordan, and Jericho on the far side, since the height in front of the church door, where we were standing, jutted out over the valley. In fact from there you can see most of Palestine, the Promiséd Land and everything in the area of Jordan as far as the eye can see.

(EGERIA, 105–106)

Trans-Jordan Area (towards Amman and Jerash)

St. Mary of Egypt

St. Cyril of Skythopolis in the sixth century wrote down a version of this very popular story, which spread throughout East and West, growing as it was retold. Like Elisha the prophet, Mary lived in the desert with very little food, like Christ she walked on water, and like learned men she knew Scripture, though she was a woman and never had a chance to study.

Mary was a girl who wandered the streets of Alexandria, Egypt, as a prostitute. Out of curiosity, she joined pilgrims going to Jerusalem. She began to seduce them and then other people in Jerusalem. She tried to enter the church of the Holy Sepulcher on the feast of the Exaltation of the Holy Cross with other pilgrims, but she was held back by a spiritual force. The prostitute began to weep and Mary the Mother of Christ appeared to her and led her to repentance. Mary went to Jericho, to the desert near the Jordan where John the Baptist had been, and eventually to an isolated place across the Jordan where she prayed and fasted for over 40 years. A priest, Zossima, saw this solitary ascetic, whom he thought was a man at first, and begged to hear her story. Zossima was greatly inspired by the holy woman and kissed the

MARY OF
EGYPT

ground on which her feet had stood. Mary begged him not to tell anyone, but to return the following year on Holy Thursday to bring her Holy Communion which she had not had in years. The next year he obeyed her request and went to the edge of the River Jordan, but as he waited he was very afraid that he would not get to see this holy one again.

While he was praying and weeping in this way, another thought struck him: "What will happen if she does come? How will she cross the Jordan since there is no boat? How can she come to me, unworthy as I am? Alas, I am wretched; who is keeping such beauty from me?" The old man was turning these things over in his mind, when lo, the holy one came, and stood on the other bank from whence she had come. When Zossima saw her, he arose rejoicing and greatly exulting he glorified God. And again the thought seized him that she could not cross the Jordan, but when he looked he saw her signing the waters of the Jordan with the sign of the Cross. For the darkness was lit by the full splendour of the moon, since it was that time in the month. As soon as she had made the sign of the Cross, she stepped on to the water and walking over the flowing waves she came as if walking on solid land. Zossima was amazed and began to kneel, but she stopped him, calling over the water and saying, "What are you doing, father, you who are a priest of God and carrying the holy mysteries?" At once he obeyed her words. When she came up from the water, she said to the old man, "Give me a blessing, father, give me a blessing." He replied with great haste (for a great stupor had come over him at so glorious a miracle) and said, "Indeed God does not lie when he promises that we shall be like him, insofar as we have been purified. Glory to you, Christ our God, who have shown me by your handmaiden here how much I should consider myself below the measure of true perfection." When he had said this the woman asked him to say the Holy Creed and then he began the Lord's Prayer. When he had finished the Our Father, the holy one as is the custom, gave the kiss of peace to the old man. And then she received the life-giving gifts of the sacrament, groaning and weeping with her hands held up to heaven, she cried out, "Lord, now let your servant depart in peace, according to your word; for my eyes have seen your salvation" (Luke 2:29). And she said to the old man, "Forgive me, father, and fulfil my other wish: go now to the monastery and may the peace of God keep you. Return in a year to the stream where I first met you. Do not fail me in this but for God's sake, come. It is the will of God that you see me again." He answered her, "Would that it were possible now to follow your footsteps and have the precious fruit of the sight of your face! Tarry, mother, grant a little request of an old man and deign to accept a little food which I have brought." Saying this he showed her the basket he had brought with him. She touched the lentils with the tip of her finger and taking three grains placed them in her mouth, saying that the grace of the Holy Spirit is sufficient to keep whole the substance of the soul. Then she said to the old man, "For God's sake pray for me, and remember me always as a sinner." He touched the feet of the holy one and with tears begged her to pray for the Church, for the Kingdom and for himself and so, weeping, he let her go, for he would not detain her any longer if she did not will it.

So once again she made the sign of the Cross over the Jordan and crossed over, walking on the element of water in the same way that she had when she came. And the old man went back full of joy and fear, reproaching himself that he had not asked the holy one her name; but he hoped to do so the following year.

So when a year had again passed, he went again into the huge solitude of the desert, having done everything according to custom, and he hurried towards that marvellous sight. He walked through the desert without finding any indications that this was the place he was looking for, so he looked right and left, turning his gaze in all directions as if he were a huntsman wanting to capture a much coveted animal. But seeing no movement anywhere he began to weep bitterly. And looking up to heaven he began to pray, "Shew me, O Lord, that angel in the flesh of whom the world is not worthy."

Having prayed in this way, he came to the place which looked like a stream and on the other side he saw the rising sun, and when he looked, he saw the holy one lying dead, her hands folded and her face turned to the East. Running up to her he watered the feet of the blessed one with tears; otherwise he did not dare to touch her. He wept for some time and said the appropriate psalms, then the prayer for the dead, and then he said to himself, "Is it right to bury the holy body here?" And then he saw by her head these words written in the earth: "Father Zossima, bury in this place the body of Mary the sinner, return me to the earth of which I am made, dust to dust, having prayed to the Lord for me, who died on the first day of the Egyptian month of Pharmuti called the fifth of the Ides of April by the Romans, on the self-same night as the Passion of the Lord after making her communion of the Divine and Mysterious Supper."

When he had read what was written, the old man wondered who it was that had written those words, since she had told him that she was unlettered, but he rejoiced to know the name of the holy one. He realised that as soon as she had received communion from the divine mysteries by the Jordan, in that same hour she had come to the place where at once she had passed from this world. The same journey which had taken Zossima twenty days with difficulty, Mary had covered in an hour and then at once passed on to God. So Zossima glorified God and shed tears on the body, saying, "It is time, Zossima, to fulfil the command. But how, wretched man, are you going to dig out a grave with nothing but your hands?" Then he was not far away from a small piece of wood, thrown down in the desert. Picking it up he set about digging. But the ground was dry and very hard, and would not yield to the efforts of the old man. He grew tired, and poured with sweat. He sighed from the depths of his soul and raising his eyes he saw a great lion standing by the body of the holy one and licking her feet. When he saw the lion he trembled with fear, especially because he remembered that Mary had said she had never met any animals. But protecting himself with the sign of the cross, he believed that he would be kept from harm by the power of the one who lay there. As for the lion, it walked up to him, expressing friendliness in every movement. Zossima said to the lion, "Greatest of the beasts, you have been sent by God, so that the body of the holy one should be buried, for I am old and have not enough strength to dig her grave. I have no spade and I cannot go back all that distance to fetch suitable tools. So do the work with your paws and we shall be able to give to the earth the mortal tabernacle of the saint."

While he was still speaking the lion had already dug out with its front paws a hole big enough to bury the body in. Again the old man watered the feet of the holy one with tears and then, with the lion standing by, he called upon her to pray for everyone; he covered her body with earth; it was naked as it had been before, except for the torn monastic cloak which Zossima had thrown across her and with which Mary, turning away, had partially covered her body. Then they both withdrew. The lion went off into the depths of the desert as meekly as if it were a lamb, and Zossima went home, blessing and praising God and singing hymns of praise to our Lord Christ. When he reached the monastery, he told the monks everything that he had heard and seen, hiding nothing. From the very beginning he told them everything in memory of the saint in fear and love. As for abbot John, he did find a few in the monastery in need of correction, so that none of the saint's words proved useless or inexplicable.[5]

Notes

[1] "Martha," translated from *Acta Sanctorum martyrum et Sanctorum* 2:233–41, in Paulus Peeters, ed., *Bibliotheca Hagiographica Orientalis* (Brussels: Bollandist Society, 1910) 698, as quoted in *Holy Women of the Syrian Orient*. Intro. and trans. Sebastian P. Brock and Susan Ashbrook Harvey (Berkeley: University of California Press, 1987) 68–71.

[2] I Esdr 4:13-32 as cited in Leonard Swidler, *Biblical Affirmation of Woman* (Philadelphia: Westminster Press) 129–30.

[3] Carey A. Moore, *Daniel, Esther, and Jeremiah: The Additions.* AB 44 (Garden City, N.Y.: Doubleday, 1977) 77.

[4] Savina J. Teubal, *Sarah the Priestess: The First Matriarch of Genesis* (Athens, Ohio: Swallow Press, 1984).

[5] Sophronius, bishop of Jerusalem, *Life of St. Mary of Egypt,* translated into Latin by Paul, deacon of the holy church of Naples. *MPG* 87 (3), cols. 3693-3726. English translation in Benedicta Ward, *Harlots of the Desert. A Study of Repentance in Early Monastic Sources* (London: Mowbray, 1987) 52–56.

CHAPTER TWELVE

LEBANON AND SYRIA
(See maps on pages 248 and 142.)

Lebanon

Beirut (Bayr⁽t)

St. Matrona of Perge

During the Roman period Beirut became famous for a School of Law, one of three in the ancient world. The city was a significant cultural center until the sixth century C.E. Many artifacts in the National Museum and the Museum of the American University give some context for this fifth-century C.E. saint who was born in Perge, but lived in Constantinople and in Beirut.

St. Matrona of Perge's *Life* reveals a number of themes frequently seen in women saints' stories. While a laywoman, she led an ascetic existence with many acts of charity. She endured an abusive husband. As a nun she dressed like a man to avoid notice, and she was the abbess of a convent. Her story is not typical in that it gives women prominence, reveals her extensive travels, and notes that a male monastic habit was worn by her nuns. Matrona was born about 430 and died about 510 or 515. She returned to Constantinople about 475. When she was elderly, historical evidence indicates that she opposed the emperor's support of Monophysitism, which lasted from 491 to 518. The *Life* may have been written in the mid-sixth century by a monk of the male monastery where she stayed, but it certainly adds pious legends to the actual facts about her.

The author begins the *Life* by praising Matrona because she "displayed the traits of holy men in the midst of monastic men and mastered the feats of accomplished solitaries. That she was no ordinary woman or in any wise deficient, but rather, greater than those women who had already distinguished themselves in asceticism."[1] This was apparent by how many chose to follow as her flock. Her parents had her married to Dometianos and she bore a daughter. Matrona went to Constantinople and visited the shrines of the saints and cared for the poor and those in need. She went to all-night prayer vigils, but her husband thought that she was out at night to be a courtesan and he became angry and forbade her to go. Matrona felt a very strong calling to be a nun and she found a friend, Susannah, who was happy to mother her daughter. Matrona believed that her husband would cause trouble for any convent that accepted her, so, following a vision, she dressed herself as a male and entered a monastery of men, the famed house of Bassianos in Constantinople. There she lived for three years and was known for prayer, fasting, and charity.

One day, while Matrona was working in the garden, a fellow monk noticed and asked her why her ears were pierced. The head of the monastery, Bassianos, had a dream that she was a woman; he called her in and asked for an explanation. She told her story, explaining that her husband would insult her, quarrel, strike, and even threaten her. She feared that he would do harm to a convent. Bassianos was sympathetic and said that surely God would guide her in what to do next. Matrona returned to Susannah and learned that her daughter had died. Her husband had heard that she was in the monastery and he went there in a rage. He was told that the monk who was there had left. Bassianos feared for Matrona's life, so the monks arranged for her to go by ship to Syria, to the monastery of Hilara. She lived peacefully there until she prayed for a blind man who was miraculously cured. Her fame spread and Dometianos heard of her. He went to Syria to try to take her back. She escaped and set off for Jerusalem with only a pilgrim's staff, the hair shirt she wore, and what was left of blessed bread given her by Bassianos.

Dometianos pursued Matrona to Jerusalem and told pious women that he was seeking the holy woman and that he would reward them if they would help him find her. Matrona saw him and hid. When the women came to her she said to tell him that she was going south to Mount Sinai. Actually she disguised herself again and went north toward Beirut.

> She found there a temple of idols and dwelled therein, choosing to be devoured by demons or beasts rather than fall into the hands of her husband. Said she, "If I serve God, demons cannot harm me. As for beasts, if I truly and piously pursue virtue, perhaps they will respect me; but if my husband gets hold of me, he will treat me more cruelly than demons and beasts." Taking up her abode, then, in the idols' temple, she performed without ceasing the order of psalmody that had been handed down to her.

Now it happened once, as she performed the nightly psalmody, that demons sang most fervently in response, for she heard the voices of many men singing. Taking fright and fortifying herself with the sign of the cross, she completed the psalmody, considering within herself and saying, "This place is deserted and the house unhallowed; there is no village in this place, nor have any passersby approached; whence, then, come these voices?" With these thoughts in her mind she went outside the temple, to find out whence the voices came. But neither finding nor seeing anyone, she went back inside the idols' temple. These voices continued to be heard for many days thereafter, so she fasted for three days and prayed intently to the Lord that He should reveal to her the cause. Swift to hearken unto those who cry out to Him by night and by day, the Lord God overlooked not her prayer, but hastened to make the revelation unto her. For as she completed her psalmody on another day, the demons began to sing impiously and to utter discordant, shameful sounds and to bring fire to the door of the temple. But the blessed one sealed herself continuously [with the cross] and rebuked them, and they fled with the fire into the mountains. Recognizing this to be the doing of the Enemy [i.e., the Devil], she looked this way and that, to see what had become of [the demons] or whither they had run off; and looking up she saw the mountains shrouded as it were in a sort of darkness.

Sometime later she was oppressed by great thirst, and going a short distance from the temple she found blossomy, tender greens. Picking some of these she pressed them to her lips and tongue, in order to assuage her thirst and alleviate the extreme dryness. But the merciful and compassionate Lord, seeing such great endurance and patience, wrought an ancient miracle: not feasting an ungrateful people but nourishing a soul which loved Him, not showering down a marvelous rain of plenteous manna, but providing her with a spontaneous meal in this desolate place. For though all the place was dry and without water, she did find one spot which was moist; and beseeching God and taking Him as assistant, she came to this spot and dug in the earth with her hands. After much toil she came to sharp stones, and in them she dug a small hole; and the further her hands went down [into the ground], the more moisture she felt. Having found a bit of water she withdrew, reckoning that it was the hour of psalmody. But when she returned on the morrow after completing her morning rule, she found the hole which she had dug the day before filled with water. Kneeling, she thanked the Giver of good things, and standing up she picked a few greens. For the place where the water was abounded in them, as the *gifts* of God are *perfect* and unfailing and they require no season to come to perfection. She washed them in water, and letting the water run off because of the dirt, she took the greens and went inside. Now, wherever the water ran out of the hole, it brought forth tender, leafy greens. Coming, then, every day after her morning prayers and picking and washing the greens, she would let the water run off and then stop it again when it was clean; and eating the greens and drinking from the water, at the customary hour of repast after the evening psalmody, she glorified God for all His gifts to her. Thus did that place supply her ever after, as if by way of tribute, with the amplest daily nourishment.

For a long time the blessed one enjoyed such meals and made progress in her intense asceticism, but then the evil demon, unable to bear seeing her rejoice in the Lord, armed himself with another device against her. Transforming himself into a woman fair of face and . . . of solemn and noble bearing, he approached the holy one and addressed her with no little flattery: "What are you doing here, madam, you who are young and quite fair of form? This is no place for you: it is a dwelling of idols and demons. Come to Beirut, for it is a beautiful and hospitable city, which provides for all people. It is desolate here: there is no provision for the necessities of life. Furthermore, heaven forbid that any of those men who often come here should do you harm, desirous of committing sin with you." Recognizing that this was the Tempter, the blessed one answered saying, "I have greens. I have water. Christ my Master provides for me in abundance. I am satisfied with these things and seek nothing else." Hearing this the demon withdrew, saying, "Out of consideration for you have I counseled you to do that which I know to be to your advantage, nor shall I cease to counsel you. For the rest, it is for you to test and do that which is good." After a few days he came again in the same guise and said to her, "I do indeed take thought for you, madam, and have compassion for your youth. I am troubled and concerned lest such great beauty and comeliness should wither and perish in the harshness of this place. Wherefore I pray you, heed my fitting counsel: come to my mistress, Beirut, where there is a hospice worthy of you and everything requisite for your protection and service." But replying with great wisdom and understanding, "It is not beauty of the body I seek but of the soul, and if I make my comeliness without to wither, I renew that within," she put the woman to shame and chased her off.

Nevertheless, the mischievous one would not desist from tempting her. Abiding but a short time he assumed the form of an old woman, common and ugly, with fiery eyes, and set upon her, insolently threatening and menacing her, uttering mindless things in keeping with his purpose. When she made no reply whatsoever, on account of the disorder of his speech, he became all the more frenzied with rage and fired with anger, and he said to her, "I have used such words toward you, in such a manner on such matters, and you answer me nothing?" But the blessed one fortified herself, as she was wont, with the sign of the cross. Then putting his hands to his head, he rent and tore them in pieces with his teeth and cried out in a loud voice, saying, "Shall I, who have vanquished many with force and worsted yet more, not be able to defeat you? Just give me time. For even if I cannot deceive you in your youth, I shall bring the most dreadful things upon you in your old age. And lest you now escape my hands, I shall incite Beirut against you, especially those who delight in this place and are enslaved to the worship of the idols; I shall drive you from this entire country." Having said this and similar things the evil one vanished. To such an extent, then, did the malignant one annoy her; but he found it impossible to deceive her in any wise, and he durst not annoy her in an obvious manner, for God's grace overshadowed her. Wherefore, after such great trials, she was seized with joy, and the snares of the demons gave way to a beauteous vision. For as she said the evening prayers there appeared to her three men; and whether they were men or angels, she neither knew then nor said later, though it would be impious and indeed wholly alien to Christians not to think this visitation divine. For God, in condescension to our weakness and for our benefit, is wont to present visions of the Incorporeal Ones [i.e., angels] in the form of embodied men. As she sang, then, [these three] entered and remained kneeling behind her for a long time. Though the blessed one was afraid, she did not cease singing, but directed her gaze this way and that, desiring to see what they were doing; she did not, however, turn round. When she began the psalmody of the evening office, the men rose from their prayer, and telling her three times, "Pray for us, O servant of Christ," they withdrew and vanished.

19. But thereafter there was talk of her in Beirut, and many went out unto her, both men and women, and especially noblewomen, for in a few days report of her had spread everywhere. All told of how her angelic way of life and splendid purity had routed the demons in the temple and put them to flight. Now, among the many who came together to see her and receive her blessing, there came also a certain woman with her daughter, whose name was Sophrone. When this Sophrone, then, saw the blessed Matrona, she was moved to compunction, and could not bear to leave the blessed one or

follow her mother, saying, "From henceforth is this holy one both mother and father to me." Though her mother did her utmost and pressed her, that she should at least take leave of her own family, she would in no wise assent to depart. On this ground did other daughters of heathen [parents] also attach themselves to the blessed Matrona: coming to her they fell down at her knees, crying, and said to her, "Deliver us, holy mother, from the vanity of the idols and deception of the demons, and lead us unto the God you serve." Receiving them the blessed one first tempered their bodily habits and then, once she had strengthened their spiritual reasoning and prepared them, over the course of many days, for the hope that lies in store for Christians, she would have the rites of chrismation and baptism performed upon them. Keeping these women, together with the first one, and teaching them letters and poring over Scripture with them, especially the blessed David, she made them children of God.[2]

Sidon

Melania the Younger and the Empress Eudocia

An earthquake destroyed Sidon in the sixth century and now it is only a small port city with few of its Roman ruins. It is located about fourteen kilometers south of Beirut.

The Martyrion of St. Phocas was claimed to be the place where this holy woman of the early church lived. While in Constantinople, Melania the Younger had encouraged the Empress Eudocia to go on a pilgrimage to the holy places. They agreed to meet in Sidon, where the Canaanite woman was said to have lived. Both Melania and Eudocia were strong, independent women, and perhaps this place of a strong woman who talked to Jesus and of the woman martyr Phocas appealed to them.

> Melania therefore met the empress in Sidon and returned thanks for the surpassing love which she had shown her in Constantinople. She stayed at the shrine of Saint Phocas, where it is said that the faithful Canaanite woman lived, who said to the Lord in the holy Gospel, *Yes, Lord, but the dogs eat from the crumbs which fall from their masters' table.* Thus the blessed lady used to be eager to please the Lord, in her home, in her conversation, and in every other activity. When the empress, who was dear to God, saw her, she welcomed her with all possible respect as her true spiritual mother, and rightly so, for it was a glory to the empress to honor her who truly glorified the King of Heaven. The saint, accepting her

faith and appreciating the toils of her journey, encouraged her to make even more progress in well-doing. The godly empress replied to her in these memorable words: "I have discharged a two-fold vow to the Lord; to venerate the holy places and to see my mother, for I wished to have the honor of seeing Your Holiness, while you are still serving the Lord in the flesh." Because of her surpassing spiritual love for Melania, the empress hastened to reach the saint's monastery. After she had entered it, she looked upon the virgins as her own sisters. Much refreshed by her visit, she wanted also to visit the men's monastery and to receive a blessing there. The deposition of the holy relics in the shrine that Melania had recently built was about to take place, as we have stated above. The empress asked that the festival should be held in her presence.

The enemy of the good was once again envious of such great spiritual devotion, and prepared at the very moment of the deposition of the holy relics to crouch down on the empress' foot and to cause an extraordinary groaning as a result. No doubt this all happened to test the saint's faith. After she had escorted the empress to the church of the holy Resurrection, she herself settled down at the same time by the relics of the holy martyrs. She remained apart with her virgins in unceasing prayer and fasting, and in mourning, until the empress sent for her. Her pain had now gone.

When the empress' pain had been cured, the blessed lady did not give up her battle with the devil, who wanted to make mischief between them. After Melania had spent a few days with the empress and had given her considerable help, she escorted her as far as Caesarea. They were scarcely able to tear themselves away from each other, for they were bound very closely together by the tie of spiritual love. The saint returned once more to her ascetic way of life, praying that the godly Empress might be kept safe right up to the end of her journey and might be restored in good health to her husband. The God of all things granted her this wish.[3]

Tripoli, Tarᶜbulus

St. Mary/Marinos

Tripoli has been a major port and trading center since Phoenician times. In 1103 Crusaders built St. Giles Cathedral, which can be seen today.

The story of Mary was very popular and early Syriac, Latin, Coptic, Ethiopic, Armenian, and Arabic texts of it have been found. Some scholars believe that it originated in the Tripoli area. St. Mary/Marinos of the fifth century is one of the so-called transvestite nuns, who disguised themselves as monks. Stories of such nuns were very common in Byzantine hagiography between the fifth and ninth centuries. Over a dozen stories exist, including those about Anastasia Patrikia, Matrona of Perge, Suphrosyne of Alexandra, Appollinaria/Dorotheos, Eugenia/Eugenios, Susannah/John, and Theodora/Theodore. Perhaps these stories reflect the ambiguity or tension growing in Christianity as males were valued more than females. Yet a primary Christian text, Gal 3:28, said that "there is neither male nor female, all are one in Christ Jesus."

The story of Mary/Marinos was probably written in the sixth or seventh century in Syria, but it did not say where Mary lived. While dressed as a monk, she was accused of raping the daughter of an innkeeper. She did not deny it and was severely punished. After the child was born she took care of it. Marinos was popular in both East and West in the Middle Ages. February 12 is celebrated as her feastday.

> 2. When the young girl grew up, her father said to her, "My child, behold, all that I own I place in your hands, for I am departing in order to save my soul." Hearing these things [said] by her father, the young girl said to him, "Father, do you wish to save your own soul and see mine destroyed? Do you not know what the Lord says? That the *good shepherd giveth his life for his sheep*?" And again she said [to him], "The one who saves the soul is like the one who . . . created it."

> 3. Hearing these things, her father was moved to compunction at her words, for she was weeping and lamenting. He therefore began to speak to her and said, "Child, what am I to do with you? You are a female, and I desire to enter a monastery. How then can you remain with me? For it is through the members of your sex that the devil wages war on the servants of God." To which his daughter responded, "Not so, my lord, for I shall not enter [the monastery] as you say, but I shall first cut off the hair of my head, and clothe myself like a man, and then enter the monastery with you."

> 4. The [father], after distributing all his possessions among the poor, followed the advice of his daughter and cut off the hair of her head, dressed her in the clothing of a man, and changed her name to Marinos. And he charged her saying, "Child, take heed how you conduct yourself, for you are about to enter into the midst of fire, for a woman in no way enters a [male] monastery. Preserve yourself therefore blameless before God, so that we may fulfill our vows." And taking his daughter, he entered the cenobitic monastery.

5. Day by day, the child advanced in all the virtues, in obedience, in humility, and in much asceticism. After she lived thus for a few years in the monastery, [some of the monks] considered her to be a eunuch, for she was beardless and of delicate voice. Others considered that [this condition] was instead the result of her great asceticism, for she partook of food only every second day.

6. Eventually it came to pass that her father died, but [Mary, remaining in the monastery], [continued] to progress in asceticism and in obedience, so that . . . she received from God the gift of healing those who were troubled by demons. For if she placed her hand upon any of the sick, they were immediately healed.

7. Living together within the cenobitic monastery were forty men. Now once a month four of the brethren were officially sent forth to minister to the needs of the monastery, because they were responsible for looking after other monks as well, the solitaries, [who lived] outside [the community]. Midway on their journey was an inn, where both those going and those coming were, on account of the great distance, accustomed to [stop and] rest. Moreover, the innkeeper provided [the monks] with many courtesies, accommodating them each with particular solicitude.

8. One day, the superior, summoning *abba* Marinos, said to him, "Brother, I know your conduct, how in all things you are perfect and unwavering in your obedience. Be willing then to go forth and attend to the needs of the monastery, for the brethren are annoyed that you do not go forth unto service. For in doing this you will obtain a greater reward from God." At these words, Marinos fell down at his feet and said, "Father, pray for me, and wherever you direct me, there I shall go."

9. One day, therefore, when Marinos had gone forth unto service along with three other brethren, and while they were all lodging at the inn, it came to pass that a certain soldier deflowered the innkeeper's daughter, who thereupon became pregnant. The soldier said to her, "If your father should learn of this, say that 'It was the young monk who slept with me.'" Her father, upon realizing that she was pregnant, questioned her closely, saying, "How did this happen to you?" And she placed . . . the blame on Marinos, saying, "The young monk from the monastery, the attractive one called Marinos, he made me pregnant."

10. Thoroughly outraged, the innkeeper made his way to the monastery, shouting accusations and saying, "Where is that charlatan, that pseudo-Christian, whom you call a Christian?" When one of the stewards came to meet him, he

said, "Welcome." But the [innkeeper] replied, "The hour was an evil one in which I made your acquaintance." In like manner he said to the father superior, "May I never see another monk," and other such things. When he was asked why he was saying these things, he answered, "I had but a single daughter, who I hoped would support me in my old age, but look at what Marinos has done to her, he whom you call a Christian—he has deflowered her and she is pregnant." The superior, "What can I do for you, brother, since [Marinos] is not here at the moment? When he returns from his duties, however, I will have no recourse but to expel him from the monastery."

11. When Marinos returned with the three other monks, the superior said to him, "Is this your conduct, and is this your asceticism, that while lodging at the inn you deflowered the innkeeper's daughter? And now her father, coming here, has made us all a spectacle to the laity." Hearing these things, Marinos fell upon his face, saying, "Forgive me, father, for I have sinned as a man." But the superior, filled with wrath, cast him out saying, "Never again shall you enter this monastery."

12. Leaving . . . the monastery, [Marinos] immediately sat down outside the monastery gate, and there endured the freezing cold and the burning heat. Thereafter, those entering the monastery used to ask him, "Why are you sitting outdoors?" To which he would reply, "Because I fornicated and have been expelled from the monastery."

13. When the day arrived for the innkeeper's daughter to give birth, she bore a male child, and the girl's father took the [infant] and brought it to the monastery. Finding Marinos sitting outside the gate, he threw the child down before him and said, "Here is the child which you have wickedly engendered. Take it." And immediately the innkeeper departed.

14. Marinos, picking up the child, was filled with distress and said, "Yes I have received the just reward for my sins, but why should this wretched babe perish here with me?" Accordingly he undertook to procure milk from some shepherds, and so nursed the child as its father. But the distress that overwhelmed him was not all, for the child, whimpering and wailing, continually soiled his [Marinos'] garments.

15. After the passage of three years, the monks entreated the superior saying, "Father, forgive this brother; his punishment is sufficient, for he has confessed his fault to all." But when they saw that the superior remained unmoved, the brethren said, "If you do not receive him back, then we too will leave the monastery. For how can we ask God to forgive our sins, when today marks the third year that he has been

sitting in the open air . . . beyond the gate, and we do not forgive him?"

16. The superior, considering these things, said to them, "For the sake of your love, I accept him." And summoning Marinos he said to him, "On account of the sin which you have committed, you are not worthy to resume your former position here. Nevertheless, on account of the brethren's love, I accept you back into our ranks, but only as the last and least of all." At this Marinos began to weep and said, "Even this is a great thing for me, my lord, for you have deemed me worthy to come inside the gate, so that I might thus be given the honor of serving the holy fathers."

17. Consequently the superior assigned him the lowliest chores of the monastery, and he performed them [all] scrupulously and with great devotion. But the child was forever following him about, crying and saying, "Dada, Dada," and such things as children say when they wish to eat. Thus, in addition to the [usual] trials and temptations that beset a monk, Marinos was continually anxious about procuring and providing sustenance for the child. When the boy grew up, he remained in the monastery, and having been raised in the practice of virtues he was deemed worthy of the monastic habit.

18. One day, after a considerable passage of time, the superior inquired of the brethren, "Where is Marinos? Today is the third day that I have not seen him singing in the choir. He was always the first to be found standing there before the start of the service. Go to his cell, and see whether he is lying ill." Going . . . to his cell, they found him dead, and informed the superior, saying, "Brother Marinos has died." But the [superior] said, "In what state did his wretched soul depart? What defense can he make for the sin that he committed?" [Having thus spoken, the superior then] directed that [Marinos] be buried. But as they were preparing to wash him, they discovered that he was a woman, and shrieking, they all began to cry out in a single voice, "Lord, have mercy."

19. The superior, hearing their cries, asked them, "What troubles you so?" And they said, "Brother Marinos is a woman." Drawing near and seeing [for himself], the [superior] cast himself down at her feet, and with many tears cried out, "Forgive me, for I have sinned against you. I shall lie dead here at your holy feet until such time as I hear forgiveness for all the wrongs that I have done you." And while he was uttering many such lamentations, as well as things yet more remarkable, a voice spoke to him saying, "Had you acted knowingly, this sin would not be forgiven you. But since you acted unknowingly, your sin is forgiven."[4]

Tyre, S^cr

Hadrian's Gate

The Syro-Phoenician Woman

The Roman Emperor Hadrian traveled widely in this area and built an arch, colonnaded street, and other monumental structures. Tyre is about twenty miles south of the coastal city of Sidon. Near Sidon is the site of a Phoenician temple, Euchmoun, with a throne of Astarte with winged lions on each side. The two areas together are considered the center of the Phoenician people, who were seafaring merchants, descendants of the Canaanites. Tyre was a flourishing commercial city. Hiram of Tyre sent cedar and fir trees and workers to assist Solomon in the building of the Temple in Jerusalem. The people of Tyre worshiped a Tyrian form of Baal, who like all the Baals was a fertility god. In the scene on Carmel in 1 Kings 21 Elijah was in competition with this Baal, the deity worshiped by Jezebel, queen of Israel and daughter of the priest/king of Tyre. The story depicts a power contest between Tyrian Baal and YHWH, the God of Israel.

In popular language Jezebel is synonymous with evil. She was dishonest in taking Naboth's vineyard and cruel in killing Naboth, as David was dishonest in taking Bathsheba and cruel in killing Uriah, her husband. Western literature and art have tended to portray strong women as dangerous. Women should be weak and passive, or they are suspect.

In this public area one can remember Jesus, who preached in Tyre (Mark 3:8; Luke 6:17; Matt 11:20-22) and there performed a miracle. Jesus seemed to be challenging the limited faith of his disciples in his conversation with the Syro-Phoenician woman. Doug Adams in *The Prostitute in the Family Tree: Discovering Humor and Irony in the Bible* suggests that while the disciples think of the Syro-Phoenicians as dogs and unworthy of their favor, Jesus and the woman have a rapport. Their repartee is to break down this prejudice of his own disciples and show up their prejudice.[5]

> 24 From there he set out and went away to the region of Tyre. He entered a house and did not want anyone to know he was there. Yet he could not escape notice, 25 but a woman whose little daughter had an unclean spirit immediately heard about him, and she came and bowed down at his feet. 26 Now the woman was a Gentile, of Syrophoenician origin. She begged him to cast the demon out of her daughter. 27 He said to her, "Let the children be fed first, for it is not fair to take the children's food and throw it to the dogs." 28 But she answered him, "Sir, even the dogs under the table eat the children's crumbs." 29 Then he said to her, "For saying that, you may go—the demon has left your daughter." 30 So she went home, found the child lying on the bed, and the demon gone.
> (Mark 7:24-30)

Zarephath of Sidon

The widow who helped Elijah

Though she was in need, a poor widow was willing to help Elijah and was blessed for her generosity. In the synagogue in Nazareth, when the people were not ready to accept him, Jesus mentioned how God sometimes used people outside the "chosen ones" like the widow with Elijah or the leper with Elisha to carry on God's plans. (Luke 4:26)

> 7 But after a while the wadi dried up, because there was no rain in the land.
> 8 Then the word of the LORD came to him, saying, 9 "Go now to Zarephath, which belongs to Sidon, and live there; for I have commanded a widow there to feed you."
> (Read: 1 Kings 17:7-24)

Syria

Damascus (Dimashq)

The Great Mosque

Aʾisha Bint abi Bakr, *Muhammad*'s Wife

The Great Mosque of the Umayyads was built on a Byzantine Christian Cathedral. Aʾisha, *Muhammad*'s youngest and beloved wife, is said to have been in this mosque for many years studying and sharing the wisdom of the Prophet. The mosque is a starting place for the pilgrimage to Mecca.

Aʾisha was known for her strong will, fine logic, intelligence, and eloquence. She had the ability to stand firm on issues that she believed were right. She entered into frank dialogue with her husband and was not afraid to disagree. Not only did she stand up to him, but she also did with other men. She expressed her thoughts clearly and strongly. One day while *Muhammad* was seated in the middle of a group of men, he pointed her out and said to them, "Draw half of your religion from this ruddy faced woman."[6]

Aʾisha was actively involved in politics, cultural and literary activities, and theological discussions. The Muslim theologian Urwa Ibn El-Zuheir said, "I have not seen any one who is more knowledgeable in theology, in medicine and in poetry than Aʾisha."[7] She even disagreed with *Muhammad* sometimes about what he said was revelation of the Quʾran, which was coming to him from heaven. In one of these verses Allah permitted *Muhammad* to marry as many women as he wished. She angrily commented, "Allah always responds immediately to your needs."[8]

Arab women's loss of independence has been related to socio-economic changes resulting in the growing prosperity of the ruling classes and the impoverishment of the majority. In Islam those who seek equality, freedom, and justice continue to be in tension with those who cling to class privilege, feudal oppression, and male domination. Since the eighth century C.E. and the third Caliph ʿUsman Ibn ʿAffan the oppression has grown. Turkish domination, Western colonialism, and international imperialism have supported this development.

One of the most challenging incidents in Aʾisha's life is known as the "affair of the slander." *Muhammad* and his entourage, including Aʾisha in a closed litter on camelback, were traveling back to Medina. She had walked away from the group to perform her morning ablutions, but when she returned the group had left. While she was waiting for them to realize this and return for her, a young man passed by. He invited her to ride on his camel and he led it into the town. People of the town began to gossip that A'isha had done something improper with the man. Some said that she was forsaking the old prophet for a young man. She tried to convince *Muhammad* that she was innocent, but he was not sure.

I despaired and became ill, so I asked Muhammad to send me to my father's house. He sent a slave with me. When I entered I found Umm Ruman, who asked what had happened. I told her and she said, "Calm yourself. Seldom is a beautiful woman who is beloved by her husband not envied by her fellow wives and not spoken ill of by them!" I asked if my father knew. She said he did and that Muhammad knew too. Then I wept copiously.

Abu Bakr who was upstairs reading heard my voice and came down to ask my mother what the matter with me was. She said, "She has heard what is being said about her." Then his eyes filled and he said, "I urge you to return to your house." So I returned and he and my mother came with me and remained with me until Muhammad came in after the afternoon prayer. He bore witness that there was no God but Allah and praised and extolled him. Then he said to me, "A'isha, if you have been tempted to evil or done wrong, repent; for Allah accepts repentance from his servants."

Meanwhile, a woman of the Ansar had come and seated herself in the doorway and I said, "Aren't you shy of speaking of the matter in front of this woman?" Then I said to my father, "Answer," but he said, "What shall I say?" I appealed to my mother, but she too was at a loss.

Then I bore witness that there was no God but Allah and praised and extolled him and said: "If I said that I had done nothing and Allah knows that I would be telling the truth, you would not believe me for you already think me guilty. If I said I were guilty and Allah knows I am not, you would say I had confessed. Thus, all I can do is cite Joseph's father: 'My course must be fitting patience, and Allah's help is to be sought for the problem you describe.'"

Then Muhammad received a revelation after which I perceived joy on his face. He wiped his forehead and said, "Rejoice A'isha, Allah has revealed your innocence."

I became as angry as possible. My parents said I should get up and go to Muhammad, but I said, "I shall neither go to him nor praise him nor you who believed what you heard about me and did not deny it. I shall praise Allah who revealed my innocence."

Before this [i.e., the revelation], Muhammad had come to my house and asked a slavegirl about me. She said, ". . . by Allah, I know of her purity the way the goldsmith knows of the purity of nuggets."[9]

Dura Europos (south of Dayr az Zawr)

Women Who Hosted House Churches

Dura Europos was a Hellenistic fortress city near the frontier. Extensive ruins with artwork have been found there. In many places one religious group would dominate over the others and try to elimate them, but in Dura Europos a house church, a synagogue, and Greek, Roman, and Mesopotamian temples all coexisted near each other. Until Christianity was legalized by Constantine in the fourth century and church architecture developed, Christians gathered in houses. The leader of the house was usually the leader of prayer. Often women led these house church groups and there is good reason to believe that they presided at the breaking of the bread, that is, in celebrating the Eucharist.[10]

Maariyé

The People Who Brought Their Children to Jesus

Maariyé, a town in the lower southwest corner of Syria, would be in the area called Betanea, beyond the Jordan, during Jesus' time. Mark 10:1 says that Jesus went into this area. Maariyé is not far from Kochaba, where Jesus was said to have had relatives. John 10 records that he was in this area when people brought him a message that Lazarus was sick.

Though the biblical text says that "people" brought children to Jesus, considering the child care customs of the day it was probably women who brought their children to him. The male disciples apparently did not think that child care was appropriate or of significant value for a man. Men are leaders, men talk of ideas and of God. In the contemporary world United Nations reports and other studies of budget priorities reveal that money allocated for the welfare of children including basic care, health, and education is very small in relation to the allocation of money for things that are considered "important," such as armaments and political structures. Jesus not only valued the children but made the challenging remark that a child is the most important person. If Jesus' words were really believed, the most highly valued work in the world would be child care, and the greatest allocation of resources would go toward the care and empowerment of young people. In Matt 18:1-14 Jesus is described as responding to a question about who is the greatest by bringing forward a little child.

> 13 People were bringing little children to him in order that he might touch them; and the disciples spoke sternly to them. 14 But when Jesus saw this, he was indignant and said to them, "Let the little children come to me; do not stop them; for it is to such as these that the kingdom of God belongs. 15 Truly I tell you, whoever does not receive the kingdom of God as a little child will never enter it." 16 And he took them up in his arms, laid his hands on them, and blessed them.
>
> (Mark 10:13-16)

Mari (near Abü Kamä)

Sarah and Hagar

About ten kilometers north of Abu Kamal are some ruins from ancient palaces of 5000 years ago. From what is known of ancient nomadic routes and from names in the text, Sarah and Abraham are thought to have begun their journey in Ur (near Babylon), traveled through Mari, Haran, on the Euphrates, Aleppo, near Damascus, and then down to Shechem, Shiloh, Bethel, Jerusalem, Hebron, Beersheba, and finally down to Egypt. The extensive ancient texts excavated at Mari and other sites indicate something of the context in which the Bible developed. Savina J. Teubal suggests that the Bible—a patriarchal document—has fragments of earlier matriarchal stories. Some of the attributes and practices of Sarah, Rebecca, and Rachel are like those of goddesses and priestesses, but then have been integrated into the Hebrew tradition.

The story of Sarah giving Hagar to Abraham to bear children seems to have echoes of the directives for priestesses in the Code of Hammurabi of 1800 B.C.E., § 146: "If a man has married a priestess [of a certain rank] and she has given a slave girl to her husband and she bears sons, if (thereafter) that slave girl goes about making herself equal to her mistress, because she has borne sons, her mistress may not sell her; she may put the mark of a slave on her and count her with the slave girls. If she has not borne sons, her mistress may sell her."[11]

Palmyra, Tudmur

Zenobia

A huge area of restored ruins can be seen in Palmyra, which was important in the second century C.E. Zenobia was a daughter of a wealthy Arab merchant. She and her family lived in this desert city, which was significant on the caravan routes between Persia and Rome. She married Odainat, who ruled in the name of Rome. In 267 C.E., when her husband died, Zenobia declared herself Queen of the East and independent of Rome. Zenobia claimed that she was a descendant of Cleopatra. She had her armies invade Egypt and they conquered most of it, then Syria, then Asia Minor as far as the Bosporus. Thus she controlled the trade routes with Abyssinia, Arabia, and India. Zenobia was of exceptional ability and ruled an empire based on tolerance rather than coercion. Though she was neither Jew nor Christian she had cordial relationships with the Jews of Alexandria and the Christian bishop of Antioch. When the Emperor Lucius Aurelian came to power in Rome in 270 C.E. he feared Zenobia's power. He took Egypt, Asia Minor, and Palmyra, and captured her. He took her as a prisoner to Rome, but later freed her. She married a wealthy senator and opened a fashionable salon in Tivoli. One might as well make the best of life wherever one is taken.

Notes

[1] "Life of St. Matrona of Perge," from *Acta Sanctorum Novembris* 3 (Brussels: Bollandist Society, 1910) 790–813, in Alice Mary Talbot, ed., *Holy Women of Byzantium: Ten Saints' Lives in English Translation* (Washington, D.C.: Dumbarton Oaks, 1996) 34–38.

[2] While the images of demons in ancient writings may sound strange to modern readers, they are symbolic of the battles between good and evil. We may struggle, but God also comes with consolation.

[3] Gerontius, "Melania the Younger," in Joan M. Petersen, ed. and trans., *Handmaids of the Lord: Contemporary Descriptions of Feminine Asceticism in the First Six Christian Centuries* (Kalamazoo: Cistercian Publications, 1996) 348, 349.

[4] "The Life and Conduct of the Blessed Mary Who Changed Her Name to Marinos," from Marcel Richard, "La Vie Ancienne de Sainte Marie surnommée Marinos," in idem, *Opera minora* (Turnhout: Brepols, 1977) 3:67, in Talbot, ed., *Holy Women of Byzantium*, 7–11.

[5] Doug Adams, *The Prostitute in the Family Tree: Discovering Humor and Irony in the Bible* (Louisville: Westminister, 1997) 73–74.

[6] Ahmed Khairat, *The Status of Women in Islam* (Egypt: Dar El Ma'arif, 1975) 64.

[7] Abdallah Alfifi, *Al-mar'al-Arabia fi Jahilyatiha Wa Islamiha* (Egypt: Dar Ihya' Al Kutub el-Arabiyya Publishing House, 1921) 2:139.

[8] Muhammad Ibn Sa'ad, *Al-Tabakat El-Kubra* (Cairo: Dar El-Tahrir Publishing House, 1970) 32.

[9] Ahmad b. Muhammad Ibn Hanbal, *Musnad al-Iman Ahmad ibn Hanbal* 6:60, in Nabia Abbott, *Aishah, the Beloved of Muhammad* (Chicago: University of Chicago Press, 1942) 46.

[10] Elisabeth Schüssler Fiorenza, *In Memory of Her: A Feminist Theological Reconstruction of Christian Origins* (New York: Crossroad, 1983) 175–84.

[11] Savina J. Teubal, *Sarah the Priestess: The First Matriarch of Genesis* (Athens, Ohio: Swallow Press, 1984) 36. (See **Avdat, Hagar** for Gen 16:1-6.)

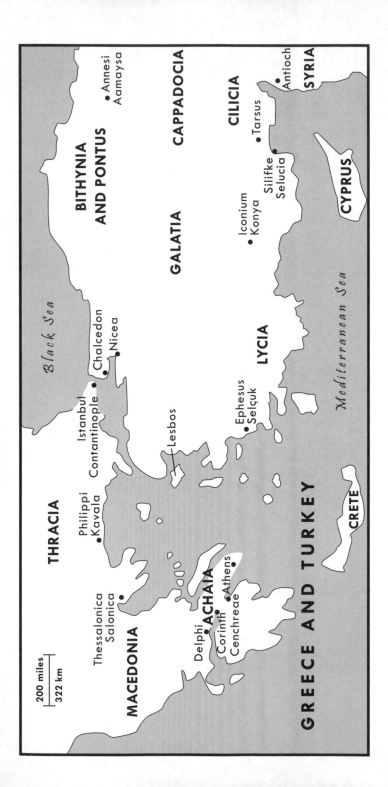

CHAPTER THIRTEEN

GREECE
AND THE MEDITERRANEAN ISLANDS

Aegina

Athanasia of Aegina

The island of Aegina, southwest of Athens, has been influenced by Crete since Neolithic times and has had inhabitants since the ninth century B.C.E. It was named for the goddess Aegina, one of Zeus' lovers. Athanasia lived in the first half of the ninth century C.E. No particular site for her exists, but she could be remembered at the Convent of Chrysoleontissa, from the 1600s, which has a fine iconostasis and an icon of the Virgin, said to bring rain. The nuns are known for hospitality and good food.

In the first half of the ninth century C.E. Athanasia, a daughter of Christian nobles, was forced by her parents to marry. Not long after that her husband was killed when the island was raided by Arabs, probably a few years after they had occupied Crete. Her parents forced her to marry again. After some years she persuaded her second husband that they should take monastic vows. She gathered a group of women, a priest gave them a convent, and eventually she became the leader. She had three churches built on the island. The following passage holds up virtues that a married woman was encouraged to have:

> One day while sitting and weaving at the loom by herself, she saw a shining star descend as far as her chest. It shed abundant light on her and then disappeared from her sight. By this [light], therefore, she was abundantly enlightened in her soul and came into an absolute hatred for the vanity of life. She intended to enter into the monastic way of life, but her parents very forcibly joined her to a husband, though she was unwilling and adamantly refused. After living with him for only sixteen days, she suddenly came into [the state of] widowhood. For, when the barbarian Maurousioi swept into

those parts, her husband went out to join battle and (by the judgments that [only] God knows) became a casualty of war.

After considerable time had passed and Athanasia was struggling within herself and directing her mind toward the monastic life, suddenly an imperial edict was issued that unmarried women and widows should be given in marriage to foreign men. So because of this, her parents drove Athanasia into a second marriage, since she had not yet attained [her goal of] monastic life. But even after this had happened, she maintained her habitual concern for her own salvation, applying herself tirelessly to the chanting of the psalms and devoting herself with assiduity to reading [Scripture], and accepting no change in her [previous] good [ways], but adorned with meekness she shone in a blessed fashion with humility of heart. Wherefore this praiseworthy woman was much loved by all who knew her good ways. She so distinguished herself in almsgiving that her household goods did not suffice, even though they were very abundant, for the generous distribution [to the poor] from her hand. She graciously received monks visiting from all over, and she plentifully provided widows and orphans and all the needy with the necessities of life.

Once after a famine arose and everyone was reduced to destitution, she generously donated food not only to her fellow believers, but also compassionately distributed [food] to the so-called Athinganoi, who were then hard-pressed by the famine and approached her. For she fulfilled that saying of the Lord which states, *"Be ye merciful as your heavenly Father, for he maketh his sun to rise on the evil and on the good, and sendeth rain on the just and on the unjust."* Not only did she provide them food, but also clothed them with garments and comforted them with other gifts. On the Lord's day and on feast days, she lovingly assembled all the neighbor women [in her presence] and read them the Holy Scriptures, gradually opening their minds and in a godly way directing them into a fear and desire of the Lord.

In this way, advancing according to God and blooming with virtues, just like a flower-laden meadow, she persuaded her spouse, who yielded to her many exhortations after some years of cohabitation, to withdraw from the world and everything in it and to enter into the sacred way of life of the monks. After [becoming a monk] and distinguishing himself in a blessed manner, he fell asleep in the Lord.

So the blessed woman, taking advantage of her freedom, totally dedicated her entire self to God. For finding other very pious women, who had the same aim and were ardent in spirit, and joining with them in full unanimity, she very soon withdrew from worldly confusion. Distributing to the poor all that she possessed according to the commandment of the Lord, along with the aforementioned honorable women she changed her worldly garb together with her way [of life]. And abiding quietly in one place at the invitation of a virtuous and blessed man who tonsured them, after three or four years she unwillingly accepted the leadership of the assembled women, called first by them in her mind considering herself the last, and fulfilling that saying of the Lord which states, *"Let the one wishing to be first among you be the last of all and the servant of all."*

So what account could explain, what tongue could present the loftiness of her great humility? For she would never allow [herself] to be served by anyone of them nor [allow] water to be poured over her hands [by anyone] during her entire lifetime, as all her fellow [nuns] assured everyone following her holy dormition, after making inquiry of each other. Considering herself unworthy to be with them, let alone be served by them (even though she was mother superior) and engaging in great abstinence, she used to partake of a little bread and a modest amount of water after the ninth hour, refraining entirely from cheese and fish, but only on the feast of Easter tasting them with thanksgiving; and during the holy days of Lent, she used to eat every other day, subsisting on raw greens alone, not partaking of any drink whatsoever during all those sacred days. And for her rest, she partook of little sleep, not on her side, but leaning on a rock that was prepared for this purpose. Not only during the holy and great Lent did she practice this discipline but also during the other two [Lents], I mean that of the Holy Apostles and that of Christmas. Her bedding set on the ground was of fairly large stones, covered above with a small goat hair [cloth], and leaning on this at the time of rest *she watered it every night with tears*, in the words of the prophet. For since the love of God abundantly inflamed her from within, she also used to shed abundant tears both in chanting the psalms and in prayers, so that one would be more likely to see a spring without streams of water than [to see] without tears her holy eyes, which continually looked to Christ.

Her inner garment was a goat hair [shirt], which irritated her flesh with its roughness, and her outer [clothing] was a ragged garment of sheep wool; and this [former garment] was the unseen one and was covering her sacred body. She kept solitary vigils and studied the Psalms of David, during each one of the *kaithismata* making a prayer with the greatest attentiveness. Then during the day, sometimes by herself and sometimes with her companions, she used to recite the Psalms, striving [to ensure] that she would spend every hour in glorifying God with her lips or mind, in accordance with the verse of the sacred psalmist David, *"I will bless the Lord at all times; His praise shall be continually in my mouth."*

From the day she became a nun until her departure to God, she never tasted any fruit whatsoever. Although enduring many tribulations, inasmuch as she was the leader of her sisters and was concerned about them, she never upbraided any of them because of the great humility she had attained. No abuse emerged from her venerable mouth, neither against the small, nor the great, neither against a slave, nor a free person, and all this even though she was often disobeyed [by her subordinates] through diabolical influence. But she was tolerant of everyone in meekness of opinion and in rectitude of heart, continually *looking forward to her future reward.*[1]

Athanasia went to Constantinople on business and was there for seven years. She had a dream that told her to return to Aegina, where she died twelve days later. Miracles of healing began to occur at her tomb. Her feast day is celebrated on April 18. While her asceticism may seem excessive to modern readers, asceticism is exercise in which one starts to focus on what and who really matters.

Athens

The Areopagus on the Acropolis

The Unknown God

At this center of learning of the ancient world, built in about the fifth century B.C.E., Paul gave a famous teaching about the unknown god (Acts 17:23). Among those who came to believe was a woman called Damaris, and the Greeks today venerate her as a saint. Paul suggests that the divine is always beyond any human description and beyond any gender. Paul's imagery of God seems to allude to being in the "womb of God."

> In God "we live and move and have our being;" as even some of your own poets have said, "For we too are his offspring."   (Acts 17:28)

Cenchreae, the Ancient Seaport of Corinth

Phoebe

Paul mentions many women among those who are spreading the faith. Unfortunately, some biblical translations through the years have obscured women and things they have done. The Greek text of Romans 16:1 calls Phoebe *diakonos*, "deacon," or "minister," the same word Paul elsewhere uses of himself. Often this word has been translated as "helper," which obscures a woman's recognized position in the community. Phoebe was the bearer of Paul's letter to the Romans. She is the only person in Christian Scriptures who has a ministerial title to a particular church. Paul goes on to speak of Andronicus and Junia as "outstanding" or "prominent" among the apostles. For centuries, beginning with the Reformation, translations have given the feminine Junia a masculine form, "Junias," concealing the fact that Paul spoke of a woman as an apostle.

> 1 I commend to you our sister Phoebe, a deacon of the church at Cenchreae, 2 so that you may welcome her in the Lord as is fitting for the saints, and help her in whatever she may require from you, for she has been a benefactor [Greek *prostatis*] of many and of myself as well. 3 Greet Prisca and Aquila, who work with me in Christ Jesus, 4 and who risked their necks for my life, to whom not only I give thanks, but also all the churches of the Gentiles. 5 Greet also the church in their house. Greet my beloved Epaenetus, who was the first convert in Asia for Christ. 6 Greet Mary, who has worked very hard among you. 7 Greet Andronicus and Junia, my relatives who were in prison with me; they are prominent among the apostles, and they were in Christ before I was.
>
> (Read Rom 16:1-16)

Corinth

Prisca (Priscilla), Nympha, and the Women Prophets of Corinth

This major seaport and business city had a famous temple dedicated to Aphrodite, the goddess of love, and the temple had both female and male prostitutes. Ruins of this can be seen in the Acrocorinth area. Paul spent about a year and a half in the city. Antoinette Clark Wire's study, *The Corinthian Women Prophets: A Reconstruction Through Paul's Rhetoric*, sheds light on women's active participation in Christianity there.[2] Paul established a friendship and worked in tentmaking with Prisca (Acts calls her "Priscilla") and Aquila. They later delivered his message to Ephesus. In that city Prisca, whose name is mentioned before that of her husband, Aquila, taught Apollos, a man from Alexandria. He then spread the gospel extensively. Paul wrote to the Corinthians in about 53–57 C.E.

> 18 After this Paul left Athens and went to Corinth. 2 There he found a Jew named Aquila, a native of Pontus, who had recently come from Italy with his wife Priscilla, because Claudius had ordered all Jews to leave Rome. Paul went to see them, 3 and, because he was of the same trade, he stayed with them, and they worked together—by trade they were tentmakers. 4 Every sabbath he would argue in the synagogue and would try to convince Jews and Greeks.   (Acts 18:1-4)

Delphi

Athanasia, a Deaconess

The Greeks called this beautiful high setting the center of the world. Since the sixth century B.C.E. pilgrims have come to this sacred spot. Eventually the shrine of the oracle was built; there three priestesses, women over fifty, would take the question of the petitionery who had offered a sacrifice for an answer. They would seek wisdom and then deliver an oracle to the person.

The people of the island were used to priestesses of the oracle. Probably when Christianity came to the island the acceptance of women leaders continued. In the past, tombstones that speak of Jewish women as heads, leaders, elders, and priestesses of the synagogue and tombstones of Christian women with the feminine forms of deacon, priest, and bishop have been belittled. They have been called titles of honor or indicators that these women were wives of men who held these positions. The scholar Bernadette J. Brooten and now many others have begun to reevaluate these in light of other sources and circumstances. The titles seem to indicate the functions the women fulfilled, as those on male tombstones indicate functions men fulfilled. In Delphi is a fifth-century C.E. tombstone of a deaconess. Often ancient tombs had a curse against someone who might plunder them.

> The most pious deaconess Athanasia
> having lived a blameless life modestly
> having been ordained a deaconess by the most holy bishop,

Pantamianos, made this monument, in which lie her
    remains.
If any other dares to open this monument, in which the
deaconess has been deposited, he will have the portion of
Judas, the betrayer of our Lord, Jesus Christ.
No less so those clerics who may be present at this
time, and assent [to the removal of]
the aforementioned deaconess . . .[3]

Lesbos

Theoktiste of Lesbos

This island, east of Greece but near the coast of Turkey, had
a significant Bronze Age culture about 1000 B.C.E. and in the
seventh and sixth centuries B.C.E. was known as a cultural center. The island is remembered as the home of Sappho (625–570
B.C.E.), a brilliant woman who wrote poetry and prose and composed music. She also taught these subjects to young women.

The story of Theoktiste of Lesbos is one of many, like those
of Athanasia of Aegina and Theodora of Thessalonike, that
deal with the trauma of the Arab pirate raids on Mediterranean
islands during the 800s. Some saints in the wilderness deal
with spiritual demons, but other saints deal with the demons of
violence and war. The Life of Theokiste resembles that of Mary
of Egypt, but the author points out the differences. An old hermit
on the island of Paros was said to have recounted this story to
the author, who stopped at the island while he was on a mission to negotiate with the Arab rulers of Crete. The hermit described a man who was hunting on the island and accidentally
met the saint. Parts of saints' bodies were highly valued as
relics and taking such parts was considered devotional; however, some people took body parts out of greed, with the intention of selling the relics. The men who tell these stories seem to
both fear and admire holy women.

In 1960 some of the relics of St. Theoktiste were transferred
from Icaria to Methymna, Lesbos, where a church was built in
her honor. Also a small church on the island of Paros is dedicated to her.

> . . . Having bagged a lot of game, we started our return to
> the ship. But while my companions walked in the direction of
> the sea, I turned aside to pursue [the object of] my prayer. I
> went into the church of our Lady and, as I was praying, I saw
> to the right of the church's holy altar something that
> resembled a thread being blown by the wind. I thought at the

moment that I was seeing a spider's web, but when I decided to step forward and determine what was there, I heard a voice saying, "Stay, [my good] man! Do not go further, nor come closer! *For being a woman, I am ashamed to show myself to you in my nakedness.*" When I heard this I was astounded by the unexpected [voice] and wished to flee. For the hairs rose on my flesh and were sharper than a thorn. For when something *unexpected* appears suddenly, *it enthralls the spirit [of a man]*, and if one thinks of himself as fearless, when taken by surprise, he stands with his mouth agape. When I recovered, I plucked up courage to ask who she was and how she came to be living in the wilderness. Again a voice reached me, saying, "*Throw me a cloak,* I beg you, and when I have covered myself, I will not hesitate to tell all that God bids me [to say]." Right away I took off my outer garment, left it and ran out the door. She took it, put it on, and when I returned after a while, I saw her standing in her original position.

She had the shape of a woman but the appearance of a superhuman being. *Her hair was white; her face was black* with an underlying tinge of whiteness; the skin alone kept the bones in place, for there was hardly any flesh. She was almost a shadow, the shape alone resembling a human being. When I saw this (he said), I was afraid, I trembled, I reproached myself, I cursed the ill-timing [of this encounter], for by being over-curious I was left behind by my companions. Trembling all over, I threw myself on the ground, begged for her prayers, and entreated her to bless me. She first turned towards the east, wishing perhaps to set my mind at ease so that I *would not suppose she was an apparition*, and *stretching up her hands she prayed in a faint whisper.* Then she turned to me and said, "May God have mercy on you, sir! But for what reason did you come to this wilderness? What necessity has brought you to an uninhabited island? But seeing that the divine will brought you here—*for the sake of my humility, I believe*—I will tell you all about my life, as you requested."

Again I prostrated myself on the ground, begging her to go on [with her story], and she began to tell [me about herself] thus: "My homeland is Lesbos, the city of Methymna. My name is Theoktiste and I am a nun by profession. Having been orphaned while still a very young child, I was entrusted to a nunnery by my relatives and assumed the monastic habit. When I was nearly eighteen years of age, I went to a village near the city [of Methymna] to visit my sister during the Easter season, for she lived near that village with her husband. But one night, Arabs from Crete under their leader, the notorious Nisiris, raided [the village] and took everyone prisoner. At dawn, after chanting the song of victory, they set sail and came to anchor at this island [of Paros]. They brought out the prisoners, and started to assess and settle the price [of each prisoner]. But I made up an excuse and, going toward the forest, I fled running until I had torn my feet to pieces, piercing them with stones and sharp twigs, and had stained the ground with my blood. Exhausted finally, I collapsed half-dead and spent the whole night in misery, unable to bear the pain from my wounds. But in the morning when I saw the abominable people sailing away, I was released from all pain and filled with so much joy as I cannot describe. And since that time—a little over thirty-five years already—I have lived here, subsisting on lupine [seeds] and *other herbs that grow in the wilderness,* or rather on the word of God, keeping in mind the divine saying that *man shall not live by bread alone but by every word that proceedeth out of the mouth of God.* I am naked, of course, for the ragged habit in which I was taken prisoner *was torn to pieces,* but I am dressed and *covered* by the hand *of God which sustains the Universe.*" With these words, she raised her eyes to heaven and gave thanks. She stood at a distance for a while and then, as she saw me *staring at the ground very quietly,* not even daring to look at her, she started to speak again: "I have told you my story, sir. I ask you now to repay me with one favor for the Lord's sake. Whenever in the coming year you are going to sail to this island for hunting (I know for sure that you will be back, God willing), *place in a clean vessel a portion of the most pure gifts, the body of our Lord Jesus Christ. For since I began to live in the wilderness I have not had the privilege of receiving this gift.*" Having said this and *enjoined me not to tell anyone at all about our [meeting],* she sent me back to my companions with her blessing. I agreed to fulfill all [her requests] and left rejoicing because God had satisfied my longing, finding me worthy to attain such treasure.

In accordance with the command of the blessed woman . . . when I was about to sail away and go on a hunt, I took in a small box a portion of the divine flesh of the Lord to bring to the blessed one. But when I reached the island and turned aside to the house of the Mother of God, I failed to find her. Whether she was there but hiding because some of my companions had come up with me [to the church], or was not there I cannot tell; only that I did not find her. The others then hurried to the forest to start hunting . . . but I slipped away and returned to the church. Right away, the holy woman appeared *wearing the cloak which she received from me* on my previous [visit]. As I threw myself on the ground, she ran [toward me] and in tears called to me from afar: "*Never do that, sir, when you are carrying the divine gift!* Do not burn me, wretched that I am, by dishonoring the divine [sacraments]." Taking hold of my tunic, she helped me to my feet and I took from my bosom the small box with the Lord's flesh. And she, falling to the ground, received the divine [eucharist] and lamenting and watering the earth with her tears, cried out, *"Lord now lettest Thou Thy servant depart [in peace according to Thy word]; for mine eyes have seen Thy salvation.* For I have received in my hands the forgiveness of my sins. Now I shall go wherever Thy power ordaineth." Having said this, she stretched up her hands to heaven for a long time and sent me back to my companions with her blessing.

We hunted for a few days, bagged an abundance of game, and started out on our return. My companions hurried down to the boat, but I ran to receive the blessing of the blessed one as a companion of my journey. When I came to the church and looked around for her, I saw her lying dead on the spot where I had previously seen her [standing]. Falling [to the ground], I kissed her venerable *feet and watered them with my tears,* and [then] remained there speechless for a long time wondering what to do. It would have been sensible and expedient as well, if I had begged God with tears and implored the blessed woman and asked [them] how to dispose of this matter properly and, in accordance with [their decree], ministered to the divine command. Had I failed to obtain this [divine guidance], I should have done the *next best thing,* as they say, I should have told the story to my companions, and with their assistance placed in a grave the remains of the blessed one and sung the [burial] hymns as best we could. But it seems that prudence is not an easy prey. Hence I too failed to do what was right and proper. Out of boorishness and simple-mindedness—indeed, being a hunter and an ignorant man, I could not have thought of anything different— I did a foolhardy thing, because of faith, as I believed, but it seems that it was not pleasing to God. For I cut off her hand, wrapped it in a linen cloth, and went back to the ship.

Late that evening, we put out from the land, set sail, and were on our way. Since favorable breezes were blowing, we were flying, so to speak, before a fair wind, and expected to reach Euboea by morning. But at daybreak we found ourselves back in the same harbor, as if the ship were held fast by an anchor or a sea monster. Fear and terror seized us all, and we looked at one another trembling, as we sought to determine the cause of this delay. We examined and questioned [one another] to find out whether we had committed an unforgivable [offense] and were held back for that reason. While one man said one thing and the other said another, being at a loss, I realized what a foolhardy thing I had done and, escaping the notice of all [my companions], I ran up to the church, placed the hand by the saint's . . . body and returned to the boat. After giving [words of] encouragement, I started on my journey with my companions. When we were far out at sea—for the ship was flying like a bird, with the sail bellying out with wind, on a straight and unimpeded course—I told my companions what had happened; how I had found the blessed one and how she had recounted the story of her life and about the holy communion and her death. I also told them that I had boarded the ship the [previous] evening with the saint's hand in my possession and that for this reason perhaps we were held back although we expected to sail away. And that now we were rightly proceeding on a straight course because I had put the relic back.[4]

Philippi in Macedonia (near modern Kavala)

Lydia, Evodia, and Syntyche

Philippi, about fifteen kilometers from modern Kavala, was the first European city reached by travelers from the East. In 49

C.E. Paul arrived here, and it was the first European community he evangelized. The Philippians always seemed to have a special place in Paul's heart. He wrote them in warm and affectionate ways, beginning his letter, "I thank my God when I think of you and when I pray, I pray with joy . . . May God who began this good work in you bring it to completion." Lydia, a businesswoman here, welcomed Paul and helped build the Christian community. (See **Dor** for **Lydia**.) The ancient excavations have a well-preserved marketplace that indicates the success of commerce in Philippi. Two women admired by Paul who were leaders in the Christian community had had a disagreement (with one another, or with Paul?), and Paul urged reconciliation.

> 1 Therefore, my brothers and sisters, whom I love and long for, my joy and crown, stand firm in the Lord in this way, my beloved. 2 I urge Euodia and I urge Syntyche to be of the same mind in the Lord. 3 Yes, and I ask you also, my loyal companion, help these women, for they have struggled beside me in the work of the gospel, together with Clement and the rest of my co-workers, whose names are in the book of life.
>
> (Read Phil 4:1-9)

Thessalonica, Salonica

Agios Dimitrios Church

Agape, Chione, and Companions

North in Macedonia on the Aegean Sea is the port city of Salonica. The main street of modern Salonica was the site of the ancient Roman Via Egnatia. Thessalonica or Salonica was next to Constantinople in importance in the area. It was named for Thessaloniki, wife of Cassander, king of Macedon in about 315 B.C.E. Agios Dimitrios Church was originally built in the 400s and rebuilt in the twentieth century after a fire. This church, the largest in Greece, and named for a male martyr, can be a place to remember these courageous women martyrs. Agape, Irene, Chione, and companions, the martyrs of Thessalonica, lived during the persecution of Diocletian and Maximian in 304, and were condemned for protecting the Christian sacred books.

> After the most holy women were consumed in the flames, the saintly girl Irene was once again brought before the court on the following day. Dulcitius said to her: "It is clear from what we have seen that you are determined in your folly, for

you have deliberately kept even till now so many tablets, books, parchments, codices, and pages of the writings of the former Christians of unholy name; even now, though you denied each time that you possessed such writings, you did show a sign of recognition when they were mentioned. You are not satisfied with the punishment of your sisters, nor do you keep before your eyes the terror of death. Therefore you must be punished.

"It, would not, however, seem out of place to show you some measure of mercy: if even now you will be willing to recognize the gods you will be released from all danger and punishment. Now what do you say? Will you do the bidding of our emperors and Caesars? Are you prepared to eat the sacrificial meats and to sacrifice to the gods?"

"No," said Irene, "I am not prepared, for the sake of the God almighty *who has created heaven and earth and the seas and all that is in them.* For those who transgress the word of God there awaits the great judgment of eternal punishment."

The prefect Dulcitius said: "Who was it that advised you to retain those parchments and writings up to the present time?"

"It was almighty God," said Irene, "who bade us to love him unto death. For this reason we did not dare to be traitors, but we chose to be burned alive or suffer anything else that might happen to us rather than betray the writings."

The prefect said: "Was anyone else aware that the documents were in the house where you lived?"

"No one else," said Irene, "saw them, save almighty God who knows all things. But no stranger. As for our own relatives, we considered them worse than our enemies, in fear that they would denounce us. Hence we told no one."

"Last year," said the prefect, "when this edict of our lords the emperors and Caesars was first promulgated, where did you hide?"

"Wherever God willed," said Irene. "We lived on the mountains, in the open air, as God is my witness."

"Whom were you living with?" asked the prefect. Irene answered: "We lived out of doors in different places among the mountains."

The prefect said: "Who supplied you with bread?"

Irene answered: "God, who supplies all men."

"Was your father aware of this?" asked the prefect.

Irene answered: "I swear by almighty God, he was not aware; he knew nothing at all about it."

"Were any of your neighbors aware of this?" asked the prefect.

Irene answered: "Go and question our neighbors, and inquire about the area to see whether anyone knew where we were."

The prefect said: "Now after you returned from the mountain where you had been, as you say, were any persons present at the reading of these books?"

Irene answered: "They were in our house and we did not dare to bring them out. In fact, it caused us so much distress that we could not devote ourselves to them night and day as we had done from the beginning until that day last year when we hid them."

Dulcitius the prefect said: "Your sisters, in accordance with my commands in their regard, have received their sentence. Now you have been guilty even before you ran away and before you concealed these writings and parchments, and hence I do not wish you to die in the same way. Instead I sentence you to be placed naked in the brothel with the help of the public notaries of this city and of Zosimus the executioner; and you will receive merely one loaf of bread from our residence, and the notaries will not allow you to leave."

And so, after the notaries and the slave Zosimus, the executioner, were brought in, the prefect said: "Be it known to you that if ever I found out from the troops that this girl was removed from the spot where I have ordered her to be even for a single instant, you will immediately be punished with the most extreme penalties. The writings we have referred to, in the cabinets and chests belonging to Irene, are to be publicly burned."

After those who were put in charge had taken the girl off to the public brothel in accordance with the prefect's order, by the grace of the Holy Spirit which preserved and guarded her pure and inviolate for the God who is the Lord of all things, no man dared to approach her, or so much as tried to insult her in speech. Hence the prefect Dulcitius called back this most saintly girl, had her stand before the tribunal, and said to her: "Do you still persist in the same folly?"

But Irene said to him: "It is not folly, but piety."

"It was abundantly clear from your earliest testimony," said the prefect Dulcitius, "that you did not wish to submit religiously to the bidding of the emperors; and now I perceive that you are persisting in the same foolishness. Therefore you shall pay the appropriate penalty."

He then asked for a sheet of papyrus and wrote the sentence against her as follows: "Whereas Irene has refused to obey the command of the emperors and to offer sacrifice, and still adheres to a sect called the Christians, I therefore sentence her to be burned alive, as I did her two sisters before her."

After this sentence had been pronounced by the prefect, the soldiers took the girl and brought her to a high place, where her sisters had been martyred before her. They ignited a huge pyre and ordered her to climb up on it, and the holy woman Irene, singing and praising God, threw herself upon it and so died. It was in the ninth consulship of Diocletian Augustus, on the first day of April, in the kingship of our Lord Christ Jesus, who reigns forever, with whom there is glory to the Father with the Holy Spirit for ever. Amen.[5]

Hagia Sophia Church

Theodora of Thessalonike

The church located on Ermou Street was built in the eighth century. St. Theodora of Thessalonike (812–892) was born on the island of Aegina and like St. Athanasia of Aegina and others of the Aegean islands was affected by the Arab raids. Hagia Sophia Church has a thirteenth-century fresco of her and she is remembered in another church that bears her name, though it is now part of a male monastery. Her father was a priest, her brother a deacon, and her sister a nun. She, her husband and father moved to Thessalonike after her brother had been killed in a raid. Her husband and two children died, and her third child was dedicated to monastic life. Then, as a twenty-five-year-old widow, she entered the convent of St. Stephen. For fifty-five years she led a simple, obedient life, and worked hard.

The writing of the Life excerpted below seems to have been encouraged by her family to attract people to her cult. This was so successful that pilgrims came from as far away as Thebes in Egypt and she got as much attention as St. Demetrios, the patron of Thessalonike. The author reveals much about healing shrines, ideas of female sanctity, and monasticism in this, the longest written biography of a female Byzantine saint. Since there had been so much controversy in Eastern Christianity about whether it was right or wrong to use icons, the author slips in an affirmation of Theodora's icon. Near the end of the story the author describes his sister's suffering and why he wrote this biography.

When my sister, who was still a very young girl (the child's name was Martha), was stricken with this disease, she remained mobile for two days. But at the end of the [third?] day, she was burning up terribly with a raging and fiery fever, which rendered her immobile. For a rupture on her right [cervical] tendon rendered each of the limbs around it, both arms and legs, paralyzed and motionless. And then the pain in her limbs became sharper and more acute so that the child often lost consciousness and lay for a long time without speaking. And for us there remained no conclusion but this: even though it was not yet the day and hour at which the fever becomes more intense, there was [already] such burning heat and bleeding (for there was no place remaining on her entire body where there were not numerous bloody [lesions] draining like small pustules), that it was clear that she would die, especially since the same thing happened to the left tendon and the parts around it soon after.

Tears come to me as I summon up in my mind the image of that child, with most of her limbs lifeless and hanging limp from every part of her body; such was the tension in both tendons from the severe hemorrhage. And it is no wonder that I am affected in this way by my sister. For if *all* of us . . . who live *in Christ are one* and Christ is the one *head* of us all, through Whom we are controlled in every way, and each of us has the same relation to the other as our limbs to each other, and *we are made all things to all men* and we share the suffering of those who are ill (even the infidels) by virtue of our natural relationship—in this case where there is a single faith and kinship and natural bonds and brotherly love, how could I possibly remain untouched in these circumstances and not share in her sufferings as best I could? At any rate that flesh-devouring and all-destroying disease spread through her entire body, which, one might well say, became one single lesion (for one could no longer rightly distinguish her limbs, as they were formed by God the master craftsman) that exuded streams of purulent serous discharge. And since her tongue was also inflamed by the countless pustules of that epidemic, the child could barely articulate her words. And who could describe the foul stench emitted from her throat? Thus, as I have said, her condition persuaded us that it was impossible for the child to escape death.

But the girl recalled the miracles of the blessed mother and being aware of the faith and love which we all had for her, she began to call upon her unceasingly with lamentation and wailing, adding the name of the supremely pure Mother of God and the glorious martyr Barbara. For as the result of extreme necessity, she was an expert at pitiable words, which could break the hearts of all and persuade God to accept propitiation on her behalf. One night the girl fell into a trance and, as she [later] told us, saw two women coming toward her from the window of the house where she lay [in her sickbed]. One of them was clad in splendid garments of silk and was adorned all over with gold, and was carrying in her right hand a wax candle and oil. She recognized the other woman, who was wearing a monastic habit, by her features as soon as she saw her. For she said that it was the blessed Theodora, clearly resembling the image on her icon, from which flows that fragrant-smelling oil. When the two women in her vision drew near, at a nod from the nun the woman who was holding the candle grasped her right arm and anointed it with oil. And she said this woman was the glorious martyr Barbara because the nun addressed her by this name. And the girl received the sensation of their grace, and filled with joy begged them to anoint her eyes as well with the holy oil. And they responded: "Know full well that there is nothing wrong with your eyes, and your arm which has been so painful is also healed." Thereupon the girl's condition improved, and after describing to us the apparition of the saints, which *occurred not in a dream, but in a waking vision*, she was relieved of the pains in her arm, but the arm remained immobile.

After suffering in this way for about fifty days, when the pustules over the lesions were drained of the fluid in them and were dried out by her fever, they formed [scabs] like black leather over her entire body. So we used a knife to cut them off her ankles and the soles of her feet, and removed her toenails as well. And we did the same thing to her arms, and, to be brief, exposed new skin on virtually her entire body. But even though she was finally unexpectedly delivered from the illness . . . her limbs were still paralyzed. And whenever we wanted to take her to the baths, we used a new-fangled type of chair which we devised, to facilitate the necessary task. And the final phase was a flux in three parts of her body, and we had to make incisions and [insert] cotton wicking for the drainage of the pus from deep [inside the body]. And the child, who was again suffering as great pain as before from the frequent replacement of the [absorbent] wicking, called upon the saint to ease her pain and restore her health. And she appeared again, alone [this time] and looking the same as she did in the first vision, and readjusting the cotton wicking, consoled her suppliant with joyful countenance, and proclaimed that from now on nothing bad would happen to her, saying, "I am Theodora, whom you summoned with lamentation to come to your aid." And indeed through her intercessions this soon came to pass. For shortly thereafter the girl became as healthy as she had been before her illness, and walking on her own feet she came with her mother to the sarcophagus of the blessed Theodora, her savior, and offered up the thanksgiving which was due to God who loves mankind and to the saint.

This extraordinary miracle inspired in me even greater love for the saint, and indeed this was the reason that obliged me to investigate and write an account of her life, something that I already wanted to do. For since two years had already passed and no one, as I said in my introduction, had written an account of her life or miracles, I was driven to irresistible zeal and began to tackle this work which is beyond my capability.[6]

Notes

[1] "St. Athanasia of Aegina." From François Halkin, "Vie de sainte Athanasie d'Aegine," *Six inédits d'hagiologie byzantine* (Brussels: Bollandist Society, 1987) 179–95, in Alice-Mary Talbot, ed., *Holy Women of Byzantium* (Washington, D.C.: Dumbarton Oaks Research Library and Collection, 1996) 142–46.

[2] Antoinette Clark Wire, *The Corinthian Women Prophets: A Reconstruction Through Paul's Rhetoric* (Minneapolis: Fortress, 1990).

[3] "Epitaph of the Deaconess Athanasia" (Delphi, 5th c.) in Ross S. Kraemer, ed., *Maenads, Martyrs, Matrons, Monastics* (Philadelphia: Fortress, 1988) 223.

[4] Niketas the Most Glorious Magistros, "The Life of Our Blessed Mother Theoktiste of Lesbos Who Practiced Asceticism and Died on the Island Named Paros," trans. Angela C. Hero, in Talbot, ed., *Holy Women of Byzantium,* 224–33.

[5] "Martyrdom of Saints Irene, Chione, and Companions," in Herbert Musurillo, *The Acts of the Christian Martyrs* (Oxford: Clarendon, 1972) 287–93.

[6] "Life and Conduct of Our Blessed Mother Theodora of Thessalonike" (*BHG* 1737, 1739), in Talbot, ed., *Holy Women of Byzantium,* 232–36.

CHAPTER FOURTEEN

TURKEY
(See map on p. 284.)

Annisa in Cappadocia, Aamaysa

Macrina

In Annisa, in northern Cappadocia toward the Black Sea, excavations to find the monastery and home of Macrina have not been attempted, but she might be remembered at places such as Goreme in central Cappadocia and others that have churches in honor of her brother, Basil. St. Macrina, born about 327 C.E., was the eldest of a family of ten children, including St. Basil, who was the bishop of Caesarea and a leader in the development of Eastern monasticism, and St. Gregory, who was bishop of Nyssa. More is known of her brothers, who did extensive writing, than of Macrina, yet this elder sister seems to have been a significant influence on them. Gregory wrote that Basil lived under Macrina's guidance in monastic life, working the soil for four years, and that he really needed this to overcome his pride after doing studies in the school of Athens. Some scholars believe that much of the wisdom in the Rule of St. Basil came from her.

In Annisa in about 357 C.E. Macrina persuaded her mother and the women of her home, both free and slave, to adopt a monastic way of life. Something of the revolutionary character of religious life is revealed in the description of Macrina baking bread. A woman of Macrina's wealth and education would never perform this type of manual work. She and her mother worked side by side with the servants.

Gregory visited his sister in 379, on his way home after the Council of Antioch. After her death he wrote of her life as a model for holy women, giving information about her manual work, study, prayer, and worship. While his writing took on something of the idealized style of Greek philosophical biographies and Christian hagiographies, it also reveals a younger brother's feelings about his beloved sister. When he arrived for his visit, though she was failing, she showed warm motherly concern for him and listened to his struggles. Macrina gave a lesson on how to die, integrating and being grateful for all of life and trusting one's failings to the mercy of God. Her feast day is celebrated on July 14.

When we were once again in her presence—for she would not let us spend our unoccupied time alone—she recalled the memories of her life from her youth onwards; she went through everything in order, like a history book. She described as much of the events of the lives of our parents as she could remember and also the events which occurred before my birth, and her subsequent life. The purpose of her recital was to give thanks to God. She showed that the lives of our parents were not so much honored and admired in the eyes of their contemporaries on account of their wealth as they were rendered significant because of their divinely inspired philanthropy. Our father's parents had been deprived of their property on account of their having confessed Christ; an ancestor on our mother's side had been put to death as the result of having provoked the emperor and all his property had been distributed to other masters. Nevertheless the property of our family was increased so much through their faith that it was not possible, at this period, to name anyone who surpassed them in wealth. Subsequently, when our parents' estate had been divided into nine portions, according to the number of their children, each child's share was increased by divine blessing in such a way that the wealth of each of the individual children surpassed the prosperity of their parents. Macrina, however, did not keep for herself the property that had been allotted to her when the estate was shared out equally between the brothers and sister, but caused it to be administered at the hands of the priest, in accordance with the divine command. Through the riches of God's grace, her life was such that her hands never ceased working to carry out the commandments of God; she never relied upon a man nor did the wherewithal for an honorable life come to her through the kindness of men. On the contrary, she sought to turn away neither beggars nor benefactors, for God secretly caused the small resources that she obtained from her work to multiply through his blessing, just as if they were seeds.

On my side, I described to her the personal difficulties in which I found myself, first of all, when the emperor Valens drove me into exile on account of my faith, and afterwards, when owing to the confusion prevailing in the local churches, I was summoned to distressing disputes. "Will you not give up your hardheartedness towards God's good gifts?" she asked, "Will you not heal the wound of ingratitude that is in your soul? Will you not compare your situation with that of your parents? Indeed from a worldly point of view, at any rate, we could take pride in this fact, that we appear as people of good birth, sprung from a noble family. Our father," she continued, "was highly thought of in his time on account of his culture, but his reputation extended only as far as the local law-courts. His subsequent fame did not reach beyond Pontus, although he was ahead of other people of his age through his skill in rhetoric, but he was satisfied with being well-known in his native country; You, on the other hand," she continued, "are a celebrated man in the cities, in the provinces and among the peoples. It is you whom some churches send and others summon, to bring help and achieve reform. Do you not see the grace that is given you? Do you not see the cause of such blessings? Is it not the prayers of your parents that have raised you to these heights, when you yourself have little or no predisposition for such things?"

While Macrina was expounding these matters, I longed to make the day last longer, that she might continue to charm our ears with her words, but the voices of the choir summoned us to the service of thanksgiving held at the lighting of the lamps. The great Macrina, having dispatched me to church, again withdrew herself into God's presence through her prayers. Night fell during these exercises. When day broke, it became clear to me from what I saw that the day which was dawning would be the limit of her life in the flesh, for the fever had consumed all the natural force that was in her. She noticed the feeble character of our thoughts and continued to distract us from our gloomy expectations; once again she dispersed the grief that was in our hearts through her beautiful words, but now she did so with a slightly troubled sigh. It was at that moment especially that my soul was torn by varied feelings over what was happening. One part of me was weighted down by depression, as was natural, because I foresaw that I should never again hear such words and I was expecting that this amazing person, the glory common to all our family, would soon pass from our human life; the other part of me, however, was carried away with emotion at what was happening and was secretly thinking that she had transcended our common human nature. She had made up her mind from the very beginning to experience, when breathing her last, not feelings of strangeness at the prospect of removal to a different place nor to fear leaving this life, but on the contrary, to engage with sublime thought in philosophical meditation right until the very end.

This attitude seemed to me to be no longer characteristic of a breathing human being. It was as if an angel had assumed human shape in the household—an angel who had no relationship with the life of the flesh nor in any way adapted to it, and whose thought remained, in a perfectly natural way, in a state of impassibility, since the flesh did not attract her to her own feelings. For this reason, it seemed to me that she revealed to those around her that pure love for the unseen Bridegroom which she cherished, hidden in the secret places of her soul, and made public the inclination of her heart to hasten to him for whom she longed, so that, once freed from the fetters of her body, she might be with him as soon as possible. In fact it was to her lover that her course was directed. No other of the sweets of life distracted her gaze from him.

The greater part of the day was already over and the sun was beginning to set. Her zeal, however, was undiminished, but as the time of her departure approached, so much the more did she contemplate the beauty of the Bridegroom and so much the greater was her haste to go to him for whom she longed. She no longer spoke (as she had done) to us who were present, but to him, upon whom she gazed directly. Her bed had been turned towards the East; she gave up talking to us and thenceforward addressed God in prayer. She stretched out her hands to him in supplication and spoke in a gentle undertone, so that we could scarcely hear her words.[1]

Constantinople, Istanbul

Hagia Sophia

Olympias, a Deaconess of Hagia Sophia

This majestic church of Holy Wisdom was build in 537 by Justinian and Theodora over the earlier church from Olympias' time, which had been destroyed in a great fire. Olympias (ca. 365–ca. 408) was of noble birth, from a very wealthy background, and was well educated under the supervision of Theodosia, a sister of the bishop of Iconium. Palladius, the historian, wrote that she entirely maintained John Chrysostom in his position as archbishop of Constantinople, as she had the previous leader Nectarius. John said that her ocean of charity went forth to the ends of the Earth. Palladius wrote that her lavish gifts to Nectarius led him even to take her advice in church affairs. Since women usually did not have a voice in such things, this is an interesting picture. He did listen to this major benefactor even though she was a woman. She generously supported many priests and bishops and engaged in dialogue with them. She was married to Nebridius, who soon died; the twenty-year-old widow refused to marry again because she wanted a religious life. The emperor Theodosius wanted her to marry because he feared that if she were independent she would use the family fortunes according to her own interests. She told the emperor that if God had wanted her married, God would not have taken away her first husband. Finally her determination prevailed over the emperor's ideas. Though sixty was set as the official age for the ordination of deaconesses, Nectarius seems to have ordained her before she was thirty. More is known of her than of most other ancient Christian women because many writers mention her. This part of her life by an anonymous fifth-century writer describes her as a young widow.

> The emperor, upon his return from the battle against Maximus, gave the order that she could exercise control over her own possessions, since he had heard of the intensity of her ascetic discipline. But she distributed all of her unlimited and immense wealth and assisted everyone, simply and without distinction. For the sake of many she surpassed that Samaritan of whom an account is given in the holy Gospels. Once upon a time he found on the road down to Jericho a man who was crushed half-dead by robbers; he raised him onto his own beast, carried him as far as the inn, and having mixed the oil of generosity with strong wine, he healed his wounds.
>
> Then straightway after the distribution and sealing up of all her goods, there was rekindled in her the divine love and she took refuge in the haven of salvation, the great, catholic, and apostolic church of this royal city. She followed to the letter with intelligence the divinely-inspired teachings of the most holy archbishop of this sacred church, John, and gave to him for this holy church (imitating also in this act those ardent lovers and disciples of Christ who in the beginning of salvation's proclamation brought to the feet of the apostles their possessions) ten thousand pounds of gold, twenty thousand of silver and all of her real estate situated in the provinces of Thrace, Galatia, Cappadocia Prima, and Bithynia; and more, the houses belonging to her in the capital city, the one situated near the most holy cathedral, which is called "the house of Olympias," together with the house of the tribune, complete with baths, and all the buildings near it, a mill, and a house which belonged to her in which she lived near the public baths of Constantinople, and another house of hers which was called the "house of Evander," as well as all of her suburban properties.

Then by the divine will she was ordained deaconess of this holy cathedral of God and she built a monastery at an angle south of it. All of the houses lying near the holy church and all the shops which were at the southern angle mentioned were torn down for the project. She constructed a path from the monastery up to the narthex of the holy church, and in the first quarter she enclosed her own chambermaids, numbering fifty, all of whom lived in purity and virginity. Next, Elisanthia, her relative who had seen the good work pleasing to God, which God gave to her to carry out, also herself a virgin, emulating the divine seal, bade farewell to the ephemeral and empty things of life with her sisters Martyria and Palladia, also virgins. Then the three entered with all the others, having made over in advance all of their possessions to the same holy monastery. Likewise also Olympia, the niece of the aforesaid holy Olympias, with many other women of senatorial families, chose the Kingdom of Heaven and disliked these lowly things which drag us down, in accordance with the grace and good favor of God who wishes all to be saved and who fosters the divine love in them. They entered also with the rest, so that all those who gathered together according to the grace of God in that holy fold of Christ numbered two hundred and fifty, all adorned with the crown of virginity and practicing the most exalted life which befits the saints. When these events had transpired in this manner by divine assistance, the noble servant of God Olympias again brought to the above-mentioned hallowed church through the most holy patriarch John the entire remainder of all her real estate, situated in all the provinces, and her interest in the public bread supply. And he also ordained as deaconesses of the holy church her three relatives, Elisanthia, Martyria, and Palladia, so that the four deaconesses would be able to be together without interruption in the most sacred monastery founded by her.

One was struck with amazement at seeing certain things in the holy chorus and angelic institution of these holy women: their incessant continence and sleeplessness, the constancy of their praise and thanksgiving to God, their "charity which is the bond of perfection," their stillness. For no one from the outside, neither man nor woman, was permitted to come upon them, the only exception being the most holy patriarch John, who visited continuously and sustained them with his most wise teachings. Thus fortified each day by his divinely-inspired instruction, they kindled in themselves the divine love so that their great and holy love streamed forth to him. The pious and blessed Olympias (who in these matters too imitated the women disciples of

Christ who served him from their possessions) prepared for the holy John his daily provisions and sent them to the bishop, for there was not much separation between the episcopal residence and the monastery, only a wall. And she did this not only before the plots against him, but also after he was banished; up to the end of his life she provided for all his expenses as well as for those who were with him in his exile.[2]

Her limitless wealth or her limitless virtue led this anonymous author to exuberant descriptions of Olympias.

And I know that this completely virtuous and divinely-inspired Olympias provided also for the blessed Nectarius, the archbishop of Constantinople, who was completely persuaded by her even in the affairs of the Church, and for Amphilochius, bishop of Iconium, and Optimus, and Peter, and Gregory the brother of the holy Basil, and Epiphanius the archbishop of Constantia in Cyprus, and many others of the saints and inspired fathers who lived in the capital city. Why is it necessary to say that she also bestowed upon them property in the country and money? And when the aforesaid Optimus died in Constantinople at this time, she shut the eyes of the great man with her own hands. In addition she relieved the piteous without measure in all ways. She sustained Antiochus of Ptolemais, and Acacius, the bishop of Beroea, and the holy Severian, the bishop of Gabala, and in a word, all the priests residing there, in addition to innumerable ascetics and virgins.

And due to her sympathy for them, she endured many trials by the actions of a willfully evil and vulgar person; contending eagerly in not a few contests on behalf of the truth of God, she lived faultlessly in unmeasured tears night and day, "submitting to every human being for the sake of the Lord," full of every reverence, bowing before the saints, venerating the bishops, honoring the presbyters, respecting the priests, welcoming the ascetics, being anxious for the virgins, supplying the widows, raising the orphans, shielding the elderly, looking after the weak, having compassion on sinners, guiding the lost and having pity on all, pity without stinting anything on the poor. Engaging in much catechizing of unbelieving women and making provision for all the necessary things of life, she left a reputation for goodness throughout her whole life, which is ever to be remembered. Having called from slavery to freedom her myriad household servants, she proclaimed them to be of the same honor as her own nobility. Or rather, if it is necessary to speak truthfully, they appeared more noble in their way of dress than that holy woman. For there could be found nothing cheaper than her clothing; the most ragged items were coverings unworthy of her manly courage. And she cultivated in herself a gentleness so that she surpassed even the simplicity of children themselves. Never any blame, not even from her neighbors, was incurred by that image of Christ, but her whole intolerable life was spent in penitence and in a great flood of tears. One was more likely to see the fount run dry in the trenches than her eyes, lowered, always gazing on Christ, leave off crying for awhile. Why go on? For to whatever extent I might provide leisure for my mind to recount the contests and virtues of this ardent soul, one will find many and poor the descriptions of the deeds. And does anyone not believe that I speak with restraint concerning the steadfast Olympias, who besides was an entirely precious vessel of the Holy Spirit? There was an eyewitness who also viewed the life of this blessed woman, her angelic regime; since he was her true spiritual friend and related to her family, much was distributed by him in accordance with her intent.[3]

Empress Theodora

As the authority in Rome weakened in the fifth century, Constantinople grew as the center of the empire. Justinian I (483–565), the heir to the Byzantine throne, married Theodora, a twenty-year-younger dancer and mime. She was supportive of her husband's efforts to rebuild the Roman Empire, but she continually opposed using warfare to do so. She encouraged the development of laws. The codification of Roman laws, which took ten years, has come to be the most respected accomplishment of their reign. She sought a better quality of life for women. During her reign divorce laws were improved, daughters were allowed to inherit as well as sons, wives could retain their dowries, and children could not be sold into slavery to pay their parents' debts. In 535 a law outlawed brothels in the major cities. Theodora purchased the freedom of five hundred girls who had been sold into prostitution and found a place for them to stay near the Black Sea. After her death her husband did little more in the way of legal reform.

St. Irene Church (Constantinople)

Elisabeth the Wonderworker

St. Irene, which means peace, is now a museum in the palace gardens next to Hagia Sophia. There one can remember St. Elisabeth the wonderworker of the fifth century C.E. She was originally from Herakleia, the Thracian capital, but she moved to Constantinople, where she was especially known as a patron of women who had problems with menstrual bleeding. Her *Life* seems to have been written between the ninth and eleventh centuries and obviously has legendary elements interwoven. Elisabeth was of a wealthy family but gave away her wealth and went to live in the convent of St. George in Constantinople where her aunt was abbess. After the aunt died, Elisabeth became the leader. She was said to have had premonitions of the great fire that destroyed much of Constantinople, including the first Hagia Sophia church, in 465.

The cult of St. George was brought to Constantinople in the fifth century. An embellishment of his legend said that he faced and slayed a dragon, which was a symbol for evil. Elisabeth, who lived in a monastery dedicated to St. George, was said to have done the same thing. (See more on **St. George** in *Lod.*) Her *Life* recounts a long list of miracles, including the following.

> Now, in this area there were the ruins of many old buildings, in which had lurked since ancient times a fearful dragon who ravaged many passersby and had made that place absolutely impassable to all. This afflicted the entire city with sorrow and helplessness since they saw no deliverance from this tribulation from any quarter. When the saint learned of this from certain people, she was seized by a divine zeal and, taking up the weapon of the venerable cross, went down to that place. Raising up her gaze to heaven and calling upon assistance from on high, she cried out to the beast and made him come out from his lair upon hearing [her]. Then, after making the sign of the cross over him, filling [her] mouth with spittle, she spat upon his head and, trampling him underfoot, she slew him, saying, *"I shall tread on the asp and the basilisk, and I shall trample on the lion and dragon, protected by the venerable cross."* And thus she completely liberated everyone in the city from harm from him. Indeed, from that time on she became hopeful, as it were, and, having received firm assurance that through [her] alliance [with Christ she would trample on] the spiritual dragon as well as the physical one and win victory over him, she boldly began her wonder-working.

As a result, her fame spread through the entire city. Now there was a man from a well-born and wealthy [family], who had an only daughter . . . with a flow of blood. He had exhausted the greater part of his wealth on doctors, but this profited her not at all, for the illness was stronger than their art. Finally, despairing of her being healed by [the doctors], he took [his] child and cast her at the saint's feet, crying out through his tears, "Save my unfortunate daughter, handmaid of God—I commit [her] to God and to your prayers and hands—and, if you wish, take all I own." She answered him, "That which is in your house, [my] child, keep as your own, for I need none of it. But if you believe unwaveringly and in accordance with the Gospel commandments, promise to be totally humble and to be merciful to the poor, your daughter will be healed." When the man immediately agreed to do these things, with a prayer [Elisabeth] anointed the child with holy oil from the great martyr George and restored her to health. And so she sent [the girl], rejoicing and giving thanks, home with her father. In addition, she similarly healed many other women who were faint with the same disease of hemorrhaging and who approached her with wholehearted faith in her, staunching their flow of blood by prayer.

Among [the people who came to her] was a man who had been *blind from birth*. Hearing of the blessed [Elisabeth's] miracles, he came up to her (led by the hands of others) and said, "Have mercy on me, faithful disciple of God, and open my eyes, so that, seeing the sweet light through you, I may glorify the Creator of all." The blessed [one] was moved with compassion by his lamentations and, without hesitation, she raised her hands to heaven in supplication, then took the saint's oil and anointed his eyes. Within seven days she made him to see most clearly, and he glorified God with a loud voice. . . . In such fashion, therefore, the saint shone with the rays of [her] wondrous miracles and illuminated those who came to her in faith.[4]

Orthodox Patriarchate (Constantinople)

Women Mentioned by Paul

In the Fener district in the old city is the church of the current leader of the Greek Orthodox Christians of Constantinople, who follows in the line from St. John Chrysostom, the archbishop in the late fourth and early fifth centuries. John gave this homily on some of the women mentioned by Paul.

Olympias, the deaconess at Hagia Sophia, was John's financial support and his friend. Did her influence contribute to the positive attitudes toward these women he shows here?

> "I recommend to you our sister Phoebe, who is a deacon of the church of Cenchreae" (one of the seaports of Corinth). See in how many ways he dignifies her. He has placed her before all the others and called her sister. It is no small thing to be called Paul's sister. But he gives her even greater importance by calling her deacon. "May you receive her in the Lord in a way worthy of the holy ones, and assist her with whatever need she has, for she has been a patroness to many including myself." Paul praises this blessed woman, and how can she not be blessed who enjoys such praise from Paul, for she was able to help the one who has helped the world. Let us then both men and women imitate this holy woman, as well as her who comes next with her husband. "Greet Priscilla and Aquila, my co-workers in Christ Jesus who have risked their necks for me, whom not only I thank, but all the churches of the Gentiles, and the church that is in their house." See these noble women, in no way hindered by nature in the pursuit of virtue. But this is quite right, for "in Christ Jesus there is no male or female" (Gal 3:28). For she was so good as to make their house a church, opening it to believers and strangers alike. These married people were quite distinguished, even though their occupation was not, for they were tent makers. . . .
>
> "Greet Mary, who has labored much among you." What is this? Again a woman is crowned with praise and proclaimed, again we men are shamed, but honored. We are honored because there are such women among us and shamed because they leave us so far behind. But if we learn with what they were adorned, we will be able to overtake them. With what were they adorned? Listen, both men and women: not with jewelry, servants and finery, but with their labor on behalf of the truth. "She has labored much" means that besides teaching, she also ministered in other ways involving risk, money, and travel. In those days the women were more ardent than lions, taking up with the apostles the labor of preaching the word. They traveled with them and performed all other ministries with them. Even with Christ there were women who followed, ministering to the teacher with their possessions (Luke 8:3).
>
> "Greet Andronicus and Junia, my relatives who were prisoners with me, who are noteworthy among the apostles," but to be noteworthy among the apostles is high praise. They are noteworthy for their labors and their righteousness. What wisdom must this woman have had, to be called an apostle![5]

Chalcedon

Euphemia

St. Euphemia was martyred in Chalcedon in 304 C.E. under the cruel ruler Galerius. When the Fathers gathered for the Council of Chalcedon in 402 they were debating over the natures of Christ and decided to turn to Euphemia for wisdom. The Orthodox Fathers wrote their thesis that Christ had a divine and a human nature on a piece of parchment. The Monophysites wrote that he had only one nature on another piece. They put these in the casket of the "holy great martyr and all-celebrated Euphemia." The next morning the parchment of the Orthodox Fathers was found in her hand and the other was under her feet. The liturgical books mention with pride and gratitude the miracle of her profession of the true faith. While live women have not been invited into the theological decision-making of the councils, a dead woman was! Her feast is celebrated on September 16 in the Melkite church.

Iconium (Konya)

Lois and Eunice, who shared the faith with Timothy

Paul was threatened in Iconium, so he fled to Lystra, which was a small town about eighteen miles southwest. Many people, like Timothy, learn faith from mothers and grandmothers.

> 2 To Timothy, my beloved child: Grace, mercy, and peace from God the Father and Christ Jesus our Lord. 3 I am grateful to God—whom I worship with a clear conscience, as my ancestors did—when I remember you constantly in my prayers night and day. 4 Recalling your tears, I long to see you so that I may be filled with joy. 5 I am reminded of your sincere faith, a faith that lived first in your grandmother Lois and your mother Eunice and now, I am sure, lives in you.
>
> (Read 2 Tim 1:1-8)

Nuseybin, Nisibis

Febronia

Between the Tigris and Euphrates in Nisibis, now called Nuseybin, St. Febronia was said to have been martyred under Diocletian (284–305). The "Life of St. Febronia" was composed in the late sixth or early seventh centuries, probably by a woman.

While there seems to have been a historical Febronia, the story is that of an "epic passion," the hagiographical genre developed to glorify and edify. These exaggerated tales should be enjoyed in themselves rather than being subjected to modern concepts of historicity.

The author claims to be the leader of the convent of St. Febronia after Bryene, the abbess at the time of the saint, had died. The writer says that most of the content she personally knew. That does not seem plausible, but the prominence of women and a sense of the psychology of women in the story suggest that it was written by a woman, perhaps of that convent.

An imperial decree ordered that the Christians in the Orient were to be killed. Soldiers went there to carry out the order, but one Lysimachos, though not a Christian, was hesitant because his mother had been a Christian. What these soldiers preferred was for the Christians to flee and hide so that they did not have to kill them. The bishop, clergy, monks, and others did flee. When the soldiers were coming to the convent of Febronia most of the women had fled, but she was determined to witness to the Christ in whom she believed. She thought this was the best way to invite others to follow him. One could call this foolishness or look on it as an example of "nonviolent resistance" that ultimately transforms the opponent. Within the twentieth century Mahatma Gandhi and Martin Luther King, Jr., have led movements with demonstrations reminiscent of the resistance of Febronia. Gandhi said that he would be willing to die for what he believed in, but he would never be willing to kill. People who witnessed Febronia giving her life began to be transformed. Febronia, like innumerable ancient women, found strength in the story of Thecla.

By the seventh century C.E. there was an oratory in honor of Febronia in St. John the Baptist Church in Constantinople in the Oxeia Quarter.

> As the soldiers were in a hurry to get going, Febronia said . . . "I beg you, mothers, send me on my way with blessings and pray for me. Let me go now."
>
> Bryene then stretched out her hands toward heaven and said in a loud voice, "Lord Jesus Christ, who appeared to your servant Thekla in the guise of Paul, turn toward this poor girl at the time of her contest." With these words she embraced Febronia and kissed her. She then sent her on her way, and the soldiers took her off. Bryene returned to the convent, threw herself down on the ground in the place of prayer, and groaned deeply as she supplicated God in her tears on behalf of Febronia.

Thomais put on laywoman's clothing and went out to watch the spectacle of the contest, as did all those lay women who used to come to the convent on Fridays to listen to the Scriptures. As they ran toward the place where the spectacle was to take place they were weeping and beating their breasts, mourning at the loss of their teacher.

When Hieria, the senator's wife, learnt that the nun Febronia was to be tried before the judge's tribunal, she got up and gave a loud wail. Her parents and everyone in the house asked her in amazement what was the matter. "My sister Febronia has gone to the court house," she replied. "My teacher is on trial for being a Christian." Her parents had tried to get her to quieten down, but she lamented and wept all the more. "Leave me alone to weep bitterly for my sister and teacher Febronia," she begged them. Her words so affected her parents that they started mourning for Febronia. Having asked them to allow her to go and see the contest, she set off with a number of servants and handmaids. As she came running in tears to the spectacle, she met on the road throngs of women also running and lamenting. She also came across Thomais, and having recognized one another, they came together, lamenting and weeping, to the site of the spectacle.

When a huge crowd had gathered there, along came the judges. When Selenos and Lysimachos had taken their seats on the tribunal, they gave orders that Febronia be fetched. They brought her in, with her hands tied and the heavy iron collar around her neck. When the crowds saw her, they were all reduced to tears and groans. As she stood there in the middle, Selenos gave orders that the clamor cease. As a great hush fell, Selenos said to Lysimachos, "Put the questions and take down the replies."

Lysimachos addressed her: "Tell me, young girl, what are you, slave or freeborn?"

Febronia replied, "Slave."

"Whose slave are you, then?" asked Lysmachos.

"Christ's," said Febronia.

"What is your name?" asked Lysmachos.

"The poor Christian woman," replied Febronia.

"It is your name I want to know," said Lysimachos.

"I have already told you," replied Febronia, "the poor Christian woman. But if you want to know my name, then I am called Febronia by my mistress."

At that point Selenos told Lysimachos to stop asking the questions, and he himself began to interrogate Febronia: "The gods know very well that I had not wanted to give you the chance of being questioned; nevertheless your gentle and meek disposition and your beautiful looks have overcome the force of my anger against you. I am not going to question you as though you were guilty, but instead I will urge you as though you were my own beloved daughter. So listen to me, my daughter. The gods are aware that I and my brother Anthimos have arranged the betrothal of a wife for Lysimachos, involving the transfer of a great deal of money and property. Today, however, I will annul the betrothal documents we made with the daughter of Prosphoros, and we will make a firm agreement with you, and you shall be wife to Lysimachos whom you can see sitting here now at my right. He is very handsome, just as you are. So listen to my advice as though I were your father; I will make you glorious upon earth. Have no fears on the grounds that you are poor; I have no wife alive or any children, and I will make over to you all that I possess; I will make you mistress of everything I have, and you shall have all this written down in your dowry. You shall recognize the lord Lysimachos as your husband and I shall take on the role of your father. You shall be the object of praise throughout the world, and all women will count you happy for having attained to such honor. Our victorious emperor also will be pleased and he will shower the pair of you with presents. For he has given his promise to raise my lord Lysimachos to the exalted throne of the glorious eparch, and he will take on that office. Now that you have heard all this, give a reply to me, your father, which will please the gods and give joy to myself. If, however, you resist my wishes and do not listen to my words, the gods know very well that you will not stay alive in my hands for another three hours. So reply as you wish."

Febronia began, "O judge, I have a marriage chamber in heaven, not made with hands, and a wedding feast that will never come to an end has been prepared for me. I have as my dowry the entire kingdom of heaven, and my Bridegroom is immortal, incorruptible, and unchangeable. I shall enjoy him in eternal life. I will not even entertain the idea of living with a mortal husband who is subject to corruption. Do not waste your time, sir; you will not achieve anything by coaxing me, nor will you frighten me by threats."

On hearing these words, the judge became exceedingly angry. He ordered the soldiers to tear off her clothes, tie her up with rags, and let her stand there undressed, an object of shame in front of everyone. "Let her see herself naked like this and lament her own folly, now that she has fallen from honor and respect to shame and ignominy."

The soldiers quickly tore off her clothes, tied her up with rags, and made her stand undressed in front of everyone.

Selenos asked her, "What have you got to say, Febronia? Do you see what a good opportunity you have lost, and to what ignominy you have been reduced?"

"Listen, judge," Febronia replied, "even if you should have me stripped completely naked, I would not think anything of this nakedness, for there is but one Creator of males and of females. In fact I am not just expecting to be stripped naked from my clothes, but I am prepared for the tortures of fire and sword, should I be considered worthy to suffer for him who suffered in my behalf."

"You impudent woman," exclaimed Selenos, "you deserve every kind of disgrace . . . ."[6]

Seleucia, Silifke

St. Thecla

A few miles outside of Selucia a church and a monastery marked the cave of Thecla. The Acts of Thecla of the second century C.E., which seem to have come from women's oral traditions, were a great source of inspiration for women. Thecla was frequently mentioned as a model for other holy women. St. Ambrose urged virgins to take Thecla as a role model second to Mary. When Macrina was born her mother had a vision of her as the new Thecla, and Jerome wrote of Melania the elder as a new Thecla.

According to the story, the virgin Thecla, who was engaged to Thamyris, sat in rapt attention for three days, listening to Paul preach. Thamyris heard that Paul was depriving "young men of wives and virgins of husbands," and introducing them to strange doctrines, so he got the officials to arrest Paul. At night Thecla secretly bribed her way into his cell and sat at his feet learning more. Paul authorized her to be an apostle spreading the gospel. Thecla was arrested and condemned her to be burned, but the fire was miraculously extinguished.

Thecla, after being released, went in search of Paul and followed him to Antioch. There Thecla was accosted by a man named Alexander. Paul did not play a very heroic role at this point: when Alexander tried to bribe Paul to hand over Thecla to him, Paul said he did not even know her! Alexander brought Thecla before the governor, who sentenced her to the beasts. While she was waiting for the sentence to be carried out a wealthy woman named Tryphaena, whose daughter Falconilla had died, took Thecla into custody. Thecla comforted her until she was taken to the arena. When Thecla was bound to a fierce

lioness the animal began to lick her feet like a pet. The crowd was astounded and the women cried out, "O God, an impious judgment is come to pass on this city!" Tryphaena took her into her home again until the next day, when Thecla was to appear in the arena again.

And when it was dawn, Alexander came to take her away—for he himself was arranging the hunt—and he said, "The governor has taken his seat, and the crowd is clamoring for us. Give me her who is to battle the beasts, that I may take her away." But Tryphaena cried out so that he fled, saying, "A second mourning for my Falconilla is come upon my house, and there is no one to help; neither child, for she is dead, nor relative, for I am a widow. O God of Thecla my child, help Thecla."

And the governor sent soldiers in order that Thecla might be brought. Tryphaena, however, did not stand aside but, taking her hand, led her up herself, saying, "My daughter Falconilla I brought to the tomb, but you, Thecla, I bring to battle the beasts." And Thecla wept bitterly and groaned to the Lord, saying, "Lord God, in whom I believe, with whom I have taken refuge, who rescued me from the fire, reward Tryphaena, who had compassion upon your servant and because she kept me chaste."

Then there was a clamor, a roaring of the beasts, and a shouting of the people and of the women who sat together, some saying, "Bring in the sacrilegious one!" But the women were saying, " Let the city perish for this lawlessness! Slay us all, Proconsul! A bitter spectacle, an evil judgment!"

Now, when Thecla was taken out of Tryphaena's hands, she was stripped, given a girdle, and thrown into the stadium. And lions and bears were thrown at her, and a fierce lioness ran to her and reclined at her feet. Now, the crowd of women shouted loudly. And a bear ran up to her, but the lioness ran and met it, and ripped the bear to shreds. And again a lion trained against men, which belonged to Alexander, ran up to her, and the lioness wrestled with the lion and perished with it. So the women mourned all the more, since the lioness that helped her was dead.

Then they sent in many beasts while she stood and stretched out her hands and prayed. And when she had finished her prayer, she turned and saw a great ditch full of water and said, "Now is the time for me to wash." And she threw herself in, saying, " In the name of Jesus Christ, I baptize myself on the last day!" And when they saw it, the women and the whole crowd wept, saying, "Do not throw yourself into the water!"—so that even the governor wept that such a beauty was going to be eaten by seals. So then she threw herself into the water in the name of Jesus Christ, but the seals, seeing the light of a lightning flash, floated dead on the surface. About her there was a cloud of fire so that neither could the beasts touch her nor could she be seen naked.

Now, the women, as other more terrible beasts were thrown in, wailed, and some threw petals, others nard, others cassia, others amomum, so that there was an abundance of perfumes. And all the beasts, overcome as if by sleep, did not touch her. So Alexander said to the governor, "I have some very fearsome bulls. Let us tie her who battles the beasts to them." Although he was frowning, the governor gave his consent, saying, "Do what you want." And they bound her by the feet between the bulls and prodded them from underneath with red-hot irons at the appropriate spot, that being the more enraged they might kill her. The bulls indeed leaped forward, but the flame that blazed around her burned through the ropes, and it was as if she were not bound.

But Tryphanea fainted as she stood beside the arena, so that her attendants said, "The queen Tryphaena is dead!" The governor observed this, and the whole city was alarmed. And Alexander, falling down at the governor's feet, said, "Have mercy upon me and the city, and set free her who battles the beasts, lest the city also perish with her. For if Caesar hears these things he will probably destroy both us and the city because his relative Tryphaena has died at the circus gates."

The governor summoned Thecla from among the beasts and said to her, "Who are you? And what have you about you that not one of the beasts touched you?" She answered, "I am a servant of the living God. As to what I have about me, I have believed in him in whom God is well pleased, his Son, on account of whom not one of the beasts touched me. For he alone is the goal of salvation and the foundation of immortal life. For to the storm-tossed he is a refuge, to the oppressed relief, to the despairing shelter; in a word, whoever does not believe in him shall not live but die forever."

When the governor heard this, he ordered clothing to be brought and said, "Put on the clothing." But she said, "The one who clothed me when I was naked among the beasts, this one shall clothe me with salvation in the day of judgment." And taking the clothing, she got dressed.

And the governor issued a decree immediately, saying, "I release to you Thecla, the God-fearing servant of God." So all the women cried out with a loud voice and as with one mouth gave praise to God, saying, "One is God who has saved Thecla!"—so that all the city was shaken by the sound.

And when Tryphaena was told the good news, she came to meet her with a crowd. She embraced Thecla and said, "Now I believe that the dead are raised up! Now I believe that my child lives! Come inside, and I will transfer everything that is mine to you." So Thecla went in with her and rested in her house for eight days, instructing her in the word of God, so that the majority of the female servants also believed. And there was great joy in the house.

Yet Thecla longed for Paul and sought him, sending all around in every direction. And it was made known to her that he was in Myra. So taking male and female servants, she got herself ready, sewed her *chiton* into a cloak like a man's, and headed off to Myra. She found Paul speaking the word of God and threw herself at him. But he was astonished when he saw her and the crowd that was with her, wondering whether another temptation was not upon her. So realizing this, she said to him, "I have taken the bath, Paul, for he who worked with you for the gospel has also worked with me for my washing."

And taking her by the hand, Paul led her into the house of Hermias and heard everything from her, so that Paul marveled greatly and those who heard were strengthened and prayed on behalf of Tryphaena. And standing up, Thecla said to Paul, "I am going to Iconium." So Paul said, "Go and teach the word of God!" Now, Tryphaena sent her a lot of clothing and gold, so it could be left behind for Paul for the ministry of the poor.

So Thecla herself headed off to Iconium . . . and threw herself down on the floor where Paul had sat when he was teaching the oracles of God, and wept, saying, "My God, and God of this house where the light shone upon me, Christ Jesus, the Son of God, my help in prison, my help before the governor, my help in the flame, my help among the beasts, you are God, and to you be glory forever. Amen."

And she found Thamyris dead, but her mother alive. And calling her mother to her, she said to her, "Theocleia, my mother, are you able to believe that the Lord lives in the heavens? For whether you desire money, the Lord will give it to you through me, or your child, behold, I am standing beside you."

And when she had given this witness, she headed off to Seleucia, and after enlightening many with the word of God, she slept with a fine sleep.[7]

Thecla was said to have retreated to a cave a few miles outside of Seleucia. In 480 C.E. a church was built over the cave, the ruins of which can be seen today. Egeria went to the monastery of St. Thecla built around the cave, both to venerate Thecla and to visit with the abbess Marthana. Though Egeria constantly met new people and was open to learning from all of them, she seems to have had a bond with this woman.

Ephesus near Selçuk

Great Theater

Economies and Divinities

Ephesus was famous for a large temple of Diana, a wonder of the ancient world. Diana, also called Artemis, was very important in the spirituality of the Roman Empire, and she had places of worship in at least thirty different cities. Hospitality for pilgrims to her temple and making silver statues of her were main sources of income for Ephesus. If people turned to the invisible God preached by Paul, their conversions could destroy the economy of Ephesus. In both ancient and modern times economics have often determined what divinity people worship. Economies based on warfare often glorify warriors, which then leads to more warfare.

The riot of the silversmiths described below took place in the theater built in the second century B.C.E. and seating 25,000; it can still be seen today.

> 23 About that time no little disturbance broke out concerning the Way. 24 A man named Demetrius, a silversmith who made silver shrines of Artemis, brought no little business to the artisans. 25 These he gathered together, with the workers of the same trade, and said, "Men, you know that we get our wealth from this business. 26 You also see and hear that not only in Ephesus but in almost the whole of Asia this Paul has persuaded and drawn away a considerable number of people by saying that gods made with hands are not gods.
>
> 27 And there is danger not only that this trade of ours may come into disrepute but also that the temple of the great goddess Artemis will be scorned, and she will be deprived of her majesty that brought all Asia and the world to worship her."
> (Read Acts 19:23-40)

House of Mary, the Mother of Jesus (Ephesus)

Theotokos

The Council of Ephesus in 431 declared that, since Christ was God and man, Mary could be called Theotokos, the Mother of God. When the church fathers came out of the session where that had been decided, the people were so delighted that they went through the streets yelling and chanting "the Mother of God." In this area where goddesses had been so important, as in many others, Mary became popular. One of the most important goddess statues excavated in Ephesus is covered with breasts, indicating a very nurturing and comforting mother with an abundance of gifts. Artistic imagery, often reflecting unconscious wisdom deeper than rational theological formulations, has shown Mary as the mother giving life, the mother giving nourishment, the mother sharing wisdom, and the mother receiving the body of the dead. These parallel the imagery of goddesses. (See *Bethlehem*, the Milk Grotto)

This "house of Mary," discovered through a vision fairly recently, has no historical foundations for its naming, but it has given the Christian minority a location in which to remember Mary. Often when people are discouraged, lacking a sense of identity or suffering from persecution, in both biblical and modern times someone has a "vision" giving hope. Community discernment is needed to determine whether this vision is helpful, healthy, and community building, or divisive, inappropriate, evil, or distracting from an authentic focus on the divine. Communities need discernment, and yet at the same time the charity and patience to live with ambiguity.

Haram

Rebecca

Haram is one of the oldest continuously occupied cities in the Middle East. In this area Abraham's servant, in search of a wife for Isaac, found Rebecca at the well. The passages reveal a little about the type of work women did, Rebecca's hospitality, and that she ran to tell those identified as "her mother's household." She had to be very strong to draw water for ten camels. The Bible consistently develops the importance of the patriarchal line, but there are glimpses of the influence of matriarchal descent.

> She went down to the spring, filled her jar, and came up. 17
> Then the servant ran to meet her and said, "Please let me sip

a little water from your jar." 18 Drink, my lord," she said, and quickly lowered her jar upon her hand and gave him a drink. 19 When she had finished giving him a drink, she said, "I will draw for your camels also, until they have finished drinking."

(Read Gen 24:10-28)

Urfa, or Edessa

Egeria

Toward the end of her Holy Land pilgrimage in the 380s C.E., Egeria described her trip to Edessa:

> Some time after that, since it was already three full years since my arrival in Jerusalem, and I had seen all the places which were the object of my pilgrimage, I felt that the time had come to return in God's name to my own country. But God also moved me with a desire to go to Syrian Mesopotamia. The holy monks there are said to be numerous and of so indescribably excellent a life that I wanted to pay them a visit; I also wanted to make a pilgrimage to the *martyrium* of the holy apostle Thomas, where his entire body is buried. It is at Edessa, to which Jesus, our God, was sending Thomas after his ascension into heaven, as he tells us in the letter he sent to King Abgar by the messenger Ananias. This letter has been most reverently preserved at Edessa, where they have this *martyrium*. And, believe me, loving sisters, no Christian who has achieved the journey to the holy places and Jerusalem misses going also on the pilgrimage to Edessa. It is twenty-five staging-posts away from Jerusalem. But Mesopotamia is not as far from Antioch. So, since my route back to Constantinople took me back that way, it was very convenient for me at God's bidding to go from Antioch to Mesopotamia, and that, under God, is what I did.
>
> Thus in the name of Christ our God I set out from Antioch to Mesopotamia. I passed through a number of different staging-posts and cities belonging to the province of Coele-Syria, which has Antioch as its capital. From there I crossed the frontier into the province of Augustophratensis, and reached the city of Hierapolis; it is the capital of this province Augustophratensis, a city of great plenty, rich and very beautiful, and it was where I had to stay, since it was not very far from there to the frontier of Mesopotamia. Fifteen kilometers after leaving Hierapolis I arrived in God's name at the river Euphrates, and the Bible is right to call it "the great river Euphrates." It is very big, and really rather frightening since

it flows very fast like the Phone, but the Euphrates is much bigger. We had to cross in ships, big ones, and that meant I spent maybe more than half a day there. So, after crossing the river Euphrates, I went on in God's name into the region of Syrian Mesopotamia.

After several more staging-posts I came to Batanis, a city mentioned in the Bible, and still there to this day. It has a church with a really godly bishop who is both monk and confessor. There are several *martyria*. And the city has a vast population, and a garrison with a tribune in charge. From there we set out again, and came, in the name of Christ our God, to Edessa.

As soon as we arrived, we went straight to the church and *martyrium* of holy Thomas; there we had our usual prayers and everything which was our custom in holy places. And we read also from the writing of holy Thomas himself. The church there is large and beautiful, and built in the new way—just right, in fact, to be a house of God. In this city there was so much I wanted to see that I had to stay there three days. I saw a great many *martyria* and visited the holy monks, some of whom lived among the *martyria,* whilst others had their cells further away from the city where it was more private.

The holy bishop of the city was a truly devout man, both monk and confessor. He welcomed me and said, "My daughter, I can see what a long journey this is on which your faith has brought you—right from the other end of the earth. So now please let us show you all the places Christians should visit here." I gave thanks to God, and eagerly accepted the bishop's invitation.

(Source: EGERIA, 113–15)

With gratitude and enthusiasm Egeria saw all that she could see. She spent over three years in the discipline and the blessings of being a pilgrim. She learned and shared her knowledge with others. Her spirit of adventure and deep faith invites others to move out of the safe and familiar. Egeria met the Holy One in new people and in new places. She knew the Holy One deep within.

Notes

[1] "A Letter from Gregory, Bishop of Nyssa on the Life of Saint Macrina," in Joan M. Petersen, *Handmaids of the Lord: Contemporary Descriptions of Feminine Asceticism in the First Six Centuries* (Kalamazoo: Cistercian Publications, 1996) 67–70.

[2] Elizabeth A. Clark, *Jerome, Chrysostom, and Friends* (New York: Edwin Mellen Press, 1979) 130–33.

[3] Ibid., 138–40.

[4] "St. Elisabeth the Wonderworker," in Alice-Mary Talbot, ed., *Holy Women of Byzantium: Ten Saints' Lives in English Translation* (Washington, D.C.: Dumbarton Oaks Research Library and Collection, 1966) 129–31.

[5] John Chrysostom, Homily on Romans 16:1-2, 6-7, *MPG* 60.663-70, trans. Carolyn Osiek in Barbara Bowe, Kathleen Hughes, Sharon Karam, and Carolyn Osiek, eds., *Silent Voices, Sacred Lives: Women's Readings for the Liturgical Year* (New York: Paulist, 1992) 216–17.

[6] "Febronia," in Paulus Peeters, ed., *Bibliotheca Hagiographica Orientalis* 302 (Brussels: Bollandist Society, 1910), from *Acta Sanctorum Martyrum et Sanctorum* 5,573-615, in Sebastian P. Brock and Susan Ashbrook Harvey, *Holy Women of the Syrian Orient* (Berkeley: University of California Press, 1987) 163–66.

[7] "The Acts of Thecla," in Ross S. Kraemer, ed., *Maenads, Martyrs, Matrons, Monastics* (Philadelphia: Fortress, 1988) 285–88.

WISDOM PREPARES A FEAST.
ABIGAIL'S STORY

Abigail (1 Samuel 25) personifies the wisdom of mediation and reconciliation. Those who journey in Bible lands and those who go on the inner journeys might celebrate her story with this service of reflection and prayer. As religious traditions through the ages in worship have remembered and celebrated the stories of men, women's stories need to be celebrated.[1] In Scripture, Wisdom has been personified as a woman who serves food to others.

(A table with a lovely cloth, flowers, an oil lamp or candles is in the center of a semicircle of chairs. Instrumental music, hymns, or songs could be woven throughout the celebration. Nearby are baskets of bread, dried raisins, figs, and a goblet of wine or grape juice. The storyteller might want to suggest that she is personifying a biblical character by wearing a shawl or a long dress. Telling the story in her own words is better than reading it.)

An opening song such as "The Circle's Larger" from Her Wings Unfurled *or "Choose Life" from* Cry of Ramah *by Colleen Fulmer[2] or "Rannanu" (Sing with Joy) from* Ancient Echoes *could be used.*

Leader: "Come, eat of my bread and drink of the wine I have mixed! Lay aside immaturity, and live, and walk in the way of insight." These words from the book of Proverbs invite us to examine the folly of our lives and of the human family. These words invite us to God who is Wisdom, justice, compassion, and love. Let us pray for open minds and open hearts as we listen to a story inspired by Abigail.[3]

Storyteller: *[This begins with an intense, almost wild energy.]* People thought my grandmother was crazy. She called aloud in the streets, she raised her voice in the public square; she called out at the street corners, she delivered her message at the city gates: "You ignorant people, how much longer will you cling to your ignorance? Violence never stops violence." Again and again my wise grandmother would say, "Violence never stops violence," and she would sing, "Fools turn to violence, Wisdom prepares a feast. Fools turn to violence, Wisdom prepares a feast."[4] *[The storyteller sings this refrain and gestures for all to join her in singing it a second time.]*

You wonder how I became the wife of the mighty king David. I was married to Nabal; his very name means "fool," and that he was, quicker to anger than to think, quicker to turn to drink than to friends, quicker to snarl than to speak. Yet Nabal had been a person of much power. We had three thousand sheep and a thousand goats. It was the season of shearing the flocks. God richly blessed us and we had an abundance of food for celebrating.

David and his men were camped nearby. David sent ten men to my husband with the message, "Peace be to you, and peace be to your house, and peace be to all that you have. I hear that you have shearers; now your shepherds have been with us, and we did them no harm, and they missed nothing, all the time they were in Carmel. Ask your young men, and they will tell you. Therefore let my young men find favor in your sight; for we have come on a feast day. Please give whatever you have at hand to your servants and to your son David." When Nabal heard of David's request, he snarled, "Who is David? Who is the son of Jesse? Shall I take my bread and my water and the meat that I have butchered for my shearers, and give to to men who come from I do not know where?"

When David heard of my husband's response to his request for food his temper was as quick as my husband's, and he said to his companions, "Every man strap on his sword!" About four hundred of David's men prepared themselves to attack our family and our helpers. Two hundred of David's followers stayed behind to guard their possessions. How is it that the men can so quickly be ready for violence, when they are so slow to respond to needs? I knew about all this from the husband of Anna, my maid. Her husband was one of the shepherds and had seen how David's men protected our flocks. Anna's husband said that David's company had been like a rampart by day and by night protecting the sheep and the goats. Anna was terrified that four hundred men would attack our home. She and her husband had three small children and a baby. We had dozens of helpers who cared for our sheep and goats. Why should they and their families be destroyed because Nabal, that fool, would not listen to a request? Why should they be destroyed because David was quick to anger when he was insulted by the fool? Anna's eyes filled with tears: "Violence never stops violence." Only fools turn a deaf ear to persons in need. Again and again my wise grandmother would say, "Violence never stops violence," and she would sing. *[The storyteller gestures for all to join her in song.]* "Fools turn to violence, Wisdom prepares a feast."

Should I try to talk to Nabal? Would he reach for more wine and then strike me again? Do I waste my words with this fool? Anna's husband said, "He is so mean that no one can talk to him." I called Anna and some of the other servant women. They had heard of the men's foolishness and rage, had held their children and wept. Anna and the others helped me prepare two hundred loaves of bread, two skins of wine, two hundred cakes of raisins and two hundred more of the finest figs. We loaded these gifts on asses. I made the women promise that they would not tell Nabal where I had gone. The fear in their eyes assured me their lips were sealed.

A few servants, the laden asses, and I hastily set out. We went through a mountain pass and I could see David and his men. As we drew nearer I heard his shouting, "Surely it was in vain that I protected all that this fellow has in the wilderness, so that nothing was missed of all that belonged to him; but he has returned me evil for good. God do so to David and more also, if by morning I leave so much as one male of all who belong to him." I trembled as I heard his words. The men have power to take life away, but we women have the power to bring life. We women have the power to bring food, to sustain life, to prepare a feast. Was it bold of me to think that I could bring life when they were ready to bring death? Was it bold of me to think thoughts of peace when they were ready for war? Was it wrong to think more of the tears of Anna, who spoke of her children, than of the reputation of my husband who said he was right and must be respected?

I dismounted and knelt in front of David, offering homage. I begged, "Upon me alone, my lord, be the guilt; please let your servant speak in your ears, and hear the words of your servant. My lord, do not take seriously this ill-natured fellow, Nabal; for as his name is, so is he; fool is his name, and folly is with him; but I, your servant, did not see the young men of my lord, whom you sent. Now then, my lord, as the LORD lives, and as you yourself live, since the LORD has restrained you from bloodguilt and from taking vengeance with your own hand, now let your enemies and those who seek to do evil to my lord be like Nabal. And now let this present that your servant has brought to my lord be given to the young men who follow my lord. Please forgive the trespass of your servant, for the LORD will certainly make my lord a sure house, because my lord is fighting the battles of the LORD." I begged him not to have innocent blood on his hands when God made him ruler. David's men were murmuring, "Do not listen to the words of a woman. Let us destroy the man who would insult your name. No man shall make fun of us and live. We must show them who has power."

I stood there silently, but grandmother's words echoed deep in my heart: "Violence never stops violence." I looked at David. He tried to look away, but then he said, "Blessed be the LORD, the God of Israel, who sent you to meet me today! Blessed be your good sense, and blessed be you, who have kept me today from bloodguilt and from avenging myself by my own hand! For as surely as the Lord the God of Israel lives, who has restrained me from hurting you, unless you had hurried and come to meet me, truly by morning there would not have been left to Nabal so much as one male." David took the gifts I had brought and said, "Go up to your house in peace; see, I have heeded your voice, and I have granted your petition." He looked into my eyes as if he wished to say more.

As I traveled back home I thought of the God who made the heavens and the earth and all that is in them, the God who made food enough for all living things, and flowers to make things beautiful.

When I got home, I was planning to tell Nabal what had happened, but I looked in and saw a party and the empty wine vessel. I heard him shouting at the servant for more wine. I quietly slipped away. Alone in my bed I thought of what I had done. I feared my husband. Would he beat me again? Giving food is a small price for saving lives. Can't we learn the ways of bringing life instead of the ways of bringing death? I think it is better to give food than to turn to bloodshed, but what do I know? I am only a woman. Yet I kept remembering the words of my grandmother: "Violence never stops violence." She would sing *[the storyteller gestures for all to join her singing]:* "Fools turn to violence, Wisdom prepares a feast."

The next morning I told Nabal that I had taken food to David and his hungry men. He began to snarl, but I firmly said, "You would be dead right now, for the four hundred of them would have attacked our household yesterday. Do not curse me that I have dishonored you. I speak of life. Fool, do you men have no more sense than to choose death?" I do not understand the ways of God. Words seemed to die within Nabal's mouth. During the next ten days he became still like a stone, and then he died. I dressed in widow's robes and mourned his passing, for all this happened so suddenly. Yet I remembered that my grandmother said that a woman's life did not have to stop with her husband's death. Then David sought me for his wife and I agreed. David brought some wisdom to God's people, but not enough. We still seek to really know God's words, God's plans, God's heart. I value David's words, but I also remember my grandmother's words: "Violence never stops violence." She would sing *[the storyteller gestures for all to join her in singing several times]:* "Fools turn to violence, Wisdom prepares a feast."

Enjoying Wisdom's Feast

Leader: Let us come and stand close around this table. Let us remember that God has prepared the abundant table of creation for all the human family.

(Baskets of pita bread, dried figs, and raisins to eat, and a sweet wine or grape juice to drink are set on the table. All gather close.)

God of life, who prepares a feast for us, you led Abigail to prepare bread and wine, raisins and figs for hungry men ready to turn to violence. You led Abigail to humble herself to bring peace, while others flaunted their power. Open our hearts to seek wisdom, open our minds to seek truth, open our hands to give service.

God of compassion, you tremble with us as we hear threats of violence. You weep with us in fear. Cry with us, until the cry becomes a mighty roar. Shout with us in the streets, in public squares, and on street corners until it is safe for all.

God of healing, may recognizing our wounds remind us that you wish our wholeness. Gently bind the deep wounds within us that can lead us to wound others. Gently touch us that we may learn to touch gently rather than violently.

May the food we share remind us that you do not leave us in need. May the sweetness of these raisins and figs remind us that you have called us to joy and not bitterness, life and not death.

(The food and drink are passed and during this the chant, "Fools turn to violence . . ." or "Tubwayhun l'ahbrday sh'lama") (Blessed Are the Peacemakers).[5]

Let us be seated and and join in conversation about this story. *[Allow time for this. The sources that inspired the story could be given.]*[6]

Suggested Questions for Discussion

1. Abigail's grandmother would say: "Violence never stops violence?" What are some examples of that?

2. The book of Proverbs portrays Wisdom as a seemingly wild woman crying out in the streets, challenging people to leave their ignorance and follow true wisdom. How were both Nabal and David foolish?

3. Nabal, David, and David's men were all concerned with "saving face," looking right. Abigail was more concerned about Anna's tears for her children than her husband's reputation. Is saving face the highest good?

4. How should one relate to a spouse or friend who is abusive?

5. How should one relate to a spouse or friend who is drunk?

6. How are women mediators of life through their sharing of nourishment?

7. How could a fairer sharing of food all over the earth stop some of the violence?

8. How could a fairer sharing of food and goods in the local area stop some of the violence?

(A prayer, sign of peace, song and/or dance could be used to close the celebration.)

Leader: Let us close our reflections and stand in a circle of solidarity. Let us pray for open hearts.

God, our Wisdom, through this sharing give us strength to be people of justice and compassion. Go with us into the streets that we may be voices for your peace. **Amen.**

(All are invited to sing and do a circle dance to "Feed our Hungry Souls" from Dancing Sophia's Circle *or "Wings Unfurled" from* Her Wings Unfurled *by Colleen Fulmer or "Ashir shirim" from* Ancient Echoes.)[6]

Notes

[1] For stories and prayer services remembering Sarah, Hagar, Miriam, Susanna, Ruth, Naomi, the woman with a hemorrhage, Martha, Mary Magdalene, and Dorcas, see Martha Ann Kirk, *Celebrations of Biblical Women's Stories: Tears, Milk, and Honey* (Kansas City, Mo.: Sheed & Ward, 1987).

[2] *Her Wings Unfurled*, cassette by Colleen Fulmer and ritual book by Martha Ann Kirk; *Cry of Ramah*, cassette by Colleen Fulmer (Albany, Calif.: Loretto Spirituality Network, 1989). *Ancient Echoes* by SAVAE, San Antonio Vocal Arts Ensemble (Schiller Park, Ill.: World Library Publications, 2003).

[3] 1 Samuel 25:1-42.

[4] The text "Fools turn to violence, Wisdom prepares a feast," can be sung twice to the melody of "Visioning Song" in Rufino Zaragoza, O.F.M., and Martha Ann Kirk, *Love's Radiant Light* (Portland, Ore.: OCP Publications, 1990).

[5] "Blessed are the Peacemakers" is on *Ancient Echoes*.

[6] 1 Sam 25:1-42; Prov 1:20-22; 9:56.

[7] Colleen Fulmer, *Dancing Sophia's Circle*, book and album on cassette or CD (Albany, Calif.: Loretto Spirituality Network, 1994).

BIBLIOGRAPHY

Adams, Doug, and Diane Apostolos-Cappadona, eds. *Dance as Religious Studies.* New York: Crossroad, 1990.

_____, and Michael E. Moynahan, S.J., eds. *Postmodern Worship and the Arts.* San Jose, Calif.: Resource Publications, 2002.

Adams, Douglas E. *The Prostitute in the Family Tree.* Louisville: Westminster John Knox, 1997.

Alfifi, Abdallah. *Al-marʾa l-Arabia fi Jahilyatiha Wa Islamiha.* Egypt: Dar Ihyaʾ Al Kutub el-Arabiyya Publishing House, 1921.

Ali, Maulana Muhammed, ed. *The Holy Qurʾan: Arabic text, English translation and Commentary.* Columbus, Ohio: Ahmadiyyah Anjuman Ishaʾat Islam Lahore, Inc., 1991.

Armstrong, Karen. "A Passion for the Holy Places," *The Sunday Times Magazine* (April 15, 1990) 32.

Ateek, Naim Stifan. *Justice and Only Justice: A Palestinian Theology of Liberation.* Maryknoll, N.Y.: Orbis, 1998.

Ateek, Naim, Hilary Rantisi, and Kent Williams. *"Our Story": The Palestinians.* Jerusalem: Sabeel Ecumenical Liberation Theology Center, 1999.

Berger, Teresa. *Women's Ways of Worship: Gender Analysis and Liturgical History.* Collegeville: The Liturgical Press, 1999.

Børresen, Kari Elisabeth, and Kari Vogt. *Women's Studies of the Christian and Islamic Traditions: Ancient, Medieval, and Renaissance Foremothers.* Dordrecht, Netherlands, and Boston: Kluwer Academic, 1993.

Bowe, Barbara, Kathleen Hughes, Sharon Karam, and Carolyn Osiek, eds. *Silent Voices, Sacred Lives: Women's Readings for the Liturgical Year.* New York: Paulist, 1992.

Brock, Sebastian P., and Susan Ashbrook Harvey, trans. *Holy Women of the Syrian Orient.* Berkeley: University of California Press, 1987; new ed. 1998.

Brooten, Bernadette J. *Women Leaders in the Ancient Synagogue: Inscriptional Evidence and Background Issues.* Chico: Scholars, 1982.

Burrus, Virginia. *Chastity as Autonomy.* Lewiston, N.Y.: Edwin Mellen, 1987.

Cady, Susan, Marian Ronan, and Hal Taussig. *Wisdom's Feast: Sophia in Study and Celebration.* San Francisco: Harper & Row, 1989.

Clark, Elizabeth A. *Ascetic Piety and Women's Faith: Essays on Late Ancient Christianity.* Lewiston, N.Y.: Edwin Mellen, 1986.

_____. "Life of Olympias," in eadem, *Jerome, Chrysostom, and Friends: Essays and Translations*. New York: Edwin Mellen, 1979.

_____. *Women in the Early Church*. Wilmington: Michael Glazier, 1983.

Cloke, Gillian. *This Female Man of God: Women and Spiritual Power in the Patristic Age*. London and New York: Routledge, 1995.

Cyril of Scythopolis. *Lives of the Monks of Palestine*. Translated by Richard M. Price, with introduction and notes by John Binns. Kalamazoo: Cistercian Publications, 1991.

Davies, John Gordon. *Pilgrimage Yesterday and Today: Why? Where? How?* London: S.C.M. Press, 1988.

Drijvers, Jan Willem. *Helena Augusta: The Mother of Constantine the Great and the Legend of Her Finding of the True Cross*. Leiden and New York: Brill, 1992.

Egeria. *Egeria's Travels*. Newly translated with supporting documents and notes by John Wilkinson. London: S.P.C.K., 1971; 3rd ed. Warminster: Aris & Phillips, 1999.

Elm, Susanna. *Virgins of God: The Making of Asceticism in Late Antiquity*. Oxford and New York: Oxford University Press, 1994.

Fernea, Elizabeth Warnock, and Basima Qattan Bezirgan, eds. *Middle Eastern Muslim Women Speak*. Austin: University of Texas Press, 1977.

Fulmer, Colleen. *Her Wings Unfurled*. Cassette and ritual book by Martha Ann Kirk. Albany, Calif.: Loretto Spirituality Network, 1989.

_____. *Dancing Sophia's Circle*. Book and CD. Albany, Calif.: Loretto Spirituality Network, 1994.

Gerontius. *The life of Melania, the Younger*. Introduction, translation, and commentary by Elizabeth A. Clark. New York: Edwin Mellen, 1984.

"Gospel of Mary [Magdalene]." Trans. George MacRae and R. McLean Wilson, in James M. Robinson, ed., *Nag Hammadi Library in English*. San Francisco: Harper & Row, 1977, 472–73.

Gonen, Rivka, ed. *To the Tombs of the Righteous: Pilgrimage in Contemporary Israel*. Jerusalem: The Israel Museum, 1998.

Grossman, Susan, and Rivka Haut. *Daughters of the King: Women and the Synagogue: A Survey of History, Halakhah, and Contemporary Realities*. Philadelphia: Jewish Publication Society, 1992.

Hickey, Anne Ewing. *Women of the Roman Aristocracy as Christian Monastics*. Ann Arbor: UMI Research Press, 1987.

Hilliard, Alison, and Betty Jane Bailey. *Living Stones Pilgrimage: With the Christians of the Holy Land*. Notre Dame, Ind.: Notre Dame University Press; London: Cassell, 1999.

Hunt, E. D. *Holy Land Pilgrimage in the Late Roman Empire, 312–460*. Oxford: Clarendon Press; New York: Oxford University Press, 1982, 1984.

Ibn Saʾad, Muhammad. *Al-Tabakat El-Kubra.* Cairo: Dar El-Tahrir Publishing House, 1970.

Johnson, Elizabeth A. *Friends of God and Prophets: A Feminist Theological Reading of the Communion of Saints.* New York: Continuum, 1998.

_____. *She Who Is: The Mystery of God in Feminist Theological Discourse.* New York: Crossroad, 1992.

Khairat, Ahmed. *The Status of Women in Islam.* Egypt: Dar El Ma'arif, 1975.

Kirk, Martha Ann. *Celebrations of Biblical Women's Stories: Tears, Milk, and Honey.* Kansas City, Mo.: Sheed & Ward, 1987.

Kraemer, Ross S., ed. *Maenads, Martyrs, Matrons, Monastics: A Sourcebook on Women's Religions in the Greco-Roman World.* Philadelphia: Fortress, 1988.

Lozada, Francisco. *A Literary Reading of John 5: Text as Construction.* New York: Peter Lang, 2000.

McNamara, Jo Ann Kay. *Sisters In Arms: Catholic Nuns Through Two Millennia.* Cambridge, Mass.: Harvard University Press, 1996.

McCarthy, Emmanuel Charles. "The Non-violent Jesus." Unpublished lecture delivered September 1996, Our Lady of the Lake University, San Antonio, Texas.

Moltmann-Wendel, Elisabeth. *The Women Around Jesus.* New York: Crossroad, 1982.

Moore, Carey A. *Daniel, Esther, Jeremiah: The Additions.* AB 44. Garden City, N.Y.: Doubleday, 1977.

Morris, Joan. *Against Nature and God: The History of Women with Clerical Ordination and the Jurisdiction of Bishops.* London: Mowbrays, 1973.

Murphy-O'Connor, Jerome. *The Holy Land. An Oxford Archeological Guide: From Earliest Times to 1700.* 4th ed. revised and expanded. Oxford and New York: Oxford University Press, 1998.

Musurillo, Herbert, trans. *The Acts of the Christian Martyrs.* Oxford: Clarendon Press, 1972.

Palladius. *The Lausiac History.* Ancient Christian Writers 34. Trans. Robert T. Meyer. Westminster, Md.: Newman Press, 1965.

Patai, Raphael. *The Hebrew Goddess.* 3rd enlarged ed., with a foreword by Merlin Stone. Detroit: Wayne State University Press, 1990.

Petersen, Joan M., ed. and trans. *Handmaids of the Lord. Contemporary Descriptions of Feminine Asceticism in the First Six Christian Centuries.* Kalamazoo: Cistercian Publications, 1996.

Pound, Omar S. *Arabic and Persian Poems in English.* New York: New Directions, 1970.

Raheb, Mitri. *I Am a Palestinian Christian.* Trans. Ruth C.L. Gritsch, with a foreword by Rosemary Radford Ruether. Minneapolis: Fortress, 1995.

Raya, Joseph, and José de Vinck. *Byzantine daily worship: with Byzantine Breviary, the Three Liturgies, Propers of the Day and Various Offices*. Allandale, N.J.: Alleluia Press, 1969.

Robinson, Martin. *Sacred Places, Pilgrim Paths: An Anthology of Pilgrimage*. London: Marshall Pickering, 1997.

Ruether, Rosemary Radford. *Sexism and God-Talk: Toward a Feminist Theology*. Boston: Beacon, 1983.

_____, ed. *Religion and Sexism; Images of Woman in the Jewish and Christian Traditions*. New York: Simon & Schuster, 1974.

_____, compiler. *Womanguides. Readings Toward a Feminist Theology*. Boston: Beacon, 1985.

Schüssler Fiorenza, Elisabeth. *In Memory of Her: A Feminist Theological Reconstruction of Christian Origins*. New York: Crossroad, 1983.

_____. *But She Said: Feminist Practices of Biblical Interpretation*. Boston: Beacon, 1992.

_____. *Jesus: Miriam's Child, Sophia's Prophet: Critical Issues in Feminist Christology*. New York: Continuum, 1994.

Smith, Margaret. *Rabiᵓa the Mystic and Her Fellow-Saints in Islam; Being the Life and Teachings of Rabiᵓa al-ᵓAdawiyya al-Qaysiyya of Basra Together with Some Account of the Place of the Women Saints in Islam*. Cambridge: Cambridge University Press, 1928.

Sölle, Dorothée, Joe H. Kirchberger, Herbert Haag, and Anne-Marie Schnieper-Müller. *Great Women of the Bible in Art and Literature*. Grand Rapids: Eerdmans, 1993.

Swidler, Arlene. "In Search of Huldah," *The Bible Today* 98 (November 1978) 1780–85.

Swidler, Leonard J. *Biblical Affirmations of Women*. Philadelphia: Westminster, 1979.

Talbot, Alice-Mary, ed. *Holy Women of Byzantium: Ten Saints' Lives in English Translation*. Washington, D.C.: Dumbarton Oaks Research Library and Collection, 1996.

Thordson, Maria. *Christians 2000 A.D. Men and Women in the Land of Christ: A Living Church History*. Jerusalem: Emerezian Establishment, 1996.

Topping, Eva Catafygiotu. *Sacred Songs: Studies in Byzantine Hymnography*. Minneapolis: Light and Life Publishing Company, 1997.

Trible, Phyllis. *God and the Rhetoric of Sexuality*. Philadelphia: Fortress, 1978.

_____. *Texts of Terror: Literary-Feminist Readings of Biblical Narratives*. Philadelphia: Fortress, 1984.

Teubal, Sarah J. *Sarah the Priestess, the First Matriarch of Genesis*. Athens, Ohio: Swallow Press, 1984.

Ward, Benedicta. *Harlots of the Desert: A Study of Repentance in Early Monastic Sources*. Kalamazoo: Cistercian Publications, 1987.

_____. *The Desert Christian: The Sayings of the Desert Fathers,* trans. Benedicta Ward, S.L.G. Kalamazoo: Cistercian Publications, rev. ed. 1984.

Wire, Antoinette Clark. *The Corinthian Women Prophets: A Reconstruction Through Paul's Rhetoric.* Minneapolis: Fortress, 1990.

Zaragoza, Rufino, O.F.M., *Love's Radiant Light.* Portland, Ore.: OCP Publications, 1990.

BIBLICAL CITATIONS AND PRAYER SERVICE SUGGESTIONS

The contents of this book could be used for prayer services on pilgrimages and in other situations. Prayer is enhanced by the use of music. The album *Ancient Echoes* is a reconstruction of music of the time of Jerusalem's Second Temple and of Jesus.[1] The texts are in Hebrew and Aramaic, the languages that Jesus spoke. The songs are listed below.

Ancient Echoes

1. *Ashir shirim* (I Will Sing Songs to God) Wedding Song
2. *Rannanu* (Sing with Joy) Chant from the Dead Sea Scrolls
3. *Abwoon* (O Father-Mother of the Cosmos)
   The Aramaic Lord's Prayer
4. *Arabian Dance* Instrumental
5. *Song of Seikilos* 1ˢᵗ-century Greek song
6. *Tubwayhun ᵖahbvday shᵖlama*
   (Blessed are the Peacemakers)
7. *Sounding of the Shofar & Shema Israel* (Hear, O Israel)
8. *Bircath Cohenim* (The Priestly Blessing)
9. *Wa yᵖdaber Elobim* (And God Spoke)
   The Ten Commandments
10. *Tubwayhun layleyn dᵖkhafnin wᵖtseyn*
    (Blessed Are Those Who Hunger and Thirst)
11. *Ze Eli meode* (This Is My Supreme God) Wedding Song
12. *Tubwayhun ᵖmiskenehᵖeh bᵖruh*
    (Blessed Are the Poor in Spirit)
13. *Psalm 114: Bᵖtseth Israel* (When Israel Came Out of Egypt)
14. *Tubwayhun ᵖbwileh* (Blessed Are They That Mourn)
15. *Abwoon* Spoken prayer
16. *Bircath Cohenim* Reprise

---

[1] SAVAE, San Antonio Vocal Art Ensemble, *Ancient Echoes*. Schiller Park, Ill.: World Library Publications, 2003. The CD jacket includes information on ancient instruments, the text of the songs, and reflections on their meanings in light of studies of ancient languages.

After the biblical citations, the numbers in parentheses indicate the numbers of the songs that would enhance a prayer service with that text. Then the page number is given.

Biblical Citations

Genesis 1:11-12; 27-29, (8, 16) p. 131
Genesis 11:28-30, (4) p. 256
Genesis 16:1-2, (4) p. 144
Genesis 18:9-12, (8) p. 184
Genesis 19:4-8, p. 165
Genesis 19:30-36, p. 257
Genesis 20:1-3, p. 208
Genesis 21:13-16, (14) p. 197–98
Genesis 22:14, (14) p. 94
Genesis 24:16-19, (11) p. 324–25
Genesis 29:30, (1) p. 137
Genesis 34:1-2, (9) p. 201
Genesis 35:16-21, (5) p. 150
Genesis 38:12-26, (14) p. 80
Genesis 39:6-10, p. 225
Genesis 49:29-33, (13) p. 174

Exodus 1:15-20, (13) p. 224
Exodus 15:20-21, (4, 10, 13) p. 231

Leviticus 12:2-4; Luke 2:22-24, p. 100

Numbers 11:12, p. 14

Deuteronomy 24:1-2, p. 135
Deuteronomy 32:6, p. 13
Deuteronomy 32:18, pp. 13, 145

Joshua 2:12-13, p. 177

Judges 4:4-8, p. 173
Judges 11:29-40, (14) p. 187
Judges 16:4-6, p. 171
Judges 19:22-23, (14) p. 182
Judges 21:20-21, (4, 10) p. 204

Ruth 1:1-2, p. 209
Ruth 1:15-17, (8) p. 156

1 Samuel 1:3-5, (1, 2) p. 204

1 Samuel 25:32-35, (6, 10) pp. 189, 328
1 Samuel 28:8-10, p. 167

2 Samuel 11:2-3, (9) p. 111
2 Samuel 14:4-7, (10) p. 206
2 Samuel 13:1-22, (10, 14) p. 105
2 Samuel 21:10, (10, 14) p. 138

1 Kings 9:16-19, p. 172
1 Kings 10:1-3, (2) p. 88
1 Kings 17:7-9, (8) p. 277

2 Kings 3:8-37, (8) p. 193
2 Kings 4:1, (8) p. 189
2 Kings 22:14-15, (7) p. 98

Judith 9:1-2, p. 187

Esther 4:12-17, p. 254

Job 28:20-24, p. 17

Psalms 22:9-10, p. 14

2 Maccabees 7:20-21, (9) p. 92

Proverbs 8:27-31, (13) p. 169
Proverbs 9:1-6, (2, 3, 10) p. 202
Proverbs 31:30-31, (10) p. 80

Song of Songs 1:13-17, (1, 11) p. 168
Song of Songs 6:1-3, (1, 11) p. 205

Wisdom 7:25-26, p. 18
Wisdom 9:17-18, p. 19

Sirach 6:27-30, p. 19
Sirach 15:1-3, (1, 11) p. 198
Sirach 24:1-2, 19-20, (13) p. 17
Sirach 51:26, p. 18

Isaiah 25:6, 8, p. 15
Isaiah 42:9, 14, p. 13

INDEX

Baal, 11, 178
Baalath, 172
Babylon, Iraq, 248, 254
Babylonian, 27, 68, 158
Bacchus, 11
Baha'I Faith, 188
Bakerwoman, 149
Banyas, or Caesarea Philippi, 142, 144
Barak, 173, 194
Barbara (St.), 69, 223
Bartholomew, 109, 110
Basil, 5, 118
Basilides, 215
Bassa, 91
Bathsheba, 67, 111, 162
Battle of the Milvian Bridge Beatitudes, 46, 175
Beatitudes, 175
Bedouin women, 29, 144, 179, 207
Beer Sheva, 144
Begin, Menachem, 131
Beirut (Bayrᶜt), Lebanon, 248, 265
Beit Sahour, 103, 202
Beloved Daughter and Wife, 190
Ben Ezra Synagogue, Coptic Cairo, 224
Benedictines, 107, 125, 175, 193
Benjamin, 138, 181, 204
Benshoff Museum, 130
Bent over woman, 164
Beruriah, 135–36
Bet Shean or Scythopolis, 142, 145
Bet Shearim, 142, 147
Bethany, 78, 103, 124–26, 142, 191
Bethel, 173
Bethlehem, 50, 103, 138, 142, 149–58, 158, 160, 324
Bethlehem University, 138
Bethphage, 103, 124, 176
Bir Zeit University, 142, 158
Bird, Phyllis, 22
Bishop Dionysius, 115
Bishop Juvenal, 129, 130
Bishop Nonnus, 112–13
Bishop of Caesarea, 159
Bishop of Canterbury, 163
Bishop of Constantinople, 129
Bishop of Rome, Leo, 130
Bishop of Zoar, 165

Bishop Theophilus, 225
Blesilla, 56
Boaz, 209
Bolsheviks, 121
British Mandate, 71
Buddhists, 162
Burrus, Virginia, 5
Byzantine, 31, 105, 124, 132–33, 180, 188, 196, 203
Byzantine Greek Church, 169
Byzantine hymnography, 133
Byzantine Lexicon, 217
Byzantine Liturgy, 133
Byzantine women saints, 10

Caesar Augustus, 166, 321
Caesarea, Maritima, 117, 142, 159, 213
Caesarea, Philippi, 142, 144
Cairo, 24, 212–13, 222–24
Campbell, Joseph, 109
Cana, 142, 159, 194
Canaan, 174
Canon Law, 162
Capernaum, 142, 160, 175, 194
Carmel, 78, 188, 189, 329
Carmelite Convent, 157
Catafygiotu, Eve, 133
Carthage, 212, 241
Catherine of Alexandria, 70, 216–17, 223
Cave of El-Khader, 189
Celtic saints, 31
Cemeteries, Mount of Olives, 114
Cenacle, 106
Cenchrae, 284, 289
Chagall, Marc, 137
Chalcedon, 130, 284
Childbirth, 162–65
Children and Jesus, 280
Chorazin (Korazim), 142, 162
Christmas Lutheran Church, 156
Church of All Nations, 121
Church of the Nativity, 152
Church of St. John the Baptist, 137
Church of St. Lawrence, 183
Church of the Ascension, 115
Church of the Holy Sepulchre, 47, 48, 70
Church of the Multiplication, 175
Church of the Pater Noster or Eleona, 116